ECDL/ICDL 3.0
Made Simple

ECDL/ICDL 3.0
Made Simple

Business Communications Development Ltd

MADE SIMPLE
BOOKS

OXFORD AUCKLAND BOSTON JOHANNESBURG MELBOURNE NEW DELHI

Made Simple
An imprint of Elsevier Science
Linacre House, Jordan Hill, Oxford OX2 8DP
225 Wildwood Avenue, Woburn MA 01801-2041

First published 2001
This edition 2002

TRADEMARKS/REGISTERED TRADEMARKS
Computer hardware and software brand names mentioned in this book are
protected by their respective trademarks and are acknowledged

British Library Cataloguing in Publication Data
A catalogue record for this book is available from the British Library

Library of Congress Cataloguing in Publication Data
A catalogue record for this book is available from the Library of Congress

ISBN   0 7506 5788 X

Typeset by Elle and P.K. McBride, Southampton
Icons designed by Sarah Ward © 1994
Printed and bound in Great Britain by Scotprint

Contents

Preface

This book was designed to cover two aspects of instruction and training: To enable the user to follow the instruction, either as part of a tutor-led course or as a self-study guide. It is specially aimed at those users who have little or no experience of computers and the applications described within it. The aim is introduce the computer and its application and then to bring added value and skill-building instruction to the user.

This book covers the ECDL syllabus version 3.0, and is based upon the Microsoft Office 2000 suite of applications.

Further information on the course in general, and availability of courses can be obtained from:

Business Communications Development Ltd
16–18 Grove Road South
Southsea, Hampshire, PO5 3QP
Telephone: 023 9275 0234
Fax: 023 9275 0161
e-mail: info@bcdgroup.com
Website: bcdgroup.com

Screenshot permissions

Microsoft: Screenshots reprinted with permission from Microsoft Corporation.

Microsoft Windows, Windows NT, Microsoft Word, Microsoft Excel, Microsoft PowerPoint and Microsoft Outlook are either registered trademarks or trademarks of Microsoft Corporation.

Apple, the Apple logo, Macintosh are registered trademarks of Apple Computers, Inc.

Business Communications Development Ltd has attempted to include trademark information for products, services and companies referred to in this guide. Although Business Communications Development Ltd has made reasonable efforts in gathering this information, it cannot guarantee its accuracy.

All brand names and product names used in this book are trade names, service marks, or registered trademarks of their respective owners. Business Communications Development Ltd are not associated with any product or vendor mentioned in the document, other than its associated company, Hitweb Ltd.

Limit of liability/disclaimer of warranty

Business Communications Development Ltd and the authors have used their best efforts in preparing this book. Business Communications Development Ltd and its authors make no representations or warranties with respect to the accuracy or completeness of the contents of this book and specifically disclaim any implied warranties of merchantability or fitness for a particular purpose. There are no warranties which extend beyond the descriptions contained in this paragraph. No warranty may be created or extended by sales representatives or written sales materials. The accuracy and completeness of the information provided herein and the opinions stated herein are not guaranteed or warranted to produce any particular results, and the advice and strategies contained herein may not be suitable for every individual. Neither Business Communications Development Ltd, nor its authors shall be liable for any loss of profit or any other commercial damages, including but not limited to special, incidental, consequential, or other damages.

Acknowledgements

The production of the EDCL/ICDL courseware was a team effort and the following are acknowledged and thanked for their input: Gareth Hinton-Jones, Julian Wright, Tracie Page, Lisa O'Connor, Eva Livingstone, Ed White, Michael Stewart, James Gregory, Rehan Butt and David Little.

1 Basic concepts of IT

Main components of a computer

Types of computer systems

Mainframe systems

The mainframe computer was once the only system generally available. IBM made its name and money selling its mainframe systems.

Mainframe systems process and store large quantities of information/data and support many users simultaneously.

The mainframe computer namely supports a network system and is to be found in many locations such as multi-national companies, defence systems, telephone companies and universities.

Minicomputer

A small computer that is intermediate between a mainframe computer and a PC in size, speed, capacity, can support time-sharing and is often dedicated to a single application.

Time-sharing is a system that allows the computer to perform two completely separate operations simultaneously, but independently of each other.

The Personal Computer (PC) IBM compatible

A PC is a computer designed for a single user and is generally used to identify an IBM compatible system. A single computer is often referred to as a 'stand-alone' system, indicating it is not connected to a network.

The popularity of PCs has grown at a phenomenal rate in recent years. They are to be found in homes, businesses, industry, the Police and the Armed Forces. The majority of PCs run on the Microsoft Windows operating system.

The Apple Macintosh computer

The 'Apple Mac' is also to be found in many homes and is the favoured system with organisations that specialise in the production of graphics, publishing and multimedia products.

The 'Apple Mac' was the first computer system to use a Graphical User Interface (GUI) which we shall discuss later.

The network computer

A network computer has a Network Interface Card installed and is connected to other computers by a cable. This allows all the computers on the network to communicate directly with other devices, such as modems and printers and supports file sharing. Networks will be discussed in more detail later.

The laptop computer

The laptop is a portable computer designed to be used in a variety of circumstances, away from the office, such as in a car, train or plane. Some laptops are designed for use under arduous conditions, such as on a military battlefield or in extreme temperatures.

Modern laptops are extremely compact and lightweight, because of miniaturisation of its component parts. Compared to a desktop PC, laptop computers are more expensive and this is due to the cost of miniaturisation.

Generally, laptop computers tend to lag behind desktops in type and speed of the processor available. This is due to the pace of processor technology, which, in recent times, has seen the introduction of number of new processors for the desktop, that await miniaturisation for laptops.

Terminals

'Dumb' terminals are usually associated with mainframe and minicomputers and are connected to a network system. Generally the terminal consists only of a keyboard and a monitor with little or no software. Often the user does not have the choice of what application to use and is automatically connected to the appropriate one. As most systems are centrally controlled, the user cannot format disks or customise the desktop display as with the Windows operating systems.

'Intelligent' terminals are usually associated with systems where the user has more control and choice on how the terminal is used with a greater choice of facilities and application use. A PC terminal is an example of an intelligent terminal.

The component parts

We are only going to look at the PC (IBM compatible system.)

Computer systems are generally referred to as either:

a desktop system

a tower system

Hardware vs. software

Hardware is the term used to describe a component part or sub-assembly of a computer system. For instance, the following items are all grouped under the term hardware:

+ The monitor
+ The computer case
+ The keyboard

Software is the term used to describe a program that is run on a computer. The following are examples of software:

+ Windows 98/Me Operating system
+ Microsoft Office Suite 2000
+ Adobe PhotoShop 6

The case

Whether the system is a desktop or tower unit is of no great importance at this time. It is what is inside the case that is of interest to us.

It is within the case that the majority of the major components of a computer system are to be found. Externally, only two, maybe three components are readily identifiable, and these are most likely from the following group:

+ The CD-ROM, CD-R, CD-RW or DVD drives
+ The floppy drive
+ Possibly a tape backup device
+ A Zip/Jazz or LS-120 (high capacity removable disk) drive

The Hp CD-Writer Plus 8100i

Plextor's internal and external CD-ROMs

A JAZ drive

All of the above items are permanent storage devices and each employs its own format to store the data. The subject of storage is discussed in more detail at Chapter 2.

Front panel controls

The controls of the front panel of the case are fairly universal, irrespective of type or manufacturer, and you may expect to find the following:

+ The main power On/Off switch
+ A Reset switch
+ A number of LEDs, (Light Emitting Diodes), discussed later

Computer interface

It is at the rear of the case, at the 'interface', that the majority of external devices are connected to the system.

Input/Output devices

Input devices, as the name suggests, input data and instructions into the computer.

Types of input devices are:

* The keyboard
* A scanner

Output devices display the result of the computation.

Types of output devices are:

* The Monitor
* Printer

The monitor

The monitor, also known as a Visual Display Unit (VDU) is an output device used to display the computer output to the user.

There are two types of monitors available:

CRT monitors

The more common monitor uses a **Cathode Ray Tube (CRT)** and is dated technology.

Mitsubishi CRT type monitor

The CRT monitor comes in a variety of screen sizes from 14 to 21 inch.

The screen size is measured diagonally from the top left corner, down to the lower right corner.

Although monitors are generally classified by their screen size there are other major factors to be considered:

* **Dot size** should not exceed 0.28. The lower the number the better but at a greater cost.
* The **refresh rate** tells you the number of times per second that the screen is updated. A rate of 85 Hz, or higher, is recommended.
* **Resolution** is the number of horizontal and vertical pixels (screen dots). Lower resolutions, 640 x 480, display larger images, so you can see the detail more clearly. Higher resolutions, 1024 x 768 or higher, display smaller images, so you can show more information on the screen.

The second type of monitor, which is becoming more available, is the **Liquid Crystal Display (LCD)**. This type of display is used in most laptop computers.

The LCD monitor employs newer technology, and offers some distinct advantages. It uses less power, is lighter in weight and takes up less space on the desk.

Mitsubishi LCD type monitor

Environmental Protection Agency (EPA)

The EPA developed an energy saving system, known as Energy Star and this system is now incorporated within the majority of monitors.

The benefits of the Energy Star technology are in reducing waste and pollution, by switching the monitor to a 'sleep' mode after a set period of inactivity.

If your is an EPA monitor, the use of a screensaver actually defeats the EPA purpose.

Ensure that the EPA aspects and controls are correctly set and do not use a screen-saver.

When purchasing a monitor, look for these signs and symbols, which indicate environmental protection through technology, and good health and safety principles in design and screen emissions.

Graphics cards

Graphic, or VGA/SVGA Video cards, will greatly affect the screen display and performance. You should consider the purchase of a monitor and a video card as one entity. If you are a keen computer gamer, then you will almost certainly require a high specification card capable of producing the special effects often required by games.

Video Graphics Array (VGA) and Super Video Graphics Array (SVGA) are standards relating to the monitor resolution.

Accelerated Graphics Port (AGP)

AGP is an interface specification that enables 3-D graphics to display quickly on personal computers. AGP has its own unique slot on the motherboard and you should always read which specification the motherboard supports before purchasing an AGP card, as this technology is regularly changing.

There are a variety of cards available, varying in cost.

The keyboard

A keyboard is an input device. Typing on it sends instructions to the computer. They come in different shapes and styles, some with specialist keys dedicated to Internet functions.

The Digital Free Wire, a cordless keyboard

The traditional QWERTY keyboard

The mouse

The mouse is a hand-held pointing device used to select or move items around on the screen. The mouse, like the keyboard, comes in different shapes and styles and some examples are shown here.

 Microsoft's Intellimouse Trackball

Microsoft's Intellimouse Pro

There are numerous types of pointing devices. The first example shown above (left) includes a wheel as well as the usual two buttons. The second example is known as a Trackerball. Instead of moving the mouse to control the cursor, there is a ball unit built into the top of the case, which the user uses to control the cursor. This eliminates the need to move the mouse.

Peripheral hardware

In computing terms 'peripheral' means a piece of equipment used by a computer, but which is not an integral part of the computer. The following items are common peripheral items that you would expect to see connected to a PC.

Touchpads are commonly used on Laptop computers in place of a mouse. The pad is sensitive to touch and the user glides a finger lightly across it and the cursor responds as if being controlled by a mouse. The user can also tap and double-tap on it to produce the same effect as clicking or double-clicking on mouse buttons.

Light pens are another form of input device. With suitable hardware and software, the user can use it to draw shapes etc, directly on the monitor screen.

Joysticks are multiple input devices used mainly by gamers. They usually have a series of buttons mounted on, or around, the main hand-held control. A joystick is essential to play a Flight Simulator where it is used to fly and control the aircraft. As more advanced games and simulations appear on the market, so do the products necessary to play them. A similar multi-input device consists of a steering wheel and pedal controls.

Communications – the modem

A modem is a device that the computer uses to communicate to other computers and fax machines over standard telephone lines. A modem can be installed inside the computer case or have its own case and be used as an external device. There are generally two types of modem available, depending on the type of telephone line you have.

Analogue modems

These use the standard telephone line and come in many shapes and styles. The current standard is known as 'V90 56K x2' and has a reasonable data transfer rate.

3COM (US Robotics) V90
56K Message Modem

ISDN modems

ISDN telephone lines are digital and use two channels to transmit and receive information and because of this, are much faster. ISDN telephone lines require specialist modems, which compared to analogue modems are quite expensive.

Zoom Telephonics ISDN
Fax/Modem

Modems are also discussed in chapter 7.

If you wish to access the Internet, then a modem is a must.

Technological advances

Technology is changing rapidly and with the introduction of digital mobile telephones, you can expect to see Internet access through a mobile telephone.

Asymmetric Digital Subscriber Line (ADSL)

This is a method of sending high-speed data, fast enough to carry feature films for instance, over an existing telephone cable. This system was introduced in the UK mid-2000. The initial cost is high.

Light Emitting Diodes (LED)

LEDs are small illumination devices which come in a variety of colours and are most commonly used to indicate a state of a device: is it on standby or is it carrying out a task, how far it has progressed with that task or has completed that task?

Where are they? You will often find LEDs on the front of devices and used to indicate if the device is switched on. In the case of a printer, LEDs indicate that it is carrying out a print task, if the printer ink or toner is running low, or if the device has a problem, such as a paper jam.

LEDs are employed on numerous devices, for instance modems and Network Interface Cards, and indicate if the device is sending or receiving data over the network.

Other peripheral equipment

Scanners

A scanner is an input device. It reads graphics and text in a manner understood by the computer and transfers that information to the screen, using appropriate software.

Suitable software, such as Optical Character Recognition (OCR) is required if you wish to use the text in a word processing application. Most scanners usually come with cut-down versions of specialist software as part of the package.

The printer

A printer is an output device. It converts electronic files to paper format, which are known as 'hard' copies. There are an abundance of printers on the market, including,

Dot Matrix printers

- Uses a ribbon to produce the image, with a set of pins, which impact on the ribbon
- Fairly low quality print, made-up from a series of dots

HP DeskJet 670C printer

Inkjet printers

- An extremely popular type of printer;
- Produces high quality print;
- The ink is usually a water-based product, which degrades over a period of time;
- Do not allow print to come in contact with water, the ink will run.

Laser printers

- High quality print output;
- Does not use ink but a toner and does not suffer the same problem with dampness as an Inkjet printer;

HP LaserJet 6P/6MP printer

- The quality of the output, particularly with graphics, still has someway to go to equal the higher end Inkjet printer.

Laser printers are generally more expensive to purchase and to run, especially colour models.

Plotters

A plotter is an output device used to produce drawings and graphs. It has a number of pens mounted on moving arms. Typically you would expect to find them in architects' drawing offices and graphic publishing houses. The plotter is connected to the computer's printer (LPT1) socket.

Speech synthesisers

Speech synthesising software is designed to assist the visually impaired and can read visual data from a computer application, convert it to speech and play it back to the user. There are numerous applications available, usually from specialist software providers, such as the Royal National Institute for the Blind.

To use Speech synthesising software, the user must have a sound card installed in the computer, with a suitable set of speakers connected to it.

Speech recognition software

Speech recognition software functions in reverse to speech synthesising software, converting the user's speech to information, which is then displayed on the computer screen.

Inside the computer

The case unit contains a number of important sub-units, or systems, that make up the computer system.

The motherboard

The motherboard is the main circuit board of the computer. All other items or units connect or plug into the motherboard.

There are various types of boards available.

The AT series of boards supporting the original Pentium processor are still available, mainly because the manufactures Cyrix and AMD series of processors use them. They are usually referred to as 'Socket 7' motherboards.

The 'Socket 7' board bus speed was only 33MHz. **The Super Socket 7 motherboard** supports faster 95 and 100 MHz bus speeds.

The TMC T16NBD Slot 1 ATX motherboard (66 – 100MHz)

RAM slots

Pentium II slot 1

Expansion facilities

AGP slot

PCI slots

ISA slots

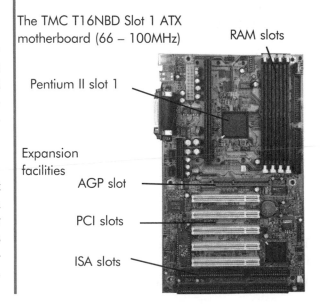

The ATX motherboard is the current series and supports both of the Pentium processors. However, Pentium II/III processors use a different socket. The name has also changed from 'socket' to 'slot 1'.

Number of on-board processors

Some motherboards will support more than one processor, usually the Pentium II series.

On-board systems

Motherboard technology has advanced in recent years. It is not unusual to find some or all of the following built-in to the motherboard,

- Two channels for the Floppy drives
- Four channel EIDE support for:
    - Hard Disk drives
    - CD drives
    - LS-120 Super Floppy drives
- VGA support for the Monitor
- Various types of SCSI support
- Sound facilities

The following items or units are to be found on the motherboard:

The Central Processing Unit (CPU)

The CPU is the main chip in the computer. It processes instructions, performs calculations and controls the flow of information through the computer. The CPU is the computer's 'brain'.

CPU names

The current range of Intel CPUs all use the name 'Pentium' and have a Roman Numeral extension which identifies the series. An example would be the Pentium III. There are several types of Pentium III CPUs available and, to further assist in identification, the CPU clock speed accompanies the name, for instance 'Pentium III 500 MHz'.

CPU clock speeds

Computer operations are performed at precisely defined intervals and therefore the processor requires a highly accurate clock to assist in its operations.

A quartz crystal clock is incorporated within the computer and the measurement of the clock rate is given in megahertz (MHz). As a general rule a PC is more powerful the higher the clock rate.

CPU manufacturers

By far the greater producer of CPUs is the Intel company. Current Intel CPUs are known by names.

- The Pentium II (PII), with speeds from 233 to 500 MHz. It is unlikely that you will be able to purchase a PII CPU as they have been superseded.

The Intel Pentium II CPU

- The Pentium III has now replaced the PII and its speed has correspondingly increased, at the time of writing the top speed is 1GHz.
- The Celeron is a fast inexpensive CPU. Based on the Pentium II, but with less built-in memory. This CPU was designed to meet the needs of home and budget users. The Celeron uses a different socket, which is referred to as socket 370.

CPU and RAM

Processor speed is measured in megahertz and the higher the number, e.g. 450 MHz, the faster the computer. However, if you have a fast processor but only have a limited amount of RAM installed, you will not achieve the maximum potential of the system. CPUs and RAM, together, produce the speed, not one or the other on its own.

Other manufacturers of CPUs

Intel is not the only company to produce CPUs. Other manufacturers include:

- AMD, who recently introduced a CPU known as the Athlon, with speeds in excess of 900MHz. This requires a specialist slot 'A' motherboard.

The AMD Athlon CPU

* Cyrix with their range of 6x86 and Media GX CPUs.

Computer technology advances in leaps and bounds. Very soon the market will see the introduction of CPUs with speeds exceeding 1 GHz.

Random Access Memory (RAM)

RAM is a temporary storage device, only active when the computer is switched on. RAM is volatile and any data still in RAM when the system is shut down, or subjected to a power failure, is lost never to be regained. RAM is discussed in detail later.

Expansion slots

There are usually a number of spare slots on the motherboard, for future expansion or upgrading. Two types are in wide use: ISA, the older slot, and PCI, the newer slot. Usually a number of each will be found on a motherboard, with the emphasis being given to the PCI type.

Take note

ISA (Industry Standard Architecture) is the bus used in standard IBM-compatible PCs to provide power to add-in boards and communication between boards and the motherboard, into which they plug. ISA is an old standard and is being replaced by the PCI standard.

PCI (Peripheral Component Interconnect). was first introduced by Intel in 1992. It is an improved standard over ISA, and has a much faster transfer rate.

Bus is a data communications connection between two or more communicating devices. Different standards operate at different speeds.

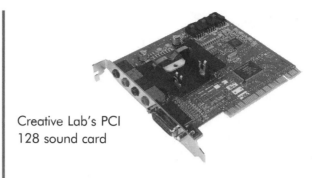

Creative Lab's PCI 128 sound card

Storage devices

The Hard Disk Drive (HDD)

The Hard Disk Drive is a permanent storage device and all of the operating system and application files reside on it, as will the majority of the files that you produce.

Most computers have at least one HDD, also known as either the fixed disk drive or the 'C' drive and it is mounted within the computer case. It is connected to the motherboard via a special ribbon cable and comes in a variety of sizes.

An internal view of a HDD

Note: HDD manufactures announced in late 1999 that they are ceasing production of HDDs below a capacity of 13GB.

The Floppy Disk Drive (FDD)

The Floppy Disk Drive is a storage read-write device. It is connected to the motherboard by the use of a similar type of cable as used by the HDD, however this cable uses a type of connector that avoids any confusion as to which cable is which. Up to 2 FDDs can be installed, though you will usually expect to find only one on most computers.

The CD drives

All computers now have a CD-ROM drive installed. It is connected to the motherboard using the same type of cable as that used by the HDD. CD drives are permanent storage devices and there are three different types. These are described in detail later.

A Yamaha internal CD ROM drive

CD-ROMs are gauged by the speed they run at and this is often referred to as 36X or 40X, which is the spindle speed of the drive motor.

ROM stands for **R**ead **O**nly **M**emory. What this means is that a file can be opened and read. Sections of it can be copied to other documents, but any changes made to the source file cannot be saved.

DVD disk drives

CD-ROMs now have competition from the Digital Versatile Disk (DVD) drive. Its external appearance is similar to a CD-ROM, it comes in two types and is discussed in detail later.

Panasonic's LF-D101U rewritable DVD disk drive

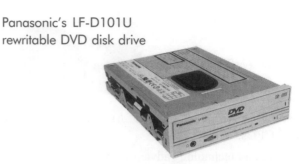

The Power Supply Unit (PSU)

There is an integral PSU installed in the case, which connects to an external, 250 volt, mains electrical supply. The PSU reduces the voltage from 250 volts Alternating Current (AC) and converts it to Direct Current (DC), with voltages between 3.3 to 12 volts.

Within the PSU is a fan that draws air out from the case to help keep the interior and components cool. Power consumption is between 200 to 250 watts. Compare that to the average light bulb of 60 watts.

The concept of storage and memory

Storage devices

Computers employ two different types of storage and these come under the headings of 'Permanent' or 'Volatile' (temporary) storage. Each is discussed with an explanation of how each functions and where it is to be found.

Types of storage devices

There are numerous types of storage devices available. Some, such as the HDDs and FDDs just discussed, permit the user to read and write to the disk any number of times. Other types of storage devices will permit 'read-only' actions.

Read-only means that a file can be opened and read, sections of it can be copied to other documents, but any changes made to the source file cannot be saved.

Connection methods

There are two common methods of connections associated with HDDs and these are Enhanced Integrated Drive Electronics (EIDE) and Small Computer Systems Interface (SCSI).

EIDE is the most commonly used method and is built into the motherboard requiring no additional hardware. A maximum of four devices can be connected, including CD-ROMs. A lower performance device than a SCSI HDD.

SCSI is a fast communications device which requires an additional (SCSI) card installed within the computer. SCSI devices are more expensive for instance a 20GB EIDE disk costs approximately £145 whereas a comparable SCSI drive costs £305.

SCSI connections are not limited to HDDs and are used to connect scanners, CD-ROMs and the like to the computer. Typically you can connect up to 6 devices to one SCSI card each device having its own identification, using what is known as a 'daisy chain' method of connecting.

With an increase in cost you get a corresponding increase in performance using SCSI devices. Gener-

ally most home and business systems use EIDE. SCSI is used in network or mission critical systems.

Permanent storage

All storage devices such as HDDs, FDDs, CD and DVDs are known as permanent storage devices. What this means is that any data written to the devices can be retrieved and reused again and again. The action of shutting down the computer and turning off the power will not result in the loss of data.

These types of drives use a magnetic or laser media on which the data is stored. It is particularly important never to use any other magnetic material in the vicinity of computer disks. The magnetic influence will corrupt and destroy the data stored on the disk.

Identifying disk drives – hard disk drives (HDD)

Most computers have one hard disk drive (HDD) installed within the computer case.

The operating system employs letters to identify the various drives installed in a computer system. If other HDDs are fitted, they will be allocated the next available letter. If only one HDD is fitted, it is always allocated the letter 'C' and this is known as the 'Root' drive.

Most computers now have a CD drive installed and it too is allocated a drive letter, usually the letter 'D'. The letters 'A' and 'B' are reserved solely for the use of floppy disk drives (FDD).

Types of HDD

HDDs are categorised as 'fixed', permanently installed within the computer case, or as 'removable', mounted in a unit which permits the removal of the disk which may then be used on another computer without the need to open the computer case.

Floppy disk drives (FDD)

It is uncommon to see more than one FDD installed and it is always allocated the letter 'A'. The letter 'B' is not available for use elsewhere, except for another

FDD. If a second FDD is installed later, the user must set up the drive through the computer BIOS; only then will the operating system see the drive. The same applies if installing further HDDs.

The capacity of the standard 3½ inch floppy disk is 1.44MB.

The super floppy ia a recently introduced drive, rumoured to eventually replace the older floppy, and is known as the LS-120. The figure 120 indicates the capacity of the disk, 120 MB, compared to the older floppy disk.

The external appearance of the LS-120 drive is almost identical to that of the old. It will also read and write to a 1.44MB floppy disk.

Ten 1.44MB disks cost approximately £5 whereas four LS-120 disks cost about £13, but compare the increase in capacity – 14.40MB vs. 480MB.

A **ZIP drive** is a storage device similar to a floppy drive, which uses a disk that has a capacity of 100MB to 250MB. Zip drives cannot read the standard 1.44MB disk and use the Parallel port, USB or SCSI connections.

The **JAZ drive** is a development of the ZIP drive and offers a storage capacity of either 1 or 2GB. The device can use either Parallel port or SCSI connections.

CD drives

CD-ROM drives are Read Only, i.e. you can read data from it but you cannot save files to it.

CD-R drives permits the user to read data from the CD, however, the write procedure can only occur once. You cannot return later and perform another write action to the same CD.

CD-RW drives permit multiple read-write operations to be performed on the same CD until such time as it is full.

CD-ROMs do not require any specialist software, other than the appropriate drivers. The CD-R and CD-RW drives do require specialist software to function and cost a great deal more.

The average CD disk has a storage capacity of 650 MB. Compare that to the everyday floppy disk, which has a capacity of 1.44 MB.

All of the CD devices mentioned above are available with EIDE or SCSI connections, with the corresponding difference in costs. For instance an EIDE CD-RW costs around £180 whereas a SCSI device will cost about £260 (not including the cost of the SCSI card).

DVD drives

DVD-ROM drives look similar to a CD-ROM drive in shape and size but stores over 26 times the amount of data. A standard DVD disk can hold over two hours of high quality video and CD quality audio. The DVD-ROM can also read standard CD disks. DVD disk storage capacities vary from 4.7 GB to 17 GB, making them ideal for distribution of large multimedia applications.

DVD players are now available for use in the home for viewing full-length feature films. You can also, with the appropriate hardware and software installed, connect your computer to your television and view feature films using your computer DVD drive.

DVD-RAM looks similar to a DVD-ROM drive and has the same features except that the user can write to the disk and store data. The DVD-RAM is a read-write system and is the equivalent of the CD-RW.

Panasonic have launched such a system, with a storage capacity of 5.2GB. It can read a standard CD disk and it will read a Panasonic optical disk. The only thing it cannot do is write to the standard CD disk.

Other permanent storage devices

Tape drives

Tape drives are used primarily to create back-up copies of data, to be used in the case of a system failure or corruption to the original data. Data stored on tape is usually stored as a block, which makes it difficult to restore individual files. Backing up to a tape drive can be quite a long and laborious job and is usually done during quiet periods.

There are numerous types of tapes available, both in size, usually 4mm, and capacity, ranging from 4GB to 50GB.

Already mentioned was the optical disk. This requires a special drive unit to write to the disk. The first series of optical disk had a storage capacity of 250 MB. The current series of disks now have a capacity of 650 MB.

Summary – permanent storage

All the devices discussed so far are known as permanent storage devices. This means that once the data has been written to the device, it is not lost when the computer is shutdown. The data is available to be reused, edited and resaved repeatedly until such time the user decides that it is no longer required and deletes it.

Most of the devices discussed are available as either 'internal' fitted within the computer case, or as 'external', with each device in its own case and connected to the computer using additional external cabling. External devices offer a greater flexibility and allow the device, such as a tape drive, to be used on other computers.

Temporary storage

When the computer is up and running and the user decides to use one of the applications, in simplistic terms, the essential elements of that application and data are loaded in to temporary memory.

Memory is referred to by a number of different names and resides in different areas, for instance built-in to the CPU or on the motherboard as RAM.

Internal cache

CPUs have a limited amount of memory, built-in as part of the overall CPU. This memory is known as Internal Cache or as Primary Cache (or L1).

External cache

Working in conjunction with the CPU cache is another memory, known as 'External Cache', which resides on the motherboard and consists of Static RAM (SRAM) chips.

Random Access Memory (RAM)

RAM, found on the motherboard, is a temporary storage device. It is only active when the computer is switched on. It is volatile and any data still in RAM when the system is shut down or subjected to a power failure, is lost, never to be regained.

There are a number of different types of RAM available with differing speeds and compatibility requirements. Some of the terms and phrases used to describe the different types of memory modules available are listed.

SIMMs, Single In-line Memory Modules, are the basic type of memory available and come in 72-pin or the older 30-pin variety. SIMMs are used on the AT series of motherboards and must be installed in pairs.

A 72-pin SIMM

DIMMs, Dual In-line Memory Modules, are the current standard for computer RAM and are used in all of the latest computers. DIMMs differ from SIMMs and can be installed singly. They come as 72-pin, 144-pin and the more common 168-pin.

Dependent upon the type of motherboard, you may also now see the bus speed quoted. The top end of the range requires the memory modules to be PC 100 compliant. This is the fastest memory currently available, and is reasonably priced.

The amount of memory on a 168-pin DIMM starts at 16MB. You can purchase DIMMs in other sizes, 32MB, 64Mb and finally 128MB. As most motherboards have 4 memory slots, in which the DIMMs fit, you could install 4 x 128MB DIMMs resulting in an overall 512MB of RAM.

There is another type of RAM available, known as RAMBUS/RIMM, which is extremely expensive. At the time of writing, the cost of 128MB of RAMBUS is in excess of £500 compared to 128MB of DIMM at around £120.

Read Only Memory (ROM)

As the name suggests ROM can only be used to retrieve information.

ROM comes in many forms and can be found burnt into a chip that resides inside the computer.

One use of the chip is that which contains the start-up instructions for the computer. This is referred to as the BIOS or CMOS.

The BIOS or CMOS contains the basic instructions required by the computer on start-up. It contains information such as what hard drives are installed and any other devices. It also contains the instructions to enable it to carry out the 'POST' test before handing the system over to the operating system (the POST test is discussed in Chapter 2).

How memory is used

Accessing data

As already stated, a certain amount of data is loaded in to the internal cache of the CPU. If the computer cannot find the data it needs in the internal cache, it looks in the external cache. If it cannot find the data it needs in the internal or external cache, the computer then looks in the slower main memory, the RAM.

Data movement

Each time the computer requests data from RAM, the computer places a copy of the data in the memory cache. This process constantly updates the memory cache so that it always contains the most recently used data.

As a consequence of the movement of data to the internal and external cache, these memory areas will quickly become full. So not only is data going into the cache, it is also being moved out. The older data, that has not been used recently, is moved down the chain and out.

Another memory area that the computer uses is sometime called a *swap file* or dynamic memory. This is an area on the disk drive that the operating system reserves for its own use. If the computer system has limited amounts of RAM installed, this area is used more often. This process slows down the access time considerably.

Operating systems and memory

Different operating systems use memory in different ways. In the older OS Windows 3xx, the OS generally set up swap files. The user could change the file size, provided the hard disk size was adequate and there was available space on it. Windows 95/98 uses a dynamic system. This means that the OS automatically adjusts the size of the file as and when necessary.

Summary – temporary memory

Memory is not a permanent means of storing data. The data remains in the memory only as long as the computer is switched on and operating. When the computer is shut down, or the electricity supply fails, any data still in RAM is lost forever.

Do not confuse storage with memory. In reality both are memory media, however in computer terms they are quite different and should not be confused, otherwise you will almost certainly end up losing data because of the confusion.

Measuring memory

Before introducing the concepts and terms used in measuring memory, it is useful to understand that computer arithmetic is performed, at the most basic level, using a system called *binary*. This format uses only two values, '0' and '1', where '0' represents 'no value present' and '1' represents 'value present'. A good analogy is a light switch where '0' is 'off' and '1' is 'on'.

The following definitions are from the New Webster's Dictionary.

Bit: A single character of a language having just two characters, such as either of the binary digits 0 or 1.

A unit of information storage capacity, as of computer memory, (binary digit).

Byte: A combination of 8 binary digits is referred to as a byte. Each byte represents a single character or letter. For example: The capital letter A = 01000001.

A group of bits of information, typically eight, treated as a unit in a computer process.

The space occupied by a single character in a computer store.

Kilobyte: 1 kilobyte (Kb) is 1,024 bytes or characters. In terms of a document, it is approximately equal to one page of double-spaced text.

Megabyte: One megabyte, (MB), is 1,024 KB or in real terms a reasonable size book

Gigabyte: gigabyte, (GB), is 1,024 MB, equivalent to a shelf of books in a library.

Terabyte: A terabyte, (TB), is 1,024 GB, approximately the same storage as a reasonable size library.

Record: A small amount of data that is stored, processed, and retrieved as a single convenient unit.

A record is a group of related facts describing one item contained in a number of separate locations called 'fields'.

Databases are made up of fields and records. Any number of fields can be used to create a record. For instance, if you are creating a database of your contacts, the database may have a field for each of the following: first name, last name, address line1, address line2, address line3 and so on. Each of these fields will finally make up a record for each of your contacts.

The rows of data within a table of a database, are its records. Each row of information is considered a separate entity that can be accessed or sequenced as required.

File: A set of data with an identifying label held in a computer storage device.

Files are the end result of writing a letter, of creating a spreadsheet or the database the user created. Applications may well call their particular end product by a different name. For instance when referring to the letter created in MS Word, it is usually called a document.

Remember the three letter extension after the filename and the period, 'doc'. This is an abbreviation for the Word 'document'.

It is irrelevant which application, or how that application refers to its own end product, because in computer terms they are all grouped under the name of file.

Summary – computer performance

The subject of a computer's performance has been discussed a number of times during this and the previous chapter and will now be summarised.

The higher the CPUs speed the greater the performance but that alone is not sufficient. RAM plays a vital part in the overall performance. You should consider the RAM requirement, as the operating system Windows 2000 requires a minimum of 64MB. Each application you intend to run will require a given amount of RAM and if you intend to run a number of programs simultaneously, you will require more RAM per application. Basically, the CPU and RAM work together and the more RAM the greater the performance.

You can further increase the performance by ensuring that you use high speed disk drives, or better still install all SCSI storage devices, CD-ROMs and CD writers which run faster than EIDE devices with a corresponding increase in cost.

Finally, you spend a great deal of time looking at the monitor, invest in a good one but do not forget that the video card is an important element. A higher specification card will return a clear crisp image and help reduce the health and safety hazard of eyestrain.

Operating systems software

An operating system (OS) ensures that all the components that comprise the computer system, function efficiently together.

The operating system functions below the applications software, and provides the platform for them. Without it, the applications cannot function.

The term 'platform' refers to the type of operating system used by a computer.

Types of operating systems

MS-DOS

Microsoft Disk Operating System, MS-DOS, was the earlier OS and it functioned by displaying lines of text only, on the screen. The user performed tasks by typing in short commands, which the computer then performed.

Windows

Windows is the follow-on OS after MS-DOS and again is a Microsoft product.

Windows is a Graphical User Interface operating system. Instead of typing commands, the user performed tasks by selecting icons (small images) or selecting commands from menus.

First generation Windows OS still required the presence of MS-DOS, because the two systems functioned together. MS-DOS was required to be installed first, followed by Windows, which sat on top of MS-DOS, with the GUI. Windows still used various MS-DOS facilities.

Graphical User Interface (GUI)

The GUI, pronounced 'gooey', uses small pictures (known as icons) and menus to perform tasks. GUIs makes it easier to use the OS, speeds up operations and is more user friendly.

Unix

Unix is a powerful OS that has been around for sometime and is currently enjoying a revival.

Unix is used on many computer systems that support the Internet.

The Apple Macintosh OS

The Apple company produced the first GUI for computers. However, due to Apple's marketing policy and strategy, they lost the market share to Microsoft.

Unix and Apple Mac's OS are mentioned simply to indicate that there are other operating systems available, other than Microsoft products.

Linux

Linux began to gain popularity in 1998 and is a GUI OS similar to Microsoft Windows.

A short history

MS-DOS was basically the first OS for PCs and, over time, numerous versions of the OS were released.

GUIs arrived with Windows and most users first encountered Windows at version 3. Windows was upgraded to version 3.11.

Windows version 3, was a major step forward in operating systems for PCs.

In Windows 95 the GUI had undertaken a major revamp. It was even easier to use and allowed the user to carry out tasks and actions much quicker.

Various patches and upgrades appeared for Windows 95, until the arrival of Windows 98.

Windows 98 still uses the 95 GUI, with increased functionality and facilities.

New Technology (NT)

During the transition and development of the variously mentioned operating systems, Microsoft was developing another system, which was called New Technology, NT for short.

The earlier versions of Windows NT used the same style GUI as that used in Windows 3x operating systems, up to and including NT version 3.51.

With the introduction of Windows NT version 4, the

switch was made to the Windows 95/98 style GUI.

Windows NT was developed specifically as a more powerful and secure operating system for business and industry.

Windows NT OS appears in two forms, the Workstation user system and the Network version, known as NT Server.

Windows 2000

Windows 2000 is Microsoft's latest OS and is available in a number of different configurations, starting with Professional, the workstation version, and moving up to Server of which there are several versions.

You cannot run any Windows applications on MS-DOS, though you can run most MS-DOS applications on the older Windows platforms. This is because Windows has what is known as 'backward compatibility'.

Within Windows, there is a section of the software that is specifically written to cater for MS-DOS applications.

More applications are being written for specific versions of OS platforms. This is particularly so with Windows 2000.

Functions of the OS

As well as ensuring all the components of the computer function together, the OS has many other areas of responsibility and functionality.

File management

It is the OS that is responsible for all file management on the computer. To this end, a particular program exists within the OS to carry out file management. It is called Windows Explorer.

File naming

With the introduction of Windows 95 there came a far more sensible file naming system. Under MS-DOS and Windows 3, file names consisted of a maximum of eight letters followed by a full stop (a period) and then a three-letter extension i.e. '.doc'.

Windows 95 introduced long file names. This system allowed the user to use up to 255 characters. The name is still followed by the period and an extension, normally three letters, though shorter and longer are possible. This system now allows the use of more descriptive names, thus making file recognition and management that much easier.

For more on file management, refer to Chapter 2 .

Utilities

The OS also provides a number of utilities, smaller programs, as integral elements of the OS to assist in the efficient performance of the computer.

When these programs are run, they appear seamlessly integrated, as part of the OS, when they are actually programs in their own right. For example:

Disk formatting

Before a disk can be used on a computer, it must be formatted, in a manner that the OS will recognise.

It is the OS that provides the necessary program that will format the disk.

Computer performance

If the computer finds a fault or error on any disk, there is a program within the OS to deal with this problem. The program is called Scandisk.

Scandisk conducts a series of checks on the disk and will attempt to fix any faults found.

Scandisk will advise the user on the current status of the disk on completion of the scan.

Defragmentation

Because of the way data is stored on disks, there will come a time when you will notice a slowing down of the system when attempting to open files.

This is due to the fact that often the file is broken down in to smaller sections. These sections are then stored in different locations on the disk, known as fragmentation.

The procedure used to overcome fragmentation is known as 'defrag'. This program basically locates the various sections of the files and moves them, if possible, next to each other, in contiguous locations.

This will assist in opening the files quicker and free up wasted space on the disk.

Networking

Windows 95/98 supports networking, with the necessary software included as an integrated part of the OS. The only additional requirements to establish your own network, assuming that you have two or more computers, are to install the Network Interface Cards (NIC) and the cabling and connectors.

Plug and play

Windows 95/98/2000 supports 'Plug and Play' technology. This means that the OS will detect any new hardware you install and load the necessary drivers to allow that item to function.

File storage

FAT16

MS-DOS, Windows 3xx and Windows 95 use a file storage system known as FAT16.

FAT stands for 'File Allocation Table'. It is the FAT that remembers where all the various parts of a file are located on the disk.

FAT16 is wasteful in the way it stores data on the disk. To overcome the problem of wasted space, Windows 98 introduced a new system known as FAT32.

FAT32

FAT32 is more economical in the manner that it stores data on the disk. Less space is lost and the system is more efficient.

However, only Windows 98 recognises FAT32. Be careful if you elect to use FAT32, as you do have a choice.

If you pass files to colleagues and friends who are running MS-DOS, Windows 95 or Windows NT, then those disks must use FAT16.

NTFS 4

New Technology Filing System 4 (NTFS4) is used by Windows NT 4 operating systems. Only NT OSs can read this filing system and it is through the use of NTFS that Windows NT gains some of its increased security features.

Windows 2000

With the introduction of Windows 2000, yet another filing system has emerged, NTFS5, which only Windows 2000 can read.

Customisation

All Windows programs permit the user to customise the computer set-up and the user interface. Windows 98 provides increased functionality in this area.

Twin monitors

Windows 98 allows for up to two monitors to be connected to the same computer. This is particularly useful if you give presentations. You may have your own monitor adjacent to the computer or you may set it up, along with the second monitor for audience use.

To run two monitors, you must install a second video card in the computer, and of course you will require longer cables.

Other features

There are more features within the OS and they are not all listed here.

Read the appropriate user handbook, failure to even scan the handbook briefly will almost certainly result in you not being fully aware of the capabilities and functionality of the OS.

Internet browser

Microsoft includes its Internet Browser software with the operating systems. The browser is necessary if you intend to access the Internet. See Module 7 for more details.

Summary

All computers require an operating system. Without the OS, the hardware will not function, nor will any applications software.

You must have the appropriate operating system, the Platform, loaded to run particular application software.

The graphical user interface

Windows and Macintosh operating systems use a Graphical User Interface, GUI (pronounced 'gooey').

A GUI is a visual means of interacting with the computer and provides an easy means of issuing commands without the user having an extensive knowledge of commands and programming by using windows, icons and mouse pull-down menus

The GUI system uses small pictures, known as icons to represent actions and commands. The interface is also made up of a series of menus. The menus, once activated, open a drop down list containing further commands. Even more menus may be concealed with the initial drop list and this system of menus is known as 'cascading'.

Icon method

Icons are a visual means of issuing instructions, for instance 'print the document', by the use of one mouse click on the icon.

To issue the same instruction to the computer, using the menus, would require three separate mouse actions, which is still quicker than the older method of command line instructions.

Menu method

Though the use of icons are usually a quicker method of issuing instructions, the menus often offers greater flexibility.

Suppose you only want to print one page, then the icon method could not be used as it prints the entire document.

Using the menu method opens a print dialog box, which offers a number of options for printing the document including,

- Print one page
- Print a range of pages
- Change the printer properties
- Change choice of printer for the current print job

The application window

Each application window consists of a number of different areas.

For the MS Word application window, starting at the top of the window:

- The blue strip along the top is the title strip
- When it is coloured blue it indicates that it is the active window
- The title strip will also list the document name and subject to customisation the file path
- Below the title strip is the menu bar, usually with nine drop-down menu lists
- Below the menu bar is the first of the toolbars, usually the Standard toolbar
- Below the Standard toolbar is usually the Formatting toolbar

The menu bar and toolbars can be customised, with additions and subtractions being made to the content of the menus and likewise to the toolbars.

The overall appearance, such as which colour scheme the user prefers, whether the ruler is displayed, and any additional toolbars that the user may wish displayed permanently, can all be customised.

Command line options

Later versions of some products provided a simple drop-down menu display, none however with the flexibility of the Windows platform.

Standardisation

With the majority of application suites, standardisation and integration has greatly improved. For instance:

- The majority of the icons that appear on the MS Word Formatting toolbar will also appear on the MS Excel Formatting toolbar
- This increases the users productivity, in that the user, having already used one application can

19

immediately apply that knowledge to the second application

- The same applies to the drop-down menu contents, to such a degree that different software companies are conforming to a common layout.

Customisation

Customisation allows the user to set up the screen display, menus, toolbars and more, to best suit the user preferences.

Image sizes

Within the operating system, there exists a means of changing the screen resolution.

This is particularly useful if the user is visually impaired. By changing the resolution to a lower setting, the images will appear larger on the screen, thus improving the visibility for the user.

Productivity

Productivity is increased. This is due to the fact that the user can often, on the click of a mouse button, issue instructions extremely quickly and then proceed to another task without having to wait for the last instruction to be performed. This speeds the work process tremendously.

To gain the maximum use of any application, the user should experiment and try out the various options available.

Use the online help system, via the help menu on the menu bar.

Summary

GUIs have made learning and using a computer extremely easy, with a corresponding increase in overall production.

Applications

Applications, such as those in the Microsoft Office 2000 suite, are programs specifically written to accomplish specialist tasks and functions.

These applications are used to write letters, manage finances, to create databases, to draw pictures and to play games.

Take note

You must have the appropriate operating system loaded to run the application.

When application software is released, it has a name and a version number. Inevitably, even after considerable testing, the software will have faults in it, known as 'bugs'. The software manufacturer will periodically issue an update or 'patch', designed to correct the various problems. When applied to the applications the patch will also update the version number of that product.

It is important to be aware of what version your software is, particularly if access and security are concerns to you.

Summary of some applications

MS Word – word processing

This application is used to produce letters and a variety of other types of documents, which would, until the introduction of computers, have been produced on a typewriter.

MS Excel – spreadsheets

This application was written to manage and analyse finances and information as well as create charts and graphs. Excel can also be used to create simple databases.

MS Access – databases

This application was specifically written to create databases, to enable information and data to be assembled and collated.

Access is a powerful application that lends itself to simple databases, such as a list of names and addresses of your friends, as well as being able to handle large and complex tasks such as stock control and ordering in warehouses and supermarkets.

MS PowerPoint — presentations

This is a presentation application that produces a series of slides, including audio and video inserts, to be assembled for presentation to audiences.

MS Outlook

Outlook is a Personal Information Management (PIM) system that lists your contacts, assists you to organise your time and much more.

If your computer is connected to a Network, Outlook provides a group working facility to enable a team, for instance, to collate their activities, meetings and so on.

Outlook is worth investigating more deeply in your own time. There are many features not readily apparent on the surface, such as tracking and logging the time you spend working on a particular document, spreadsheet or database. This feature is particularly useful if you are self-employed and charge for your time by the hour.

E-mail

Outlook and Outlook Express creates and manages your e-mail.

Desktop Publishing (DTP)

Numerous programs exist which assist the user in producing newsletters, brochures, notices and suchlike. Microsoft's own application is Publisher 2000, which, through the use of wizards, can assist the novice to produce good DTP publications.

Web design software

In addition to DTP applications there are numerous applications available that are used to create Websites. One such application is Microsoft's FrontPage. This is reasonably inexpensive and the user quickly develops sufficient skills to create simple, or using the built-in wizards, fairly complex Websites or pages.

The applications previously described are all Microsoft products. There are of course numerous other applications on the market. You should carefully investigate and identify what your requirements are and what funding you have available, before buying.

Application integration

All applications within the MS Office suite are written by Microsoft and therefore support cross-application functionality.

This means that, instead of each application performing similar functions independently, the same functions are centrally located and each application accesses these functions.

Through the use of integrated functions, the applications do not waste precious space on the hard disk. Furthermore, as a consequence of integration, many of the menus and toolbars within the applications are much the same with regard to look, content and feel.

Naturally there are specialist menus and toolbars specifically related to the particular application.

Because of the similarity and layout of the application GUI, user training is much easier and experience quickly transferred.

Summary

Applications will not function without the appropriate operating system and are Platform specific.

Integrated applications are frequently cheaper to purchase than buying each application singularly. Furthermore, by purchasing a suite of applications, cross application and functionality is greatly enhanced.

Do not forget to use the online Help for more information, particularly regarding customisation.

Computer-based systems

Systems developement

Business use

When an organisation, or an individual, decides that it requires a computer system, either from new or upgrading current systems, there are a series of procedures that should be followed. It is essential to identify what the requirements are.

Systems analysis: Identify all the input, output and control mechanisms operating in the current system.

A feasibility study: Is the proposal economically, technically and socially practicable?

Systems design: Specifying the input and output processes and control for a new system, designed to overcome the short-comings of the old system.

Program design: Using a high level language to write the programs necessary to perform the processing operations required by the system specification.

Program testing: With real time and test data to iron out any bugs and test the system to extremes.

Implementation: Either parallel, direct, phased in, or a pilot system.

Training: If re-training is required, prioritise the training. Key personnel should head the list.

Conversion of files: Will the new system read old formats or will manual conversion be required.

Maintenance and monitoring: To deal with any problems that arise after implementation and also to maintain and upgrade the system when required, either in programming or through the introduction of new hardware/software.

Home use

As an individual, the procedure is much less complicated and the overall deciding factor will almost always be that of finance – what can one afford?

The following are a number of questions that you should take into consideration when thinking of buying a computer for personal use.

Finance: How much can I afford? If money is unimportant then the assessment is somewhat easier, though it should still be carefully thought out.

Requirement: What do you expect the system to do? For example, is the use solely for adults or will children have access to the system?

Security: Is security going to be of importance? If so, then the type of operating system should be carefully considered. For general home and low-level office use Windows 98 would be satisfactory.

If security is likely to be a problem then Windows NT/2000 may meet the requirements. The increase in security has a corresponding increase in price.

Applications: What applications will you require? Will the built-in Windows 98 word-processor meet your requirements, or will you require compatibility with applications in use at the office.

Multimedia: Almost all systems come pre-packaged with CD drives, sound cards and speakers. It is worth checking just to be sure.

Brand Names: Do you choose a brand name or buy by mail order and have a 'clone'. There are many good deals to be had at lower prices.

Monitors: It is suggested that the minimum size that should be considered is 15 inch.

Games: Do you intend to play games, if so then a good quality joystick is required. You are limited when using a mouse to control games.

Disk Size: This is less of a problem today than it used to be, however still check the size.

RAM (Memory): The CPU will be degraded by a lack of RAM. The more RAM the better.

Warranties: Ensure you understand the warranty offered, and do you purchase an extended warranty?

Pay particular attention to the warranty on monitors. Many mail order houses offer a swop-out warranty. If the monitor becomes faulty, a telephone call will generally have a fully re-conditioned monitor at your door the next working day. The delivery man will return the defective monitor.

Information network services

A network is a group of connected computers, sharing files and printers and in some cases, applications.

All information on a network is potentially shareable. The sharing of information reduces duplication and helps to increase the productivity of the workgroup.

There is also a capital saving to be made by the sharing of printers and other devices. Networks offer greater utilisation of computer resources and availability of information.

Network connections

There are different types of systems used to connect computers to create the network, which vary in size and complexity.

The number of computers on a network will vary in quantity, subject to a number of factors such as traffic volume, workgroup design, function, style and more.

A workgroup

A workgroup is usually used to describe a small group of people, within a small establishment and often employing peer-to-peer networking.

Peer-to-peer

In peer-to-peer networking, all the people on the network usually store their files on their own computers and give access to some, or all of the files to other users.

Printer sharing

Resources, such as printers, can be used by other users, even though the printer is connected to another person's computer.

A Local Area Network

A Local Area Network (LAN) may describe a number of computers connected together, in one room, on one floor, in one building or in an immediate locality.

LAN systems usually employ what is known as a 'client/server' network.

The **client** is the computer at which the user sits, the workstation which is connected to the server.

All workstations are connected to the **server**. This is a central computer that stores all the files commonly used by the company or organisation.

A number of other shared facilities, such as printers and modems, may also be running off the server.

Wide Area Networks

Wide Area Networks (WAN) interconnect smaller networks. These networks can be close or at a great distance from each other.

The Internet is a series of smaller networks interconnected, to create the Internet.

Standard network topologies

All network designs stem from three basic topologies, methods of connecting computers.

Bus

The bus topology is the simplest to install and maintain. It consists of a single coaxial cable, known as a truck, backbone or segment, that connects all the computers together in a single line.

There are advantages and disadvantages of the system. For instance if a cable fails in any way, the complete network will 'crash', cease to function.

Star

The star topology connects all the computers by individual cable runs to a centralised component called a *hub*.

Unlike the bus topology, if one cable fails, the network as a whole will not crash. However, one hub failing may cause a network crash.

Token ring

The token ring topology connects the computers to a single circle of cable. The signal travels around the cable in one direction and passes through each computer in turn. Each computer acts as a repeater to boost the signal.

The failure of one computer may have an impact on the entire network and cause a crash.

Telephone systems in computing

Telephone systems play a major part in computer networking.

Modem

Modem means **Mo**dulator – **Dem**odulator.

Computers are generally, and almost always in home use, connected to the Internet or a company's network by the use of modems.

Modems are electronic devices that convert binary data from the computer to analogue tones and voltages that are suitable for transmission over standard dial-up or leased telephone lines.

Many modems also have a fax capability and, in addition, many now offer voice mail facilities, via the software bundled with the modem.

Dial-up networking

Dial-up networking is a means used to access the Internet by most home users and, for instance, by company personnel working out of the office who require access to the company network.

For dial-up networking to function, the user requires a suitable modem, access to a telephone line or a suitable mobile telephone and its associated hardware.

The user must also have the necessary authority to access the respective network, usually in the form of a particular telephone number, an approved logon name and the correct password.

The user dials the respective number and, subject to the software and network set-up, may be prompted to logon and provide a password.

Some software packages store the logon name and password, thus speeding up the dial-up process. There are of course security implications in such a system.

The modem, before it can start transmitting data, carries out a '*handshake*' with the remote modem. This establishes how they will exchange information.

Once the handshake has been completed, the modems are ready to pass or receive data as required.

Data compression

The transmitting modem will compress the data, then send it to the remote modem, which will decompress the data. The modems will use what is known as error control to ensure that the data reliably reaches its destination.

Speeds

Modems have the option of using different speeds to transfer data. When communicating modems must use the same speed. A fast modem can talk to a slow modem, but both modems will communicate at the slower speed.

Current standards

The current standard for most common modems is V90 56K x2.

Terminology definitions

You are constantly being introduced to terminology that you may not have heard of, or unsure of what it is, or its meaning. The list that follows explains what the terminology is and gives a basic explanation of how it functions.

Online

The user is 'online' when the modem has connected to another modem and is ready to exchange information.

Offline

When the modem is not connected to another the user is 'offline'.

Integrated Services Digital Network (ISDN)

Instead of using standard telephone lines and a modem, many companies use an ISDN line. ISDN digital technology transfers information four times faster than the standard modem. ISDN requires the use of a specialist modem, called a 'terminal adapter'. Along with faster speeds there are high costs associated with ISDN.

Asymmetric Digital Subscriber Line

Asymmetric Digital Subscriber Line (ADSL) is a more advanced telephone system and was introduced in the UK mid-2000.

In its initial introduction phase, it will allow downloading at speeds of 512KB, compared to the average current modem speed of 56KB. The final planned download speed is planned to be around 2MB, which will allow the user to view full-length feature films with TV quality.

Public Switched Data Network

Public Switched Data Network (PSDN) is a method and system for accessing multimedia and data over a Public Switched Telephone Network.

Public Switched Telephone Network

Public Switched Telephone Network (PSTN) is a circuit switched analogue network which makes connections for the duration of the telephone call.

Analogue

Analogue conveys data as electronic signals of varying frequency or amplitude that are added to carrier waves of a given frequency. Broadcast and phone transmission has conventionally used analogue technology.

Digital

Digital describes electronic technology that generates, stores, and processes data in terms of two states, positive and non-positive. Positive is expressed or represented by the number 1 and non-positive by the number 0. Thus, data transmitted or stored with digital technology is expressed as a string of 0's and 1's. Each of these state digits is referred to as a bit (and a string of bits that a computer can address individually as a group is a byte). Bits and bytes have been discussed previously.

Digital technology is primarily used with new physical communications media, such as satellite and fibre-optic transmission.

Baud

Baud was the prevalent measure for data transmission speed until replaced by a more accurate term, bps (bits per second). One baud is one electronic state change per second. Since a single state change can involve more than a single bit of data, the bps unit of measurement has replaced it as a better expression of data transmission speed.

The measure was named after a French engineer, Jean-Maurice-Emile Baudot. It was first used to measure the speed of telegraph transmissions.

Satellite

There are hundreds of wireless reciever/transmitter satellites currently in operation around the earth. They are used for such diverse purposes as weather forecasting, television broadcast, amateur radio communications, Internet communications and the Global Positioning System.

Fax

A fax is the telephonic transmission of scanned-in printed material (text or images), usually to a telephone number associated with a printer or other output device.

The original document is scanned with a fax machine, which treats the contents (text or images) as a single fixed graphic image, converting it into a bitmap. In this digital form, the information is transmitted as electrical signals through the telephone system.

The receiving fax machine reconverts the coded image and prints a paper copy of the document.

Telex

A Telex machine resembles a typewriter, which is connected to a telephone line. The operator types in data which is usually converted to punch tape as well as producing a paper copy.

When the operator has finished typing in the data, the recipients telephone number is dialled, and provided both Telex systems recognise each other, the data is transferred over the telephone lines. The recipient machine receives the data and produces a typewritten copy.

Telex technology is extremely dated and few systems still exist in companies, being replaced by the Fax and e-mail systems.

The Internet and e-mail

Internet

The Internet, sometimes called simply the Net, is a worldwide system of computer networks. A network of networks in which users at any one computer can, if they have permission, get information from any other computer (and sometimes talk directly to users at other computers).

The Internet was conceived by the Advanced Research Projects Agency (ARPA) of the U.S. Government in 1969 and was first known as the ARPANet.

The original aim was to create a network that would allow users of a research computer at one university to be able to 'talk to' research computers at others.

A side benefit of ARPANet's design was that, because messages could be routed or re-routed in more than one direction, the network could continue to function even if parts of it were destroyed in the event of a military attack or other disaster.

Today the Internet is a public, co-operative and self-sustaining facility accessible to hundreds of millions of people worldwide.

World Wide Web

Technically, the World Wide Web is 'all the resources and users on the Internet that are using the Hypertext Transfer Protocol (HTTP)'.

A broader definition comes from the organisation that Web inventor Tim Berners-Lee helped found, the World Wide Web Consortium (W3C). 'The World Wide Web is the universe of network-accessible information, an embodiment of human knowledge.'

The most widely used part of the Internet is the World Wide Web (often abbreviated to WWW or the Web).

Internet browser

To access the Internet you must have a suitable Internet Browser which translates the Internet data in to a usable visual display on the screen. During this course we will be using Internet Explorer 5.

Search engines

Many newcomers to the Internet worry about how they are going to find the addresses of Websites that might be of interest to them. There is no equivalent of a phone book for the Internet, but it is remarkably easy to find what you are looking for.

The nearest you will get to a telephone book are the search engines. They are directories of millions of Web pages that have been indexed to allow you to track down topics by typing in keywords.

Electronic mail (e-mail)

For many Internet users, e-mail has replaced the postal service for short, written transactions. E-mail is the most widely used application on the Net.

E-mail can be exchanged with anyone around the world, provided of course that both parties have access to the Internet and have an e-mail address.

You can access your e-mail from anywhere in the world, simply by dialling the appropriate telephone number for your ISP and your e-mail can be accessed using a logon name and password.

E-mail is fast, easy, inexpensive and reduces the use of paper, envelopes and stamps, thus creating a saving of resources.

During this course we will be using Microsoft Outlook Express.

Voice over the Internet

In the near future, greater use of the Internet will be made in the field of voice communications.

Fax over the Internet

There are specialist systems in place that now allow a user, who has the appropriate software, to send and receive faxes over the Internet.

For more detailed information regarding the Internet please refer to Chapter 7, which covers the subject of the Internet and e-mail in greater detail.

Computers and daily life

Background

Throughout history there have been numerous technological advances that have had major impacts upon our way of life and approach to manufacturing.

The arrival of the computer, though slow to initially make change, has in recent years seen tremendous changes to almost all ways of life and work.

The computer, whether it be a mainframe, mini-computer or a PC, has impacted in varying degrees on almost everyone's life. This may take the form of a person actually using a PC at home or in the office, or in the way they work, for instance in a car plant where much of work is now automated.

Computers are ideal for performing unattended repetitive actions, with a very high degree of accuracy. This is seen particularly in manufacturing industry.

Computers have also lessened the risk to man by their use in dangerous areas and processes, for instance in the nuclear industry and in bomb disposal.

The above fields were mentioned particularly to highlight the use of multimedia. In both of these fields visual, and often audio, requirements exist. The use of a computer coupled with video and audio is one form of multimedia.

Future development

Development continues at a pace within the computer industry, in the form of new CPUs arriving on the market, new systems of data storage such as the DVD RAM, and the continual upgrading of operating systems and applications.

Surrounding the introduction of the new or upgraded applications there is also the introduction of new or expanded use of computer systems and applications.

Computer systems in business

There exist numerous systems and platforms in use in business today, including those outlined here.

Banking

- Automatic Transaction Machines or better known as cash machines
- Automatic cheque readers that not only read the cash details, but also monitor the number of cheques issued by the individual or company, by the use of magnetic strips or other medium to determine if the user requires a new cheque book
- Internet banking
- Cash transfer, whether national or international

Stock exchange

Trading on numerous Stock Exchanges is now conducted by the use of computers. There were some problems in the earlier days when the systems were designed, and programmed, to monitor the sale of stocks and shares and should there appear to be a run on them, automatically initiate sales. This in turn was picked up by other Exchanges and the computer systems actually started a panic selling spree.

Advertising

Advertising has seen the introduction of the computer work to its advantage, particularly in the mail-shot (or junk mail).

The mail merge feature of the word-processing and Desktop Publishing (DTP) programs has introduced the automation of bulk mail addressing.

Accountancy

The use of spreadsheets has introduced an automation capability to accountancy.

The spreadsheet can be used as a modelling tool for simple forecasting and the use of the 'what if' feature can assist in the development of strategy and business planning.

Management

Specialist software exists to assist management in the executive decision-making process.

Project management

Project Management software is available to assist in the management of many different types of projects.

This software will program in events, sequences, etc. and will warn of over-runs or conflicts between events.

Group working

Many tasks involve group working.

Information must be available to more than one person, hence the development of group working through the use of networking.

The network allows the sharing of information and resources, thus speeding up processing time and production of documentation in relation to the projects.

Office automation

Numerous areas within an office now have automated features, such as:

- Customer Administration
- Company calendars
- Production of in-house publications
- Company contacts and address book
- E-mail is a fast and cost effective method of communications and with suitable communications hardware and applications installed, the transmission of text and graphics can be achieved quickly and easily

Computer systems in industry

Already discussed was the car industry, which has seen, over the last ten years, completely new systems of work introduced.

The manufacture of a motor vehicle is extensively an automated process, where large areas of the car plant are manned by a few personnel, mainly technicians in attendance of the robots that actually assemble the car body and shell.

Advantages

There are numerous advantages to be gained by the use of computer controlled robotic systems:

- **Reliability:** The system performs repeatedly the same actions without the problem of fatigue.
- **Accuracy:** The same actions, no matter how often performed are consistently accurate.
- **Re-programming:** All systems can be re-programmed quickly and easily from one focal point
- **Staff training:** With manual handling and assembly by staff, there exists a requirement to retrain staff when changes are introduced. A consequence of robotic assembly and of re-programming is that the need for staff training is minimal and therefore reduces the likelihood of error in the assembly of the product.

Disadvantages

- **Loss of employment opportunities:** The introduction of robotic assembly lines saw a major reduction in numerous car plant work forces. The Banking industry has also seen the impact of the computers affect their manpower situation with the introduction of automated systems and Internet banking, less and less personnel are required.

Computers in education

When computers were first introduced into schools, the British Broadcasting Corporation (BBC) used a computer system that was known as the 'Acorn'.

The Acorn in its early days was far-sighted, however, it required its own hardware and specially written software. Cross platform compatibility did not exist.

It can still be found in many schools today but is now in decline, with the introduction of PC's, Windows based systems.

The Acorn was available to the general public however, due to the limited quantities sold, costs of the system, including software, was high.

In 1997 the UK government decided that all schools would have current systems introduced as soon as possible.

In addition and as part and parcel of the government initiative, the "schoolnet" was introduced. The idea was to link schools and to give access to the Internet.

Educational software

With the introduction of the PC into schools, the availability of educational software has increased and its cost has correspondingly reduced.

The software available ranges from basic applications for use in primary schools, to more advanced applications for senior schools and colleges.

There is one particular application that employs multimedia, which is an interactive Desktop Publishing application and is aimed at Junior schools. The children can assemble a story or project for presenting to other members of the school. The application incorporates sound, video and hyperlinks.

Advantages

* The student can quickly and easily return to a passage and carry out the same task, or re-read the same passage for clarification
* The student can pace his or her own study rate
* Some applications will monitor and test the student progress and advise if there is a problem

Disadvantages

* The student cannot question the tutor for clarification or request assistance
* The computer is impersonal and offers only limited feedback to the student

Computers for home/hobby use

The majority of home based computers are multimedia systems, incorporating CD-ROM drives and sound systems.

Software

* If the system is to be used for business then the applications used should be those used at the office to ensure compatibility

Home accounts

* If the system is to be used to run household accounts and your bank details, including online banking, then specialist software exists to meet your requirements

* The Microsoft product, 'Money Financial Suite', provides online banking, assists in tax returns and manages your share portfolio
* There are other applications that will also peform the same functions

Hobbies

It is impossible to list everything that one could do using a computer, however a sample includes:

Family history

* If you are keen to assemble your family history there are applications packages that will assist you in this area (try www.familysearch.org)

Research

* By the use of the numerous CDs that are available, you can conduct research into a vast array of subjects and topics
* Do not forget the availability of the Internet for research as well

Home study

* There exists an ever-increasing number of CDs for home study and revision. Whether it is for GCSEs or for the Open University, the computer is an excellent tool to assist with revision and of course, the final presentation of the course work.

Computers in everyday life

Computers are encountered in our everyday life to such an extent that we are sometimes not aware of their presence. Some examples are:

Supermarkets

Barcode reader

At the checkout, the barcode reader is connected to the store's computer.

When the product is passed in front of the barcode reader, the details are read and passed back to the computer, which in turn identifies the item and advises the checkout of its price. The details are printed out on to the customer's receipt.

Stock holdings

As well as recognising the item and pricing it, the computer will also advise its stock holding section that the item has been sold.

Re-ordering

The stock holding section will have built-in, as a feature of the software, a re-order code. Once a certain level of stock is reached, the system will automatically scan to see if stock is already on-route, when it is due to arrive and what the quantity is.

In the event that there is a rush for certain products and the on-route stock quantity maybe inadequate, then a further request for stock is placed on the company warehouse for future delivery.

Stocktaking

Stocktaking is conducted very much quicker. The staff will download, to a hand held device, the details of the stock on hand; such as the name and code.

The staff then count the items on the shelves and enter the quantity on the device. The two figures are tallied back on the main computer, taking into account damaged goods and write-offs.

Another method is again a hand held device, but this time with a barcode reader. Each item has a stock number displayed on the front of the shelf. The reader is swiped across the code and the quantity on the shelf is also entered.

The detail is in turn downloaded at the main computer.

Pricing

Because all pricing is handled at one point, the computer changes can be quickly implemented.

Libraries

Computerisation of library holdings has now re-placed most of the old methods and computers lend themselves to this area particularly well.

The master list

The library will have a master list of all publications on its inventory. This list is in turn arranged into categories such as crime, historical, etc.

Each item will also be listed by title, author and date of publication, with some specialist publications having a keyword list on which the staff may conduct searches.

The borrower

For a person to borrow a publication, that person must first be registered at the library.

The registration will include some form of identification, usually a number, which identifies the borrower, along with that person's details such as home address, etc.

Library smart card

Some libraries issue the borrower with a swipe card, which records the above detail. The borrower presents the book to the library staff, who in turn passes the card through a card reader.

The detail is transferred to the computer and the book details are also entered. The date for return of the book is recorded on the computer. At this stage, the system returns to that of the old system, where the library staff then stamps the return date on the sheet inside the book.

Accountancy procedures

Different libraries have different procedures. How-ever at some stage the system will perform a check on all loaned publications and produce a list of those overdue. This list will contain the details of who the book was loaned to, the person's address, etc. for further action.

Smart cards

Smart cards come in many shapes and forms and include: Bank debit cards, credit cards, supermarket loyalty cards, fuel cards, etc.

The use and potential use of smart cards is endless and is only currently limited by the need for greater security measures.

The range of uses is as diverse as:

Hotel use

In hotels to replace doors keys. The card is pro-grammed to open the room allocated to the client.

Bank use

For use with Bank cash machines. The card is issued to a bank customer with a personal identification number (PIN).

The customer inserts the card into a slot and the card is read by the system. The user is then asked to type the PIN, which is transmitted back to a central location and checked as correct.

Once confirmed correct, the user is offered a number of options, including the option to withdraw cash.

The bank cash machines are another form of computer network. All the banks who own machines are ultimately connected to the main system, where all the customers details are stored.

In addition to their own machines, a majority of banks allow other banks' customers to withdraw cash from their machines, via the network of interconnected systems. Some banks offer this service for free, whilst others impose a surcharge.

Doctors surgeries

More and more doctors surgeries are using computers to store patients' details and records as well as treatment received. These are bespoke systems, especially written for the task and are not available from the average computer/software retailer.

This is an area where security implications are enormous. The system must protect the patient's rights of confidentiality and the data must be access protected.

Driving licences

The recently introduced driving licence is a smart card and has given some organisations a growing concern in respect of the "Big Brother" syndrome.

The card will record the driver's details on the face of the card and possibly more on a chip in the card.

Computers in government

Computers have been in use with the government probably longer than with most private organisations.

Uses range from the basic office computer producing the everyday letter, to those running the countries finances.

In 1999, the UK passport office switched to a computerised system for issuing passports.

In 2000, for the local elections held on 4th May, a trial was conducted using computers for voting. It is likely that computers will replace the old ballot box.

The National Health Service has an extensive computer system, which is still being developed. One purpose is to enable doctors in any area of the country to access a patient's documents if that patient is taken ill away from home.

The computer vs. man

There are undoubtedly situations where a computer system, either as a computer on a desk or controlling a robotic device, can perform functions better than a person does.

The occasions when this may be the case include:

*   Repeated action tasks
*   Actions that require accuracy and speed
*   Rapid processing of large quantities of information
*   Hazardous operations involving nuclear materials, deep-water operations and the like

Man vs. computer

There are also occasions when man is the better choice for a certain task such as:

*   When the task is a one-off and the time spent programming a computer would not prove cost effective
*   When the information relating to the task or action is free-flowing and the computer would either have to be re-programmed or to have, as part of its programming, a learning function (again most likely non-cost effective)
*   Situations when interpretation on the ground is vital to the task as the computer cannot see or hear, at this point in time, to assimilate the data
*   A situation develops where no programming has foreseen the circumstances or likelihood of such an event

IT and society

Information society

Information society is a term for a society in which the creation, distribution, and manipulation of information has become the most significant economic and cultural activity. An information society may be contrasted with societies in which the economic underpinning is primarily industrial or agrarian. The tools of the information society are computers and telecommunications, rather than lathes or ploughs.

The information age

This is the age of information. Never before has information been so freely and easily accessible by so many people, to such an extent that there is almost too much information available, hence the term 'information overload'.

The abundance of information has lead to the development of specialist applications, designed to sort, filter and present the information in various formats.

Impact on society

- The way in which information is handled has resulted in a massive loss of jobs in administration, for example in payroll staff
- The computer is more accurate and is extremely fast when compared to a human performing the same or similar tasks
- Everything is required and expected to be delivered instantly, resulting in an increase of stress-related problems

Information super highway

The term Information Super Highway was originally used to describe the Internet and the World Wide Web. It is not often used now and has been replaced by the terms 'Internet', 'Net' or 'Web'.

Year 2000 issues

The year 2000, (also known as 'Y2K'), raised issues for anyone who was dependent upon programs in which the year was represented by a two-digit number, such as '97' for 1997.

Many programs, written 10 or 15 years ago when storage limitations encouraged such information economies, are still running in many companies. The problem was that when the two-digit space allocated for '99' rolled over to 2000, the next number was '00'. Frequently, program logic assumes that the year number gets larger, not smaller - so '00' could wreak havoc in a program that had not been modified to account for the millennium.

So pervasive was the problem in the world's legacy payroll, billing, and other programs that a new industry arose dedicated to helping companies solve the problem. IBM and other major computer manufacturers, software houses, and consultants offered tools and services to address this problem.

Electronic commerce

'E-commerce' (derived from such terms as 'e-mail') is the conduct of business on the Internet, not only buying and selling but also servicing customers and collaborating with business partners.

One of the first to use the term was IBM when, in October 1997, it launched a multi-million dollar campaign built around the term.

Today, major corporations are rethinking their businesses in terms of the Internet and its new culture and capabilities. Companies are using the Web to buy parts and supplies from other companies, to collaborate on sales promotions and to do joint research. Exploiting the convenience, availability, and worldwide reach of the Internet, many companies, such as Amazon.com, the book sellers, have already discovered how to use the Internet successfully. Increasingly, much direct selling (or 'e-tailing') of computer-related equipment and software is taking place on the Internet.

One of the first to report sales in the millions of dollars directly from the Web was Dell Computer.

Travel bookings, directly or indirectly as a result of Web research, are becoming significant. Custom-made golf clubs and similar specialities are considered good prospects for the immediate future.

Computer viruses

A virus is a piece of programming code inserted into other programming to cause some unexpected and, for the victim, usually undesirable event.

Viruses can be transmitted by downloading programming from other sites or be present on a diskette. The source of the file you are downloading or off a disk you have received is often unaware of the virus. The virus lies dormant until circumstances cause its code to be executed by the computer. Some viruses are playful in intent and effect ("Happy Birthday, Ludwig!") and some can be quite harmful, erasing data or causing your hard disk to require reformatting.

Generally, there are three main classes of viruses.

File infectors

These viruses attach themselves to program files, usually selecting '.COM' or '.EXE' files. Some can infect any program for which execution is requested, including '.SYS', '.OVL', '.PRG', and '.MNU' files. When the program is loaded, the virus is loaded as well.

System or boot-record infectors

These viruses infect executable code found in certain system areas on a disk. They attach to the DOS boot sector on diskettes or the Master Boot Record on hard disks.

A typical scenario is to receive a diskette from an innocent source that contains a boot disk virus. When your operating system is running, files on the diskette can be read without triggering the boot disk virus. However, if you leave the diskette in the drive and then turn the computer off or reload the operating system, the computer will look first in your A drive, find the diskette with its boot disk virus, load it, and make it temporarily impossible to use your hard disk.

(Allow several days for recovery.) This is why you should make sure you have a bootable floppy 'Emergency Repair Disk' (ERD).

Macro viruses

These are among the most common viruses, and they tend to do the least damage. Macro viruses can infect your Microsoft Word application and typically insert unwanted words or phrases.

Anti-virus protection

The best protection against a virus is to know the origin of each program or file you load into your computer.

Since this is difficult, you can buy anti-virus software that typically checks all of your files periodically and can remove any viruses that are found.

Norton AntiVirus or McAfee are two examples of protection software.

On occasion you may receive an e-mail message warning of a new virus. You should normally ignore these. Do not send them on to your contacts. The vast majority of these are hoaxes, and by sending them on you will simply waste other peoples time.

E-mail attacks

In recent times there have been a number of major attacks transmitted by e-mail.

Melissa was such an attack, which was attached to an e-mail and when read by the recipient, located the e-mail address book and automatically created 50 copies of itself. The 50 copies were then transmitted and the whole episode was repeated. The result was that major companies and ISPs were swamped with e-mails to such an extent that they either closed down or collapsed under the strain.

The US government ordered the FBI to investigate and eventually apprehended the person who sent the original e-mail and he is, at the time of writing, awaiting trial.

Health and safety and ergonomics

Health and safety considerations

The European Union issued a series of publications, which became known as the six pack.

One of the publications specifically dealt with computer workstation ergonomics and the following areas were addressed.

- Display screens
- Keyboards
- Work desk/surface
- Work chair
- Space requirements
- Lighting
- Reflections and glare
- Noise
- Heat
- Humidity
- Computer/user interface

All the above items will, in some way or another, have an impact on the working environment of the user. For example,

- Glare from the monitor screen or from a glossy desktop
- A strong light behind the monitor, i.e. windows
- A chair that is not adjustable or does not meet the safety standards laid down in the regulations
- Cramped and restraining working space
- Poor lighting conditions that reflect on to the monitor screen
- The monitor set either too high or, most commonly, too low

Breaks

The user must take short breaks if involved with prolonged work at the screen. The break does not necessarily mean leaving the location of work, but a change of activity away from the screen and keyboard.

Eye tests

- Regulation 5 of the UK Health and Safety (Display Screens Equipment) Regulations 1992 gives the user, or those about to become users, the right to have an eye and eyesight test as soon as practicable after request and at regular intervals
- Special corrective appliances are to be provided by the employer for users where normal ones cannot be used
- The costs of the tests and special corrective appliances are to be met by the employer of the user
- The term 'special appliance' will be those prescribed to meet vision defects at the viewing distance (anti-glare screens are not special corrective appliances)

Further regulations

There are a number of further regulations that the employer and casual user should be aware of.

The regulations are not simply for guidance but are to be implemented as a matter of law.

Common sense

Most problems can be quickly overcome by the application of a common sense approach. However, common sense must not override the application and enforcement of the Rules and Regulations that apply to the working environment, etc.

If in doubt, contact your local Health and Safety Executive (HSE) office for advice.

Repetitive strain injury

Repetitive strain injury (RSI) was originally denied by the medical profession, however it is now recognised that an injury can occur if the same actions are repeated over and over.

RSI has been associated with IT when personnel employed on data inputting, sat at a keyboard for a prolonged period of time typing in data, suffered swelling and stiffness to fingers, wrists and arms.

- Short breaks should be taken which will involve the use of hands and arms but in a different manner to that of typing
- If you have any concerns regarding RSI you should seek medical advise, do not put it off because if there is a problem, the situation could get worse if left untreated

Workstations

The Health and Safety Executive, (HSE), publishes Display Screen Equipment regulations, which lists the key areas concerning a workstation, including seating, posture etc.

Seating and posture for typical office tasks

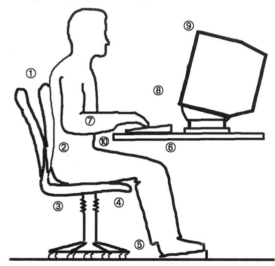

① Seat back adjustability
② Good lumber support
③ Seat height adjustability
④ No excess pressure on underside of thighs or backs of knees
⑤ Foot support if needed
⑥ Space for postural change, no obstacles under desk
⑦ Forearms approximately horizontal
⑧ Minimum extension, flexion or deviation of wrists
⑨ Screen height and angle allow comfortable head position
⑩ Space in front of keyboard to support hands/ wrists during pauses in keying

Workstation schedule and requirements

① Adequate lighting
② Adequate contrast, no glare or distracting reflections
③ No distracting noise
④ Leg room and clearance to allow postural change
⑤ Window covering
⑥ Software: appropriate to task, adapted to user, provides feedback on system status, no undisclosed monitoring
⑦ Screen: stable image, adjustable, readable
⑧ Keyboard: adjustable, detectable, legible
⑨ Work surface: allow flexible arrangements, spacious, glare free
⑩ Work chair: adjustable, with footrest if needed

Workplace safety

A problem with computer systems is the abundance of cables that connect the various items of the system. Ensure that cables are kept tidy and are not likely to cause accidents, for example people tripping over them, with the effect of the actual item possibly being pulled off the desk, further compounding the problem.

In the workplace, it is the employer's responsibility to provide a safe working environment. Likewise it is the home users responsibility to ensure that the home environment is also safe.

In the office environment, the employer should ensure that the correct office furniture is purchased and installed. For instance:

- Desks with cable management systems for all computer workstations

- Printer stands that allow stacking if so required and also permit the correct paper feed, for the type of printer in use

- Some dot matrix printers, particularly the larger machines, can be very noisy and the printer should be placed inside a noise reducing cabinet

- During the printing process, the Laser series of printers will, over time, exude fine particles of toner, therefore the printer should not be in a position that will allow the particles to be blown over people working nearby

Mains power points

Never overload the mains power point.

Never use the double adapter units that allow more than one plug to be inserted into a socket outlet.

Because most computer items only use low power consumption, it is acceptable to use an extension type lead. Remember to keep the lead as short as possible and do not coil it up if it is too long. Cut it to the required length.

There are appropriate means available to permit the running of a number of computer items from one socket.

Always ensure that the appropriate fuse is in the plug-top. Most plugs, when purchased, will have a 13-amp fuse installed. That is too strong a fuse for the average computer item.

If in doubt, seek professional advice.

Ventilation

Good ventilation is important, particularly if you have a laser printer near your workstation.

You should ensure that any airflow around your workstation and the printer does not direct the toner to you.

Lighting

Lighting, both electrical and natural, is extremely important and can cause major problems for computer users. Care must be taken to ensure that lighting does not produce glare, shadows or reflections.

The HSE also published Display Screen Equipment regulations, which lists the key areas concerning a workstation with regard to lighting.

Security, copyright and the law

Software copyright

Programs are usually covered by copyright. You are personally liable if you contravene the copyright of the software.

You break the law if you:

* Copy the software and later distribute the copies
* Lend the software to friends to install on their computers

You may make a copy of the software solely as a safeguard, in the event that the original disk becomes damaged.

Licences held

You may only load the software on the number of computers that you hold licences for.

Security

You must afford the original disks and any legally held copies the same level of security.

You must retain all copies of licences for all software used and you must maintain a list of where and on what computers the software is loaded.

Freeware

This is software that is freely available, such as demonstration disks, or some educational programs. Read the licenses supplied, to ensure that you are not inadvertently contravening any agreements.

Shareware

This is software that is made freely available for a limited time, to enable you to decide whether or not you wish to buy it.

If you decide that you wish to continue using the software after the trial period, you will be required to register the product and pay a fee.

Delete the software at the end of the trial period if you are not interested in it, otherwise you will be liable to pay the producers for the product.

Software on the Internet

Pirated copies of software are sometimes available on the Internet. Be sure to check before downloading such software.

End user licence agreement

The End User Licence Agreement (EULA) is included as part of the installation program on all software.

As the installation of the software progresses, the user is prompted to agree to the terms and conditions of the EULA or to discontinue the installation.

A section of the EULA states that if you do not agree with the EULA the user should not continue with the installation and return the software to the supplier from where it was purchased.

The supplier however, generally, has in his small print a clause that states that should the cellophane wrapping be removed, the product will not be accepted for any other reason than faulty disks.

Be aware. Ensure you know what you require before you buy.

Data protection act 1998 (DPA)

The DPA act was introduced to meet the concern arising from the threat of misuse of the power, that computing equipment might pose to individuals.

This concern derives from the ability of computing systems to store vast amounts of data, to manipulate data at high speed and, with associated communications systems, to give access to data from locations far from the site where the data is stored.

All public and private organizations that hold data about individuals or companies on computer systems must register with the Data Protection Commissioner, giving the purpose for which the data is held.

Data held can only be used for the purpose specified.

Individuals can obtain a copy of the data held about themselves. A fee will be charged.

Data users must register:

* what data they hold
* how they use it
* how it is obtained
* disclose it if requested

An Extract from the UK Data Protection Act 1998

Schedule 1

The Data Protection Principles Part 1

1. Personal data shall be processed fairly and lawfully and in particular, shall not be processed unless:

(a) at least one of the conditions in schedule 2 is met, and

(b) in the case of sensitive personal data, at least one of the conditions on Schedule 3 is also met.

2. Personal data shall be obtained only for one or more specified and lawful purposes, and shall not be further processed in any manner incompatible with that purpose or purposes.

3. Personal data shall be adequate, relevant and not excessive in relation to that purpose or those purposes, for which they are processed.

4. Personal data shall be accurate and, where necessary, kept up to date.

5. Personal data processed for any purpose or purposes shall not be kept for longer than is necessary for that purpose or those purposes.

6. Personal data shall be processed in accordance with the rights of data subjects under this act.

7. Appropriate technical and organisational measures shall be taken against unauthorised or unlawful processing of personal data and against accidental loss or destruction of, or damage to, personal data.

8. Personal data shall not be transferred to a country or territory outside the European Economic Area unless that country or territory ensures an adequate level of protection for rights and freedoms of data subjects in relation to the processing of personal data.

Rights of Data Subjects – Part II

Subject to the following provisions of this section, and to sections 8 and 9, the individual is entitled

(a) to be informed by any data controller whether personal data of which that individual is the data subject arc being processed by or on behalf of that data controller

(b) if that is the case, to be given by the data controller a description of -

(i) the personal data of which that individual is the data subject,

(ii) the purpose for which they are being or are to be processed, and

(iii) the recipients or classes of recipients to whom they are or may be disclosed.

The UK Data Protection Act 1998 is a complex document and the extracts quoted were taken from the reprinted copy of the DPA 1998 published 1999. For further information visit the Website **www.dataprotection.gov.uk**.

A full version of the data act can be obtained from The Stationary Office Ltd. See their Website at **www.tso-online.co.uk**

Security

Computer security not only covers the aspects of theft of the computer and its associated equipment, but the security of the data stored on the computer itself.

Data

Only legitimately held data can be stored on a computer, as covered by the Data Protection act.

Passwords

Computer passwords must be guarded carefully. In particular that of the person afforded administrator rights on the computer system.

Copies of the passwords should be maintained and sealed in an envelope and then locked in a secure container, i.e. the company safe.

Instructions as to who may open the envelopes should be clearly written on the outside.

Any person permitted to open the envelopes should sign a document stating why and by what authority, that the person is accessing the password lists.

Backup policy

In the event of any data becoming damaged, lost or otherwise destroyed, there should exist a policy for creating back-up copies of all important data.

Subject to the degree of importance attached to the data, the requirement might exist for a daily backup or more frequent.

Incremental Backup

The backup policy may only require the backing-up of new or recently amended data, termed incremental backup.

Full backup

A full backup occurs less frequently. During the course of backing up data it is important to use a number of tapes for different days, due to possible tape damage such as tape stretch or breakage.

Backup storage

Naturally one copy of the Backup tapes should by held on site in the event that they are required.

Equally important, at least one copy of the Backup tapes should be held off site in the event of a fire or theft.

Backup procedures

Backup procedures must be documented and clearly understood and practised by the staff responsible for creating the Backups.

Restoration

Equally important is that the Backup Restore procedures must be tried and tested. It is not enough to have a document detailing the Backup and Restore procedures unless the system is fully and regularly tested.

Virus protection

All systems should employ some form of anti-virus protection, not just in the form of anti-virus software, but including company policy as to who may load programs, what disks may be used and how they should be transported.

See Chapter 10 for additional information.

Power failure

Security also comes in the form of protection against power failures or power surges.

Uninterrupted power supplies

There are numerous types of Uninterrupted Power Supply (UPS) systems available.

These systems contain powerful batteries that are on constant standby and will switch on if there is a power failure.

The batteries are not usually powerful enough to allow continuing use of the computer system, but are designed to have sufficient power to give the system adequate time to perform an orderly shut-down without losing any data.

UPS systems have specialist software working in conjunction with the power supply, designed to sense power problems.

Anti–surge protection

Power supply systems are often not running at the correct voltage, etc., due to strain on the systems or adverse weather.

These conditions create power surges, increases and falls in the output, which if powerful enough could cause data corruption.

Sufficiently powerful surges may actually cause some systems to re-boot, particularly in times of storms.

UPS systems can provide considerable protection, by the way of built-in circuitry, and reduce the likelihood of data loss.

Home users can also benefit from such protection by purchasing smaller protective devices, rather than a full UPS system, which can be costly.

Data loss

If your computer does suffer a crash or a problem, the end result could be the loss of data. The file you were working on may be corrupted or you may simply lose the data that you had on the screen at the time.

This subject has been covered elsewhere in module 1, however, a reminder.

RAM is volatile, which means that any data in RAM at the time of a crash or power failure is lost. That is one reason why you are repeatedly advised to save your work.

Sce page 12 for additional information on RAM.

Transferring files

Transferring files across a trusted network usually presents no problems, though it can

sometimes be slow, subject to the speed of the network and the volume of traffic being passed. The Internet is a good example.

Occasionally problems may occur and result in data loss or corruption, either due to network failures or due to a virus attack on the network server.

If at all possible ensure that your data is regularly backed-up, as discussed previously.

Summary

Computer security comes in many forms and covers not only the possible loss through theft, but includes equipment failure resulting in data loss or damage, to destruction in the event of fire.

Written procedures are all well and good, but do they work in practice and do the staff responsible for the security aspects understand and practice the procedures?

2 Using the computer

Systems start-up and configuration

Module 1 gave you a basic introduction to computer hardware and software. We now move on and look at what we have to do to get the computer running, what the system is doing during this phase and finally what the display should look like. It is assumed that your operating system is Microsoft Windows 95/98.

Switching on the computer

Before you switch on the system always check that there is not a floppy disk in the drive unit.

The on/off switch is usually located on the front panel of the main unit. An electrical power unit built into the computer supplies all the components with power and you will hear the fan unit run and the hard disk drive start up.

System start-up

Before the computer loads the operating system, it performs a number of actions.

The start-up display

On initial start-up the computer will read a set of instructions that are stored in the BIOS/CMOS and execute them. You will see a series of lists appear on the monitor. These vary with the type and version of your BIOS/CMOS.

The first list identifies the make, type and version of the BIOS or CMOS chip, which contains the start-up instructions. These do basically the same thing but use different names. You may see something like:

Award Modular BIOS v4.51PG, An Energy Star Ally
Copyright © 1984-00, Award Software, Inc.
AMD-K6™-2/450 CPU Found
Memory test: 131072K OK

The next list may identify the 'Plug and Play' section of the BIOS and will list those items installed on the computer. The following list will include:

BIOS/CMOS

At this stage a message will appear, usually in the lower area of the screen, which will tell you how you can get into the BIOS/CMOS, from where you can change certain settings, such as the Hard Disk Drives (HDD) types. The message may vary slightly but you could expect to see something like:

Press DEL to enter SETUP, ESC to skip memory test

If you press the 'Delete' key at this stage, the BIOS/CMOS stops loading and the Setup screen will appear. Do not go into the Setup at this stage, however. If you decide to investigate this section, write down all the settings and store them in a safe place. There is no reason for you to change anything in this area. It was set-up when you acquired your computer, which is assumed to be working correctly. Be very careful, because if you do change anything and the new settings are incompatible with your system, it may not function until the correct settings are re-installed. You have been warned!

The second part of the message relates to the test the system performs on the memory (RAM) to ensure that it is functioning. You can bypass the test by pressing the **[Escape]** (ESC) key.

The POST test routine

At this stage the computer performs a self-test on itself, to determine that everything that should be there is present and functioning.

The self-test is known as the POST routine (**P**ower **O**n **S**elf **T**est) and the instructions for the test are stored in a permanent memory chip on the computer motherboard.

Detecting HDD Primary Master	Quatum Fireball SE3.2A	*This is a hard disk drive*
Detecting HDD Primary Slave	Quatum Fireball CR8.4A	*Another hard disk drive*
Detecting HDD Secondary Master	LS-120 VERA 07	*Panasonic LS-120 disk drive*
Detecting HDD Secondary slave	CRD.8480B	*This is a CD drive*

44

During the course of the check you will see a number of actions taking place on the screen and these will include:

- Identifying what make and type of processor is installed

- Confirmation and identification of the floppy and hard disk drives, along with that of any other devices installed, such as the CD-ROM and maybe a Super Floppy Disk drive such as the Panasonic LS-120

- Checking that the various systems are functioning and attempting to detect any errors

In the event that the POST discovers a problem, for instance with the floppy drive, it will return an error message, which in this case will appear on the screen as 'Floppy Disk Drive Failure'.

At some stage the screen will display a table listing all the above mentioned items, as shown below.

CPU Type	AMD-K6™-2
Co-Processor	Installed
CPU Clock	450
Diskette Drive A	1.44 3.5 IN
Diskette Drive B	1.44 3.5 IN
Pri Master Disk	LBA, UDMA 33, 3228 MB
Pri Slave Disk	LBA, UMDA 33, 8455 MB
Sec Master Disk	LS-120, Mode 4
Sec Slave Disk	CD.ROM, Mode 4
Base Memory	640K
Extended Memory	130048K
Cache Memory	512K
Display Type	EGA/VGA
Serial Port(s)	3F8 2F8
Parallel Port(s)	378
Bank0/1 DRAM type	None
Bank2/3 DRAM type	None
Bank3/4 DRAM type	Sync. DRAM

If you were to change any of the settings within the BIOS/CMOS Setup, those changes will appear in above list.

The list identifies the different type of disk drive units installed and where they are installed. Refer to Module 1, ' *Main components of the computer*' and you will recognise a number of the items listed above.

An area of particular interest lists the type of memory (RAM) and where it is installed on your computer.

If you have any SCSI (Small Computer System Interface) devices installed, e.g. a scanner, they will also be detected at this stage.

Numerous errors can be detected by the POST routine. However, successful completion of the test routine does not guarantee that your system is actually free of all errors and problems.

On completion of the POST routine, we will assume that the system is fully functional. The system then loads the routines that are imperative to the operation of the computer into the memory (RAM).

The operating system (OS), Windows 95/98, Windows NT or any other OS is loaded as required as are the special files that adapt the OS to the hardware requirements.

Finally the Windows interface is loaded and the Desktop appears. You are now ready to start using the computer.

The Desktop display

The Desktop

The Desktop is the screen that you see when the operating system has loaded. Because Desktops are configurable by the user to suit their requirements and preferences, there is no such thing as a standard display. There are, however, certain items that most people retain on their Desktop. The Desktop display consists of a number of areas and items.

If a wallpaper background had been loaded, it would appear in the white area of this image.

Usually a coloured background or pattern is used. A light colour is used in this diagram for printing purposes only.

This whole area is what is known as the desktop.

Background

The Background may be a plain colour or may consist of patterns and images. These are referred to as the 'wallpaper' and a number are included in the Windows 95/98 operating system. You can create your own backgrounds if you wish.

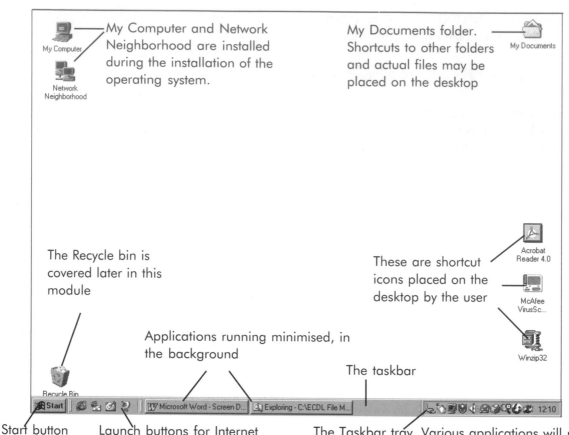

My Computer and Network Neighborhood are installed during the installation of the operating system.

My Documents folder. Shortcuts to other folders and actual files may be placed on the desktop

The Recycle bin is covered later in this module

These are shortcut icons placed on the desktop by the user

Applications running minimised, in the background

The taskbar

Start button

Launch buttons for Internet Explorer, Show Desktop, View Channels. Windows 98 onward

The Taskbar tray. Various applications will place items in the tray. This has a shortcut to the modem, mouse, display panel and date/time

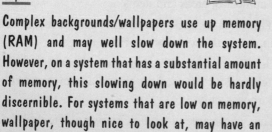

Tip

Complex backgrounds/wallpapers use up memory (RAM) and may well slow down the system. However, on a system that has a substantial amount of memory, this slowing down would be hardly discernible. For systems that are low on memory, wallpaper, though nice to look at, may have an adverse effect on the efficiency of the system.

Customisation

You can customise your computer in a number of ways, create shortcuts and change the way your Desktop looks to suit your preferred way of working.

Desktop icons and shortcuts

An icon is a picture which represents a program, disk drive, folder or other item. A shortcut is an icon that links to a file or folder. When you double-click a shortcut, the original item opens.

Moving icons/shortcuts

It is possible to move the icons and shortcuts to different locations on the Desktop. To move an icon or shortcut

Basic steps

1 Place the cursor over the item
2 Left-click and hold the button down
❑ The selected object will change colour, usually dark blue.
3 With the left button still depressed, drag the item to the desired location and release it
❑ The object will remain selected until such time that you either select another object or click on a blank area of the Desktop.

Creating a Desktop shortcut

It is often very handy to have quick access to a file or folder that you regularly use, and one method is to create a shortcut on the Desktop to it.

We will create a shortcut to the courseware CD, so that you have an alternative method of starting the course.

Basic steps

1 Right-click on a blank area on the desktop and a pop-up menu will appear
2 Select New, then Shortcut
3 At the Create Shortcut dialog box, click the Browse button

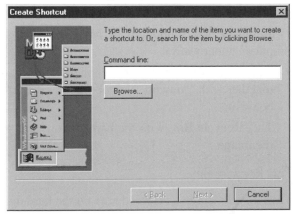

4 When the Browse dialog box opens, in the Files of type slot select *All Files*
5 Using the Look in slot, navigate to the CD drive. The folders and files on the CD disk will appear in the dialog box.
6 Find and click on the file called *Default.htm*
7 When highlighted, click the Open button
❑ The Browse dialog box will close and the file name will appear in the Command line slot.
8 Click the Next button
❑ When the next dialog box opens you are given the option of changing the name or accepting the default name.
9 Change the name to *ECDL Course*
10 Click the Finish button

The dialog box will close and the shortcut will appear on your Desktop. For the Shortcut to function, you must have the CD in the CD drive, otherwise a message will pop-up and advise you that the CD is not ready.

Your ECDL course CD will automatically start when you first place the CD in the drive. With this shortcut you can exit the course and leave the disk in the drive. When you later return to continue, double-click on the shortcut.

Test the shortcut when you next exit the CD program.

You can create a shortcut to any folder, file or program by simply following the sequences outlined and substituting the name where appropriate.

Deleting shortcuts or icons

Basic steps

1 Select it
2 Press the Delete key on the keyboard
or
3 Right-click over the object and from the pop-up menu select Delete
❑ A dialog box will open asking you to confirm that you wish to send the object to the Recycle Bin.
4 Click Yes to delete

47

The Taskbar

It is from the Taskbar that you generally select and start the applications you wish to use. The Taskbar is usually located along the bottom area of the screen and has a number of regions that are independent of each other.

At the extreme left edge of the Taskbar is the **Start** button ![Start]. This button has the word Start on it, as well as the Microsoft Flying Window logo.

◆ Move the cursor over the 'Start' button and pause. A tool tip box will pop-up.

◆ Click on the Start button to see what happens

Remember, because of the ability to customise display, yours may not exactly match the examples shown.

The Start menu

The Start menu is divided into three regions, separated by horizontal lines.

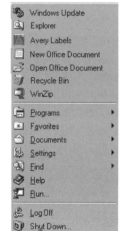

The lower region will usually have only one or two options available, which will include the **Shut Down** command. It is from here that you will close the system down (see page 53).

Move the cursor back to the **Start** button menu to check out the middle region.

This has a further six (or more) menu options. To the right of the top four of these options are right-facing arrows. These indicate that there are secondary menus available and by moving the cursor over the appropriate item, a further menu will open. This type of system is known as a cascading menu.

Basic steps

1 Point to ![Programs]

2 Click on it once (this will keep the menu

open should you accidentally move off the menu area)

❑ The secondary (cascading) menu has now opened and you can see immediately that there are more right-facing arrows adjacent to some of the items listed.

3 Do not select any item

4 Move the cursor back over the main menu

5 Click on it

❑ The Programs menu will now close

The upper region of the main menu is a customisable area, where you can insert or remove items.

Ensure that the Taskbar is still visible and look to the extreme right-hand side. What you will see is dependent upon how your computer has been set up, however, there is usually at least one item in this region and it is a digital clock.

◆ Move the cursor over the clock and pause. In the area above it the current date will be displayed.

Once an application is open, the name of that application will appear on the Taskbar. If you have multiple applications running, all names will appear. It is from the Taskbar that you can switch between applications. Simply clicking once on the required application name will bring it up on the screen.

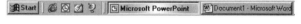

Elsewhere on the Desktop are a number of icons. This again is subject to how the computer has been configured and personalised. Where the icons appear is irrelevant to the operation of the system. You generally see:

◆ An image of a computer with 'My Computer' underneath it

◆ An image of two computers connected together with 'Network Neighborhood' below it

◆ The 'Recycle Bin' with the name below the image

The Recycle Bin

The Recycle Bin is a reserved area on the hard disk

drive and usually occupies 10% of the disk space.

When you delete an object, it is sent to the Recycle Bin. It is not deleted immediately, but held in storage in case you decide to use it again.

Basic steps

To reclaim the object:

1 Double-click over the Recycle Bin icon to open the Recycle Bin folder

2 Select the appropriate object

3 From the menu bar select File > Restore. The object will then reappear in its original location

❑ To change the Recycle Bin settings:

4 Right-click over it

5 From the pop-up menu select Properties

Take note

Be careful when making adjustments, particularly if you change the default and opt to delete objects without first sending them to the Recycle Bin.

Should the Recycle Bin become full, it will automatically delete the oldest files to make room for the newer files. Check the Recycle Bin contents periodically and empty some or all of them. Investigate the Recycle Bin more but exercise caution if you decide to make any changes to the settings.

We will end our brief tour of the Desktop at this point.

Starting applications

Basic steps

1 Ensure that the Taskbar is visible

2 Click the Start button

3 Move the cursor up to the Programs area

4 Pause and a cascade menu will open

5 Click on PowerPoint

Microsoft PowerPoint will open and you are ready to either edit an existing presentation or start a new one.

The control buttons

Two sets of control buttons appear, usually as a group as follows.

The application control buttons

These are to be found on the top right-hand side of the application Window in the Title bar area.

■ **The Minimize button:** Clicking on this will reduce the window to a button on the Taskbar. If the application is reduced to the Taskbar, left-clicking once on the application button will re-store it to its previous location and size.

□ **The Maximize button**: Left-clicking on this button will open a previously reduced window to its maximum size.

▣ **The Restore button**: The Restore button will shrink your window to a smaller size, enabling you to then adjust the window to the desired shape, size and position. This method is discussed later.

☒ **The Close button**: Left-clicking on this button will close the window.

File control buttons

It was mentioned previously that two sets of control buttons will appear with most applications.

In Microsoft PowerPoint you will find one set of control buttons which control the application, as described above, and another set will appear for each open document and subject to your preferences, may appear below the application buttons.

The **File Control** buttons function in the same way as the **Application Control** buttons except for the **Minimize** button ■. Click this and the document is reduced to an icon, usually in the lower left area of the application window. Left-clicking on the **Restore** or **Maximize** buttons will return the document window to its original size and position.

Experiment and see the way the application window changes and decide which display suits you best.

49

Maximizing an application window

To demonstrate the next section we need PowerPoint's application window to be at its maximum size.

If the control buttons match that shown, then the window is at its maximum size, indicated by the middle button ▬ ▣ ✕ .

If however, the control buttons are as shown here, left-click once on the **Maximize** button (middle) ▬ ▢ ✕ . The application window will open out to its maximum size and the button will change to that shown in first example.

Starting a second application

Perform the same procedure described above, except this time select Microsoft Excel. Excel will now open ready for you to open an existing workbook or start a new one.

Basic steps

1   Ensure that Excel's application window is at its maximum size, if not perform the procedure above.

Excel should now occupy the full area of the screen and you should no longer be able to see the PowerPoint application window. It is still there, however Excel is now on top of it.

On the taskbar you should see that there is a button for PowerPoint and a button for Excel. Notice that the Excel button is slightly different, it appears to be depressed compared to the PowerPoint button. This is because Excel is currently the active application.

2   Click on the PowerPoint Taskbar button.

❑   The applications will switch and PowerPoint will appear on the screen. Do not close either application just yet.

Displaying two applications simultaneously

There will be occasions when you will want two applications open and displayed simultaneously. This is possible, though the efficiency of the display will depend upon the monitor screen size – the larger the better.

There are a number of ways that you can display multiple windows simultaneously and the first method is to right-click over a blank area of the Taskbar. A pop-up menu will appear as shown.

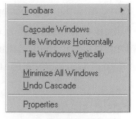

Experiment by selecting the options in turn .

To perform the next section, it is necessary to restore the applications to full screen display. Right-click on the Taskbar and click on the **Undo Cascade** option.

Manual resizing

The second method is for you to manually re-size the application windows.

Basic steps

1   Ensure that both of the application windows' control buttons look like these ▬ ▢ ✕

2   Move the cursor to the lower right-hand area of the application window

❑   When the cursor is over the edge of the application window it will change to that of a diagonal double-headed arrow.

3   Left-click, hold the button down and drag to the left until the window occupies approximately half the screen

4   Release the mouse button

5   Now select Excel

6   This time place the cursor over the left border of the application

7   When it changes to a diagonal double-headed arrow, click and drag the cursor to the right edge of the PowerPoint application

8   Release the mouse button

Both applications should now be viewable, with the active application being Excel, because it was the last to be selected. To switch between applications, simply click on the required application's window and it will become active.

Moving windows on the Desktop

With both of the applications, PowerPoint and Excel still open and having completed the exercise of re-sizing the windows, we are now going to move the windows to different positions on the Desktop.

Basic steps

1 Click on the PowerPoint window.

This will make PowerPoint the active application. You can confirm this by checking PowerPoint's title bar which will be blue if you are using the default colour settings. The title bar of Excel will be a different colour, probably grey.

2 Click on the Excel window. Its title bar will change colour, indicating that it is now the active application.

3 Place the mouse cursor over Excel's title bar

4 Click and hold

5 Drag the mouse cursor down about an inch, so that you still see the PowerPoint window

6 Drag to the left until it almost covers the PowerPoint window

7 Release the mouse button

8 Now select PowerPoint and repeat, but move the application in the opposite direction

9 When you have finished moving the applications, close PowerPoint and Excel.

Tip

Any window or dialog box can be repositioned on the screen, by clicking over its title bar and dragging it to the required location.

Changing the Desktop configuration

The background display has already been mentioned briefly. We will now investigate this and other options you may wish to change.

The Control Panel

It is from the Control Panel that the majority of configuration adjustments and changes are made. We are going to select background setting for the Desktop and investigate what other changes and selections can be made.

Basic steps

1 Click on the Start button

2 From the pop-up menu select Setting > Control Panel

3 At the Control Panel, double-click on the Display icon

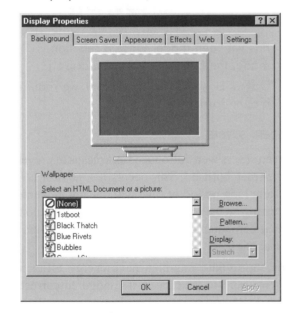

Selecting a background

Basic steps

1 Click on the Background tab

2 Select a choice from the Wallpaper pane. The image will be displayed on the Preview

3 Click the Display options down-arrow and experiment with the settings

4 If you find a Wallpaper that you like, select it and click the Apply button. (This is dimmed in the example as no wallpaper selection

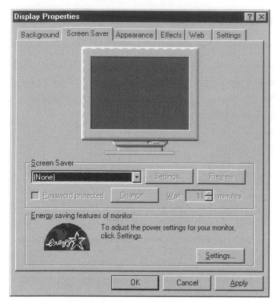

has yet been made. Once a selection is made, the button will become active.)

❑ Do not close the dialog box yet, we require it open for the next exercise.

Screen savers

Screen savers were introduced as a means of preventing 'screen burn-in'. This occurs if a monitor is left on for a long period of time without any movement occurring on the screen. The image will burn into the screen permanently and the monitor would then be unusable.

More up-to-date monitors have energy efficiency systems built-in, and these, if configured correctly, make screen savers redundant. However, people like them and some can be fun.

Basic steps

1 Click on the Screen Saver tab.
2 Click on the Screen Saver slot down-arrow
3 Select any option. The Screen Saver will be displayed in the Preview
4 Click Preview to see the effect on your monitor. Adjustments can be made to the screen saver settings . Experiment with the options. Do not close the dialog box.

In the lower section of the dialog box, you will find the Energy Saving features. Click the **Settings** button to select or change the various energy saving features, provided you have a suitable monitor. Other devices are now featured in this section so experiment and check what options are available.

Various other changes can be made within the **Display Properties** dialog box. Select the other tabs to investigate what can be changed, such as the colour schemes, resolution settings, etc. These are all dependent upon your monitor and video card permitting the various options available.

When you have finished making all the adjustments click on **OK** and the dialog box will close.

Regional configuration

Changes to the date and time settings can be made from the Control Panel.

Basic steps

1 Click the Start button
2 Select Setting > Control Panel

There are two icons which affect the date and time settings. The first is the **Regional Settings** icon, with an image of the globe, which is used to configure the system to recognise where in the world you are.

Regional Settings

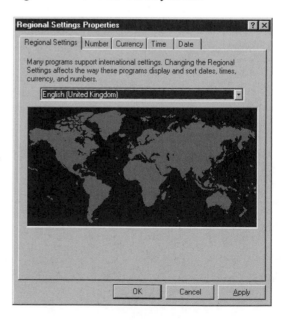

52

Double-click over the icon and the **Regional Settings Properties** box will open.

The setting for the United Kingdom is displayed in the example.

Before experimenting, make a note of the current settings to ensure that the system can be returned to its correct configuration.

Experiment with each of the settings to learn their respective functions and formats.

When you have finished investigating the options, return your settings to the original configuration.

Date/time formats

It is from the 'Regional Settings' that you will set your preferences for the format of date and time display.

Your motherboard has an on-board clock (powered by an automatically rechargeable battery), which you can adjust.

Again, make a note of the current settings and then investigate what other options and formats are available. If you decide that you prefer an alternative format, select that option and click the **Apply** button.

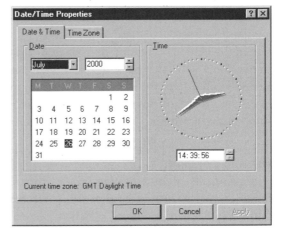

When all options have been investigated, re-set any of the changes, if appropriate, click on **OK** and the dialog box will close.

Adjusting the date/time

The Day/Time settings are usually set when the operating system is first loaded or after a reload. Having dealt with the Regional icon which sets the formats and preferences, now we will adjust the date and time. The second icon is also in the Control Panel.

Basic steps

1   With the Control Panel open, double-click on the Date/Time icon. The Date/Time

You can also access this dialog box by double-clicking on the clock which appears on the Taskbar.

Date changes
The day, month or year can be set individually.

1   Ensure the Date & Time tab is selected

2   To change the day, click the day number

3   To change the month, click the down-arrow by the Month slot and select from the list

5   To change the year, click on the up or down arrows, to increase or decrease the year

Changing the time
The time is displayed in the right area of the window in the form of a clock and in digital format.

❑   Click over the item to be changed, e.g. the hours. To the right of the display slot are two small arrow buttons, one for adjusting the clock forward and the other to turn it back.

Experiment with all the above facilities but remember to reset your correct local date/time when you have finished.

Clicking on the **Time Zone** tab will open the **Regional Settings Properties** dialog box.

Applying the changes

When all changes have been made:

❑ Click the Apply button then the OK button. The dialog box will close and you are back at the Control Panel. If no further changes are necessary, close the Control Panel.

Seasonal adjustments

It should be noted that the operating system will recognise local seasonal time adjustments, for instance in the United Kingdom the change to British Summer Time and later back to Greenwich Mean Time. When the time for the changes to be implemented is reached the operating system will make the change and will prompt you to check and confirm that the changes made are correct.

Multimedia adjustments

Any adjustments such as turning up, or down, the volume control for CD music are performed from the 'Multimedia Properties' panel, which is also to be found within the 'Control Panel'.

Basic steps

1 Open the Control Panel

2 Double-click on the Multimedia icon and the Multimedia Properties dialog box will open

3 Select the CD Music tab

4 Place the mouse cursor over the slide control and drag to adjust the volume

❑ Investigate the various other options available within the dialog box. Not all options may be available. This will depend upon what hardware is installed on your computer, such as Sound cards and Midi systems.

5 To exit the Properties dialog box, left-click on the OK button.

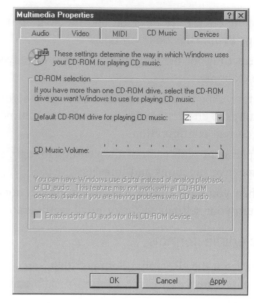

System shut down

You should never switch off the your computer just by using the power on/off switch. There is a set procedure that must be performed to close the system down and the computer itself will tell you when it is safe to switch off.

Basic steps

To shut-down the computer:

1 Close all programs

2 Click the Start button

3 From the pop-up menu select Shut Down

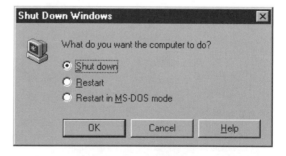

❑ The Desktop background will dim and the Shut Down Windows dialog box will open.

4 If you want to close down the system, select the Shut down option

If you selected the Shut Down option, the system will carry out a series of checks and save any changes that you may have made to the Desktop, etc.

Once this phase has been completed the message '*It is now safe to switch off your computer*' will be displayed on your screen.

Switch off the computer and any other peripherals that maybe connected to it.

If your system has an ATX motherboard installed it may switch off automatically.

Re-starting the computer

There will be occasions when you may want to shut down the computer and re-start it immediately.

There are a number of reasons why this may be necessary, for instance, if you have just installed new software. For the operating system to recognise the presence of the application, it is often necessary to re-start, or to give it another name, 're-boot' the system.

Consult the **Shut Down Windows** dialog box image and you will see that the option to restart the computer exists. Select **Restart** and click the **OK** button and the computer will shut down and then automatically restart.

Remember it is extremely important to close the computer down correctly. Failure to do so may well cause problems in the future.

Should you find that the computer will not respond and appears to have stalled and locked up, wait a short while in case it is busy.

The Ctrl+Alt+Del action

Should the system still fail to respond there is one course of action left.

Press the 'Control' (Ctrl), 'Alternative' (Alt) and 'Delete' (Del) keys simultaneously and a dialog box appear.

Read what it reports. Look for any application(s) reported as not responding. Highlight the offending item and then click on the **End Task** button and with luck, the offending item will close down and free up the system, resolving the problem.

If this fails and the system remains frozen and unresponsive, you will have to resort to turning the computer off, using its on/off switch.

If your computer has an ATX motherboard installed, press and hold the power on/off switch for 5 seconds. This should override the automatic control.

Sometimes even this is not possible. The ATX motherboard, if correctly configured, will automatically shut the computer down and if the system is locked up the On/Off switch may be inoperable. Should this be the case, the only option is to then switch off the power supply at the wall socket or carefully remove the computer plug from the socket.

If a problem persists, seek technical support from the supplier from whom you purchased the computer.

Take note

If you press the 'Ctrl+Alt+Del' keys twice in quick succession, you will cause the computer to shut down and restart. You may find that any files that are open and being used may be lost or corrupted. This is not the correct method of re-starting your computer and you should use the methods described above.

File management

File management is about filing or storing, in a logical and orderly manner all the documents, spreadsheets, databases and images that you create on the computer. A Word document or an Excel spreadsheet, or any other document, in file management terms, are all the same and known as 'files'.

Imagine having no system or management of the files already on the computer, before you even start saving any new files. We would spend more time looking for files than actually using them.

Included within Windows is a program especially designed to assist in file management, called Windows Explorer.

Before we actually open Explorer, an explanation of some of the terms and expressions particularly associated with file management. There is no requirement to differentiate between a Word document and an Excel workbook.

All items are referred to as *files* and are stored within *folders*.

Many computers only have one hard disk drive and in computer terms this is referred to as the 'C' drive, or 'root' directory. Do not concern yourself too much at this stage about remembering all the names and alternatives. We will return to this subject in more detail later.

Think of the 'C' drive as a large filing cabinet that has a number of drawers. Within these drawers are a number of folders. 'Folders' is the same term as used by Explorer. These folders serve the same purpose as those in the filing cabinet with one exception – the folders in Explorer are electronic ones.

You can do most things with the computer folder that you can with those in a real cabinet. You can move the folder from one drawer to another. You can insert documents (files) into the folders and likewise you can remove items. If you so decide, you could throw the folder away for good, by deleting it.

You can copy a file, so that you have two identical files. Be careful though, this could lead to confusion and Windows will not allow you to do this in some instances. Using a computer to copy a file is far quicker than standing over a photocopier, copying each individual item, then putting all the items into their respective folders.

It is now time for us to take a look at Windows Explorer.

Basic steps

1   Click **Start** – the Start menu will pop up
2   Point to Programs to open its menu
3   Click on Windows Explorer
❑   After a short while it will open. Initially it may look daunting, however do not worry as all will be explained. Check the diagram opposite and we will identify the main areas of interest to us at the moment.

Exploring Windows Explorer

Windows Explorer is a stand-alone program, within Windows 95/98, that manages all the folders and files on the computer.

Examine the example. Starting at the very top of the window is an icon that represents the Desktop.

Imagine that you are sitting at a conventional desk and all your various items and equipment are placed on the Desktop.

The principle is the same here, the Desktop is the visual focal point of the computer.

You will see that the system is laid out in an hierarchical system comprising of different levels.

The highest level is the *Desktop*.

The second level down after the *Desktop* is *My Computer*, with other items below.

You will also see that a number of the items shown have a '+' adjacent to them, to the left. Clicking once

Windows Explorer

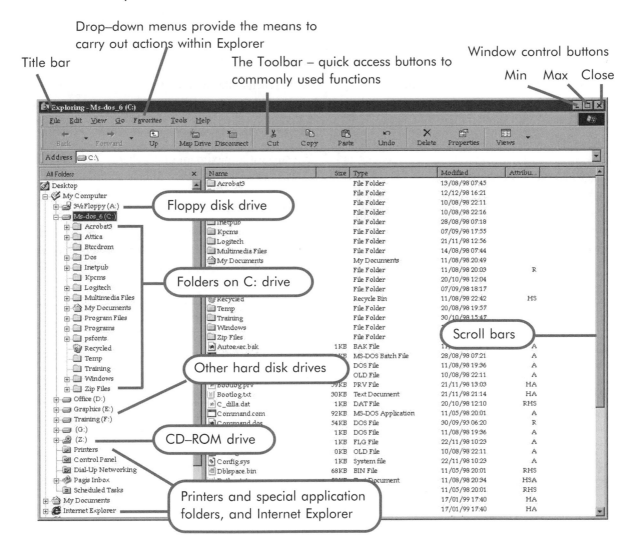

Drop–down menus provide the means to carry out actions within Explorer

Title bar

The Toolbar – quick access buttons to commonly used functions

Window control buttons

Min   Max   Close

Floppy disk drive

Folders on C: drive

Other hard disk drives

CD–ROM drive

Scroll bars

Printers and special application folders, and Internet Explorer

on the '+' sign will open a branch below that item.

Return to the top of the window and you will see a number of drive units.

The first drive listed is the 3½ Floppy Drive, the letter 'A' identifies it.

Below the Floppy drive is the first Hard drive, and it is identified by the letter 'C'. In the example it is shown as 'MS-DOS_6(C:)'.

All storage units are assigned identifying letters.

The letters 'A' and 'B' are reserved and assigned to the floppy drives, even though only one floppy is usually fitted in most computers today.

Below the Floppy drive is the 'C' drive, usually the only hard disk drive in most computers.

CD-Rom drives, usually known as the 'D' drive, and any other types of unit are also assigned drive letters. If your computer is connected to a network, letters will be assigned to identify the various network connections and drives.

You can assign up to the 26 letters of the alphabet to drives.

57

Folders and files

Before we investigate folders and files in more detail, we shall look at some rules and conventions regarding the naming of folders and files.

Folder names

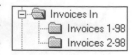

Windows 95 introduced long file names to the PC. Prior to its arrival, MS-DOS rules applied and you could only use up to 8 letters in a file name.

Using the long file name rules and conventions, you can use up to 256 characters, including hyphens and spaces when naming 'folders'.

There are a number of characters that are reserved for the operating system, such as the colon ':' and full stop '.' which means you cannot use them. The operating system will prompt you if you attempt to use them and will give you the opportunity to change the name.

Folder structures

When naming folders and files, make sure that you use names that are unambiguous and relate to their content. For instance, if you deal with invoices, the first level folder should be named 'INVOICES IN' and another folder called 'INVOICES OUT'.

Within each folder, a subfolder might hold files for each quarter, possibly called 'INVOICES 1-98', 'INVOICES 2-98', etc.

We suggest a maximum of 15 characters. Too many characters will only serve to cause confusion.

File Extension List

The following list contains some common file extensions and the applications they are associated with. The list is not extensive and shown as a guide only.

Extension	Type of File	Extension	Type of File
DOC	Microsoft Word document	TXT	Text files (e.g. Notepad)
XLS	Microsoft Excel spreadsheet	BMP	Bitmap graphic *
MDB	Microsoft Access database	PCL	HP Laser printer format
MPP	Microsoft Project document	EPS	Encapsulated Postscript document*
PPT	Microsoft PowerPoint presentation	TIF	Tagged Image File Format *
CAL	Microsoft Schedule + document	CGM	CGM Vector graphic *
WP5	WordPerfect document	PM6	PageMaker 6 document
WPD	WordPerfect 6 document	WRI	Wordpad document
PDF	Adobe Acrobat document	PCX	PCX format bitmap graphic *
MMF	Microsoft Mail File	WMF	Windows MetaFile graphic *
EXE	Any program	DGN	Microstation drawing
BAT	A batch file	PLT	HPGL plot
DRW	Micrografx designer drawing	HTM	Internet/Intranet document
CDR	CorelDraw drawing	ZIP	PKZip/WinZip compressed file
DWG	AutoCAD file	PST	Microsoft Outlook file

* These are image files that may originate from a digital camera, or from an image being scanned.

Naming files

The rules and conventions for file naming is much the same as for naming folders. One can use upper and lower case letters, as well as hyphens and spaces, up to 256 characters.

The notable exception when naming files is the use of what is known as an extension. The extension consists of a full stop followed by a group of three letters. The letters indicate what type of file one is looking at.

In this example there are two files, each with a different extension. The top one, '6Test.doc', is a Word document, indicated by the extension '.doc'.

The second example, '7Test.xls', is an Excel spreadsheet, indicated by the extension '.xls'.

File management and folders

Let us take a look at how we manage our files and copy and move them from one location to another on the computer. We use folders to store our files (the electronic documents) in. Take a look at the following series of diagrams.

We are now looking at the folder called *Logitech*. This folder is on the 'C' drive and has a '+' sign to the left of the folder.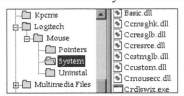

Note the '+' sign next to some of the folders. This indicates that there are other folders, sub-folders, within that particular folder.

Click once on the '+' sign.

In this example note that the '+' sign has now changed. It now indicates a '−' sign and we see that there is another folder within the 'Logitech' folder. This new folder is called 'Mouse' and it too has a '+' sign next to it.

In this example the 'Mouse' folder has been opened to reveal a further three folders.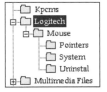

Note the absence of any '+' or '-' signs adjacent to the three folders.

In this example the folder called 'System' has been opened. In the window on the right you can see the files that are stored in the 'System' folder.

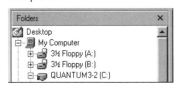

Take note

In Windows Explorer, folders appear in the left and right panes. Files reside in folders and only appear in Explorer's right pane, once a folder is opened. Files never appear in Explorer's left pane.

Creating folders

You can create folders as required. Folders can be created within folders, and are referred to as 'sub-folders'. For this exercise we will create a number of folders, using the names given.

Basic steps

1   In Windows Explorer, click on the 'C:' drive, in the left pane

2   Click on File > New > Folder

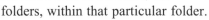

3   A new folder will appear in the right pane of Explorer, with the name, *New Folder*. The name box is highlighted and the cursor already in it, waiting for you to type a name for the folder.

4 Type in the name '0Student' (Note the '0' is a zero not a letter 'O') and press 'Enter'

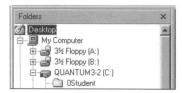

5 Now press the 'F5' key

❑ This will refresh the screen display and the folder that you created will now appear at the top of the 'C:' drive listings.

Take note

The reason for the prefix '0', before the name, is to make it easier for you to locate the folder. With '0' at the beginning of the name, Explorer will place the folder at, or near the top of the 'C:\' listings.

You have just created your first folder. However, we require a number of folders to complete this exercise, so carry on as outlined.

Create another folder, following the sequence already described.

Basic steps

1 Select the 'C:' drive in the left pane first.

2 Follow the steps as before, but call the new folder *1Student* (figure '1', not the letter 'l')

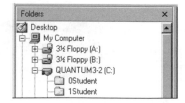

❑ We require another folder, but this one is to be placed in the one you have just created.

3 Click on the folder *1Student*, in the left pane

---

4 Complete the sequence for creating a folder by selecting File > New > Folder

5 The new folder will appear in the right pane. Name it *Exercise*

6 The folder *1Student* now has a '+' sign next to it. Click the '+' and the folder *Exercise* will appear below the folder *1Student*.

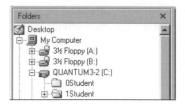

❑ Note that the '+' sign has now changed to a '-' sign.

7 Click on the '-' sign and the *Exercise* folder is no longer visible

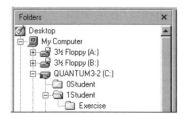

Configuring Windows Explorer

Before we proceed and create any files, we first must ensure that Windows Explorer is configured correctly for this course.

Basic steps

1 If necessary open Windows Explorer and find the folder called 'Windows'

2 Click on it and look in the right pane

3 At the top of the pane you will see a considerable number of folders. Scroll down until you can see the files below them

❑ Check if the file extensions appear after the file names.

File extensions were discussed earlier, but if you are unsure, an example of a file with its extension should look like 'CDPLAYER.EXE', with the '.EXE' element being the extension of the file name.

If you can see the file extensions, you can skip the remainder of this section and move to the next one, '*Creating Files*'. If however you cannot see the file extensions, you will need to re-configure Windows Explorer.

4   On the menu bar select View > Folder Options

❑   The Folder Options dialog box will appear.

5   Select the View tab

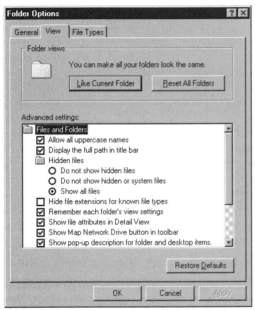

6   Ensure that your settings match the items shown circled in the example by clicking on the button squares and circles

7   Click Apply then OK

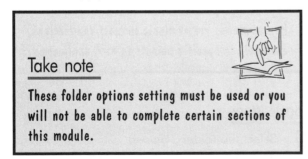

Take note

These folder options setting must be used or you will not be able to complete certain sections of this module.

Creating files

At this stage we have created three folders, which are empty. Imagine them as containers, with no files in them yet. We will now create a number of files and

place them in these folders. For the benefit of this exercise we will create a number of files without actually opening any applications.

Basic steps

1   Ensure that Windows Explorer is open

2   Select the folder *0Student*

3   Open the File menu

4   Select New, then move the cursor down and click on Microsoft Word Document

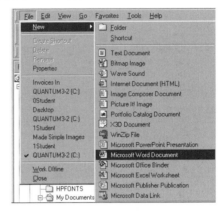

Look in the right pane of Explorer and you will see a new file, called *New Microsoft Word Document*. The name may have an extension of '.doc' on the end.

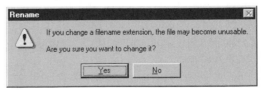

Note that the file name is highlighted ready for you to type in the name. As soon as you start typing, you will overwrite the name in the box.

5   Type in the name *2Test.doc* (do not include any spaces)

If you do not type in the full-stop and 'doc' extension, the following dialog box will appear.

Rename
⚠ If you change a filename extension, the file may become unusable.
Are you sure you want to change it?
[Yes]   [No]

6   Should this occur, simply click the No button. Re-type the name, with the full stop and doc ('.doc')

7   When finished press Enter

To continue with this exercise we require a number of additional files. Continue following the instructions and create the files, with the names given, in the stated folders.

We are now going to create a further two files, except this time we will create two workbook files. Follow the procedures for creating the Word document but in this instance select Microsoft Excel Worksheet.

Before you type in the name, note that the last three letters, the extension, now reads '.xls'. This will identify the file as an Excel workbook.

Basic steps

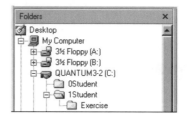

1 In the folder *0Student*, create another Microsoft Word document called *3Test.doc*

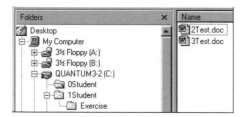

2 Now create two files in the folder *1Student* named *4Test.xls* and *5Test.xls* (do not to insert any spaces in the names)

3 Finally, create one Word and one Excel file (in the sub-folder *Exercise*) named *6Test.doc* and *7Test.xls*

We now have all the folders and files needed to enable us to move onto the next phase of the exercise, which is to copy and move files around between different folders.

Copying and moving files

Remember that Windows Explorer is the dedicated file management program.

Basic steps

1 Ensure that Explorer is open

2 In the left pane of Explorer, click once on the '+' sign adjacent to the folder *1Student*. This will expand the folder and reveal the subfolder *Exercise* inside it. We will require access to this folder shortly.

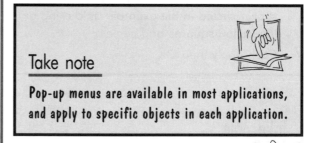

The Copy command

The Copy command is a means for you to copy a file and place the copy in a different location.

As is usually the case with Windows, there are a number of ways of performing the action of copying a File. For this exercise, we will use the right-click pop-up menu method.

> ### Take note
>
> **Pop-up menus are available in most applications, and apply to specific objects in each application.**

Basic steps

1 Select the folder *0Student*

2 Place the cursor over the file *2Test.doc*

3 Do not select the file but right-click once over it and a pop-up menu will appear

❑ Take a moment to investigate the options available.

❑ Note that your pop-up menu may not match that shown opposite. This is subject to your computer's configuration

```
Open
Print
New
Quick View

Send To          ▶

Cut
Copy

Create Shortcut
Delete
Rename

Properties
```

Explanations

Think of the 'Cut' command as meaning 'Move'.

Cut will remove the file, or folder, from its current location. The item is temporarily stored in the Clipboard (see below) and when you select its new location, you **Paste** it in that location.

Copy, as its name suggests copies the file, or folder, which is also then held in the Clipboard, ready for use in a different location.

Paste completes the **Copy** or **Cut** command and inserts the file, or folder, in its new location, but does not appear in the content menu at this stage.

The Clipboard

The *Clipboard* is a specially selected area within the computer memory (RAM). It is the means of copying or moving text, images, etc, Windows applications. You will encounter the Clipboard repeatedly in all Windows applications, and you will frequently use it, sometimes without realising so.

The standard Clipboard

In earlier versions of Microsoft Office, the Clipboard can only hold one item at any time. Anything placed in the Clipboard would remain there a **Copy** or **Cut** commands was used again, when it will be over-written by the new item.

Office 2000 Clipboard

With the introduction of Office 2000, Microsoft upgraded the functionality of the Clipboard and it can now hold up to twelve copy blocks.

> ## Take note
>
>
> **Each item copied to the Clipboard is referred to as a block.**

How does it Work?

When you copy an item, Office 2000 will copy the first block to the Clipboard and you will not see the action take place. However, if you then copy a second block to the Clipboard, the Clipboard Toolbar will appear and possibly the Office Assistant, assuming that you have not disabled it.

The Office 2000 Clipboard Toolbar

The Title bar, showing that there are 3 items currently in the Clipboard.

The Menu bar, point to an item and a tool-tip will pop-up to identify its function.

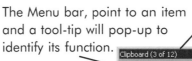
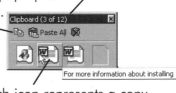

For more information about installing ...

Copy blocks – each icon represents a copy block. Here, the first icon is an image and the two remaining icons are Word text. Pointing to a block will result in a pop-up box displaying the first line of text, or for images, the message 'Picture 1' or as appropriate.

Displaying the Toolbar

There are two methods of displaying the Toolbar. The example shown above is a *floating* toolbar. By clicking on its Title bar, you drag and drop it to any location on your screen.

The other method is known as a docked toolbar. By clicking on its Title bar and dragging it to a position below another toolbar will result in it remaining in that location, docked.

> ## Take note
>
>
> **If the toolbar is not on display and you want it, right-click on any toolbar and select Clipboard.**

As you copy more blocks to the Clipboard, it will expand until twelve blocks are displayed. If you attempt to copy a thirteenth item, a warning message will

appear and advise you that it will delete the oldest of the twelve items currently stored in the Clipboard. You do have a choice if you are happy to over-write the oldest item, click OK to continue.

Inserting Blocks

To insert (Paste) a block from the Clipboard, left-click over the appropriate block and it will be inserted into your document. If you have more than one block in the Clipboard, you can insert the blocks in any order to suit your requirements.

Emptying the Clipboard

To empty the Clipboard click the **Clear Clipboard** button on the menu bar.

Summary

The increased functionality of the Clipboard is a welcome addition to the Office 2000 Suite of applications. It is however important to remember that it is primarily designed to work within Office 2000 and that many other applications cannot access it, and that the Clipboard is a reserved area of the memory (RAM) and is therefore volatile. Switch off the computer and all is lost.

The Cut, Copy and Paste icons

The **Cut**, **Copy** and **Paste** commands are available from a number of locations within Windows.

If you were to use the toolbars for these actions, it is the icons shown that you would select.

This icon ✂ represents the **Cut** command.

This icon 📋 represents the **Copy** command.

This icon 📋 presents the **Paste** command.

There are still more ways of performing these commands. Check the **Edit** menu and you will find the same commands there. You will, in time develop your own preferred way of working.

Basic steps

1 Open the folder *0Student*
2 Move the cursor back over the file *2Test.doc*
3 Right-click and select Copy
4 In the left pane in Explorer, right-click over the folder *1Student*, and select Paste from the pop-up menu

❑ At this point you will not see the result of the Copy command because Explorer is still looking at the *0Student* folder.

5 Click on the folder *1Student* to select it

❑ Now look in the right pane of Explorer and you will see that there is now an additional file, *2Test.doc*, in the folder.

6 Click on the folder *0Student* and you will see that there is still a file called *2Test.doc*.

7 Right-click on this file, and select Cut

8 Right-click on the folder *Exercise*, and select Paste. Check the right pane and you will see that the file *2Test.doc* is no longer displayed and that there is only one file remaining in the folder. Look in the *Exercise* folder and you will see the file *2Test.doc* is now in it

Take note

If you try to copy a folder or file to a folder that already contains one with the same name, the following prompt will warn you of the problem.

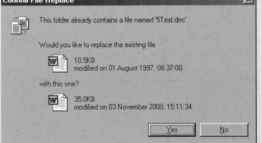

If in doubt click No at the prompt. Investigate the file, and decide what course of action to take.

9 From the folder *0Student*, move the file *3Test.doc* to the folder *1Student*

10 Open the folder *Exercise*, right-click on the file *2Test.doc* and select Delete

11 A prompt will ask you to confirm that you want to send the file to the Recycle Bin, click Yes

❑ Open the folder *0Student* and you will see that there are no longer any files in it.

Recovering files from the Recycle Bin

Basic steps

1 Resize and move Explorer to the right so that it occupies approximately half of the screen

2 Open the *Exercise* folder so that you can see its contents

Recycle Bin

3 Open the Recycle Bin by double-clicking on it

4 When the window opens, resize it so that it and Explorer can be viewed simultaneously

5 In the Recycle Bin right-click over the file *2Test.doc*

Restore
Cut
Delete
Properties

6 Select Restore. The file will disappear from the Recycle Bin and should reappear in the *Exercise* folder in Explorer

❑ The same procedure will also restore a folder from the recycle bin

7 Close the Recycle Bin

Moving folders/files using drag and drop

Here is another way to move files and folders, known as 'drag and drop'.

Basic steps

1 In the left pane select the folder *1Student*

2 In the right pane, click on the folder *Exercise* and keep the button pressed

3 Now drag the folder (keep that left button pressed) from the right pane and place it over the folder *0Student* in the left pane

❑ This folder will become highlighted as the cursor moves over it.

4 Once the folder, *0Student*, is highlighted release the mouse button. A '+' sign will appear next to the *0Student* folder and disappear from the folder *1Student*.

5 Open the folder *0Student* and confirm the presence of the *Exercise* folder

Multiple file deletion

You can select and delete files in a group.

Basic steps

If the files are listed sequentially:

1 Select the file at the top of the list

2 Press and hold the [Shift] key down

3 Select the last file that you wish to delete

❑ All the files in the group will be highlighted. Double-check that you have selected only those files that you wish to delete.

4 Press [Delete] and the files will be moved to the Recycle Bin

Deleting non-adjacent files

1 Select the first file

2 Hold down [Ctrl] and click on each file

3 When all files are selected, release [Ctrl] and press [Delete]

Should you make an incorrect selection:

5 Keep [Ctrl] pressed and click once more on the file. It will then be deselected

Deleting folders

Deleting folders is performed in the same manner as that used to delete files.

Basic steps

1 Open the *Exercise* folder so that you can see its contents (3 files) in the right pane

65

2   Right-click over the *Exercise* folder in the left pane and select Delete

❑   A prompt will ask you to confirm that you want to send the folder and its contents to the Recycle Bin

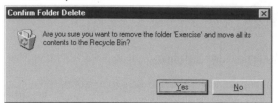

3   Click on Yes

❑   The folder and all of its contents will be moved to the Recycle Bin.

Take note

When a folder is deleted all the files contained within that folder are also deleted.

Renaming folders/files

There will come a time when you will want to change a folder or a file name. Remember that Explorer is the program in which you should make these changes.

Basic steps

Renaming a folder:

1   Right-click over the folder that you want to rename

2   From the pop-up menu select Rename

3   The folder name will become highlighted. Type in the new name

4   When you have finished, press [Enter] to apply the change

Renaming files:

1   Open Explorer

2   Left-click on the folder *1Student* in the right pane you will see four files

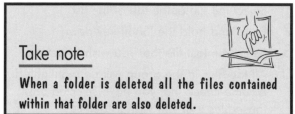

3   Right-click on the file *4Test.xls* and select Rename from the pop-up menu

4   The file name will become highlighted. Type the new name *Excel.xls* and press [Enter]

❑   You must type in the extension (.xls) or you will be prompted for a response.

An alternative method

You could rename a file by selecting **File** on the menu bar and then selecting **Rename**. You must however select the file first.

Examine a folder

Basic steps

When you look at a folder in Explorer few details are shown. To find more information about a folder:

1   Right-click over the *1Student* folder and select Properties – a dialog box will open

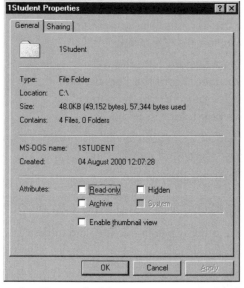

From the 'Properties' box you can reset the following attributes:

♦   **Read-only** prevents a folder or file from being changed or deleted.

♦   **Hidden** prevents the operating system from displaying the folder or file in a directory list.

♦   **Archive** controls which files are backed up.

Examine a file

When a file is saved, certain other information is saved in addition to the file itself. This information is extremely useful in many ways and will assist you, for example, to find a file when you have forgotten its location.

If when using Windows Explorer you should find that you do not have the same display as in the example shown, you will need to change what is known as the **View** mode within Explorer.

1 Select the Views button on the Toolbar, or View on the Menu bar

2 Select Details

❑ Once selected a small dot will appear next to Details

Examine the files shown below and you can see from the detail when the various files were last modified or created.

Name	Size	Type	Modified	Attributes
2Test.doc	11KB	Microsoft Word Do...	01/08/97 08:37	A
3Test.doc	19KB	Microsoft Word Do...	03/11/00 15:27	A
4Test.xls	14KB	Microsoft Excel Wo...	03/11/00 15:29	A
5Test.xls	16KB	Microsoft Excel Wo...	03/11/00 15:30	A

For example, file '*2Test.doc*' was modified at 11.09 hrs (am) on 5 July 1999. The file is 19KB in size and it is identified as a Microsoft Word Document.

If you cannot see all of the detail, such as the type, place your cursor to the right of the heading and when it changes its shape to a double-headed arrow, double-click and the Type column will expand and you will see all of the detail.

You can do the same on any of the other areas as well.

You can also manually adjust the size. When the cursor changes to the double-headed arrow, click and drag left or right as required, then release the button.

Searching for folders and files

There will be occasions when a file is misplaced or simply not used for so long that you may have forgotten where it is stored. To assist with locating files there is a 'Find' facility which can be used to search for files and folders.

There are two ways to launch the 'Find' facility.

Basic steps

1 Click on the Start button

2 Point to the Find option and from its menu select Files or Folders.

Or

3 In Windows Explorer, open the Tools menu, point to Find and select Files or Folders.

❑ The Find: All Files dialog box will open

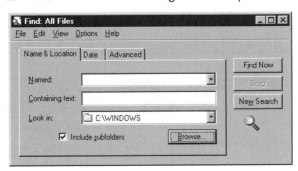

We will conduct a simple search for a file that is included in the Windows system and is one of the files used to create the background for the Desktop.

4 Type the details as shown. As the file we are looking for is in the Windows folder, remove the tick from the Include subfolders slot. This will speed-up the search

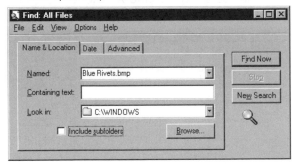

7 When complete, click on the 'Find Now' button

❑ The dialog window will expand to reveal an additional window. Assuming that the file is present on the computer and the search was successful, the location of the file and its details will be listed here.

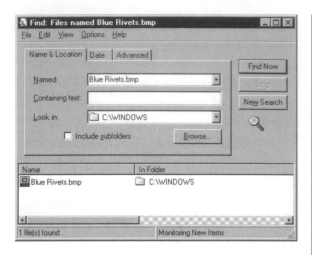

Searching on date criteria

If you have an idea when the file was created or last modified, you can conduct a search using dates to assist and speed up the search.

Basic steps

1 Ensure that the Find dialog box is open
2 Click on the Date tab
❑ The window will change to that shown
3 Select the between option
❑ When selected the Find All Files option will also become active

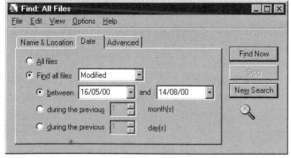

4 Leave the selection as *Modified*
5 Type in the dates that may apply to the file
6 Click on the Find Now button

New search

If the search was unsuccessful and you wish to perform another search, but with different criteria:

7 Click on the New Search button
❑ This prompt will open

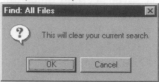

8 Click on OK to clear the old search criteria
9 Enter the new search criteria and start again

Advanced searches

The advanced search is not included in the syllabus of this course, but a brief introduction is given below.

This feature allows you to search for specific items, for instance, all of the PowerPoint presentations on a drive. You can further refine the search by selecting a date range and the file's size range.

Basic steps

1 Open the Find: All Files dialog box
2 Select the Name & Location tab
3 In the Look in slot select the drive that you wish to search (normally the 'C' drive)
4 Click on the Date tab and set a date range
6 Click on the Advanced tab

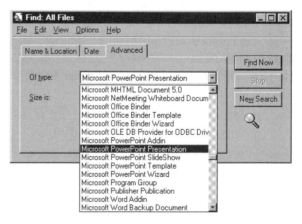

7 Select the appropriate item from the drop-down list Of type
8 Click Find Now. The Find dialog box will now expand.

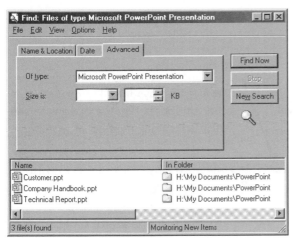

All of the PowerPoint presentations files that met the search critieria, will be displayed.

If you want to open one of the items listed, simply double-click over the name and the appropriate application will run and display the file you clicked on.

Saving files

Files are saved from within the application where they were created. For example, if you use Word to create a document, you must use the 'Save' function in Word to save it.

Earlier we created Word and Excel files without opening the applications. These files are empty and do not contain data. Once data is inserted the application used to create that data must be used to save the file.

Path

The term 'path' is used to identify the location of a file. Let us assume that we have just saved a file, using the name *Sales*, in a folder called *August* and that folder is on the *A:* drive.

Using the path method of description it would appear as *A:\August\Sales*. This is a quick and simple method of describing the file's location. The path always starts with the drive, followed by any folders, sub-folders and eventually the file. The backslash (\) is used to separate each location.

Here is another example:

C:\ My Documents\Excel\August Invoices.xls

This is structured as follows:

C: is the hard disk drive on which the item is stored.

My Documents is a folder on the *C:* drive

Excel is a sub-folder within *My Documents*.

August Invoices is the file name.

.xls is the extension, identifing it as an Excel file.

Which storage device?

When saving files you have the option of where, or more accurately, which storage device will be used to store the file. In most cases you will select either the hard disk drive (C:) or the floppy disk drive (A:).

Other storage devices are available and are being used more frequently. For the sake of simplicity however, we will use only the 'A:' and 'C:' drives.

File name

Earlier in the course the subject of creating folders and managing file was discussed, with a number of recommendations and suggestions regarding how to structure a filing system.

When initially saving a file you can select the **Save** option from the menu bar, **File > Save** or by clicking the **Save** icon on the Standard Toolbar.

When a file is saved for the first time, the **Save As** dialog box will open. This is because the system recognises that the file does not yet have a name. Once allocated a name the document will be saved.

If you want to save the same file using a different name, the **Save As** option should be selected. This option allows you to modify a file to suit your requirement whilst retaining a copy of the original.

New Office 2000 Dialog Boxes

If you have used any previous version of Microsoft Office, you will immediately notice that in Office 2000 the **Save As** and **Open** dialog boxes have changed and each offers you more control and functionality. The two dialog boxes are the same size and, in the main, contain the same controls and have the same functionality. The obvious differences are in the name of each box. Other differences will be highlighted as we explore the boxes.

Save As Dialog Box

Shown below is the **Save As** dialog box, which enables you to save files to different locations or in different formats. Explore the diagrams and explanations to identify and determine what each item is.

Create a new folder

Views – displays the file name and/or other attributes. Try the options to see which suits your method of working

The current storage device or folder

Back – open the last used folder

Up one level

Delete

Tools – open the dropdown menu and investigate the options, in particular the General Options...

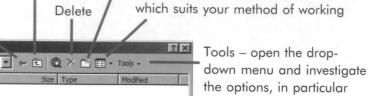

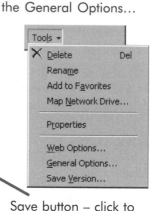

Places bar – see below

File name – type a name to save the file under. Word inserts the first word(s) of the document as a suggested name

Save As Type slot – click the down arrow to open a list of the file formats that Word can save the document in. By default, Word will use its own format, *.doc*.

Save button – click to complete the process and close the dialog box

Cancel button – if you decide not to save the file, click to close the box without saving.

The Places bar

This is another new feature, adding increased functionality.

The **History** folder stores shortcuts for every file that you have used and lists them in date order, with the most recent first. If you have worked on the same file several times, the shortcut takes you to the latest version. Practice using this feature, as it will certainly save you a great deal of time.

My Documents is Word's default document folder. It places all your newly saved files here, unless you specify a different location.

Desktop is the top-level on your computer. Although you probably won't store files in the Desktop folder, it gives you a high-level view of your drives. You can navigate to just about anywhere from this location.

Favorites also stores shortcuts, however in this instance they are to files that you use regularly. Use Word's on-line Help to learn more on this subject.

Web Folders gives you quick access to folders on your Web server, which contains the files that you have published on your Intranet or Web site. Use Word's on-line Help to learn more on this subject.

The Open dialog Box

The **Open** dialog box is almost identical to the **Save As** dialog box. The first obvious difference is the name in the title bar and the **Save** button is replaced by the **Open** button, which offers a number of options for opening a file. Finally, the other difference is not apparent until you open the **Tools** menu. Investigate the examples and explanations shown below.

Click **Tools** on the dialog box menu bar and the drop-down menu will appear

You must first select a file to Delete, Rename, Print or Add to Favorites. To print a file, you do not have to open it.

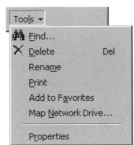

You can now also carry out a search for a file directly from the **Open** dialog box . Click on **Tools > Find** and the Office 2000 **Find** dialog box will open.

The Find Dialog Box

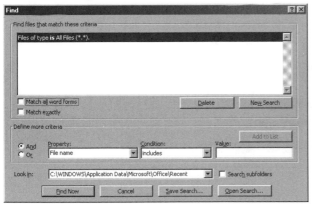

This is an area that you should investigate in more detail later. The options are quite straightforward to understand and use. Navigate to where you store your files. Set up your search criterion and then click on the **Find Now** button

Practice searching with different search criteria and remember to use the on-line Help to learn more of this feature.

The Open button

Open – select the file that you wish to open and then click on the Open button.

Open Read-Only – Word opens the selected file, but will prevent you from making any changes to it.

Open as Copy – Word will create a new copy of the file and will open the copy. The copy will have the same name but with '*Copy of*' in front of it.

Open in Browser – you may have created a file that you intend to use through a browser and want to check how it will look in the browser. Word will open the file in your default browser.

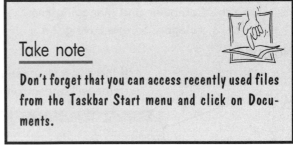

Take note

Don't forget that you can access recently used files from the Taskbar Start menu and click on Documents.

Using Microsoft Notepad

We will now use an application called Notepad for a short exercise.

Notepad is a text editor which was designed for creating specialist files for the computer. Notepad can however be used to create short notes and documents of limited size but does not have the flexibility and functionality of Word.

Basic steps

To locate Notepad

1 Click the Start button

2 Point to Programs

3 Point to Accessories

3 From its sub-menu select Notepad

Typing Text in Notepad

1 Before you type in any text, select Edit > Word Wrap. This will ensure that the text fits the width of the display.

2 Type 'This is the ICDL/ECDL Module 2, Using the Computer and Managing Files. Version 3, category Simple Editing 2.4'

3 Select File > Save and save it as *Module 2* in the *My Documents* folder

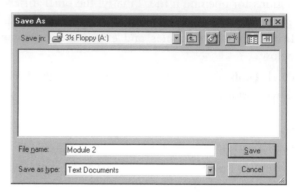

❑ There is no need to type the file extension, as Notepad will assign the correct extension (txt) to the file.

4 Ensure that there is a floppy disk in the 'A:' drive

5 Re-select File from the menu bar and this time select the Save As option

6 At the Save As dialog box click on the down-arrow of the Save In slot and select the *3½ Floppy (A:)*

Notepad

Title bar

Menu bar

If there is a file open in Notepad, the name will appear on the title bar.

Control buttons – see page 47 if you need a reminder of these

Clicking on any of the menu headings will open a drop-down list of commands, many of which are common to most Applications.

There are two scroll bars, one for vertical control and the other horizontal control.

Untitled - Notepad

File   Edit   Search   Help

This is the ECDL Module 2, Using the Computer and Managing Files.

This is syllabus version 3 category Simple editing 2.4

This is the working text area where you type in your text.

7 Note that the original name is highlighted in the File Name slot. Retain the same name and click on the Save button

8 Close Notepad by selecting File > Exit from the menu bar

What you have just done is create a simple text file using Notepad and then save the file to the *My Documents* folder located on the hard disk drive, usually the C: drive.

Following on from this, the same file was re-saved except this time to a different drive, in this instance the A: drive.

The result is that you now have two files with the same name but each is stored on a different storage device. One is stored on the hard disk drive and the other on a floppy disk, thus ensuring that if one disk failed, you would have a backup copy of the file. A quick and simple method of creating backups.

The same procedure can be applied to most applications by using the option **Save As**. The limiting factor when saving files to the floppy disk is their size. Remember that standard 3½ inch floppy disks are limited to 1.44MB.

We will return to the file that was just created later in the module when printers are discussed.

Backing up data

The term 'backup' means to make copies of your important data in the event that a disaster occurs and the original data is corrupted or is destroyed.

Companies who have vast quantities of data will have backup systems and procedures in place in the event that they experience a crisis, even to the extent of having empty offices with duplicated computer systems running in parallel to the operational system.

There are a number of different, and some complex, methods of backing up data. The hardware involved could be as simple as a floppy disk. However, for large quantities of data other methods are used.

On networks, the hard disk drives are connected in a manner known as 'mirroring'. When data is saved, it is saved simultaneously to two or more hard disks. If a drive fails, the other drives will continue to function and data is not lost. A drive failure occurs when either the drive becomes unserviceable, that is, develops a fault, or a poor cable connection occurs.

Another method used in conjunction with the above are backups to a tape drive, which holds large amounts of data using a specialist tape cassette. A different tape is used each day and copies are stored off-site for additional security, for instance in the event of a fire.

Creating backup files

We are not going to duplicate computer systems, but we will make backup copies of some files. As these are not large, will be stored on a floppy.

Basic steps

1 Open Windows Explorer
2 Insert a floppy disk in the disk drive
3 Right-click on the folder *1Student* and on the pop-up menu point to Send To. A second menu will open, listing a number of options

Explore
Open
Find...

Sharing...
Send To   ▶

Cut
Copy

Create Shortcut
Delete
Rename

Properties

5 Select '3½ Floppy (A)'

❑ You will see a visual display of the files being copied to the floppy drive.

6 Now click on '3½ Floppy (A:)'

❑ You will see the folder '1Student' has been copied to the floppy disk.

Take note

Remember the standard floppy disk can only hold a maximum of 1.44 MB of data.

Identifying file details

Once you have made copies of your important data, you must remember to change the backup copies each time you amend the master files. How do you do this? Remember that when you save a file, additional information that will assist in managing backups, such as the date, is also saved. (See page 67.)

Microsoft Backup

Included in the Windows 95/98 operating system is a backup tool and, though it is not discussed here, you may want to look at it.

1 Click on the Start button
2 Select Programs > Accessories > Systems Tools > Backup

The 'Microsoft Backup' dialog box will open.

Use the online Help to learn more about this program and then decide if it meets your requirements.

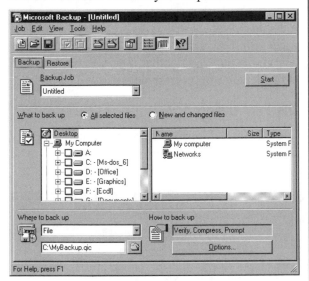

Third Party Products

There are numerous ways of backing up data, which usually require third party products.

The term third party product means an application or utility produced by a company or organisation other than the operating system vendor. The product is not supplied as a part of the operating system and must be purchased separately and then loaded on to the computer.

Most of these products will employ a compression method. What this does is 'squeeze' the data, which makes the file smaller, therefore taking up less space.

However, there are drawbacks to this method, mostly in that it takes quite a long time to backup large quantities of data and it is not always easy to recover a single file rather than whole blocks of data.

Winzip

A well-known and often quoted product, that is extremely handy for the home user, is Winzip. This product is given free with most computer magazines. There are one or two limitations of the free version of the product but it is still a very useful utility to have for home and small office use.

Summary

Module 1 covered the subject of backing up data and stressed that backup systems must be carefully thought out. It requires discipline and procedures to ensure that the backup will function in a crisis. Always practice the procedures, which may look good on paper but must be carried out to work.

Selecting printers

The computer is a tool to produce letters, spreadsheets, databases and much more. The end products of most of these are frequently required to be printed for distribution. To this end a printer is installed and connected to the computer.

More than one printer can be installed on a computer, although usually there is only one port where the printer is connected. This is 'LPT1' (Line Printer Terminal 1). Additional ports can be installed.

There are a number of ways that you can connect additional printers to the computer using switch boxes or, more commonly these days, using the USB ports available with Windows 98. Refer to your computer manual for further details.

Another method of connecting to a different printer is to use a network connection. The printer is connected directly to the network and configured so that anyone on the network can use it, or has a password list which will authorise access if necessary.

Another network connection could be used where another computer is connected to the network and its printer is 'shared'. What this means is that the printer is set up to be available to anyone, provided they are on a network, hence the term 'shared'.

When more than one printer is installed on a computer, one is designated the default printer. This is always selected and printing will be performed by that printer, unless you select a different one.

If you were to view the default printer in the 'Printers' folder, it will have a tick next to it, indicating that it is the default printer.

These icons are those that you will usually encounter in Windows in relation to printing and printers.

 A default stand alone printer

 A networked printer

 A shared printer

 Toolbar printer icon

A document can be sent to the printer in a number of ways. The first method is by clicking the **Printer** icon on the Standard toolbar. This will send the data to the default printer from where it will be printed.

The Print dialog box

File > Print will open a dialog box, where you may change the printer selection, number of copies to be printed and other factors affecting the printing.

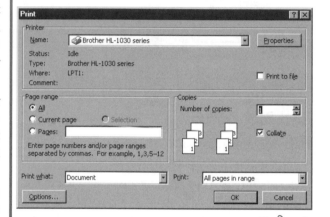

Basic steps

To change the printer:

1 Click the arrow by the Name slot and select

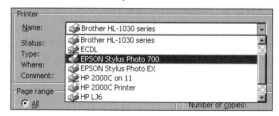

To print selected:

2 Select *Current page* from the Page range section, or specify the *Pages*, seperating page numbers by commas

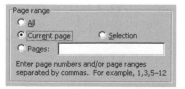

To print more than one copy:

3 Click the up-arrow next to Number of copies slot and set the number you require

4 Click the OK button to print the document

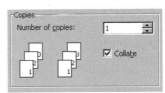

Changing printer properties

You can change the default settings and select specialist options by using the printer 'Properties' button on the 'Print' dialog box.

The 'Properties' button will open a further dialog box from which you may make adjustments to the quality of the printing, select specialist paper if you are using a colour printer and change the printer resolution.

We are not going to make any adjustments at this time, but you should be aware of this facility.

Changing the default printer

You may want to change the default printer, rather than having to keep opening the 'Print' dialog box and selecting a different printer.

Basic steps

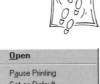

1 Click the Start button

2 Select Settings > Printers

3 When the Printers folder opens, right-click over the printer that you want to set as your default

4 Click on the Set as Default option

❑ A tick will appear next to the printer icon in the folder and it will remain as the default until such time that you change it

To print a document or change the printer selection is as easy as that.

> **Open**
>
> Pause Printing
> Set as Default
>
> Purge Print Documents
>
> Create Shortcut
> Delete
> Rename
>
> Properties

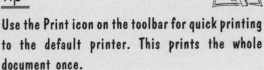

> **Tip**
>
> Use the Print icon on the toolbar for quick printing to the default printer. This prints the whole document once.

Printing a Document

We are now going to print a document. You will recall that we created a small text file in Microsoft Notepad earlier in the module. It is this file, 'Module 2.txt' we are going to print.

Before we print the document we are going to add a little more text to the document, so that it will take a little longer to print. This will then enable you to check the print process.

Type in at least two paragraphs of at least two lines each, re-save the file and then close it.

There are a number of ways to print the file and we will investigate two methods as outlined below.

Printing from Explorer

Basic steps

1 In Windows Explorer locate the file saved as *Module 2.txt* in the *My Documents* folder

2 Right-click on the file *Module 2.txt*

3 From the pop-up menu select Print. The file will then be sent to the default printer.

Printing from Notepad

1 In Notepad, open the file *Module 2.txt*

2 Open the File menu and select Print

You will have noticed that there is no 'Printer Set-up' option available in the menu list.

When Notepad prints a document, you are not given the option of changing any of the print options. Nor are you presented with the 'Print' window that you would normally see with applications such as Word or Excel. Notepad prints directly to the default printer.

Viewing print process

When you send a file to be printed, it goes into the 'print queue'. This occurs even if there is only one file to be printed. If there is more than one file to be printed, each joins the queue and is printed in the order that they were sent.

Many printers, in addition to loading printer drivers, also load a printer manager. This will run automatically when the printer starts to print a document.

It is from the 'print manager' that you can determine how the document is progressing through the print queue, whether it is actually being printed and how far through the print process the document is.

Take note

The print manager, or Status Monitor, is a program supplied with the printer that runs independently of the Windows printer controls and is designed to run with a specified printer.

Shown here is the Status Monitor for the Epson Stylus Photo 700 colour printer.

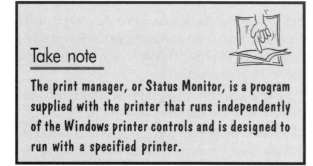

The monitor provides feedback on a number of different areas of the printer's activity such as:

- The progress bar indicates the status of the print job
- The file type, in this instance a Microsoft Word document is being printed
- The time remaining to complete the print task – this should not be relied upon to be accurate

This Epson printer uses two ink cartridges, one for the black ink and the other providing the coloured inks. The content of each cartridge is also monitored.

The detail button will also provide other information as shown in the example.

Running in the background, minimized, and monitoring the print task, is this window.

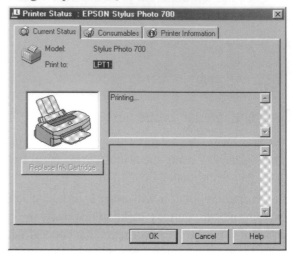

You can delete, pause, restart or cancel the print job.

Using Windows print monitoring

There is another method of monitoring the progress of a print job.

Basic steps

1 While a document is being printed click Start

2 From the menu, move to Settings and select Printers. The Printers window will open

❑ This computer has three printers installed.

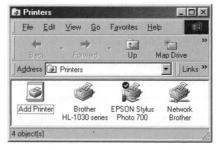

3 Double-click over the printer

❑ The monitor window will open

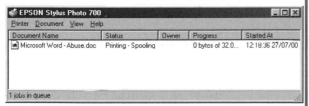

Considerable information is given: what the document is, the progress of the printing (i.e. 148KB of 299KB has been printed) and what time the printing started, complete with date.

Deleting a print task

There will be occasions when having sent a document to a printer you then decide that the print task is not required and want to terminate it.

This can be done through the printer monitoring software using either the Windows or the printer's own software.

Basic steps

To end a print task using the Windows software:

1 Click Start
2 Select Settings > Printers
3 Double-click over the required printer
4 When the monitor window opens, select the file that you want to stop printing

5 When the file is highlighted, select Document > Cancel Printing from the menu bar

❑ Alternatively select Printer > Purge Print Documents to end all printing

Either method is slow and will often leave you wondering if anything is happening. Eventually the print task will terminate.

It is recommended that, if possible, you should investigate the monitoring software that is provided with the printer. It is usually more efficient and quicker than using the Windows options.

Summary

Remember that there are two basic methods of printing documents and these are:

♦ Selecting **File > Print** whereupon the **Print** dialog box will open. It is from here that all the various adjustments can be made relating to the printer connected to the computer.

♦ By using the **Print** icon on the Standard toolbar. By clicking on this icon the complete document to be printed is sent directly to the printer bypassing the **Print** dialog box.

♦ To print a single page of a multiple page document, you must select **File > Print** and make the appropriate selection in the dialog box.

It is possible to create a macro that can be placed on the Standard toolbar that would avoid the necessity of opening the **Print** dialog box and send a single page to the printer direct. Macros are outside this courseware and you will need to use the on-line Help for more information on their creation and use.

Disk drives and formatting disks

Floppy disks and hard disks consist of platters, which are coated with a magnetic surface. It is this magnetic material that is the storage medium and actually stores the data by rearranging the magnetic pattern on the disk.

Damage and misuse of disks can result in data loss. Floppy disks in particular are susceptible to damage simply by being left too close to items that have a magnetic influence. Do not bend or touch the disk inside the plastic casing.

We have identified and spoken of the floppy and hard disk drives. What was not mentioned was the requirement that all disks have to be formatted before they can be used.

Formatting disks

What is formatting? For data to be stored on a disk in an orderly and logical manner, some form of structure is required. Formatting creates this structure on the disk. It creates sectors on the disk, each with a unique address which is used to find it and its content. This address applies to the whole sector so only one file (or part of a file) can be stored in it.

Depending upon the disk size, these sectors are of different sizes and are not easily changed once set. Basically, the larger the disk, the larger the sector.

When you save a file to disk, the file may well be smaller – or greater – than the sector size on the disk. When the file to be saved is greater than the sector size, it is saved to disk and fills up one sector; with the remaining part of the file placed in another sector. If this portion of the file does not fill that sector, the remaining area cannot be used for saving any other files. It becomes wasted space.

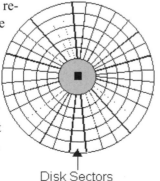

Disk Sectors

To keep track of where all the individual pieces of file are stored, a particular area on the disk is reserved and is known as the 'File Allocation Table', 'FAT' for short. It is the FAT that keeps track of all the various parts of the files stored on the disk.

File fragmentation

Now imagine that you had originally saved a file to disk, then deleted it. The FAT takes this into account and when you next save a file, this space is available and maybe used. Because available space like this is almost certainly spaced out around the disk, file fragmentation occurs. What this means is that the file is not saved as one long continuous file but sections of the file fill up any space available, irrespective of where on the disk the space is.

Over a period of time, fragmentation can actually become a problem and slow down the time it takes to find and open programs and files. To assist in overcoming this problem, the operating system includes a number of tools. For more information and to find what system tools are loaded on your computer click **Programs** > **Accessories** > **System Tools** and use the online Help.

It is important to remember that should you format a disk that originally had data saved on it, once formatting is complete that data is lost and cannot be recovered. So, think carefully before formatting a disk, always check the disk content first.

Basic steps

1   Close down any programs that maybe running and return to the Desktop

2   Place the floppy disk into the disk drive, the metal shutter end in first with the label uppermost. Double-click on the My Computer icon

3   Place the cursor over the 3½ Floppy (A:) and right-click.

4 At the pop-up menu, click on Format

❑ At the Format dialog box, select your format options.

5 Leave the Capacity slot set on the default 1.44MB (3.5"). Below in the Format type section select *Full* and then click on Start

❑ When the formatting starts, the progress is indicated by a blue bar at the bottom of the dialog box.

On completion of the formatting, a Format Results window will open. This window will give information relating to the disk, its capacity and will confirm that the formatting is complete.

7 Click the Close button

8 Return to the My Computer window and double-click on the 3½ Floppy (A:) and its window will open

The window is empty because you have just formatted the disk. Any data that was on the disk prior to formatting has now been lost and cannot be recovered.

That is all there is to formatting but remember the words of caution, formatting destroys data, check and if necessary recheck before formatting. Never rush this process.

Caring for floppy disks

Never leave disks exposed to direct sunlight

Do not bend the disk

Never expose disks to magnetic or electrical fields

Do not open the shutter and touch the disk directly

Store disks at room temperature

2: Using computers

Online Help

The operating system (Windows 98) and each application has its own specialist online Help system. The systems used to look and function much the same, but with the introduction of Office 2000, the application Help has changed considerably. Both systems will be discussed, starting with the operating system.

Accessing Windows 98 online Help

The Help functions for Windows can be accessed in two ways, from the Start menu and from the Help menu in Windows Explorer.

Basic steps

1   Select Start > Help

Or

2   In Windows Explorer, select Help > Help Topics.

3   At the Windows Help dialog box ensure that the Index tab is selected

4   Type the word *Help* in the Index slot.

❑   As you type, the lower left pane will scroll to list all the occurrences of the typed letters/ words. When you have finished, you will find the word *Help* at the top of the list.

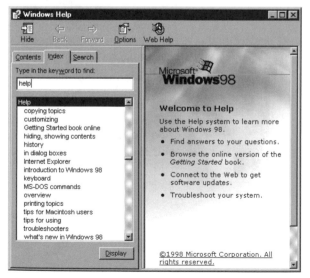

5   Left-click on the Display button and the Topics Found dialog box will open

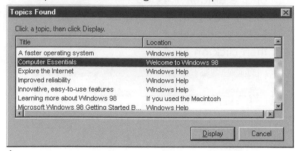

6   Select the subject *Computer Essentials*

7   Click Display. The dialog box will close and the topic appear in the right-hand pane

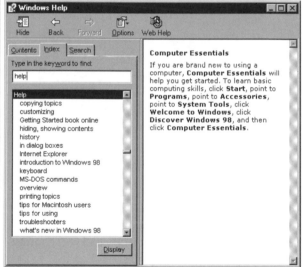

8   To print the topic, open the Options menu and select Print

Explore the Help facility to see how Microsoft uses names, and lists, various actions and commands. Also investigate the **Contents** and **Search** tabs and become competent in their use.

The operating system online Help is not dissimilar to that of the various applications such as Word or Access. However, it does not have the flexibility or, in the case of Access online Help, the interactivity with the application. Experiment and you will learn a lot from the Help system.

Applications Online Help

With the introduction of Office 2000, Microsoft revamped the online Help. The new system can be customized to suit your preferred way of working.

The Office Assistant

The default online Help option is the Office Assistant. This provides Help and tips on tasks as you work. You can customize or turn off the assistant if you find it irritating, though it can be quite amusing at times.

One face of the assistant – 'Rocky' the dog.

Selecting an assistant

Basic steps

1 Right-click over the assistant.
2 Click Choose Assistant and the Office Assistant dialog box will open.
3 Use the Back or Next buttons to scroll through the eight available options.

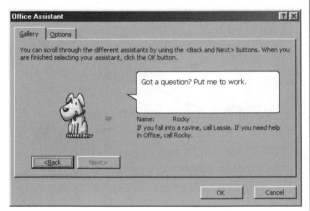

4 Follow the on-screen prompts

Customising the assistant

Basic steps

1 Right-click over the assistant
2 Select Options
3 Make your selections by clicking in each checkbox to insert or remove a tick.

Getting Help

The first time that you use Help the dialog box shown will appear.

You get Help by asking the assistant questions, for instance 'how do I create a table'.

Basic steps

1 Press the [F1] key
2 Click in the slot 'Type your question here' and type in your question
3 Click Search or press [Enter]
4 Select the appropriate item
5 The Help dialog box will open, to the right of the application window.
6 You may have several options – select as required.

Take note

You will always be offered the option 'None of the above, look for more help on the web'. This can be initially confusing, as it suggests that by selecting this option you will immediately be connected to the Web for further assistance. This is not the case, the online Help dialog box will appear. How to use this box is discussed later.

Disabling the assistant

You can disable, or 'Hide', the assistant and use the more conventional online Help option.

Basic steps

1 Right-click over the assistant
2 Select Options
3 Click in the Use the Office Assistant check box to remove the tick
4 Click on OK to accept the change and close the dialog box

Help without the Assistant

Online Help is still available, even though Office assistant has been disabled, by using the [F1] key.

Take note

If you disable the assistant, it can be reactivated from the Help menu and clicking on 'Show the Office Assistant'.

Basic steps

1 Press the [F1] key
2 The Help dialog box will appear

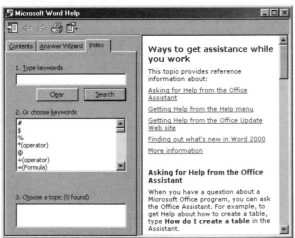

3 Type in your keyword
4 Click Search
5 If a match is found, it will appear in the Choose a topic slot

6 Select a topic and it will appear in the right pane

Take note

The Help dialog box offers you three methods of accessing Help – Contents, Answer Wizard and the Index. Select each tab in turn to discover how it functions.

You can move and/or resize the dialog box to your requirements.

The Help menu

The Help dialog box now has a toolbar. The first button is a toggle switch. In the example it is set to 'Hide'. Clicking on it will result in the left pane of the Help dialog box closing, and it will switch its mode to 'Show'. Clicking on it in this mode will result in the left pane reappearing.

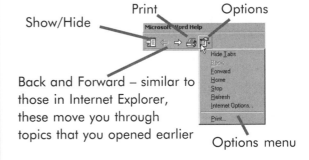

Back and Forward – similar to those in Internet Explorer, these move you through topics that you opened earlier

Printing a topic

Having found a topic you may want to print it, thus allowing you more flexibility when following detailed instructions.

Basic steps

1 Locate your topic
2 On the Menu bar click the Print icon
Or
3 Open the Options menu and select Print...

4   The Print dialog box will open

5   Ensure the correct printer and options are selected

6   Click OK to print topic

> **Tip**
>
> **If the assistant looks like it will get in the way of your work, don't move it, it will automatically move out of the way.**

Getting Help from Office Update Website

Microsoft has a Website dedicated to Office 2000 applications and provided that you have Internet access, you can quickly access it for more information and help.

Basic steps

1.   Click on the application Help menu

2.   Select the Office on the Web option

3.   Internet Explorer will open and connect to the Office Website

> **Tip**
>
> **If you press [F1] and decide that you do not want to use Help, press [Esc] and the dialog box will close.**

Using Help with Microsoft Access

When used in Microsoft Access, Help provides greater interactivity and an example is given in Module 5. This feature is particularly useful, and is a good learning aid, and should be investigated in more detail when you have completed module 5.

3 Word processing

Introduction to Microsoft Word

Microsoft Word is the word processing application included within the Microsoft Office Suite.

You will recall from the File Management module that any document, spreadsheet or database, produced by a computer is an electronic document and you can manipulate it. This means you can change, move, copy or delete various sections and imagery can be inserted, as can tables and columns.

Starting Word

As with many Windows based applications, you can start Word a number of different ways. If Word is installed as part of the Office Suite a shortcut bar is also installed and you can start the applications from it. We will use the **Start** button method.

Basic steps

1 Click Start
2 In the menu, click Programs
3 In its submenu, click Microsoft Word

Menus and toolbars

You should remember that Microsoft applications can be customised by you, the user, and you may find that some of the examples shown in this courseware do not match exactly what you see in your application window. Do not concern yourself because we will only use the standard menus and toolbar commands when telling you how to perform a particular procedure.

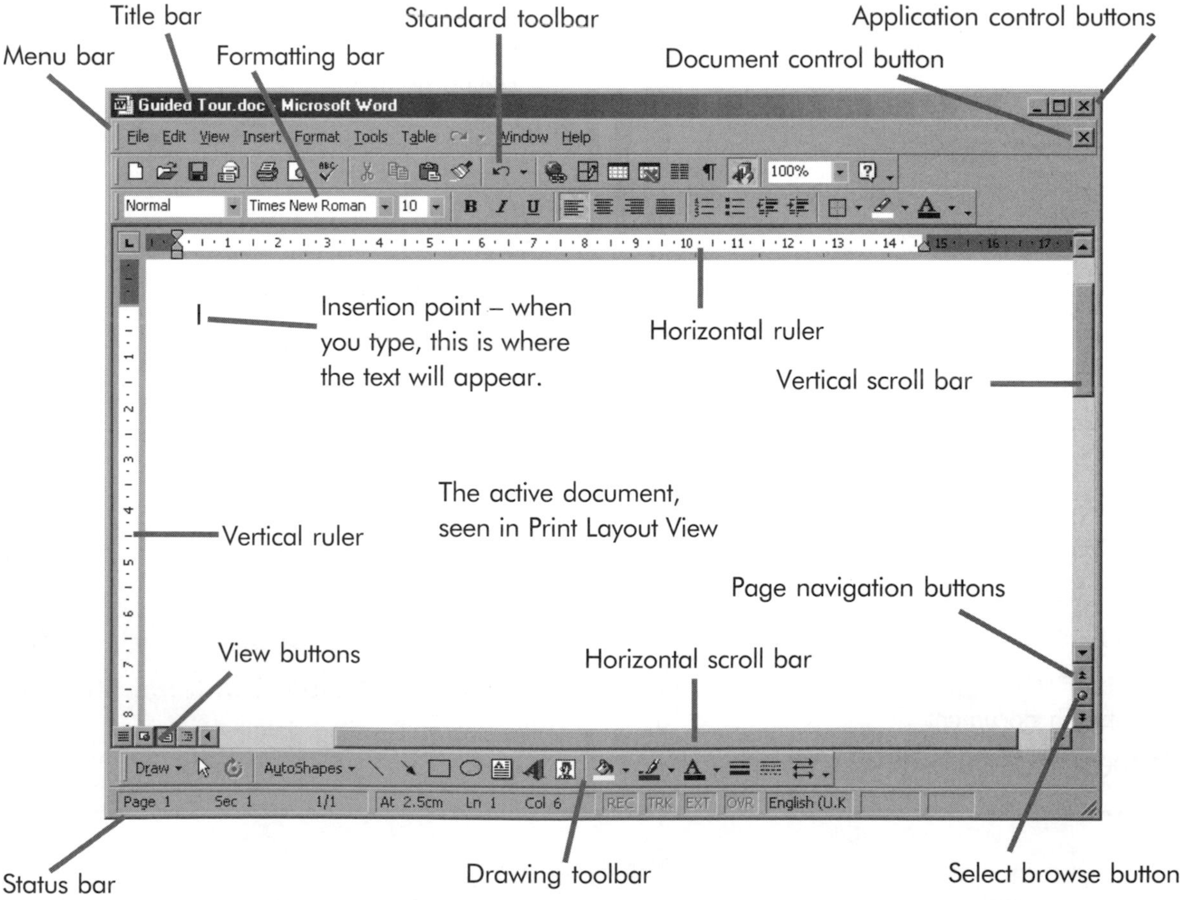
Title bar
Standard toolbar
Application control buttons
Menu bar
Formatting bar
Document control button
Guided Tour.doc - Microsoft Word
Insertion point – when you type, this is where the text will appear.
Horizontal ruler
Vertical scroll bar
The active document, seen in Print Layout View
Vertical ruler
Page navigation buttons
View buttons
Horizontal scroll bar
Status bar
Drawing toolbar
Select browse button

The Menu bar

This is immediately below the Title bar. It is from here that most commands and functions are located.

When you initially open a menu, it will, by default, only list a short version of its contents. At the bottom are two chevrons. Place your cursor over them, pause and the menu will reveal its full contents.

Customisation

By default, Word will monitor your use of the menus. If you do not use commands, Word will remove them from the initial list, and those that you use most will be moved to the top. To turn off this option and have the full menu content displayed each time you access a menu, do the following:

Basic steps

1 From the Menu bar select Tools > Customise.
2 Go to the Options tab.
3 Select *Menus show recently used commands first* then click Close.

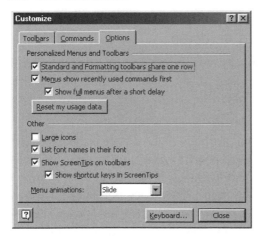

Toolbars

When you first open Word, Excel or PowerPoint, you will find the Standard and Formatting toolbars share one row, rather than each having its own row and appearing one below the other.

The Standard toolbar

The Standard toolbar gives you one-click access to the commands and functions that are most commonly used in Word. As you move the cursor over the icons, a tool tip will appear to identify the purpose and function of the respective buttons.

Shown below is the default Standard toolbar as it appears when it shares the same row with the Formatting toolbar.

The first group of buttons opens a new blank document, an existing document, saves a document and, finally a new feature, which applies e-mail headers to a document. More on this item later.

The Cut, Copy and Paste buttons form the second group. These were discussed in Module 2.

The Formatting Toolbar

Shown below is the Formatting toolbar, as displayed when it shares a row with the Standard toolbar. It is from this toolbar that the majority of text-based formatting can be performed.

There are a number of different ways that you can access commands. If you open the **Format** drop-down menu, you will find that the Formatting toolbar duplicates a number of the menu options.

Customising Toolbar Displays

To display Standard and Formatting toolbars separately turn off the share one row option on the Options tab of the Customize dialog box (see left).

You can customise various aspects of Word. You can add or remove buttons to the toolbars, remove the default toolbars from view or add additional toolbars to the display.

Standard toolbar

Formatting toolbar

Adding or removing buttons

In previous versions of Microsoft Office you could customise toolbars however, it has been made much more easier to do so in Office 2000.

Basic steps

1 Click the chevrons ⟫ at the right of the toolbar

2 A drop-down menu will appear, carrying the buttons that are hidden due to the compressed view of the toolbar. Click Add or Remove Buttons.

3 A list will open showing all the buttons available for that toolbar. Click on a button to add or remove it from view.

Displaying toolbars

You can choose which toolbars to show.

Basic steps

1 Open the View menu and select Toolbars

Or

2 Right-click on any toolbar.

3 If a toolbar is open there will be a ✓ by its name. Click on the name to add or remove a toolbar.

4 For further customisation click Customize... at the bottom of the menu.

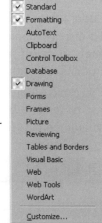

5 In the Customize dialog box you can specify which commands appear on menus and toolbars. This is outside the scope of this course and you should use the online Help for more information on this subject.

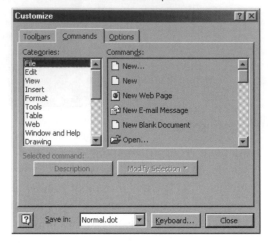

Introduction to the mouse

The mouse is essentially a pointing device and is extremely important, as many actions in Windows based applications rely totally on it to initiate actions or functions. This short section will introduce you to a number of mouse actions and the terminology used in association with the mouse throughout this course.

Types of mouse

You may recall from Module 1 that there are different types of computer pointing devices (mouse) available.

All standard devices have the following:

Within the body of the device is a heavy roller ball, which responds to your movements of the mouse and moves the on-screen mouse pointer, known as the cursor, in the vertical and horizontal plains.

Mouse buttons – There are always two mouse buttons located on top and to the front of the device body. The buttons are referred to simply as:

♦ **The left mouse button** – This is generally the most used button and is used to select, highlight or in drag and drop operations. The term used is 'click'.

- **The right mouse button** – This button has recently been given more functionality and has acquired an increased importance in Windows applications. The most common result of using the right mouse button is to open a content or pop-up menu. The term used is 'right-click' on or over the specified item or area.

During this course, you will be directed to click and drag. For instance to highlight a section of text. This means that you first press the left mouse button then, keeping the left button pressed, drag the cursor in the direction stated in the instruction until the desired effect or location is reached. Then you release the mouse button. Remember this, as you will be using it extensively throughout the course.

Shortcut keys

There are certain actions that, when performed using the mouse can actually slow you down. For instance if you are typing, with both hands on the keyboard and decide to save your work. To do this requires you to remove a hand from the keyboard and place it on the mouse then move the cursor up to the Standard toolbar and then left-click on the **Save** button.

This takes time. However, you can keep both hands on the keyboard and use the shortcut combination method 'Ctrl+S' (simultaneously press 'Control' [Ctrl] and the letter 'S' keys). Whatever you are working on is saved (this action is not case sensitive, you can use upper or lower case letters). This method is much quicker and is common to all Windows applications.

Other shortcut keys

There are numerous other shortcut key combinations, that are common to most Windows-based applications, and these will be discussed as the course progresses.

A summary of the main shortcuts key combinations is given in the table below.

For further information on shortcut keys available within Microsoft Word, look up 'shortcut' in the online Help.

Shortcut	Action	Shortcut	Action
Ctrl+S	Save current work	**Ctrl+X**	Cut selection to Clipboard
Ctrl+Z	Undo last action	**Ctrl+C**	Copy selected text/image
Ctrl+V	Paste Clipboard contents	**Ctrl+A**	Select entire document
Ctrl+Right Arrow	Move one word to the right	**Ctrl+Left Arrow**	Move one word to the left
End	Move to end of line	**Home**	Move to start of line
Ctrl+End	Move to end of document	**Ctrl+Home**	Move to start of document

Documents

On each occasion that Microsoft Word is opened, a new blank document is displayed, which is based on the 'Normal' Template (templates are discussed later in this course).

Default name

If you check the Title bar you will see that Word has given the document a default name. If the document is the first to be opened since Word was first started, it will have the name *Document1*. The number at the end of the word *Document* will increase as you open subsequent new documents.

Opening documents

We will use the toolbar buttons to open documents, though you can carry out the same functions by using the **File** > **Open** menu command.

Basic steps

To start a new document:

1   Click on the Standard toolbar

To open an existing document:

2   Select File > Open from the menu bar

Or

3   Click 🗁 on the Standard toolbar
❑   The Open dialog box will appear
4   Navigate your way to where the required document is stored
5   Double-click on it
❑   It will then open ready for use.

Take note

If in doubt as to how to locate files, refer to Chapter 2, Using the Computer and Managing Files.

How documents are displayed

If a single document is open, a document Close button will appear below the application control buttons. Click on it to close the document.

If more than one document is open, Word will open each in a full application window. This is known as 'Single Document Interface' (SDI). Each open document will have an icon on the Taskbar. The document Close button will not appear in subsequent windows.

To switch between documents, use the Taskbar icons or open the Window menu and select from the list.

To close a document

From the menu bar select **File** > **Close**. If you have not saved any changes, you will first be prompted to save the changes and when you have responded to the prompt, the document will close.

Or, if only one document is open, click the document Close button. Word will perform the same procedure described above and then close the document.

To close Word

From the Menu bar select **File** > **Exit**. If you have a document open and it has not been saved, Word will prompt you to do so, then close the application.

Or click the application **Close** button, which is located to the right of the application title bar.

Document cursors

Word 2000 has introduced three new document cursors. Ensure that Word is open with a blank document on display and try this short exercise.

Place your cursor about 2 inches from the top of the document and move it slowly towards the left margin. As you near the margin the cursor will change to I≡. Any text typed now will be left aligned

Move the cursor towards the centre of the page and notice that it changes to I≡. Any text typed now will be centre aligned.

Move the cursor to the right and as you approach the margin it again changes its shape to ⫤T. Any text typed now will be right aligned

These cursors allow you to point and double-click on any blank area of a document and immediately start typing. No more having to keep pressing [Enter] to move to a blank area of the document. Experiment, and note that you can double-click on any blank area, not just at the left, centre or right positions.

Document views

When a new blank document is opened, there are a number of different ways in which you may view the document, and these are **Normal**, **Web Layout**, **Print Layout** and **Outline**.

Basic steps

To switch between the views:

1 Open the View menu

2 Select a view from the top part of the menu

❑ For now ensure that the Print Layout is selected

In the example, the **Print Layout** has been selected – note that the button by its name is depressed.

Normal view is a trade-off between accuracy and speed. The overall appearance of the document is that of a continuous length of paper, with dashed lines indicating the different pages. Exceptions are:

- You will not see any headers and footers, assuming there are any in the document.

- You will not see any imported images. Should you try to use any of the Drawing tools, the view automatically changes to Print Layout view.

- If working in multiple columns, only one column will appear.

Print Layout view displays the document exactly as it would appear when printed, complete with the headers and footers. The overall appearance of the displayed page is that of a single sheet of paper with clearly defined breaks between each page. All images and columns will be displayed.

A minor disadvantage is that Print Layout is slightly slower than Normal view, but on a reasonably good computer the difference in speed is hardly noticable.

Web Layout view is designed to show how the text will apear in a browser. It wraps text to the width of the screen, as does a browser.

Outline view displays the outline structure of the document and if using the features mentioned above, you will have exceptional control over the document. It is possible that you will not see too much difference between Outline view and other views unless you are using Word Heading Styles or Outline Levels. Outline Levels are not covered within this course, but you should investigate these in the online Help.

The Document Map

The Document Map feature is not covered in depth in this course. However, it is a subject well worth investigating more, using the online Help.

The Document Map is used in-conjunction with Word Heading Styles (styles are discussed later in this module). To select the Document Map, choose **View > Document Map** from the menu bar.

The Document Map will display a map of the document, which is based on the section or paragraph headings. The display area is split into two. The map appears on the left and displays the headings and sub-headings of the document. You can move to a particular location within the document just by clicking on the appropriate heading or sub-heading, listed in the Document Map section.

The text appears to the right of the map area.

The system functions in much the same way as a hyperlink on a Web page. Clicking on an item, in the document map will result in the text area scrolling up and the cursor moving to the selected text.

Summary

You will, in time, find the best view to suit your way of working. In general it is suggested that you use the Print Layout view for this course.

You will find examples of a number of view options later in this module.

Saving documents

You should develop the practice of always saving a new document as soon as it is opened. There are a number of ways to save a document. We will discuss three methods, which includes the use of the menu **File > Save** method, the **Save** icon on the Standard toolbar and the shortcut key method **Ctrl+S**.

The File > Save approach

Basic steps

1   Open a new blank document
2   Select File > Save. Because this is a new document that is being saved to disk for the first time, the Save As dialog box opens.

3   Navigate your way to the folder that you wish to store the file in or select the appropriate disk drive or floppy disk by clicking on the drop-down arrow of the Save in: slot
4   Press [Tab] until the cursor appears in the File Name slot
5   Type in the name that you wish to save the document with. In this example, the name *'Using the Computer and Managing Files'* has been used. Use that name for this exercise.
6   Click the Save button
☐   The document will be saved and the dialog box will close

Take note

For more information regarding file extensions, refer to Chapter 2, where you will find a list of commonly used extensions. It is important that you understand and know them.

Microsoft Word automatically applies an extension to the end of the document name. You may recall that various applications use extensions to recognise the type of file or application used to create the file.

Microsoft Word appends a period (a full stop) and the letters 'doc' to the file name. Use the **File > Open** command or click the **Open** button and you will now find that the file that you just saved is called '*Using the Computer and Managing Files.doc*'. Remember that the file name is also displayed on Word's Title bar.

Using the Save button

The **Save** button can be used to save an already named document, or will open the **Save As** dialog box if saving a document for the first time. Once a document has been initially saved, clicking on the **Save** button will save all changes to the document, without the **Save** dialog box opening.

Using the shortcut key

Ctrl + S is the shortcut for **File > Save** in Word, as in all Windows applications.

Take note

Microsoft Word 2000 has introduced a new Save As dialog box, which is discussed in Chapter 2.

Formatting the page layout

Page layout

Page layout covers such items as paper size, paper source, margins and layout. During the installation of the Microsoft Office Suite, or just Word, you are given an option to set-up default settings, including what the paper size should be. You should be aware of the following:

The UK and Europe use a paper size that is prefixed by the letter 'A', followed by a number. The default size, for most uses, is A4 and measures 210 x 297mm. The paper size used by the USA is different. It is known as *Letter 8½ x 11 inch*.

If during the installation of the software, the correct paper size is not selected, the default American size will be set-up for use.

Tip

Should you find that when printing out a document you have unexpected results, for example excess blank space on the printout, check the Page Setup. A4 should be selected in the paper size section.

Changing the Paper size

Before you can make any changes to the page layout, you must first have a document open.

Basic steps

To check that the computer that you are working on is set to the European A4 paper:

1 Open a new blank document
2 From the menu bar select File > Page Setup
3 When the Page Setup dialog box opens click on the Paper size tab to see details of the default paper selection

❑ If on UK settings, your computer should display the size in centimetres and not inches. You can change the option if required.

4 Click on the drop-down arrow of the Paper size slot

5 Select the *A4 210 x 297 mm* option

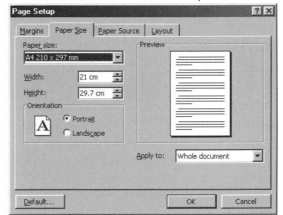

❑ So that you do not have to have to keep changing the setting to the European A4 size:

6 Click the Default… button (located in the lower left area of the dialog box)

❑ A prompt will advise you that the change will affect all of the documents based on the Normal Template.

7 Click on the Yes button

❑ From now on, each new document will be based on the European A4 paper size.

Other paper and envelope choices

It is from the **Paper size** list, that you can select a different size and type of paper as well as envelope sizes. In addition to the pre-set options, you can create your own paper size by selecting the *Custom size* option at the end of the drop-down list.

Margins

The default settings for Word margins are as shown in the table below and will change subject to your choice of paper. There are a number of items listed that we are not concerned with currently, so ignore them. We are only concerned with the margins.

Feature	Setting
Top and bottom margins	1 inch (2.54cm)
Left and right margins	1.23 inches (3.1cm)
Header and footer margins	.5 inches (1.3cm)
Paper Size	Letter 8.5 x 11"
Paper Orientation	Portrait
Paper Source	Printer-dependent
Section Starts	On a new page
Headers and Footers	The same throughout the document
Vertical Alignment	Top
Line Numbers	Off

Basic steps

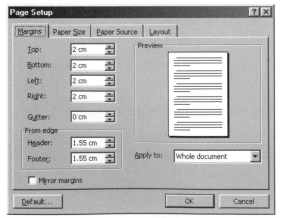

1 At the Page Setup dialog box select the Margins tab.

The settings displayed on your computer may be different to that shown. The Preview shows how the settings will affect the text layout in the document.

To change the margins:

2 Use the arrow buttons to the right of each of the settings to increase or decrease the value

Or

3 Double-click in the slot of the setting that you want to alter, and type in your changes

4 To move to the next setting press [Tab]

5 Make the following changes:

Change the Top and Bottom margins to 3 cm (or 1.25 inches)

Change the Left and Right margins to 2.5 cm (or 1 inch)

6 Ensure the Apply To slot has *Whole document* selected if not, select it

7 Click OK and the settings will be applied

Page orientation

In the **Page Setup** dialog box the page orientation can be set to either *Portrait* (shortest edge horizontal) or *Landscape* (longest edge horizontal).

> **Take note**
>
> If you are producing wide tables, *Landscape* is probably the better choice of paper orientation.
>
> As not all areas shown in the **Page Setup** dialog box have been covered, look at the online Help for further information.

Font default

For continuity and to ensure that your work matches the exercises used throughout this module set your font default as 'Times New Roman', size '12'.

Basic steps

1 From the menu bar select Format > Font

2 In the Font list select *Times New Roman*

3 In the Font Style list select *Regular*

4 In the Size list select *12*

5 Click Default...

6 When prompted to confirm, click Yes

Working with text

Typing in text

Basic steps

1 Open a new blank document
2 Place a floppy disk in the 3½ Floppy (A:) drive
3 Save the new document to the floppy disk and use the name *Colliery*
4 Type the text shown in the box, including any spelling mistakes, or type in some text of your own, but do make some mistakes. They are required to highlight certain features within Word

> ### The Colliery
>
> The news had just leaked out that the Pit was to close. Pop had never known any other work, except of course when he was sent to France during the First World War. Pop, as man and boy, from the age of fourteen had worked this pit, and now it was all to end.
> The closure programme was to be formally announced later that afternoon, even so, the news swept around the colliery in no time at all. Even the men at the coal-face knew the news before they even came up from underground. They quesioned the man at the gate guard as they stepped out of the cage, 'is it true, are they really closing us down?'they asked. Just the look on his face was suficient to confirm their worst fears.
> Some four hundred men worked the colliery, and a high percentage of them were in their late forties and early fifties. Although some of the men would move to other collieries, the future looked bleak for the majority of the men.

Editing and enhancement of text

We are now going to change the font type and size as well as changing the header line to all capital letters.

Ignore the spelling mistakes, which appear with a red wavy line under the mis-spelt word.

This short exercise will show how quick and easy it is to make major changes to the appearance of the text. We will return to text editing and enhancement later in the course.

Basic steps

In order to change the heading to all capitals and to increase text size:

1 Place the cursor to the left of the line '*The Colliery*'. The cursor will change to an arrow
2 Click once and the heading will be highlighted
❑ This method of highlighting text is quick if you wish to highlight the entire line.
3 On the Formatting toolbar, click on the down-arrow by the Font Size slot
4 Select *14*. Word will change the highlighted text from its current size to 14.
5 With the text still selected, press [Shift] and [F3] together. This will change the text to capitals.
7 Select the word '*fourteen*' in the first paragraph, by double-clicking in the middle of the word
8 Click the *Italic* button ⬛ on the Formatting toolbar, to change the word to italic style
9 Deselect the highlighted text by clicking on a blank area of the document
10 Save the changes to the document, using the Save button ⬛ on the Standard toolbar
❑ Do not close the document

Creating a second document

Open a new blank document and save it as '*Colliery2*'. Enter the following text including the spelling mistakes, or more of your own

After the shift change, and when the men had washed and showered, the shift assembled in the canteen. One of the Deputies caled for order and the Manager walked in. The canteen fell silant and the men waited forlornly for the formal announcement of the closure.

The Manager, Jack Harkins, not used to adressing such a large audience, cleared his throat and started to speak. 'I'm sure that you have all heard, at least something to the effect, that the colliery is to close. Gentlemen, I am afraid that the rumour is true, and the colliery will close in four months time'.

The men, even though they were expecting the whorst, groaned loudly. They turned to their pals and the noise in the canteen rose from a deathly silence to such a level that the Manager could not be heard, and he had to bang on the table to regain the men's attention.

Spell and grammar check

Depending on how Word is configured, you may have noticed that a red wavy line has appeared below some words. This indicates that Word has not recognised them and they require checking.

Basic steps

1 Put the cursor at the start of the document
2 Click on the ABC button 🔤 on the toolbar to open the Spelling and Grammar dialog box
❑ The suspect word is indicated in the upper pane, in red if it is a spelling error and in green if it is a grammar query.

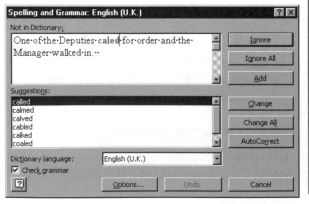

❑ In the lower pane, Word offers its suggestion, 'called', which is correct.
2 To accept the suggested word, click Change
3 Complete the spell check
4 Save the changes but do not close the document

Switching between open documents

You should now have two documents open, though you may only see one, subject to how your screen display is set up. We will assume that you can only see the one document, so the question is 'how do you switch between the two documents?'

Basic steps

To switch between documents:
1 Open the Window menu
❑ You will see the two document names in the lower section. The tick (✓) by *Colliery2.doc* indicates that it is the active document – the one you currently working on.
2 Click on the required document. It will then become the active document.

Copying text between documents

We are now going to copy the text from the *Colliery2* document and paste it in the first document that we created called *Colliery*. Ensure that *Colliery2* is the active document.

We are going to use the shortcut key options to copy and paste the text from one document to the other.

Copy

There will be occasions when you will want to re-use or duplicate a section of text, or an image, either in the same or a different document. Before you can copy text, or images, you must first select it.

There are a number of ways that you can invoke the copy or paste commands.

Use of buttons. The **Copy** and **Paste** buttons appear on the Formatting toolbar.

Use Menu Bar. The **Edit** menu lists the **Copy** and **Paste** commands.

Shortcut keys. In all Windows applications the shortcut keys for **Copy** are the combination of the Control and letter 'C' keys, written as **Ctrl+C**. For **Paste** use the key combination **Ctrl+V**.

Right-click menu. Once the text, or image, has been selected, right-click over the selected area and a pop-up menu will appear. The **Cut**, **Copy** and **Paste** commands appear in the menu.

Basic steps

1 Ensure that the *Colliery2* document is active
2 Press Ctrl+A. This combination selects everything that is in the document, in this case all of the text.
3 With all the text highlighted, press Ctrl+C to copy the text to the Clipboard
4 Deselect the text by clicking in the right margin area. The highlight will be removed.

Tip

It is important that you are familiar with the Office 2000 Clipboard and how it functions. Refer back to page 63 if necessary.

The Paste command

The Paste command, when activated, looks in the Clipboard and copies whatever it finds to the new location indicated by the user.

Basic steps

1 Switch to the *Colliery* document
2 Place the cursor at the end of the last line of the document, after the full-stop
3 Press [Enter] twice to create two blank lines

4 As we have only one block in the Clipboard, we can use the key combination Ctrl+V, to paste the text into the new location. If there are several copied blocks, the Clipboard toolbar is displayed and we can paste from there by clicking on the desired icon.
5 Perform another spell check
6 When completed save the changes using the shortcut key combination Ctrl+S

Selecting text

We used the shortcut key method to select the text and then copied it. The shortcut key **Ctrl+A** selects everything in the document, which on this occasion was satisfactory because we required all of the text. There will be times when only a section of text, or an image, is required.

You can select a section of the document with the drag method.

Basic steps

1 Place the cursor to the left of the first word of the section to be copied
2 Click, hold the mouse button down and drag the cursor to the end of the section you require
3 Release the button. The text will remain highlighted
4 Copy the selected area, using one of the previously described methods.

At this stage both documents are open. We only require the Colliery document at this time, so switch to the *Colliery2* document and close it by selecting **File > Close**.

Formatting selected text

We are now going to change the formatting on selected text, which will involve the use of the **Center** and **Underline** commands and changing the typeface to **Arial**.

Basic steps

1 Select the heading text 'THE COLLIERY'

2 On the Formatting toolbar, click the Center button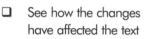

Or

3 Use the Ctrl+E shortcut.

The heading 'THE COLLIERY' will move to the centre of the page.

4 With the text still selected, click the Underline button U or use the Ctrl+U shortcut.

❑ Click the down-arrow to open the Font list

5 From the list select *Arial*

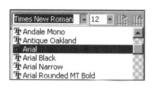

6 De-select the text

❑ See how the changes have affected the text

7 Save the changes by clicking the Save button or by using Ctrl+S

❑ Do not close the document because we will require it for the next exercise

Hyphenating text

To make any changes to the hyphenation settings, you must have a document open before you can open the **Hyphenation** dialog box.

There will be occasions when you find that Word may be breaking up words and applying a hyphen where you consider it inappropriate. You can control how the hyphen feature functions or you can turn it off and apply your own hyphenation manually.

Hyphenation helps to eliminate gaps or 'rivers of white' and to maintain even line lengths in narrow columns.

If you hyphenate manually, Word searches the document for words to hyphenate and then asks you whether and where to insert a hyphen.

Use an optional hyphen to control where a word such as 'AutoFormat', breaks at the end of a line, for example, 'Auto-Format'. Use a non-breaking hy-

phen to prevent a hyphenated word, such as 'CD–ROM', from breaking if it falls at the end of a line.

Basic steps

Hyphenate text automatically

1 Ensure that the *Colliery* document is open

2 From the menu bar select Tools > Language > Hyphenation

3 Click the Automatically hyphenate document slot and a tick will apperar

4 In the Hyphenation zone box change the amount of space to be left between the end of the last word in a line and the right margin to *1.5cm*

5 Click OK

Take note

You may find that only one, maybe two, words have been split and a hyphen applied. Experiment by increasing and decreasing the hyphenation zone, and observe the changes.

To reduce the number of hyphens, make the hyphenation zone wider. To reduce the raggedness of the right margin, make the hyphenation zone narrower.

In the Limit consecutive hyphens to box, enter the number of consecutive lines that can be hyphenated, if required.

To ensure continuity throughout this course reset the hyphenation settings as shown here:

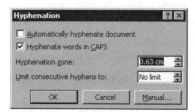

Further assistance

If **Hyphenation** does not appear on the **Language** sub-menu, you need to install the hyphenation tool. Refer to the online Help for more information, particularly if you wish to manually control hyphenation.

Tip

It is a good idea to wait to hyphenate your document until after you have finished writing and editing, because adding and deleting text may affect the way lines break.

Inserting additional text

Re-open the *Colliery* document, start a new paragraph and type in the text shown in the box. Check and correct the spelling and grammar as necessary and save the file. Use [F7] to start the spell check and **Ctrl+S** to save.

> The talk in the pubs and clubs that evening was only of the forthcoming closure. Wives had joined their husbands, all hoping that someone else knew a little more than they did, only to find that there was no further news.
>
> A number of the young men thought that they would be better off leaving the indudtry altogether, the question was, where else was there to go? The general consensus of opinion was that the closure would be the death of the valley.
>
> The Manager waited until there was silence, he then told the men that the majority of the equipment underground, that could bt used elsewhere, would be removed. This meant that there would be a requirement, after the mine had formally closed, for a limited work force to remain ot remove the equipment. The response from the men was utter silence. The shock of the closure, and its speed of implmentation, was still working its way home for most.
>
> Any resemblance to actual events, or to persons alive or dead, is purely coincidental.

More text formatting

Currently the document is formatted *left aligned*. This means that the text on the left of the page is aligned with the left margin, while the right margin is ragged, with lines of different lengths.

We will now change the formatting to *Full Justified*. The application will adjust the text and space it out evenly across the page width, within the margin settings. The text closest to the right margin will now line up and the ragged edge will disappear.

Basic steps

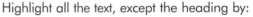

Highlight all the text, except the heading by:

1. Placing the cursor at the top of the document to the left of the first line starting 'The News'
2. Simultaneously press the Shift+Ctrl+End keys
- All of the text will be highlighted
3. Left-click on the Full Justification button on the Formatting toolbar
- The text will adjust and you will see the difference, mainly in the right margin area, which will be aligned vertically
4. Save the changes to the document

Moving text

Before we start, ensure that the Clipboard toolbar is display.

Some of the text is in the wrong place within the general story line and should be moved.

Basic steps

1. Place the cursor at the beginning of the paragraph '*The Manager waited until there...*'
2. Drag the cursor to the right and down to include the full stop after the word '*most.*'
- All the paragraph should now be highlighted
3. Click the Cut button ✂ or use Ctrl+X
4. Click to place the insertion point directly below the fifth paragraph

5   Press [Enter] once to insert an additional line
6   Click the appropriate icon on the Clipboard toolbar
❑   The text will appear at the insertion point
7   Save the document changes

Make any necessary adjustments and ensure the space above and below the inserted paragraph is consistent, i.e. one blank line between paragraphs.

Indenting text

Basic steps

1   Place the cursor to the left of the first word of the first paragraph, starting '*The news ...*'
2   Press [Tab]. The first line of text will move to the right. This is '*First Line Indentation*'.
3   Place the cursor at the start of the paragraph '*The Manager waited until...*'
4   Use the shortcut key Ctrl+M and the whole paragraph will adjust and move to the right

---

Take note

Use the Ctrl+M option if the paragraph is a sub-section of the previous paragraph. Press the same keys to move the text further to the right.

We do not actually want the text indented this way – it was used to demonstrate the difference between tabulation and indentation. Move the paragraph back to its original position, against the left margin.

5   Place the cursor adjacent to the paragraph starting '*The Manager waited until...*'
6   Use the key combination of Ctrl+Shift+M to move the paragraph to the left – repeat, if required, until such time that paragraph is at the left margin
7   Create a First Line Indentation for each and every paragraph
8   Save the changes and close the document.

Creating a new document

We are now going to practice some of the techniques previously taught and introduce some new ones.

Basic steps

1   Open a new blank document
2   Save this document as '*Colliery3*' on the 3½ Floppy (A:) drive (or wherever you saved the previous documents)
3   Type in the following text or some new text on your own topic, and to save the document

---

Six months after the colliery had closed, and all the equipment that was worth removing had gone, the demolition started. Reinforced retaining walls were built at the shatf bottom. The wals were there to stop the in-fill spilling out into the galleries. Ton upon ton of rock and gravel was poured down the shaft until it was full, and finally a plug was set in at the top of the shaft.

Mid-way through March a short service was held at the pit head, to remember men and boys lost in accidents over the long years that the mine had been worked. Pop Jones, Alun Davis and Jim Walker stood together, each thinking back to when the number four gallery had flooded. The speed and rush of water was such that, even though they were some considerable distance from the source, they were swept off their feet. In all the cofusion and chaos they lost sight of their pal Peter Dillion. It was not for some time after the evnet that Peter was found dead, trapped between two drams that had overturned

Eventually the winding gear and superstructure was dismantled. The filling of the shaft seemed to most to be the end of the colliery, but in actual fact it was the removal of the winding gears and towers that really brought home the fact that the pit was no more.

Any resemblance to actual events, or to persons alive or dead, is purely coincidental.

---

4   Perform a Spell and Grammar check
5   Save the document

Examine the document just typed and you will see that it does not follow a logical order. We will now rearrange the text to correct this.

Basic steps

1 Place the cursor to the left of the word '*Eventually*' (the start of the penultimate paragraph)

2 Select the complete paragraph and cut it

3 Place the cursor after the last word of the first paragraph, '*shaft*'

4 Press [Enter] twice to insert two additional blank lines

5 Leave the cursor at this position

6 Click the appropriate icon on the Clipboard toolbar. The text will be inserted between the two paragraphs.

7 Format as required, such as deleting the double line spacing between the paragraphs

8 Save the changes and close the document

Inserting a file

We are now going to combine two separate documents and produce one new document. This procedure is extremely useful, particularly if two people have been working on a project and each has produced a separate document on the subject.

The procedure that we are about to perform will result in the two original files remaining intact, with an entirely new document being produced. We will use the documents *Colliery* and *Colliery3*.

Basic steps

1 Open the *Colliery* document

2 Place the cursor after the paragraph ending '*death of the valley*' at the end of the document

3 Press [Enter] twice to insert two new blank lines

4 From the menu bar select Insert > File

5 At the Insert File dialog box, ensure that the 3½ Floppy (A:), or where you saved the document, is selected in the Look in slot

6 Select *Colliery3.doc* from the list

7 Click OK button

The file *Colliery3.doc* will now be inserted into the current document, *Colliery*, as an integral part of it. Save the document using a different name:

8 Select File > Save As

9 When the dialog box opens, save the document as *Colliery4* to the floppy disk or to a location of your choice

You will now have four documents:

The original *Colliery* document

The original *Colliery2* document

The original *Colliery3* document

Colliery.doc
Colliery2.doc
Colliery3.doc
Colliery4.doc

Colliery4 is the combined document produced after the insertion took place.

Deleting text

Save the changes to all your documents and close all except 'Colliery 4'. Look through this and you will see that there is a duplicate paragraph.

Basic steps

1 Save the changes to any documents that are currently open and then close all documents except *Colliery4*

❑ Looking through the document you will see that there is a duplicate paragraph

2 Locate the first instance of the paragraph '*Any resemblance to actual events, or to persons living or dead, is purely coincidental*'

3 Highlight the paragraph and delete it

4 Do not save the changes just yet

The Undo command

In the event that you inadvertently deleted the wrong text, stop immediately. There is a way to correct the error and restore the text by using the Undo command. It is important to remember that as soon as you make the mistake, stop.

We will use the deleted text section to demonstrate the Undo command.

There are a number of ways of restoring the deleted text.

Basic steps

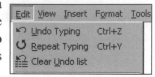

1 Use the shortcut key combination Ctrl+Z

❑ The deleted text should reappear in its original location

or

2 Left-click on the Undo button on the Standard toolbar

There are two buttons. The one on the left is the **Undo** button. The other on the right is the **Redo** button

Clicking on the **Undo** button, not the down-arrow, will undo the last action only.

Adjacent to each of the buttons are drop-down arrows. Clicking on an arrow will open a list of recent actions. Use this method if you wish to undo an action that took place previous to the last action.

Click the down-arrow and from the list click the action you want to undo. If you do not see the action, use the scroll bar.

If you later decide that you do not want the Undo action applied, click the **Redo** button or drop-down arrow and click on the appropriate action.

Select **Edit** on the menu bar and you will find the same **Undo** and **Redo** commands are there as well.

Edit	View	Insert	Format	Tools
↰ Undo Typing			Ctrl+Z	
↻ Repeat Typing			Ctrl+Y	
Clear Undo list				

If, after experimenting with the above, you still have the duplicated sentence in your document, delete it completely. We do not want duplicate entries in it.

❑ Save the changes and close the document

Fonts, typeface and size

Word offers you an assortment of fonts to use when creating your documents. Each font has a specific typeface and style, which determines the appearance of the characters. Typefaces are identified by names such as 'Arial', 'Courier' and 'Times New Roman'.

Font size

Font size is specified in points. One point is equal to 1/72 of an inch, so a 72 point font would measure 1 inch from the bottom of its lowest hanging character (g, y) to the top of its largest letter (T, I).

Fonts are classified as 'proportional' or 'non-proportional'. A proportional font such as 'Times New Roman' will use more space on the paper for the letter 'w' than it does for the letter 'I'. A non-proportional font such as 'Courier' uses the same amount of space on the paper for every letter and every space.

Some font examples

The following are examples of different font typefaces and sizes.

Basic steps

1 Open a blank new document and save it as *Fonts*
2 Type in the first line of text as shown
3 Copy the text and paste the same line six times, with a space between each line
4 Change each line in your document, as necessary, until you have the same text as shown in the examples
5 Highlight each line individually
6 Apply the font typeface and size as indicated in that line's text

If you do not have these fonts installed, go to the section later in this module and follow the instructions for installing additional fonts or use fonts of your choice.

This line of text is in Times New Roman, size 10.

This line of text is in Courier, size 10.

This line of text is in Helvetica, size 10.

THIS LINE OF TEXT IS IN ALGERIAN, SIZE 10.

This line of text is in Lucida Handwriting, size 10.

This line of text is in Times New Roman, size 14.

THIS LINE OF TEXT IS IN MATISSE ITC, SIZE 14.

You can clearly see the differences in typeface and size.

This is a topic that you should investigate. Use the online Help for assistance to learn how Word handles fonts.

Take note

Be careful not to use too many fonts in a document as this can become a distraction.

Reformat and embolden text

Basic steps

1 Open the document *Colliery4*
❑ We are going to re-format some areas of text
2 Highlight the heading '*The Colliery*'
3 Click the Bold icon on the Formatting toolbar
❑ Notice how the word expands to take up more space with the text emboldened.
4 Save the changes to the document

105

Using the format painter

There will be occasions when you will have spent some time deciding on what typeface and size to use and will have selected various other formatting options for use in a document. Later you may decide that the same formatting etc. is required in a different section of the document.

There is no need to perform the time consuming procedure of making all the selections again. Microsoft Word provides a tool, called the **Format Painter**, which applies the formatting from one section of text to another.

Basic steps

1 Open the document '*Colliery*'

2 Select the whole of the first paragraph that starts '*The news had just...*'

3 Change the font to *Algerian* size 14 (if you do not have this font installed use a font of your choice)

4 With the text still highlighted click the Format Painter icon on the Standard toolbar

❑ Note that when selected, the cursor changes to a paintbrush.

5 Place the cursor at the beginning of the third paragraph

6 Drag the Format Painter cursor over the whole paragraph

7 When highlighted release the mouse button

❑ The formatting from paragraph 1 will be applied to the text of paragraph 3, including the first line indentation.

8 Save the changes and close the document

Tip

To copy the selected formatting to several locations a document, double-click **Format Painter**. Click the icon again when you are finished.

106

Printing documents

The time has come to print a number of documents. We require one copy of each of the files shown.

Print preview

Before printing a document, you may wish to check what the document will look like when printed. Word provides a means of doing this is known as **Print Preview**. To use this, a document must first be open.

Basic steps

1 Open the three documents

2 Ensure that *Colliery4* is the active document (though it is not important in which order you print the documents)

3 Select File > Print Preview. The display will change to the preview window and the document will be displayed in the format in which it will be printed.

❑ The document may be displayed as one complete page or as a section of the page. If you wish to change the display view, to either increase or decrease it:

4 Click on the Magnifier button

5 When the cursor has changed its shape, click on the document

❑ The display will either increase or decrease in size, subject to the setting indicated on the magnifying glass icon. If the icon has a plus (+) sign in the middle of it when placed over the document, clicking on the document will increase the size of it. Or, if the magnifying glass icon has a minus (-) sign in the middle of the icon, it will decrease the display size.

An alternative method

Another method of increasing the page size and magnification is:

1 Click on the Zoom drop-down arrow, on the

Print Preview toolbar

2 Select an appropriate magnification figure from the list and the page view either increases or decreases, according to the figure selected

Viewing multiple pages

Basic steps

1 Click on the Multiple page button

❑ The button will expand as shown in the example

Up to six pages may be previewed at a time. Drag across the display to indicate how many pages you want to see at once.

Clicking on the top left and middle icons will result in the pages being displayed adjacent to each other. However, if you select the top left and bottom left icons, the pages will be displayed one above the other, which results in a smaller display

You can scroll through the entire document, assuming that there is more than one page to the document, by using the vertical scroll bar, located to the right of the display.

Experiment with this feature to gain maximum benefit. When finished, close the window by clicking on the **Close** button on the **Print Preview** toolbar.

Printing a document

Basic steps

1 With a document open, select File > Print

❑ The Print dialog box will open

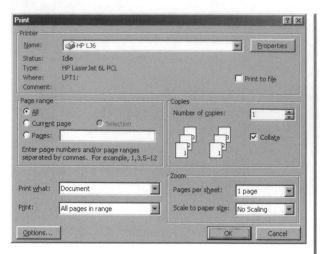

To print a range of pages

If you decide that you do not require the complete document to be printed, for example you have amended a number of pages, you can specify which pages are to be printed.

❑ Word automatically selects *All* from the Print range area. We will print all the pages for each document

2 Click the OK button

❑ The window will close and the document will be sent to the printer

3 Print one copy of each document

❑ Compare each document, starting with *Colliery*. Find the section where you inserted the file and compare it with the document *Colliery4*. Confirm that the file inserted is the same as the document *Colliery*.

Printing options

Basic steps

To print a single page
1 Ensure the document is open and that the page you require is displayed on the screen

2 Place the cursor anywhere within the page

3 Select File > Print

4 At the Print dialog box, change the Page range selection to *Current page*

5 Click the OK button

❑ Only the selected page will be printed

Basic steps

To print pages 2, 4, 5, 6, 8:
1 Select File > Print
2 In the Pages slot, type *2,4-6,8*
3 Click OK

Word will now look at the page numbers and miss out page 1, print page 2, miss out page 3 and start next at page 4. However, the hyphen between the figures 4 and 6 is an instruction to print a range of pages, in this instance, print pages 4, 5 and 6. When the range is printed, page 7 will be skipped and finally page 8 will be printed.

Further information

Take some time to investigate the **Print** dialog box and the flexibility available in the print options. Pay particular attention to the **Properties** button. Click on it and a **Properties** dialog box will open. It is not possible to describe the contents in detail because each printer has its own unique properties. You should consult your printer handbook for more detail.

Terminology

Printed copies of documents are known as *hard copies*. *Soft copies*' are the electronic files. Keep all copies of the print outs for future reference.

Using online Help

The online Help system will assist you to gain more knowledge and therefore more experience. Investigate the online help and read your printer handbook. Not all printers function the same.

Intermediate features and functions

This section will introduce you to useful features that are frequently overlooked in the early stages of learning Microsoft Word.

Headers and Footers

The Headers and Footers function is a particularly useful feature and is a means of producing the same text, or image, on each page of a multi-page document without repeatedly re-typing or inserting images. If you require each page to be numbered, it is through the use of Footers that this is achieved.

Frequently people produce documents, save them and then do not open them for some time. You may well have a paper copy of the document, however, you may not recall what the saved document was called, or where it is located on the computer. Again Headers and Footers provide a means of identifying the file name. You can save the file name, along with the name of the person who created the file and what date it was last modified or amended within a Footer.

Using Headers and Footers

The active document will adjust its position on the screen, moving up to the top of the document and you will see a broken line box, as shown below. It is within this box that the header text, etc. is typed.

In addition to the box, a further toolbar will open as shown here. This toolbar may appear centred on your screen or may be placed underneath another toolbar.

Move the cursor over each of the buttons on the toolbar, in turn and pause. A tool tip will appear indicating what its function is.

You can change the font and size, using the Formatting toolbar, within the Header or Footer, as required.

Entering text

When the document is in the **Headers and Footers** view, the cursor is placed at the beginning of the line, left justified, of the Header section.

Basic steps

1 Ensure the document is open – in this instance open *Colliery4.doc*
2 Select View > Header and Footer
3 Type your name in the Header area

Other changes can be made such as a different typeface, embolden or italic formatting.

Take note

You will only see the Headers and Footers if the document is being viewed in Print Layout View. If not already selected, change to it now.

Switching to the footer section

To switch between the Header and Footer, use this icon ⌹ or use the cursor keys on the keyboard:

1 Change the Font size to *8*
2 Press the [Enter] key once. This will move the first line of the Footer text down, one line away from the document text
3 Type in '*A:\Colliery4.doc Page*'

Header area

Header

Header and Footer toolbar

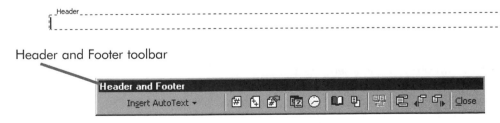

109

4 Press the Spacebar once

5 From the Header and Footer toolbar, click on the Insert Page Number button 🔲

❑ You will find that the page number appears in a different font size

6 Highlight the page number and change the Font size to *8*

7 Click the Close button and scroll up to the top of the page

❑ You will see the Header dimmed, at the top of the page, above the document text

8 Scroll to the bottom of the page and check the Footer text

9 Move to the next page, where you will find the same Header and Footer. You will see that Word has automatically changed the page numbering as you move from page to page.

10 Save the changes and close the document

Built in features

Headers and Footers in Word provide you with a number of built in features designed to save you time and effort and worthy of further investigation.

Insert AutoText

The **Insert AutoText** feature is particularly useful.

Earlier you opened a document, *Colliery4*, and inserted a Header and Footer by typing in your name and the document name, and inserted automatic page numbering. To achieve this, a specific number of individual actions were performed. However, Word could have done most, if not all of this in one go.

Basic steps

1 Open the document *Colliery3*

2 Select the Headers and Footers view

3 Switch to the Footer

4 Press [Enter] to insert a blank line

5 Change the Font size to *8*

6 Click on the drop-down arrow of the Insert AutoText button

❑ A drop-down list will appear

7 Click on the Author, Page #, Date option

- PAGE -
Author, Page #, Date
Confidential, Page #, Date
Created by
Created on
Filename
Filename and path
Last printed
Last saved by
Page X of Y

The list will close and you are returned to the Footer of the open document. Your name, the page number and current date should now appear as the footer.

So how was this done? Word has picked-up this information directly from the computer.

When the operating system was first installed, the user was requested to provide their name. Assuming a name was given, it was stored with other data. The page numbering feature has already been discussed and Word simply inserted the page number. The date was taken from the computer's built-in calendar feature.

8 Enter two blank lines in the Footer section by pressing [Enter] twice

9 Click on the Insert AutoText button and from the list select Filename and Path

Word will now check where this file is saved and enter those details. To use this feature, the file must first have been saved. If it has not been saved Word will enter the default name of the file without a location, for example 'Document2'.

10 If necessary highlight all of the Footer text and reapply the Font Size *8*

11 Close the Headers and Footers

12 Save the changes and close the document

Tables within a header or footer

There may be occasions, when you will find that the text does not appear as you want or where you want it. A simple solution is to insert a table as part of the Header or Footer. Tables offer you greater control of text, formatting and the location of items.

The subject of tables will be covered within this course shortly.

Further investigation

There are other features available for use with the Headers and Footers and you should investigate these later. For instance, using the online Help, investigate how to change the page numbering sequence if you have a large document comprising of two or more files.

Find and Replace text

The **Find and Replace** feature of Word is extremely powerful and can speed up changes to documents immensely. We are going to search for a word and then replace it with another.

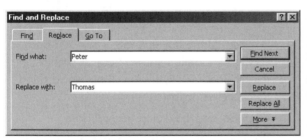

Basic steps

1 Open the *Colliery3* document
2 From the menu bar select Edit > Replace
❏ The Find and Replace dialog box will open

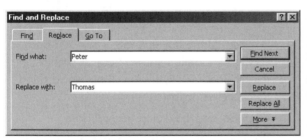

3 Type in the Find what slot what you wish to find and change
4 In the Replace with slot type in the word you wish to replace the original word with

In the above example, in the **Find what** slot is the word '*Peter*' and in the **Replace with** slot is '*Thomas*'.

Word will start to search for the word 'Peter' from wherever the cursor is at that time. To search the document from top to bottom, ensure that the cursor is at the beginning of the document. This may save you time, because if Word starts the search partway through the document, it will, when it reaches the end, ask you if you want it to start at the beginning.

5 To start the search click the Find Next button
❏ Word will commence a search and will highlight the first occurrence of the word

'Peter' that it finds and scrolls the document to enable you to see the selected word.

6 If you wish to change this occurrence of the word, click the Replace button

In this instance the word '*Peter*' should be highlighted, near the end of the document, in the sentence '*sight of their pal Peter*'. Click the **Replace** button.

Word will replace 'Peter' with 'Thomas' and move on to look for the next occurrence of the word 'Peter'. Replace the second occurrence of the word 'Peter'.

Word will continue until such time that it cannot find another occurrence of the word, then a dialog box will open and advise you of such.

7 If you are satisfied that you can safely change all occurrences of the word 'Peter', then click the Replace All button
8 Save any changes that you have made to the document

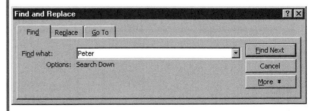

Take note

Use **Replace All** with care, as a wrong word could be replaced in error.

The Find feature

The **Find** feature functions in the same way as **Find and Replace**, except that the dialog box is smaller as shown here.

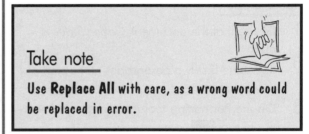

Clicking the **More** button will expand the dialog box and offer you more advanced control over how the search is conducted, including searching for specific applied formatting or items such as line breaks.

The **Find** dialog box can be changed to the **Find and Replace** dialog box by clicking on the **Replace** tab.

111

- ❑ Selecting the 'Go To' tab will offer you the option of going to a specific page, table or graphic, amongst other options.

Further information

To learn more of these features, you should experiment and use the online Help for further information.

Numbered or bulleted lists

Numbered and bulleted lists are useful formatting tools for creating lists of information in your documents.

Numbering paragraphs

Certain types of documents will require the inclusion of paragraph numbers and Word provides an automated feature for just this purpose.

Basic steps

1 Ensure that the document *Colliery3.doc* is open

2 Select the first two paragraphs at the start of the document

3 On the Formatting toolbar, click the Numbering button ▤

❑ Word will insert paragraph numbers adjacent to the two selected paragraphs.

4 Close the document but do not save the changes as we do not require the paragraph numbering.

Tip

If you know before you start, that paragraph numbering is a requirement, click the icon first and then start typing. Word will insert paragraph numbers as you progress. There are limitations with this feature, experiment to find out how best it can be used by you.

Bullet lists

Basic steps

1 Re-open the *Colliery3.doc*

2 Select the first two paragraphs

3 Select Format > Bullets and Numbering

❑ This dialog box will open

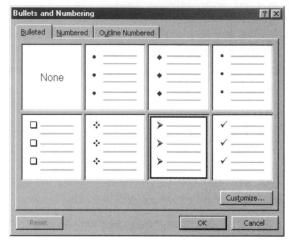

4 Ensure that the Bulleted tab is selected and click on the option shown here. A slightly thicker line, usually blue, will appear around the selected option

5 Click OK and the dialog box will close

Word will convert the text into a Bulleted list, using the selected formatting.

Using the Customize… button will open a further dialog box from where you may make changes to the selected option, such as indentation, etc.

6 Close the document but do not save the changes

Inserting Page Breaks

You will have noticed that Word automatically senses when it has reached the end of a page and inserts a new page when required. This is known as 'Page breaks' and could split a paragraph over two pages, or otherwise interfere with the page layout. You can control how and where page breaks occur.

Inserting a manual page break

There will be occasions when you will require text to appear on a new or the next page.

There are a number of different ways to achieve this. The simplest way is with the shortcut.

Basic steps

1   Open the *Colliery3.doc* in Normal View
2   Place the cursor at the end of the text where you want the new page to start from, in this case, in the blank line above the paragraph starting *'Eventually the winding gear...'*
3   Press the [Control] and [Enter] (Ctrl + Enter) keys simultaneously and release them.
❑   Word will insert a *Forced Page Break*. It will force this paragraph and all the following paragraphs on to the next page. A dashed line, with the words *Page Break*, will appear indicating the Page Break location

--------------Page Break--------------

❑   If the Page Break is in the wrong place, or simply wish to remove it:
4   Place the cursor to the left of the Page Break
5   Press the [Delete] key

There are other types of Breaks that are available within Word however, we will not cover them here. Experiment in your own time later by investigating the options available from the **Insert** command on the menu bar. Do not forget to use the online Help for further information and guidance.

6   Close the document but do not save the changes

Using tabulation

Tabulation is a method of aligning text and numbers in vertical columns or evenly spaced text on horizontal lines. By default, Word tabulations are set at ½ inch intervals. You can however customise the setting yourself.

Basic steps

1   Open a new blank document
2   Save it as *Tabulation*
3   Type in the text as shown here. Press [Tab] before the words *'Chapter'*, after the chapter number, and before the page numbers
❑   Do not attempt to align the text at this stage.

4   Save the changes

Your text should resemble the example shown here:

```
Section 1
Chapter 1   The first chapter of eight     4
Chapter 2   The second, a short chapter         8
Chapter 3   The third chapter     25
Chapter 4   The fourth chapter     35
Section 2
Chapter 5   The fifth chapter     56
Chapter 6   The sixth chapter     68
Chapter 7   The seventh chapter 88
Chapter 8   The eighth and last chapter 118
```

Tabulation options

Word has a number of Tab types, which you can apply to suit your own requirements.

The default Tab is left aligned

Centre aligned

Right aligned

Decimal aligned Tab

Basic steps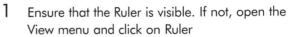

To change the default Tab setting:

1   Ensure that the Ruler is visible. If not, open the View menu and click on Ruler
2   On the left of the Ruler is a small square with a symbol indicating the type of tab currently selected – here it is a left aligned tab.

2 Click on the symbol and it will change to Centre tab. Click again to change to Right aligned, Decimal aligned, Bar, First Line Indent, Hanging Indent and then back to Left aligned

Changing tabulation settings

Basic steps

1 With *Tabulation* open, select Edit >Select All

2 Select the left-aligned symbol on the Ruler

3 Click once on the Ruler at the 2.5cm position

❑ A faint symbol will appear, indicating a left aligned tab has been set. The text will now adjust the first tab position to that position.

4 Click on the Ruler at the 6cm position

❑ The second tab is set and text will move along to align under the 6 cm location

5 Click twice on the tab setting, to change it to a right aligned tab

6 Click on the Ruler at the 12.5cm position

❑ A right aligned tab is inserted, and the text moved along to align at the 12.5cm location

| 4 |
| 8 |
| 25 |
| 35 |

Note that the numbers have aligned in numerical order alignment. Had you not selected the right aligned tab but left the selection as a left aligned Tab, the numbers would have aligned incorrectly, as shown above.

Your document *Tabulation* should now match the example shown.

Left tabs (2.5cm and 6cm)   Right tab (12.5cm)

Section 1			
	Chapter 1	The first chapter of eight	4
	Chapter 2	The second, a short chapter	8
	Chapter 3	The third chapter	25
	Chapter 4	The fourth chapter	35
Section 2			
	Chapter 5	The fifth chapter	56
	Chapter 6	The sixth chapter	68
	Chapter 7	The seventh chapter	88
	Chapter 8	The eighth and last chapter	118

❑ Save the changes and close the document

Decimal aligned tabulation

Decimal Tabs are used to align columns of figures that include decimal places.

Basic steps

1 Open a new blank document and Save it as *Decimal.doc*

2 Create a list as shown here, inserting one tab space after each item before the price

Chocolate mix	£1.45
Flour	£1.65
Sugar	£0.99
Eggs	£1.25
Milk	£0.65
Baking tin	£12.45

3 Now select all the text and numbers

4 Change the tab selection on the Ruler to Decimal

5 Click on the Ruler at the 4.5cm position

❑ Note that all the figures now align on the decimal point

| £1.45 |
| £1.65 |
| £0.99 |
| £1.25 |
| £0.65 |
| £12.45 |

6 Save and close the document

Line spacing in documents

There will come a time when you will be required to produce a document with the text formatted in double line spacing. This is often the practice when producing draft copies of documents. The reason for the double line spacing is to leave room in the document for hand written amendments to be inserted during proof reading.

Basic steps

1 Open a new blank document

2 Save the document as *Double.doc*

3 Type the following text

4   Select all the text, including the heading

5   Select Format > Paragraph

❑   The Paragraph dialog box will open

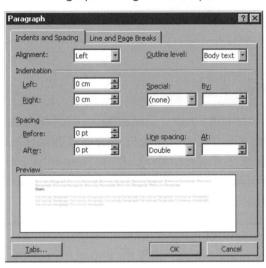

6   Look in the Spacing section and locate the Line spacing slot

7   Click on the down arrow and select *Double*

8   Click OK

❑   The text will change to double-line spacing. This selection can be made before typing

9   Save the changes and close the document

Further information

There are a number of options available using the **Format > Paragraph** command and you should study the online Help to gain maximum knowledge.

Word documents and e-mail

Office 2000 has introduced a new feature, Microsoft Office E-mail, which is accessible in Word, Excel and PowerPoint. A new icon on the Standard toolbar, see page 89, gives you access to the new feature.

Previously, to send a document, spreadsheet or a presentation to a colleague, you first had to create the item, prepare an e-mail and then attach the item to it. Image this. You are typing a document and decide that it might interest a colleague. You can now send it directly from Word, complete with formatting – in HTML – without opening your e-mail package.

> ## Take note
>
> **Using HTML format can be a problem, as not every-one can read e-mail messages in HTML format.**

Basic steps

1 Open the *Colliery4* document.

2 Click the e-mail icon 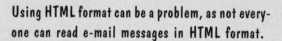. The e-mail headers and toolbar will appear above the document.

You may recognise the headers from Outlook. The document name will be in the Subject slot and can be changed if required.

3 Click on the To: button and the Address Book will open (see page 348 for more on this)

4 Insert the appropriate details and then click on the Send a Copy button

> ## Take note
>
> **If Outlook 2000 is your default e-mail package, the e-mail button will not appear until Outlook has been configured. Many of the features rely on Outlook 2000 and might work differently with Outlook Express or another e-mail package.**

If you inadvertently click the e-mail icon or decide not to send the document, click the e-mail icon once more and the headers will close and you will be returned to the standard Word window.

E-mail is discussed in detail in Chapter 7.

Using Word templates

A template is a pre-defined document that can be used time and time again. You can create templates of your own design and content. Word has a series of predefined templates that can be modified to suit your own specifications and requirements.

Good examples of a template would be:

♦ A document that has a company letterhead, with a logo at the top, and the remainder of the document blank, ready for the user to insert text, etc.

♦ Forms, such as an order form that has standard text entries with blank spaces, which the user completes

Template extensions

Templates use the extension '.dot', rather than the normal '.doc' of Word, to denote that they are different from the standard document.

Open a template

When you open a template you use a slightly different procedure to that used for a standard Word document. Templates are stored in their own individual folders, one folder for each type.

Basic steps

1 Select File > New
2 At the New dialog box, click on the Letters & Faxes tab.

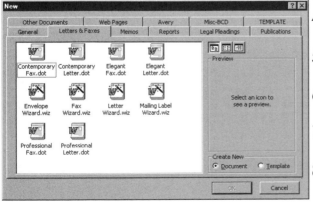

Take note

If you are using short menus, you will not see the New option unless you have used it recently. To see the full menu, click the chevrons at the bottom.

❑ In the example you will see a number of items. Some are templates and others are *Wizards*. We will return to the subject of Wizards later.

3 Open the template *Professional Fax.dot* – click on it, then click OK, or double-click on it

❑ When the template opens, you will see that several of the items in it require further action.

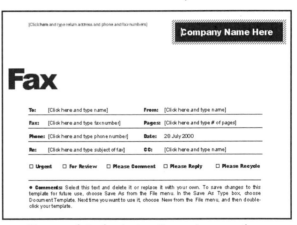

To complete the instructions given on the template and fill in your own details:

4 Highlight the existing text in the Company Name Here text box and type '*Com-tec plc*'

5 Place the cursor on the From brackets (no need to highlight the text, just type your name)

6 Place the cursor on the Phone brackets and type your telephone number

7 Place the cursor on the Re brackets and type '*High efficiency, low energy pumps*'

8 Place the cursor in the address box, top left of the document and type your address

Saving the document as a template

Basic steps

1 From the menu bar select File > Save As
2 At the Save As dialog box, click on the Save as type drop-down arrow
3 Select *Document Template*. The Save As dialog box will switch to the *templates* folder
4 Click in the Filename slot.
5 Type in the name '*My Test fax*'.
6 Click Save

Test the template

We will now open the template and confirm that the changes were correctly saved and that it functions as a template.

Basic steps

1 From the menu bar select File > New
2 Make sure that the General tab is selected.
3 Double-click on '*My Test Fax.dot*'
❑ You will find that it has retained the changes you made to it earlier
4 Close the document and if prompted do not save it

Deleting a template

You may not want to retain the template that you have just created and you can delete it if you wish. It is not required further in this course.

Basic steps

1 From the menu bar select File > New
2 Click on the General tab.
3 Right-click over '*My Test Fax.dot*' and select Delete from the pop-up menu.

Summary

Templates are extremely useful and can save you considerable time and effort. You can modify any template to suit your requirements and save it using a different name. You can also create a completely new template from scratch.

When a Template is opened for use, Word changes it to a standard Word document, thus leaving the original for further use.

Creating tables

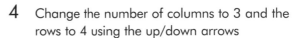

A *table* allows you to arrange information in rows and columns. You enter information in *cells* and each cell is independent of others in the table. Rows and columns can be of different sizes and you may have any number of cells within a table. Each cell can be formatted to contain a different typeface and size.

Tables can contain text, images and in Word 2000 can also contain another, nested, table. If you are using a table to create a Web page, you can add cell padding, spacing between cells and between the boundary of the cell and the text inside it.

Tables are an extremely useful feature and give you more control than tabulation or columns. In Word 2000, the options in the design and use of tables have increased and some have been simplified.

You can create a table using freehand drawing. All border styles can be changed, have colour added and individual cells, columns or rows can be shaded as appropriate. Word also has a number of predefined table layouts, known as *AutoFormat* tables.

Basic steps

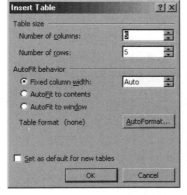

1 Open a new blank document
2 Save it as *Tables.doc*
3 From the Menu bar select Table>Insert>Table
❑ The Insert Table dialog box will open. It is here that you set the number of columns and rows, and if you wish, select an AutoFormat table layout.

> **Insert Table** ?|X|
> Table size
> Number of columns: ⊟ 3 ⊞
> Number of rows: ⊟ 5 ⊞
> AutoFit behavior
> ⊙ Fixed column width: ⊟ Auto ⊞
> ○ AutoFit to contents
> ○ AutoFit to window
> Table format (none)   AutoFormat...
> ☐ Set as default for new tables
>   OK   Cancel

4 Change the number of columns to 3 and the rows to 4 using the up/down arrows
5 Do not select any Autoformat options at this time, instead click on OK
❑ The table will appear on your screen with 3 columns and 4 rows, all the same size

Merging cells

Basic steps

1 Place the cursor in the second column of the first row, and click. Drag the cursor to the right through into the third column
❑ Note that as you drag the cursor to the right, the columns are highlighted

2 When the two cells are highlighted, release the mouse button
3 Select Table > Merge Cells. Word will join the two cells together creating one large cell.

The cell remains highlighted at this stage; click anywhere in the table to remove the selection. Your table should look like the example shown.

Formatting cells

Basic steps

1 Place the cursor in the top left cell of the top row and highlight the top row by left clicking and dragging the cursor to the right
2 Click the Bold and Center buttons on the Formatting toolbar
3 Click outside the table to deselect the cells

4 Type in all of the text as shown here

Region	Temperatures	
	Mid-summer	Mid-winter
North	85	56
West	92	61

You will now find that your top row resembles the example, but the rest of the text is left aligned.

The example table was pre-formatted; we applied Bold and Center before we typed any text. This was done to show the flexibility of formatting tables.

Centring the text
Previously we used the **Center** icon on the **Formatting** toolbar. In this instance we will use the shortcut key combination of **Ctrl+E**.

Basic steps

1 Highlight the remaining cells below the '*Region*' and '*Temperature*' cells

2 Press Ctrl+E

3 Save the changes

Region	Temperatures	
	Mid-Summer	Mid-Winter
North	85	56
West	92	61

The last exercise demonstrates that you can change the formatting after text is created. Either method functions well, but if you plan your table layout in advance, you could save yourself some time.

Inserting additional columns and rows
If you need more columns or rows in a table, you can insert either, or both, easily. We will insert three rows between the '*North*' and '*West*' rows.

Basic steps

1 Place the mouse cursor just outside of the table, to the left and adjacent to the last row that contains the word '*West*'

2 Right-click. The row will be highlighted and a pop-up menu will appear

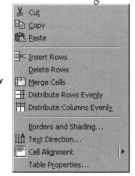

Cut
Copy
Paste
Insert Rows
Delete Rows
Merge Cells
Distribute Rows Evenly
Distribute Columns Evenly
Borders and Shading...
Text Direction...
Cell Alignment
Table Properties...

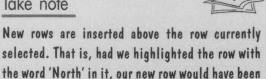

3 Select Insert Rows

4 Repeat to insert a further two rows so that we have three blank rows

❑ Investigate this pop-up menu later. It contains a number of commands that you will want to use when you become familiar with tables.

5 Type the text as shown in the table

Region	Temperatures	
	Mid-Summer	Mid-Winter
North	85	56
South	89	58
East	92	56
West	92	61

Note as you type the text, the formatting you applied to the previous rows is applied to the new rows.

Deleting rows or columns

The procedure for deleting is similar to inserting a row or column. We have a blank row which is not required and we will now delete it.

Basic steps

To delete a row:

1 Right-click adjacent to the row

2 Select Delete Rows from the pop-up menu

Deleting a column:

3 Highlight the column to be deleted

4 Right-click over the highlighted area

5 Select Delete Columns

Draw Table
Insert
Delete
Select
Merge Cells
Split Cells...
Split Table
Table AutoFormat...
AutoFit
Heading Rows Repeat
Convert
Sort...
Formula...
Hide Gridlines
Table Properties...

Alternative method

There are other ways to delete rows or columns, such as using the **Delete Rows** and **Delete Columns** options in the **Table** menu.

Changing the cell height

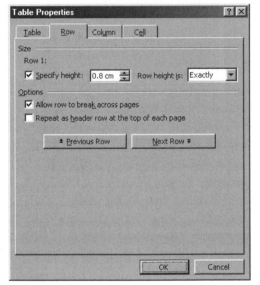

Basic steps

1 Ensure that the '*tables*' document is open
2 Highlight the top row of the table
3 From the menu bar select Table > Table Properties
4 At the dialog box select the Row tab
5 Tick Specify height then enter the detail as shown here and click OK to apply the changes

Cell alignment

We will now align the text in the top row centrally in the vertical and horizontal planes.

Basic steps

1 Highlight the top row again
2 Right-click over the highlighted row
3 From the pop-up menu select Cell Alignment
❑ The cascade menu shown here will open. Take a moment to investigate the contents of this menu.

4 Select Align Center

❑ The text will be centrally located, in the vertical and horizontal aspect of the cell.

5 Save the changes

Changing the table border

There are many ways to brighten up a table and one method is to apply a different border style other than the default, single line border. It is not necessary to highlight the table to change a border.

Basic steps

1 Right-click on any cell
2 Select Borders and Shading from the pop-up menu
3 At the dialog box ensure that the Borders tab is selected
4 Copy the settings shown here

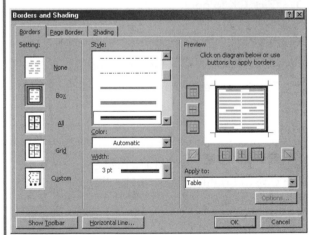

5 Click OK

❑ The Borders and Shading dialog box has many options for border styles and shading. You should investigate this feature more fully.

121

6   Save the changes and keep the document open

Applying shading

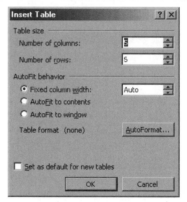

Basic steps

1   Right-click beside the top row of the table
2   From the pop-up menu select Borders and Shading
3   This time select the Shading tab

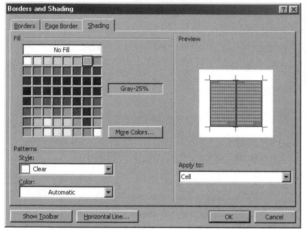

4   Select the *Gray 25%* option. This option has a 25% fill applied to it, which means that any text in the cell will show through the Gray fill.
5   Click OK to apply the shading
6   Select the cells *'Mid-Summer'* down to the last cell in that column
7   Right-click and select Borders and Shading
8   This time select *10% gray fill* and click OK

This will give a lightly coloured shading to the selected cells, which may assist the reader to concentrate on one area of text at a time.

Colours can also be applied as a Background Fill, but take care as bright colours can be difficult to read.

Changing the font colour

Basic steps

1   Select the cells North to West inclusive
2   From the menu bar select Format > Font

3   At the Font dialog box, select Color
4   From the drop-down list make your choice
5   Click OK
6   Save the changes and close the document

Automated formatting of tables

Word has several pre-formatted tables and we are going to create a table using this feature.

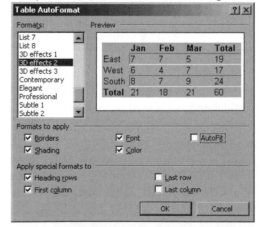

Basic steps

1   Open a new blank document
2   Save it as *AutoTable.doc*
3   Select Table > Insert Table on the menu bar

4   At the Insert Table dialog box, set the size as shown and click on the AutoFormat... button to open the Table AutoFormat dialog box

The dialog box contains the format options and as you select each option, it displays an example of the pre-formatted table style.

In the example shown, the *3D effects 2* format has been selected and you can see an example of what the pre-formatting looks like in the **Preview** pane.

Below the **Formats** and the **Preview** panes there are a number of options available, as to how and where in the table the formatting is applied.

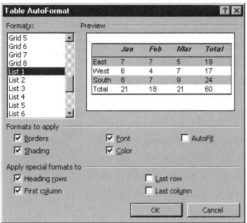

5   Select *List 1* in the Formats window

6   Do not change any other settings

7   Click OK to accept this format style

❑   You will be returned to the Insert Table dialog box. The selected table format will now appear in the dialog box as *List 1*.

8   Click OK. The Insert Table dialog box will close and the table will be inserted into the document.

Entering text

Basic steps

1   Type in the detail as shown in the example

2   Use the [Tab] key to move between the cells

❑   If you jump a cell, press the [Shift] and [Tab] keys simultaneously to move back one cell.

❑   When the cursor reaches the last cell in a row, it will move to the next row when the tab key is next used.

	April	*May*	*June*	*Total*
North	15	17	20	52
South	14	14	21	49
East	10	18	25	53
West	12	14	21	47

Manually adjusting the table size

The table size can be adjusted manually by dragging the vertical lines to the left or right.

Basic steps

1   Place the cursor over the second vertical line of the table that separates the cells that contain the region names and the April data

❑   When the cursor detects the presence of the table line, it will change its shape to that shown here.

2   Click and drag the line to the left until it reaches a position similar to that shown here

	April	*May*	*June*	*Total*
North	15	17	20	52
South	14	14	21	49
East	10	18	25	53
West	12	14	21	47

3   When you reach the required location, release the mouse button

4   Perform the same action on all of the dividing lines to achieve a similar result as shown in the example

Re-formatting the table

Although the Table was created using the AutoFormat feature, you can still change any of the formatting.

To illustrate this we will change the colour of the text in the first column, add underlining and centre the detail in several of the columns.

Basic steps

1   Select the cells '*North*' to '*West*'

2   From the menu bar select Format > Font

3   Ensure that the Font tab is selected

4   Open the Font color list and select *Blue*

5   Open the Underline Style list

6   Scroll through the list and select *Wave*

7   Select Underline color *Green*

8   To apply the changes, click OK

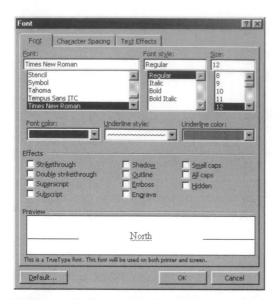

Basic steps

1 Click on the table

2 From the Table menu select Table AutoFormat

3 At the dialog box, scroll up until you locate the *(none)* option and select it, (or select a different style from the list)

4 Click OK

The AutoFormat design will be removed and you will be left with a plain style table (if you selected a different table format, it would be applied).

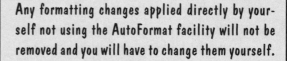

Take note

As you change the formatting, the Preview window will display the selected formatting.

Centre the numbers

Basic steps

1 Highlight all of the numbers

2 Centre them by clicking on the Center button on the Formatting toolbar or by using the shortcut keys Ctrl+E

Your table should now resemble the example shown here.

	April	May	June	Total
North	15	17	20	52
South	14	14	21	49
East	10	18	25	53
West	12	14	21	47

Removing the autoformatting

Should you later decide that you either do not like the applied style or now require a plain table, it is possible to remove all of the formatting applied by the AutoFormat feature.

Take note

Any formatting changes applied directly by yourself not using the AutoFormat facility will not be removed and you will have to change them yourself.

That completes the description of the 'AutoFormat' feature. Experiment with this feature to learn more.

Tables and mail merge

Mail merge is used to produce multiple copies of letters, containing the same information. However, each letter is customised to include personal information of each customer/client.

It is a quick and efficient method of producing mass mailing and we will return to this subject in detail later in the course.

We are now going to produce a table that you will later use in conjunction with the mail merge exercise.

Title	LastName	Company	Address1	Address2	County	PostalCode
Mr	Jones	Jones Heating Contractors	5 Marylebone Rd	Bolton	Lancs	B19 8YH
Mr	Bryon	Lington Heating Controls Ltd	12 High St	Logton	Lincs	LM8 3HJ
Mr	Kaye	Kaye's Engineering and Heating	98 Benton Rd	Longparish	York	YM6 6JK
Mr	Collins	Collins and Son Heating Contractors	56 Bridge St	Middletown	Notts	NH32 4AG

Basic steps

1 Open a new blank document

2 Save it as *Data Source Information*

3 Change the Page Setup to *Landscape*, ensuring that the Paper Size is set to *A4*

4 Change the top and bottom margins to 1.5cm (0.75") and the left and right to 1cm (0.5")

5 Create a table with 7 columns and 5 rows

❑ Do not apply any AutoFormatting to the table

6 Highlight the complete table and change the font size to *10*. This will allow greater space to accommodate the text

7 Type the detail shown in the example table

8 Ensure that, where appropriate, you do not insert any spaces between words that appear joined, such as *LastName*

9 Manually adjust the column widths so they are the same as the example

10 Save the changes to the document and then print a copy of the table

❑ Keep this safe as you will require it later when you reach the 'Mail Merge' section

11 Close the document and remember where it is stored for future use

Summary

The table just created will become what is known in mail merge as the *data source*. The table contents will be used to create the customised sections in the merged letters which are the end product of the mail merge.

Moving a table

A tables can be moved either manually – drag it to where you what it – or using the Table Properties dialog box to specify where you want it.

Table Properties dialog box

There are two ways to access the Tables Properties dialog box.

Right-click over the table and select **Table Properties** from the pop-up menu.

Click into a cell in the table and from the Menu bar select **Table >Table Properties**.

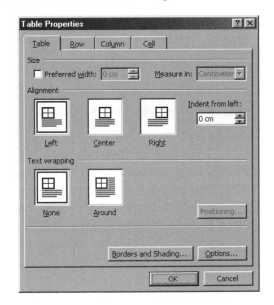

You should investigate the Table Properties box in more detail later. It offers you considerable options and flexibility when working with tables.

Drag and Drop

You can drag and drop the table to meet your requirements.

Basic steps

1 Place your cursor over the table.

2 A symbol will appear, top left of the table (see example)

3 Place your cursor over it, left-click, hold and drag the table to the required location.

4 Release the mouse button when in position.

June	July	August
25	32	38

Nested tables

The subject of nested tables was touched up on in the introduction and we will now learn how and what a nested table is and how to produce one.

Create the main table as shown in the example. Format the table, merge calls, type in and format the text as shown.

Basic steps

1 Click in the second row of the first column

2 Right-click and select Insert Table

3 Change the settings to 3 columns and 2 rows

4 Click OK

The table will now be inserted, as shown below. Carry out the same procedure placing the nested table in the second column. Carry out any formatting and alignments adjustments, using the **Table Properties** dialog box.

Resort Temperature Ranges					
Summer			Autumn		
June	July	August	Sept	Oct	Nov
25	32	38	27	20	18

Inserting an image

The subject of inserting graphics or images is discussed in detail later and only the basic procedure is show below.

Basic steps

1 Click in the cell that you want the image to appear in

2 From the Menu bar select Insert > Picture > Clip Art

3 When the Insert ClipArt dialog box opens, select an appropriate category/image

The image will appear in the selected cell and you will quite likely find that you will have to carry out some formatting such as alignment and sizing.

Summary

By now you should have recognised that tables offer you a great deal in functionality and flexibility. Use tables to gain more control over your text, images, etc. and don't forget that you can turn off the grid lines so that it is not immediately obvious that you have used a table.

To learn more on tables use the online Help.

Inserting images or graphics

Inserting an image or graphic, whether it is an actual photograph or a Clip Art image, will enhance a document's appearance.

Use it to highlight or draw attention to the subject matter and be aware that the Clip Art contained as part of the Office suite is copyright.

Practical exercise

In the following exercise, we are going to create a simple 'no smoking' sign.

Basic steps

1 Open a new document and save it as *Sign*

2 Select File > Page Setup, then the Paper Size tab

3 Select *A4* paper, *Landscape* and click OK

❑ The page orientation will now change to Landscape. This is ideal for most signs

4 Right-click anywhere on the document and select Font

5 At the Font dialog box, change the Font name to *Arial* and the size to *72*

6 Click the Color down arrow, select *Red* and click OK

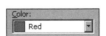

❑ The text will look better if it is centred at the top of the page

7 Click the Center button 📊 on the Formatting toolbar

8 Press [Enter] once and type '*No Smoking*' then press [Enter] again

The text is large and is coloured red (you will need to print on a colour printer to have the colour effect).

Inserting clip art

If you have used any previous version of Office you will see that the **Insert ClipArt** dialog box has changed. It is now a one-stop resource centre for pictures, sounds and motion clips.

Clicking on the category image will open it up to reveal its content. Be aware of the *Keep Looking* feature, which is located at the end of the all of the images. Use it to find more or similar images.

Basic steps

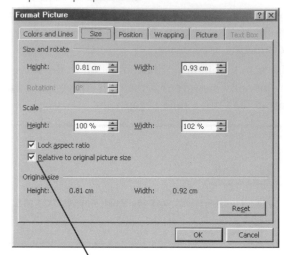

1 Select Insert > Picture > Clip Art
2 In the Search for clips slot type in '*smoking*' and press [Enter]
4 Select the smoking cigarette or an appropriate alternative

5 Double-click on the image to insert it

Resizing the image

When the image appears on the page, it is not usually where you want it or the required size. We will now resize the image.

Basic steps

1 Click on it and the re-sizing handles, small squares in the image frame, will surround it
❑ Use the handles to resize the image, but use with care, otherwise you could easily distort it.
2 Place the cursor over the lower-right square
3 When it changes to a double-headed arrow ↖ click and slowly drag the cursor down and to the right. The image will increase in size
❑ Try to keep the image's proportions correct
4 When you have a reasonable size image, release the mouse button

An alternative method

Using handles can be inaccurate. There is a more accurate method of re-sizing an image.

Basic steps

1 Right-click over the image
2 From the pop-up menu select Format Picture
3 At the Format Picture dialog box, select the Size tab

4 Ensure that Lock aspect ratio and Relative to original picture size have ticks in their slot. Selecting these options will retain the overall picture proportions.

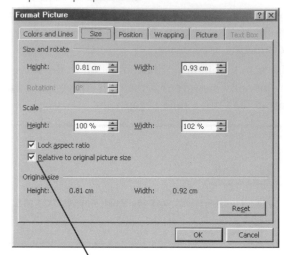

Because we have ticks in these slots, we only have to make an adjustment in one of the Size slots, either the Height or Width and the other adjustment will be made automatically for us.

5 Double-click in one of the Size slots and type in the value, or use the up and down arrows to the right of the slots to change the size
6 Click OK

The window will close and the new size will be applied to the image. If necessary re-adjust to achieve a suitable size.

Positioning the image

Basic steps

Ensure that you can see the full page size. If not:

1 Select *Whole Page* from the Zoom drop-down list on the Standard toolbar. This feature is available at any time within Word and can greatly assist you when working, where accuracy is of importance.
2 Place the cursor over the image and it will change to ✥

3 Click and drag the image to the centre of the page below the text '*No Smoking*'

4 Release the mouse button

5 Save the changes and close the document

Inserting images is as simple as that. Obviously Word offers more options and features when working with imagery and you should experiment later.

Using the drawing tools

Word, like all Office applications, has a number of freehand drawing tools. Included in the tools are predefined shapes known as *AutoShapes*. We will use this feature now.

Basic steps

1 Open a new blank document

2 Save it as *AutoShape*

3 If not already visible, display the Drawing toolbar

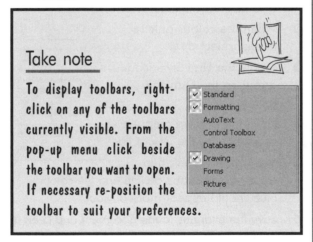

Take note

To display toolbars, right-click on any of the toolbars currently visible. From the pop-up menu click beside the toolbar you want to open. If necessary re-position the toolbar to suit your preferences.

- Standard
- Formatting
- AutoText
- Control Toolbox
- Database
- Drawing
- Forms
- Picture

The Drawing toolbar

Shown at the bottom of this page is the Drawing toolbar. If yours does not look exactly the same, do not worry. The toolbar shown has been customised and has a number of additional icons. You will recall that customisation was discussed at the start of the module.

Investigate the various options on the toolbar, for instance, click on the **Draw** button, which is located on the extreme left and check the pop-up menu. When finished, click on the **AutoShapes** button and investigate each of the pop-up menu features.

Remember that passing the cursor over each icon and pausing will bring up a tool-tip that will identify the icon's function.

Creating AutoShapes

What is an AutoShape? AutoShapes are pre-defined shapes, triangles, 3D boxes, circles, etc, which when selected and drawn by you, are automatically created with little or no effort other than moving the mouse.

Basic steps

1 Click on the AutoShapes button

2 From the pop-up menu select Basic Shapes

3 Click on the shape indicated in the example

Lines
Basic Shapes
Block Arrows
Flowchart
Stars and Banners
Callouts

Draw ▾ AutoShapes ▾

❑ The menu will close. Note that the cursor has changed its shape to that of a thin black cross

4 Move the cursor up to the top left-hand corner of the document, next to the flashing cursor

5 Left-click, hold and drag it down and to the right to create an image approximately 2 inches square

6 Release the mouse button

You will notice that as you dragged the mouse down and to the right, an image is drawn in the selected style. When you released the button, the image displayed a number of resizing handles, indicating that the image is active.

Draw ▾ AutoShapes ▾

The image can be re-sized, rotated, have colour added or have its basic shape changed by use of the 3D tools.

There are a number of different methods of applying colour, etc to the shape, using the icons on the Drawing toolbar or from the right-click **Format AutoShape** dialog box. We will use the dialog box method first.

Basic steps

1 Right-click over the image

2 From the pop-up menu select Format AutoShape

3 When the dialog box opens, ensure that the Colors and Lines tab is selected

4 Open the Fill Color drop-down menu

5 Select Red from the colour palette

6 Close the Format AutoShape dialog window by clicking on OK

❑ The colour will be applied to the shape

Converting an image to 3D

We will now change the overall appearance of the shape from that of a flat object to a 3D object.

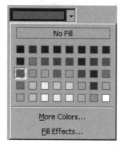

Basic steps

1 Ensure that the shape is selected

2 From the Drawing toolbar select the 3D icon (circled in the example). The menu will open

3 Select the 3D shape indicated in the example. The menu will close.

❑ The selected 3D shape will be applied to your image and should resemble the one shown

4 Save the changes and keep the document open

Combining AutoShape and images

It is possible to combine 'AutoShapes' and images to create a new image. First we will change the image back to a flat object.

Basic steps

1 Select the 3D image in the document

2 Click on the 3D icon on the Drawing toolbar

3 When the 3D menu opens select the *No 3-D* option located at the top

❑ Your image should revert to that of a flat two-dimensional image

4 With the shape still selected, click on the Line Color icon

5 When the colour palette opens, select *Blue*

6 Locate the Line Style icon arrow on the Drawing toolbar

7 From the pop-up menu click once on the 2¼ pt line

❑ You will now see an increase in the shape outline and the colour blue should appear more obvious

8 Save the changes to the document and keep it open

Incorporating an Image

We will now add an image from the 'Clip Art Gallery' to create another no smoking sign, which this time is visual without any text.

Basic steps

1 Select Insert > Picture > Clip Art

2 Enter 'smoking' in the Search for clips slot.

130

3 Double-click on the cigarette image and close the Insert ClipArt dialog box

4 Right-click on the cigarette image and select Format Picture

5 Select Layout and click on the In front of text option then click OK

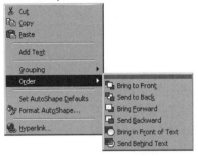

6 Move the cigarette image over the No symbol.

7 Right-click on the cigarette image and select Order > Send to Back

The cigarette image will now appear behind the AutoShape, which appears to be on top of it and resembles the more familiar no smoking sign often seen on buses and trains, etc.

Creating a group

Basic steps

You can create a group using two or more objects. This simplifies matters for the user, for instance when moving the image. Instead of having to deal with two items and reposition each in relation to one another, one at a time, the group is moved as one.

1 Select the image

2 Hold the [Shift] key down and click on the AutoShape

3 Release the [Shift] key

4 Right-click over the selected images

5 From the pop-up menu select Grouping > Group

- You can split the group if required. Just right-click over it and select **Ungroup**.

Practice this action and experiment using the **Regroup** command as well.

Summary

The Drawing tools and the AutoShape feature should be experimented with. With practice, you will quickly gain experience and realise their potential.

Investigate the features and icons on the Drawing toolbar and remember the right-click pop-up menus that give you quick access to numerous commands.

Investigate how to rotate objects, how to change an AutoShape without having to draw another image.

You can actually have a great deal of fun with the Drawing tools, so experiment.

Formatting the display

This next exercise will show just how quickly and simply, certain formatting changes can be applied to text and paragraphs.

Basic steps

1 Open a new blank document

2 Save it as 'Formatting Display'

3 Press 'Enter' once to insert a blank line at the top of the document

4 Type in the text shown here (ensure that you apply all the line spacing)

An introduction to USB

Developed by leading computer and peripheral manufacturers the Universal Serial Bus (USB) is designed to solve problems. Microsoft, Intel, Apple, etc understand that if you want to add a traditional peripheral device to your computer, you're going to have some issues to deal with.

Add a printer, a joystick, a scanner, a digital camera, digital speakers, etc. and you're likely to have to deal with several different types of cables and interfaces. USB makes it remarkably easy to avoid these issues because there's only one kind of plug and one kind of port for it to plug into.

USB is about simplicity, ease and convenience.

---

5 Leave a blank line after the last line of text

Adding a border to text

Basic steps

1   Select all of the text and be sure to include the blank line above and below the text so that the border will not sit too close to the text

2   Select Format > Borders and Shading

3   When the Borders and Shading dialog box opens, ensure that the Borders tab is selected

4   Select the same settings as in the example here

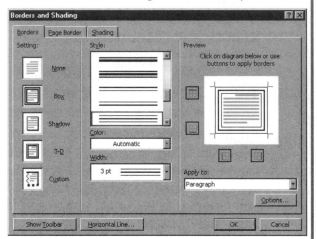

5   Click OK to apply the changes

6   Click anywhere on the document to remove the highlighting

The text should now have a triple line border.

In Introduction to USB

Developed by leading computer and peripheral manufacturing the Universal Serial Bus (USB) is designed to solve problems. Microsoft, Intel, Apple, etc understand that if you want to add a traditional peripheral device to your computer, you-re going to have some issues to deal with.

Add a printer, a joystick, a scanner, a digital camera, digital speakers, etc and you're likely to have to deal with several different types of cables and interfaces. USB makes it remarkably easy to avoid these issues because there's only one kind of plug and one kind of port for it to plug into.

USB is about simplicity, ease and convenience.

Types of borders

The border in the example was a *Paragraph Border*. There is another type, the *Page Border*, which fits around the whole page area. We will not use a page border, but you should investigate this feature later.

Inserting additional text within the border

We are going to insert some additional text within the border that you have just created and as you type the text, you will see that the border automatically expands to accommodate the extra text.

Basic steps

1   Place the cursor at the end of the last sentence, ending '*...and convenience.*'

2   Insert two blank lines

3   Type the text as shown here

Using USB devices

USB defines a class of hardware that makes it easy to add serial devices to your computer.

USB support is built to the specification so that future updates of Windows will support current drivers.

To install a USB device, plug the cord from the device into any USB port on your computer and follow the on-screen prompts.

---

4   Save the changes to the document

Applying colour to text

We are now going to apply some colour to a number of text areas to demonstrate the effect and enhancement that colour can bring to a document. To gain maximum effect in the printed document you must have access to a colour printer.

Basic steps

1   Highlight the last sentence of the document

2   Right-click over the highlighted area

3   Select Font from the pop-up menu

4   At the Font dialog box, change the colour to *Blue*

5   Click OK to apply the change

Repeat for the first paragraph, below the heading '*An Introduction to USB*' and change the colour to Teal.

Changing alignment

The subject of alignment has been discussed previously. We will now apply different alignments to various paragraphs.

Basic steps

1 Highlight the second paragraph starting '*Add a printer...*'

2 Using the shortcut key, Ctrl+R, apply right alignment to the paragraph

3 Highlight the second heading '*Using USB devices*'

4 Apply Centre alignment using Ctrl+E

5 Highlight the first paragraph

6 Apply full alignment using Ctrl+J.

❑ Notice that Word has stretched the paragraph so that both the left and right sides align on their respective margins. Word will increase spaces between the paragraph words to create the stretched version as necessary and you many find that there are large white gaps between words.

7 Select the paragraph starting '*Add a printer...*'

8 Change the alignment to Centre

Notice how Word deals with variation in line length. Centre alignment can be used to good effect when creating posters, banners and suchlike.

By now the document should look quite untidy, with various paragraphs aligned to the Left, Centre and Right. Remember that the document was created to demonstrate and show the differences in alignment.

9 Save the changes and keep the document open

Exceedingly large fonts

You may have noticed that the maximum size that appears in the font size drop-down slot is 72 pt. Word can produce a font size of 1,638 pt. If printed, these letters would be nearly two feet high.

So how do you do it?

Special characters and symbols

First we are going to learn how to insert the special characters and symbols that are available in Word and are often forgotten, then we shall enlarge them beyond the standard 72 pt. We are going to insert a symbol from the Wingdings font.

Basic steps

1 Place the cursor at the end of the last line of text in the '*Formatting Display.doc*'

2 Insert two new lines outside of the border

3 Insert a page break, using the shortcut Ctrl+Enter. A new page will appear.

4 Put the cursor on the second page and keep pressing [Enter], inserting blank lines until the cursor is approximately halfway down

5 From the Standard toolbar, click on the drop-down arrow and change the Zoom setting to *Page width* so that you have a better view

6 Select Insert > Symbol. The Symbol dialog box will open.

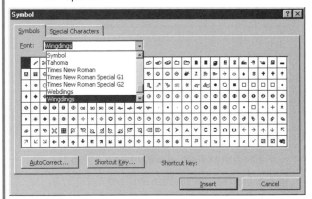

7 Ensure that the Symbols tab is selected and click on the Font drop-down arrow

8 Scroll down the list and select *Wingdings*. The symbols will change to that of the 'Wingdings' font group

❑ Initially you may think that the images are rather small and they are, but do not worry

9 On the top line count in nine squares from the left and click on the ninth square

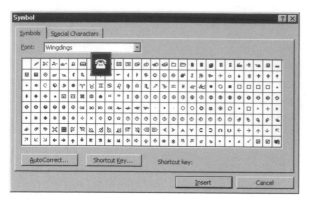

❑ The image should enlarge and you will see that it is a telephone image

10 To insert the symbol, click on the Insert button or double-click on the symbol.

❑ The symbol will appear rather small and this is where we will learn how to increase the size beyond that of 72 pt

11 Highlight the symbol

12 Click in the Font size slot (not on its down-arrow) on the Formatting toolbar

13 Type in the number *325*

14 Press [Enter]

Tip

If you require a size above 999 pt, select **Format > Font**, to open the Font dialog box. Its **Font size** slot will accept sizes above 999 pt, which the one in the Formatting toolbar will not.

Reposition the symbol

Basic steps

1 Select the telephone symbol and centre it using the shortcut key Ctrl+E

2 Reposition the symbol by either decreasing or increasing the number of blank lines above it, so that it appears central on the page, in the vertical and horizontal aspects

❑ To ensure that everyone knows that you created the image and to practise the procedure, we will now insert another symbol:

3 If necessary press [Enter] to insert the appropriate number of new lines, so that your cursor is at the bottom of the page

4 Select Insert > Symbol and at the dialog box click on the Special Characters tab

5 In the Character pane, double-click on the copyright symbol © to insert it into the document

6 Close the dialog box

7 Leave a space after the symbol and type your name

❑ If the copyright symbol is too small:

8 Select it and type the required size in the Font size slot

9 Press [Enter] to apply the change

Summary

The *Formatting Display* document layout is unconventional and was produced so that you could visually see the difference in alignment, font size and colour. Investigate the use of special characters and symbols and what other images are available.

Applying styles

Microsoft Word has 90 built-in *styles*. Although not all are available at any given time, they can be powerful time-savers.

A style is a set of formats that can be applied to a paragraph or to specific characters, with one action.

Imagine having to apply a number of different format options to a paragraph where each option has to be applied individually, clicking on toolbar buttons, using dialog boxes or shortcut keystrokes. All time consuming. Then imagine that sometime later you decide that you want to apply the same formatting to a different section of text. Do you have to go through the same drawn-out procedure of applying each formatting option again? No, use styles.

Types of styles

Paragraph styles control formatting of entire paragraphs. Any manual formatting that you can add to a paragraph can be included in a paragraph style. For instance, any formatting that is found in the Font, Paragraph, Tabs, Borders and Shading (but not Page borders), Bullets and Numbering or Tools > Language dialog boxes.

Character styles can only be applied from the text formatting options found in the Font, Borders and Shading and Tools > Language dialog boxes.

How styles interact

Character styles may be superimposed on paragraph styles, however some clash between the two types of style may occur and you should experiment to gain a greater understanding of how styles function. Remember the online Help in Word, which will assist you on this subject.

Where are the styles in Word

Styles are available from the Formatting toolbar or the **Style** dialog box.

Your list may not be the same as shown in the example, due to customisation.

If you know the style that you want, then the quickest way to apply a style is to use the Formatting toolbar option.

In the example, *Heading 1* is selected. This applies the formatting:

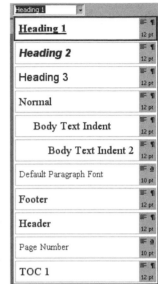

- ◆ Font, Times New Roman, size 12
- ◆ Left justified
- ◆ Bold and underlined

To apply all the formatting listed above would have taken five or more actions, whereas to apply the style only required two actions.

If you wish to confirm what formatting the style includes, then the better option of selecting a style would be to use the **Format > Style** comand.

Select **Format > Style** from the menu bar and the **Style** dialog box will open. This provides a visual display of how the formatting will look and written details of the formatting.

Investigate the various styles by clicking on different names in the **Styles** pane, e.g. click on the name *Heading 1*. The display will show the style layout and formatting. Click on one or two of the other style names to understand how the names are used and their formatting options.

Basic steps

❑ To apply a style from the dialog box:

1 Select the required style name

2 Click Apply. The dialog box will close and the style will be applied

3 Open the '*Formatting Display.doc*' document that you created earlier

135

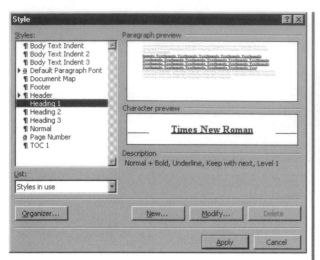

We will apply one or two styles to the existing text, but first we remove the borders from all sections of text. This will avoid possible conflicts between borders and styles. We will then reset the document alignment to left aligned.

4 Ensure that the cursor is within the border area

5 Select Format > Borders and Shading and at the dialog box, select the Borders tab

6 In the Setting area of the dialog box, select *None*, then click OK

7 Select all the text using the shortcut Ctrl+A

8 Apply left alignment, using the shortcut Ctrl+L

9 De-select the text by clicking on a blank area of the document

Applying styles

Basic steps

1 Highlight the heading '*An Introduction to USB*'

2 From the Formatting toolbar click on the Style drop-down arrow to open the list of styles

3 Select the style *Heading 1*

4 Highlight the text '*USB is about simplicity, ease, and convenience.*'

5 Select the style *Heading 2*. Note that the font size is 14 pt and the text has italic formatting. Note also the line spacing.

6 Select the text '*Using USB devices*'

7 Apply the style *Heading 1* and save the changes

Take note

Do remember that there may be minor variations between that described and what appears on your screen. This is usually due to customisation of the local computer, however the principles still apply.

To demonstrate this feature more realistically we need more text in the *Formatting Display* document.

8 Insert a blank line at the end of the document

9 Type the text shown in the example

10 Apply the style *Heading 1* to the heading

What is Memory?

A computer uses random access memory to hold temporary instructions and data needed to complete tasks. This enables the computer's central processing unit, or CPU, to access instructions and data stored in memory very quickly.

A good example of this is when the CPU loads an application program, such as a word processor or publishing package into memory thereby allowing the application program to run as quickly as possible. In practical terms, this means you can get more work done in less time.

11 Save the changes and keep the document open

Using the Document Map

You will recall that the Document Map was mentioned earlier. The Document Map and styles can be used to great effect and save you time when working with large documents.

Basic steps

1 Click the Document Map icon ▣ on the Standard toolbar

Or

2 Select View > Document Map

❑ The page view will change to that shown here. The left pane will display the document headings. In this instance there are only four.

The way 'Document Map' functions is:

◆ All the headings and sub-headings in the *Formatting Display* document have styles applied

◆ The Document Map looks for all style headings and lists them in their own window, the left pane (this is known as the *Document Map*).

Click once on the heading '*Using USB devices*' and watch what happens in the document window. You should see the cursor locate the selected heading. This is *linking*. You will have seen something similar if you have used the Internet and clicked on an address or a key word, which opens a new page or moves you further on in the page. These *hyperlinks* are discussed in the Internet chapter.

Imagine if this had been a large document with numerous headings, sub-headings etc. To move from one area to another, can at times be long and laborious. The Document Map is a great time saver, but you must use style headings to gain the maximum benefit from the feature.

Save any changes to the *Formatting Display* document.

Summary

Styles apply consistent and accurate formatting throughout a document, which can be reproduced at a keystroke, thus saving you time and effort.

There may come a time when you will have to create a particular section of a document and apply formatting, for which there is no suitable 'Style' available. You may also wish to apply the same formatting to another section of the document later.

You have two options:

◆ If you think that you will want to re-use the format style in the future, stop and create a new style.

◆ Apply the formatting style to the relevant section and should you find later that you wish to apply the same formatting to another section, use the **Format Painter** ✑ (see page 106).

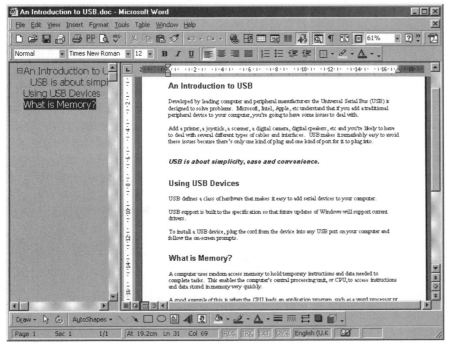

The Document Map

Alternative file formats

Saving documents as Web pages

Word 2000 is extremely Web-oriented and can save documents in a number of different formats, which can be read by other word processing applications or Web browsers. In this section we will use the *Formatting Display* document to demonstrate how easy this process is and view the same document using Internet Explorer.

Basic steps

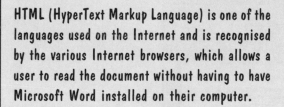

1 Open the *Formatting Display* document
2 Select File > Save as Web page
❑ The Save as dialog box will open. This is the same the dialog box thar you have already met, except in this instance, the format the document will be saved in is HTML

Take note

HTML (HyperText Markup Language) is one of the languages used on the Internet and is recognised by the various Internet browsers, which allows a user to read the document without having to have Microsoft Word installed on their computer.

❑ The name used to save the document will be picked up by the Save as dialog box and displayed in the File name slot
3 Accept this name
4 Click Save

The conversion may take a moment or two. Check Word's status bar to monitor progress.

The page view in Word will now change to Web Layout, which displays the document in a similar manner as if you are viewing the document using an Internet browser.

Tip

It is suggested that if you decide to use this feature of Word, that you always save the document as a standard Word document first and then convert it to HTML. This could save you considerable time if the converted document fails in some way.

Viewing the document in a browser

Basic steps

1 Close the document.
2 Open Internet Explorer.

Depending on how your browser is configured, you may find that it immediately attempts to dial-up your Internet Service Provider. If this is the case click on the **Stop** icon ▨ on the toolbar and then select the **Work Off-line** option.

Alternatively you may be presented with a dialog box which offers you the option of connecting to the Internet or working off-line. If so, select off-line.

3 Select File > Open from the menu bar.
❑ The Open dialog box will appear.
4 Click the Browse button.
5 Navigate to where you stored the *Formatting Display.htm* document, and double-click on it.

6 You will be returned to the Open dialog box and the file name will appear in the Open slot. Click OK.

The document will be loaded into the browser where you can view it. The document cannot be edited in the browser, because it is a *Read-only* application.

Summary

You may feel a little disappointed with the appearance of the document, but remember that Word is not a dedicated Web page design application and that this page was created from a simple Word document.

If creating Web pages is important and you plan to create a number of pages, then you should investigate the templates that are installed as part of Word. Start with **File > New** and in the **New** dialog box, select the **Web Pages** tab and investigate each of the templates.

If this fails to meet your requirements then you should consider purchasing a dedicated Web page application, such as Microsoft FrontPage. Included on the Microsoft Office CD is a cut-down version of this, called FrontPage Express, which you may wish to look at before buying the complete product.

Other file formats

Word offers you a wide range of different file formats when it comes to saving documents. You should be aware that certain formatting features may be lost in the saved file, if you select any other format other than the dedicated Word default option of '.doc'.

Shown below is the **Save As** dialog box. You have encountered this box previously, however we have not investigated all of the options available in the **Save as type** slot, shown open.

You may save a document in a format suitable for Word on a Macintosh system or for WordPerfect 5.1 for MS-DOS. Use the scroll bar to view the options and when finished click **Cancel** to close the dialog box.

Saving the document as Rich Text Format

Rich Text Format (RTF) saves all formatting. RTF converts formatting to instructions that other programs, including compatible Microsoft programs, can read and interpret. We are going to save a copy of the *Formatting Display.doc* document as an RTF document.

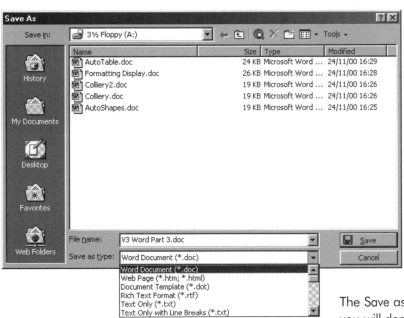

The Save as type options available to you will depend upon the export filters that were selected during installation

Basic steps

1 Open the *Formatting Display.doc* document
2 From the menu bar select File > Save As
3 At the Save As dialog box, click on the drop-down arrow next to the Save as type slot
4 Select the option *Rich Text Format (*.RTF)*
5 Accept the same file name and click Save
6 Click the Open icon on the Standard toolbar
7 When the Open dialog box opens, navigate to where you stored the document
8 Click on the down-arrow of the Files of type slot and select the *All Files* option

❑ If you have saved all of the copies of the *Formatting Display* document in the same folder, you should see a number of files, with the same name but different file extensions.

9 Open each document in turn and check for any changes to the formatting and layout

Summary

Saving documents in another file format is as easy as that. However, be aware that some changes and or loss of formatting may occur.

This will normally be set to only show Word documents

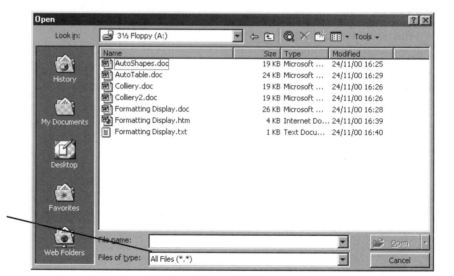

Mail merge

One of the many features of Microsoft Word is *mail merge*. This is designed to assist the user who has to produce numerous copies of similar letters which are sent to a large number of clients. Each letter will contain the same content, though personalised in its salutation and address details.

Imagine you have a database of several hundred clients and you wish to inform them of a change in a specification to an item they have an interest in. In the days of typewriters, to personalise the letters would have meant someone typing each individual letter. However with mail merge you can produce bulk mailings from two previously prepared documents.

Take note

Word uses particular names in the merge process, so it is important to remember these names and exactly what they are.

Mail merge requirements

The form letter

The *form letter* is the skeleton of the letter that contains all the common content that each client will receive. One of the advantages of using a form letter is that should you later have to amend it, you only have one document to amend. You can create a reusable series of form letters for different uses.

Take note

It is not strictly necessary to create the form letter first; in time you will choose your preferred method of working.

The data source

The *data source* is the document that contains all the personal details of the client, including name, how you address the client and their address. Data sources, like the form letters, are reusable. You can produce a data source in Word or use a file from another application as the source, such as Access.

Other data sources

You can use names and addresses of contacts in your Outlook Contact list, as a data source, with the mail merge. However this can only be done after the creation of the form letter.

Basic steps

1 Open Word and select Tools > Mail Merge
2 Click Get Data
3 Click Use Address Book
4 Select Outlook Address Book

For powerful sorting and searching capabilities, use Access or Excel to edit longer lists of data.

Tip

As you are most likely to be using other lists or applications for data, it is worth spending time investigating if these sources can be utilised. One reason for using a computer is to store and reuse information without duplication.

The main document

It is from the form letter and the data source, that the *main document* is produced. This is the document that will actually be sent out to the clients after the mail merge has been completed.

Creating the components

We will use Word to create the various components necessary for the following exercise, and will start by creating the form letter.

Creating the form letter

Basic steps

1 Open a new blank document
2 Save it as *Form Let1*
❑ We will use the standard business layout for the form letter. To save time and space, we have omitted our company details, logo, etc. from the letter, which would usually appear between the Ref and client address sections.

Example:

> Ref: JAW/ct
>
> Date *(Read the guidance notes below)*
>
> Dear
>
> *Heading*
>
> This is to advise you that we have once again reduced the cost price of our low energy, high efficiency water pumps.
> As a valued client, we thought that you should be amongst the first to be advised of the price reduction. Furthermore, with your customer discounts applied, this will add up to a substantial saving to you.
> We look forward to receiving your orders, which will receive our prompt attention.
> Yours sincerely
>
> John A Worthington

❑ You can insert an automatic date entry. Select Insert > Date and Time. When the dialog box opens select the format '25 July 2000' (the date on your PC will indicate today's date). Tick the Update automatically checkbox. This will ensure that each time the form letter is used, Word will insert the current date.

3 Once you have completed the form letter, save the document
4 Select Tools > Mail Merge
❑ The Mail Merge Helper dialog box will open. Note that currently you only have the Create option available

5 Click Create. At the next dialog box select Form Letters…

6 This prompt will appear. We have already produced the form letter and it is open, so select Active Window

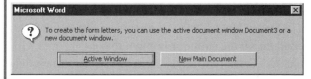

❑ You will be returned to the Mail Merge Helper box. However, you will now see that there is an additional option. This is the Edit button, located to the right of the Create button. Ignore this button for the time being.

Note that the Data Source, Get Data button has also become active.

Creating the data source

Basic steps

1 Click the Data Source > Get Data button

2 Select Create Data Source and another dialog box will open. Word has set up a number of common fields and you can include additional fields. For this exercise we will use the fields provided, with the following exceptions.

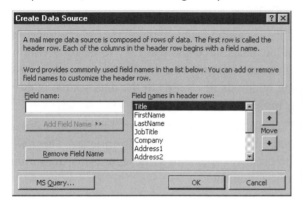

3 Select *FirstName*, *JobTitle*, *State*, *Country*, *HomePhone* and *WorkPhone*

4 Click the Remove Field Name button

5 Click OK

❑ The Save As dialog box will open. You will be prompted to save the data source, even though you have not entered any data yet

6 Save it as *Data Source1*

❑ When the data source has been saved the Save As dialog box will close and a further dialog box will open offering you a choice of Edit Data Source or Edit Main Document.

7 Select Edit Data Source. The Edit Data Form dialog box will open

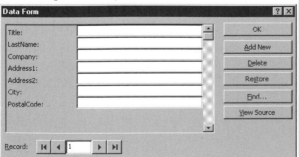

It is in this box that we will enter our clients' details. You will note that only seven fields are available, as we deleted the others.

Refer to the document that you created earlier and saved as, *Data Source Information*. Use the information contained within this document to enter client details, as shown in the respective fields in the data form window.

8 When you reach the last field, for the first client, click the Add New button. A new blank form will open

9 Continue entering the clients' details until all have been entered

10 Click OK

You are now returned to the form letter. Look for the *Merge* toolbar – it should appear adjacent to the Formatting toolbar.

Inserting the merge fields

Basic steps

1 On the form letter, place the cursor at the end of the date line and press the [Enter] key twice

2 Click the Insert Merge Field button on the Merge toolbar

3 From the drop-down list select the *Company* field. It will appear in the form letter

4 Move down one line at a time by pressing [Enter] and insert the four remaining address fields, each on its own line

5 When all fields have been entered, ensure there is a blank line between the address block and the salutation

6 Place the cursor after the salutation starting '*Dear*'

7 Insert a single space after '*Dear*' (or the words will run in to each other)

8 Click Insert Merge field

143

9 Select the field *Title*, followed by the *LastName*

Enter a space between the field names *Title* and *LastName*. These fields are to appear on the same line one after the other.

Once all the necessary fields have been inserted, the Form letter should look like the example shown.

Ref: JAW/ct

Date

<<Company>>
<<Address1>>
<<Address2>>
<<City>>
<<PostalCode>>

Dear <<Title>><<LastName>>

We are now at the stage ready to perform the actual merger of the documents.

10 Click the Merge to New Document button

Take note

If you use the **Tools > Mail Merge** method, the Merge window will open and the default option is to *Merge to a new document*. Accept this option and click on the **Merge** button.

The completed merge

On releasing the **Merge** button, the dialog box will close and the merge process will commence. Word will now produce a four-page document.

This document is, in fact, four different letters separated by page breaks. This is the final product – the merged document.

❑ Save as *Merge* and close all documents

Summary

This was a simple merge involving only four records in the data source and was easy to perform without any complications. To carry out a merge task, accessing hundreds of records in the data source is more complex.

You would have to select the clients who have an interest in the subject of the form letter. There will almost always be fields in the records that are surplus to requirement.

This section should be practised a number of times to gain confidence in using the feature. Use the online Help to learn more about 'Mail Merge' and how you can perform more complex 'Mail Merge' tasks.

Importing a spreadsheet

It will only be possible to practice the following if you have already completed the module on Microsoft Excel and that you have Excel installed on your PC. Information such as a Microsoft Excel worksheet can be stored within a Word document, either by copying or linking it to the document.

Exchanging data between Word and Excel

Imported data can be up to 4,000 rows by 4,000 columns, but charts can display no more than 255 data series (the elements that make up a chart).

If you are importing an Excel worksheet and want the imported data to begin at a cell other than the top-left cell, select the starting cell first.

To open in Word a file created in another program, select the relevant file format from the **Files of type** box, locate the folder that contains the file you want and double-click the file you want to import.

If the data is in an Excel work*book* created with version 5.0 or later, select the sheet you want to import. You can import only one sheet.

To import all the data on the worksheet, click *Entire sheet* under **Import**.

To import part of the data, click **Range**, and then type the range. For example, to import cells A1 through B5, type *A1:B5*. If the range is named, you can type the name instead of the reference.

To analyse the data from a Word table in Excel, you can copy and paste the data to a new Excel workbook.

Definitions

The following are extracts from Excel online Help which explains the meaning of the terminology used to describe the various methods available to copy, or link data from Excel worksheets to Word documents.

Source file contains the information used to create a linked object or embedded object. The object exists in the destination file. In the source file, when you update the information that the linked object was created from, the linked object in the destination file is updated automatically.

The destination file is where a linked or embedded object is inserted into. The file that contains information used to create the object is the source file. When you change information in a destination file, the information is not updated in the source file.

Linked object – Information (the *object*) created in one file (the *source* file) and inserted into another file (the *destination* file) while maintaining a connection between the two files. The linked object in the destination file is automatically updated when the source file is updated. A linked object does not become part of the destination file.

Embedded object – Information (the object) inserted into a file (the destination file). Once embedded, the object becomes part of the destination file. When you double-click an embedded object, it opens in the source program it was created in. Any changes you make to the embedded object are reflected in the destination file.

There is a great deal of information contained in the previous section, which describes the definitions used when copying or linking information between applications. It is particularly important that you understand the differences and various methods available to you when exchanging information between different applications. Using the appropriate method will reduce the long-term effort when you may have to update the information.

Practice embedding data

You will require an Excel workbook that contains data, or must create a simple spreadsheet to demonstrate this feature. If you have to create a worksheet before continuing, ensure that you close it when finished and remember where you saved it.

Basic steps

1 In Word, open a new blank document
2 Save it as *Importing*

145

3   From the menu bar select Insert > Object

4   When the Object dialog box opens, select the Create from File tab

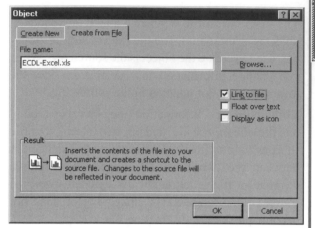

5   Type in the path to the workbook or click Browse and locate and open the file through the Browse dialog box

6   Tick the Link to file checkbox. This will allow Excel to open when you double-click on the data, once it is in your document.

7   Click OK. The dialog box will close and the data will be inserted in your document.

8   Double-click over the data area and Excel will open. You may now update or change any of the data as required

9   Change some figures (remember which ones)

10   When finished Save the changes and close Excel

11   Check the figures that you changed and you will see that Word reflects the change made in Excel

An alternative method

Basic steps

❑   Perform the above procedure except this time:

1   Save the document as *Importing2*

2   Select Insert > Object.

3   Remove the tick in the Link to file checkbox

4   Finish the procedure to import the data

	B	C	D	E	F
2			Quarterly Sales		
3	Region	Jan	Feb	Mar	Area Totals
4	North East	50,985.00	45,987.00	48,755.00	145,727.00
5	North West	47,800.00	47,855.00	47,522.00	143,177.00
6	South East	51,200.00	46,585.00	52,456.00	150,241.00
7	South West	49,125.00	52,100.00	47,800.00	149,025.00
8					
9	Monthly Totals	£199,110.00	£192,527.00	£196,533.00	£588,170.00

Sheet1 / Sheet2 / Sheet3 /

5   Double-click over the data area. Note that the data area changes to that shown here. Word Menus and toolbars have changed to those of Excel, but Excel has not opened in the same manner as it did in the previous exercise.

6   Practice by making one or two changes to the data

7   Click on a blank area of the document above the column headers

The Excel menus and toolbars will close, you will be returned to the Word document view, and the changes will appear in your document.

8   Save the changes but do not close the document

Importing a chart

The previous two exercises demonstrated how to import an Excel worksheet. In this exercise we are going to import a chart. To assist with this exercise, an Excel file has been included on the Course CD. It is located in the *Course Resources* folder and is called *Excel Chart Sheet.xls*.

Basic steps

1   Ensure that the *Import2* document is open

2   Place the cursor below the Excel worksheet and press [Enter] three times

3   Open Excel and open the file *Excel Chart Sheet.xls*

4   The file contains a chart. Place the cursor over the upper left area of the chart – a tool-tip will appear with the message *Chart Area*. If you get a different message, move the cursor until it does show the tip *Chart Area*.

5   Copy the chart using Ctrl+C

6   Switch to Word

7   Select Edit > Paste Special

8   At the Paste Special dialog box, change your settings to correspond to those shown here

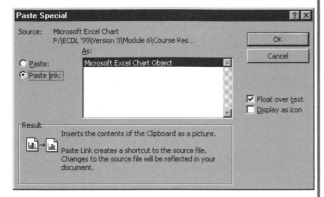

9   Click OK. The chart will now appear in your document

10 Double-click over the chart – Excel will open and you can carry out any amendments necessary to the worksheet.

❑   When complete, close Excel and you are returned to your document in Word

Experiment with the features described in the previous exercises, using Excel worksheets, to gain experience and to realise their full potential.

Summary

When you copy information between Excel and another Office program or any program that supports Object Linking and Embedding (OLE), you can choose to copy the information as either a linked object or an embedded object.

Use linked objects if you want the information to be updated when the original data changes in the source file.

The source application must be installed on your computer.

To maintain the link to the original data, the source file must remain available on your computer or network.

Use embedded objects if you or others will be using the destination file on another computer, or if you don't want changes to the original data to affect the copied information in the destination file.

An embedded object becomes part of the destination file and thus increases the file size. You can insert objects you've already created in other programs that support OLE or you can start the program and create new objects while you work in Microsoft Excel.

For more information about the differences between linked and embedded objects use the on-line Help.

4 Spreadsheets

Introduction to Microsoft Excel

What is a spreadsheet?

A spreadsheet is a tool for managing numerical data and performing calculations. It consists of columns and rows in which you record data, on which a formula is used to perform various calculations.

Excel enables you to perform a variety of functions including sorting and selecting from lists. Automatic calculations mean that you will always have up-to-date results in your spreadsheet. Excel includes an easy-to-use chart-creating feature.

Excel also has a linking feature that allows you to enter data in one location and use it in other spreadsheets or documents, which are automatically updated from the source. This improves productivity, and reduces the chances of errors being introduced.

Excel allows you to experiment with the design and layout on the screen before actually printing the final product.

At the bottom of this page is an example of a simple spreadsheet.

The above example is extremely simple in design and appearance. The calculations performed by the spreadsheet are simply to total the sales figures, down by region and across by month.

Calculation operators in formulas

Before we start creating our first spreadsheet you need to understand how Excel carries out certain tasks, how it applies precedence in formulas, what an operator is and how Excel uses it.

Operators specify the type of calculation that you want to perform on the elements of a formula. Excel includes four different types of calculation operators: arithmetic, comparison, text, and reference.

Arithmetic operators perform basic mathematical operations - such as addition, subtraction, division or multiplication; combine numbers; and produce numeric results. Examples are shown later.

There are specific rules when entering formula in spreadsheets. Should you find that your results are not what you expected, always check how the formula was entered. If you have not used mathematics for sometime, this is an area where a little practice could save time in the future.

The order of operations in formulas

If you combine several operators in a single formula, Excel performs the operations in the order shown below. If a formula contains operators with the same precedence, for example, if a formula contains both a multiplication and division operator – Excel evaluates the operators from left to right. To change the order of evaluation, enclose the part of the formula to be calculated first in parentheses ( ).

If you are completely new to computers, the symbols used to indicate multiplication and division may be different to what you are normally accustomed to using.

- Multiplication is indicated by the symbol *.
- Division is indicated by the symbol /.

Region	Quarterly Sales			
	Jan	Feb	Mar	Area Totals
North East	50,985.00	45,987.00	48,755.00	145,727.00
North West	47,800.00	47,855.00	47,522.00	143,177.00
South East	51,200.00	46,585.00	52,456.00	150,241.00
South West	49,125.00	52,100.00	47,800.00	149,025.00
Monthly Totals	199,110.00	192,527.00	196,533.00	588,170.00

Examples

Try out these examples in Excel later. The calculation will produce two different results if the rules are not applied, i.e.

- (2+2)*3 = 12, because: 2 + 2 = 4, then 4 * 3 = 12.
- 2+2*3 = 8, because: 2 * 3 = 6, (multiplication is always carried out first), then 2 + 6 = 8.

Operator	Description
: (colon)	Reference operators
, (comma)	(single space)
–	Negation (as in -1)
%	Percent
^	Exponentiation
* and /	Multiplication and division
+ and –	Addition and subtraction
&	Concatenation – joins two strings of text
= < > <= >= <>	Comparison

Actual use of operators will be discussed later in the course and at this stage all that is required is that you remember that the operators are listed above for future reference.

Starting Excel

In common with many Windows applications, you can start Excel a number of different ways. Only one method will be described here.

It is assumed that the computer has been switched on and that the operating system is fully up and running normally.

Basic steps

1 Click **Start**.

2 Point to Programs and click Microsoft Excel

❑ Microsoft Excel will open and display a screen similar to that shown

> **Take note**
>
> Refer to Chapter 3, page 89 for more information on toolbar customisation.

Menu bar

Standard toolbar

Formatting toolbar

Formula bar

Control buttons
Top three for Excel
Bottom three for Workbook

Scroll bars

Row number

Active cell A1

Worksheet number – up to 16 per workbook

Drawing toolbar

Column header

Starting a new workbook

Excel opens with a new blank worksheet. For this section of the course we will close this workbook and open another new workbook. The reason for doing this is to identify where and how you select a new workbook.

Closing the workbook

In the example shown there are two groups of control buttons. The top group of buttons are used to control Excel, the application.

The second group of buttons relate to the workbook. To Close the workbook, click on the circled button. If prompted to Save the workbook, click on No.

Take note

See page 49 for more information of the purpose and function of the control buttons.

Basic steps

1 On the menu bar select File > New
❑ The New dialog box will open

2 Ensure that the General tab is selected
3 Click on the *Workbook* icon

4 Click OK
❑ A new worksheet will now open similar to that shown previously

By default Excel opens the workbook at sheet 1 with the cursor in cell A1.

Workbook options

There are a number of options that you can change, some of which are now listed.

The number of sheets contained within a workbook can be changed to meet your requirements. For example, you can change the default number of sheets (3) in a workbook, so that each time Excel opens you have, for example, 16 sheets inserted in the workbook.

A maximum of 255 worksheets can be inserted within a workbook.

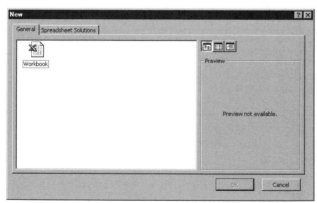

Basic steps

To change the 3 to 16:
1 Select Tools > Options
2 Select the General tab
3 In the Sheets in new workbook area change the setting to 16
4 Click OK

No changes will occur until you next open a new workbook.

Excel allows the following:

◆ A maximum of 32,000 characters in a cell.

◆ A maximum of 65,536 rows by 256 columns per worksheet.

◆ A maximum of 16 Undo actions. If you accidentally delete a range of data, you can use the Undo feature to retrieve it (Undo is covered in detail later in the course).

◆ A maximum of 56 colours per workbook.

Saving the workbook

We will now start entering text and figures in our worksheet, however before we actually commence we will save the workbook.

The Save routines are the same as in Word (see page 86). Save the new workbook on the A drive, calling it 'ECDL1'

Naming worksheets

By default, Excel names the worksheets contained in workbooks as '*Sheet 1*', '*Sheet 2*' and so on. To make worksheet names more relevant and easier to remember:

Basic steps

If the worksheet default name is Sheet 1:

1 Double-click over the name tab
2 When highlighted type in the required name
3 Press [Enter] or click on the worksheet to apply the change

> \ **Sheet1** / Sheet2 / Sheet3 /

Before and after the change

> \ **Autumn 1999** / Sheet2 / Sheet3 /

Renaming worksheets

Basic steps

1 Double-click on the worksheet name to be changed
2 When highlighted type in the new name

or

3 Right-click on the worksheet name
4 From the pop-up menu select 'Rename'
5 When the worksheet name is highlighted type in the new name

Inserting worksheets

Basic steps

To insert an additional worksheet in a workbook:

1 Select the last worksheet or where you want the new worksheet
2 From the menu bar select Insert > Worksheet
❑ A new sheet will be inserted

Excel will place the new worksheet to the left of the selected worksheet. For instances, if you select Sheet 2 and then insert a new worksheet, it will appear between Sheets 1 and 2.

> \ Sheet1 \ **Sheet4** / Sheet2 / Sheet3 /

Moving worksheets

Basic steps

To move the position of a worksheet within a workbook:

1　Select the worksheet name tab
2　Drag the sheet to the required location

Before and
after the move

Moving within the worksheet

There are a number of methods that you can use to move the cursor from one cell to the next within a worksheet and the most common are now listed.

Tab key: To move forward from cell A1 to B1 use the [Tab] key, which will move the cursor horizontally within the worksheet.

Shift-Tab keys: Use the [Shift]-[Tab] key combination to move the cursor back to the previously selected cell.

Cursor keys: The four cursor keys will move the cursor one cell in the direction of the selected key as appropriate.

Mouse: Use the mouse, left-click in the require cell.

Closing the application

So far we have only created a new workbook, saved it using the name 'ECDL1' and not yet entered any data in it. To enable us to demonstrate the next section of the course, we will close Excel, as follows:

❑　From the menu bar select File > Exit and Excel will close

Entering text and figures

Open Excel, using your preferred method.

Locate and open the workbook 'ECDL1' and ensure that cell A1 is the active cell. The active cell is denoted by a thick rectangle surrounding it.

Typing in data

Basic steps

1 Type '*QUARTERLY SALES FOR AUTUMN 1999*' and press [Enter]

2 Leave a blank row and in cell B3 type '*October*'

☐ Look closely at the active cell, particularly the lower right corner, where you will see a small square

	A	B
1		
2		
3		October
4		

3 Place your mouse cursor over the square

When correctly placed, it will change its shape to a thin black cross

4 With the cursor indicating a thin black cross, press and hold the left mouse button

5 Drag the cursor to the right over the two cells C3 and D3

As you drag, you will see that Excel has recognised that you have entered a calendar month name. Because you are dragging the cursor to the right, Excel assumes that you require the following months, November, December, entered in the respective cells. This feature is called *AutoFill*.

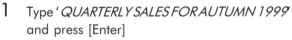

In this instance, as you typed in 'October', Excel automatically inserts 'November' and 'December'.

6 When you have the necessary months displayed, keep the cursor on the last cell in this case '*December*'

7 Release the mouse button

Take note

If you had dragged the cursor to the left, Excel would have inserted September, August and so on.

Excel has a number of similar features and you should investigate these later by going to the menu bar and selecting **Tools** > **Options** > **Custom Lists**. You can also create your own requirements within the Custom Lists. We will be using a number of these features in due course.

Continue to enter the following detail in the cells as indicated using capital letters throughout.

Cell location	Detail
A4	FOOTWEAR
A5	CLOTHING
A6	TOILETRIES
A7	MISC

You may find that some of the text appears to have run into the adjacent cell.

The current situation regarding the display is not satisfactory but we shall rectify that shortly.

Your worksheet should look similar to the example shown.

	A	B	C	D
1	QUARTERLY SALES FOR AUTUMN 1999			
2				
3		October	November	December
4	FOOTWEAR			
5	CLOTHING			
6	TOILETRIES			
7	MISC			

This is the text that appears to have over run into the adjacent cells.

Adjusting column width

There are a number of ways to display the text correctly and we will investigate two of these options.

155

Basic steps

Method one

1 Move the cursor to the column headers, between A and B. The cursor will change to a double arrow

2 Press the left mouse button and hold it down

3 Drag the cursor to the right until you are satisfied with the positioning

❏ Do not release the button yet

4 Drag it back to the left so that the text appears to be overflowing again

5 Release the button now

There is a quicker method, but if you carry out these adjustments at this stage, you will not achieve the desired results. This is because there is a longer piece of text already in cell A1 and Excel will open the column to accommodate that text. The width will be excessive.

To overcome this problem, we will first carry out some formatting to the text in cell A1.

Basic steps

1 Place the cursor over the cell A1

❏ The cursor should resemble a cross ⊹

2 Press the left button to select the cell A1

3 Drag the cursor to the right and select the cells A1 to D1 inclusive, then release the button

4 Click the Merge and Centre icon ▤▤▤▦ on the Formatting toolbar

The text will merge and become centred within the four cells.

You will hardly notice any visual change, in respect of the text placement. What you will see is that the four cells are enclosed in a bold rectangle without any text highlighted.

We will now return our attention to adjusting the width of column A.

Basic steps

Method two

1 Move the cursor up to the column headers, just between the headers A and B. The mouse cursor will change to the double arrow ◄╂►

2 Double-click on the left mouse button. Excel will automatically open out the column to the correct width

❏ The width will be opened out to accommodate the text contained within cells A4 to A7. Compare the before and after examples.

	A	B	C	D
1	QUARTERLY SALES FOR AUTUMN 1999			
2				
3		October	November	December
4	FOOTWEAR			
5	CLOTHING			
6	TOILETRIES			
7	MISC			

Before column width adjusted

	A	B	C	D
1	QUARTERLY SALES FOR AUTUMN 1999			
2				
3		October	November	December
4	FOOTWEAR			
5	CLOTHING			
6	TOILETRIES			
7	MISC			

After column width adjusted

Continue to enter the data as shown here.

	A	B	C	D
1	QUARTERLY SALES FOR AUTUMN 1999			
2				
3		October	November	December
4	FOOTWEAR	3980	3285	4120
5	CLOTHING	5740	5566	5990
6	TOILETRIES	2541	3500	2654
7	MISC	1500	1750	1458

Formatting numbers

When entering text into cells Excel will align all text to the left. All figures will be aligned to the right.

There is still considerable formatting to be carried out on the figures yet. The figures as they stand could mean anything, when actually they are monetary sums.

We will now format the figures to show only whole currency, that is to say we will not show any denomination less than £1.

There is a quick way to format all twelve cells together, rather than having to apply the formatting to individual cells.

Basic steps

1   Highlight all the cells that contain the sales figures by placing the cursor over the cell B4, then dragging it down and to the right until the cells B4 to D7 are highlighted

3980	3285	4120
5740	5566	5990
2541	3500	2654
1500	1750	1458

2   Release the button
3   Right-click over the highlighted area
4   From the pop-up menu, select Format Cells...

❏   The 'Format Cells' dialog box will open. This box contains a large number of formatting features and should be investigated more closely in the future. However, for this exercise:

5   Ensure that the Number tab is selected
6   Select *Currency* from the Category slot
    We will not be showing any value less than £1
7   Click on the down-arrow next to the Decimal places slot until 0 (zero) is displayed
8   Click on the down-arrow next to the Symbol slot and select *None.* We do not want the '£' sign displayed in these cells

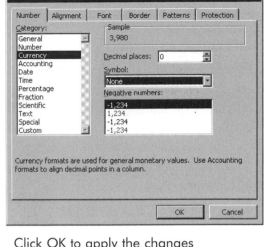

9   Click OK to apply the changes

The area will still have the highlight applied. To remove the highlight click in a blank cell.

The worksheet should look like the example shown. Ensure that the thousand marker is present.

October	November	December
3,980	3,285	4,120
5,740	5,566	5,990
2,541	3,500	2,654
1,500	1,750	1,458

Changing font style and size

The title of this worksheet in its current format is not very eye-catching. We will increase the font size and add a little colour to it to make it more attractive. Naturally you will need a colour printer to gain the full effect.

Take note

If you only have a black and white printer, be careful with the use of colours and shades. You should print a test page on your printer to determine the quality of its output and to ensure that the detail can be read.

157

Basic steps

1 Click on cell A1 to select it

2 Select Format > Cells... from the menu bar

Or

3 Right-click on the selected cell

4 Select Format Cells... from the pop-up menu

5 At the Format Cells dialog box, select the Font tab

6 Scroll the Size list and select 12

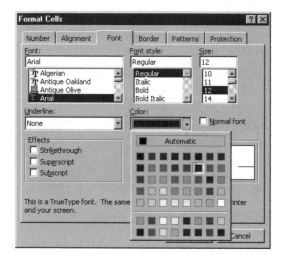

7 Click on the drop-down-arrow next to the Color slot and select *Blue* from the drop-down palette

8 Click OK to apply the changes

As you can see, the text is too big for the cell. We will rectify this problem soon.

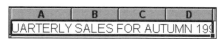

An alternative method

We will now change the font size back to 10 however, on this occasion we will use a different method. Examine the example shown.

Basic steps

1 Click in cell A1

2 Click on the Size drop-down arrow in the Formatting toolbar

3 Select the value 10

❑ You should now be able to see all of the text

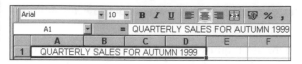

There is still considerable formatting that we have to apply to the worksheet and this will be listed on the following pages.

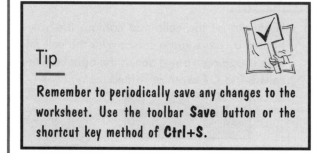

Tip

Remember to periodically save any changes to the worksheet. Use the toolbar Save button or the shortcut key method of Ctrl+S.

We are now going to format the text October through to December and make it stand out from the rest of the text.

Basic steps

1 Place the cursor over the cell B3, *October*

2 Drag the cursor to the right, to highlight the three cells

3 On the Formatting toolbar, click the Bold icon

4 Left-click once on the Centre icon

Now carry out any other formatting requirements, for instance the width may require adjusting to compensate for the change in the text, because bold text occupies more space.

Your worksheet should now look like this. Note how the names stand out now when formatted with Bold.

	A	B	C	D
1	QUARTERLY SALES FOR AUTUMN 1999			
2				
3		October	November	December
4	FOOTWEAR	3,980	3,285	4,120
5	CLOTHING	5,740	5,566	5,990
6	TOILETRIES	2,541	3,500	2,654
7	MISC	1,500	1,750	1,458

5   Save the changes and close the workbook

❑   We will return to this workbook later

Text orientation

Sometimes the conventional method of displaying text, horizontally, left to right, will not meet requirements. Excel supports vertical text orientation.

Basic steps

1   Open a new blank workbook and save it using the name '*Orientation*'

2   Type the words shown in each cell as indicated

B2 Text   C2 Angled   D2 Angled E2 Orientation
B4 One more C4 Example   D4 Using   E4 Justification

3   Right-click once over B2

4   From the pop-up menu select Format Cells…

5   At the Format Cells dialog box, select the Alignment tab

6   In the Orientation pane, place the cursor over the pointer as shown

✂	Cu_t
🗐	_Copy
📋	_Paste
	Paste _Special…
	_Insert…
	_Delete…
	Clear Co_ntents
📷	Insert Co_mment
📝	_Format Cells…
	Pic_k From List…

Format Cells   ? ✕

Number | Alignment | Font | Border | Patterns | Protection

Text alignment
Horizontal:
Center   Indent: 0
Vertical:
Bottom

Text control
☐ Wrap text
☐ Shrink to fit
☐ Merge cells

Orientation
T e x t   Text ——◆
0 ⬍ Degrees

OK   Cancel

7   Click and drag the pointer round to the upper-most position

8   Release the button and click OK

There are two other methods of changing the orientation, which are:

Click the up or down arrows next to the **Degrees** slot, until the desired angle is displayed within the slot.

Double-click in the **Degrees** slot and when the figure is highlighted type in the required value.

When they are displayed, left-click **OK** and observe the changes to the text orientation.

The example shows the setting adjustment for the word 'Angle', in cell C2. Apply this setting to your cell C2.

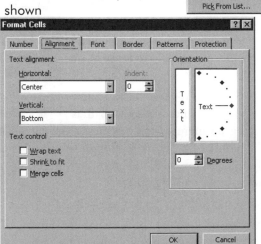

Text positioning in cells

In addition to text orientation, the position of the text, within a cell, can also be adjusted.

Basic steps

1 Right-click over the cell C4 and select Format Cells... from the pop-up menu

2 When the Format Cells dialog box opens, apply the settings shown in the example

3 Click OK to apply the changes

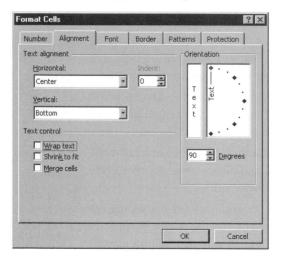

Exercise

Select each of the remaining cells, and apply the appropriate changes so that your text matches the example shown on the previous page.

When all changes have been applied, save the changes to the worksheet and close the workbook.

Changing the view mode

There will be occasions when you will want to change the view of the worksheet, rather than using Normal View. There are a number of different ways to do this.

Ensure that workbook ECDL1 is open.

Reducing or increasing the view size

Reducing the view size will show more of the spreadsheet and is useful for checking the layout and formatting consistency. If the view is greatly reduced, you may encounter difficulty in reading the text and figures.

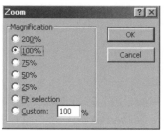

The quick method of changing the view is to select the Zoom drop-down arrow on the standard toolbar and make your selection.

An alternative method

Basic steps

1 From the menu bar select View > Zoom

❑ The Zoom dialog box will open

2 Select one of the options

3 Click OK

❑ The box will close and the worksheet view will change as appropriate

Even more alternative views

Investigate the **View** menu and you will find other options available to you for viewing the spreadsheet.

Normal is the default setting.

Page Break Preview will display the page breaks which may suit your requirements.

Custom Views is more advanced – use the online Help to learn more on this subject.

Full Screen will remove from view the toolbars and Status bar, thus freeing up more of the screen for the spreadsheet. The Full Screen button is a toggle – it is either on or off. When you want to return to Normal, or other views, click on it again.

Zoom has already been discussed.

Experiment with the above to see the varying effects that each view can bring to the worksheet.

Changing the toolbars

Removing toolbars from view

It is quite likely, as you gain experience, you will want to see more of the spreadsheet and less of the toolbars.

One way of achieving this would be to use the **Full Screen** option as discussed previously. Another way would be to remove the toolbars from view.

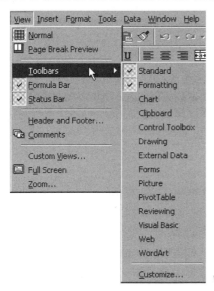

Basic steps

1   From the menu bar select View > Toolbars

❑   A further menu will open and all the Toolbars currently open will have a tick (✓) next to them

2   Click on the (✓) and the toolbar will no longer be displayed

Take note

Toolbars automatically change, subject to the task being performed. This provides you with quick access to commands and functions relevant to the task.

Selecting toolbars

Excel, like other Microsoft applications, has a considerable number of toolbars available from which to choose.

Displaying different/additional toolbars

Basic steps

1   Select View > Toolbars only this time click by the required toolbar to have it displayed

❑   Some toolbars are *floating* and you may well find they obscure an area of the worksheet. This can quickly be overcome:

2   Place the cursor over the Title bar of the toolbar

3   Click and drag it to a more suitable location

Toolbars can be docked beneath other toolbars or placed to the left, right or bottom of the screen, much in the same way that the Taskbar in the Windows Desktop can be moved around.

Experiment with all the above and when finished, close the workbook, making sure that you save any changes. We will return to this workbook later.

Creating a second Workbook

Basic steps

1 Create another new workbook

2 Save this workbook as '*ECDL2*'

❑ You may save this to either the floppy disk or your hard disk

❑ Enter the following data in the *Sheet 1*

3 In cell B1 type the title '*QUARTERLY SALES FOR WINTER 1999*'

❑ The titles should be formatted as previously described: i.e. Merge and Centre, and blue

4 Enter the months as shown using the AutoFill feature starting at cell B3

5 Continue typing the data starting at cell A4 through to D7

	A	B	C	D	E
1		QUARTERLY SALES FOR WINTER 1999			
2					
3		January	February	March	
4	FOOTWEAR	2,976	2,367	2,989	
5	CLOTHING	4,356	2,340	3,452	
6	TOILETRIES	2,350	2,956	2,870	
7	MISC	1,300	1,456	1,299	

6 Apply the same formatting as that for the worksheet *ECDL1*, i.e.

❑ Adjust the column width to accommodate the product descriptions, 'Footwear', etc.

❑ Format the sale figures to display the comma and no '£' sign or any decimal places

❑ Enbolden the month names

Take note

Remember to periodically save any changes to the worksheet. Use the toolbar **Save** button or the shortcut key of **Ctrl+S**.

Additional text and formulas

Ensure that the workbook 'ECDL2' is open - it should appear as shown.

	A	B	C	D	E
1		QUARTERLY SALES FOR WINTER 1999			
2					
3		January	February	March	
4	FOOTWEAR	2,976	2,367	2,989	
5	CLOTHING	4,356	2,340	3,452	
6	TOILETRIES	2,350	2,956	2,870	
7	MISC	1,300	1,456	1,299	

Basic steps

1 Move the cursor to cell 'E3' and type 'Quarterly Sales' and format as 'Bold'

2 In cell 'A9' type 'Total'

3 Move the cursor to cell 'A10' and type 'Monthly Sales'

4 Adjust the column widths to accommodate the newly-entered text

We are now going to enter the formula which will add together the quarterly sales figures for the months 'January', 'February' and 'March'. It will then display the result in cell 'E4'. Do not at this stage enter any detail, simply read the explanation and the guide.

When finally entered, the formula will appear in the Formula window as:

=SUM(B4:D4)

An explanation

Before we actually enter the formula, some explanation is necessary of how the formula is structured and what the meaning of the various component parts are. So how does the formula translate?

Excel is an intelligent application, but there is a saying 'Junk in Junk out'. You must tell Excel that you want it to do a specific task, such as perform a function.

Formula syntax is the structure or order of the elements in a formula. Formulas in Excel follow a specific syntax that includes an equal sign (=) followed by a function name and the elements to be calculated (the arguments). Each argument can be a value that does not change (a constant), a cell or range reference, a label, a name, or a function.

Functions are predefined formulas that perform calculations by using specific values, called arguments, in a particular order, called the syntax. For example, the SUM function adds values or ranges of cells:

$$=SUM(B4:D4)$$

This is a formula   Function name   Argument

As you build up a calculation you have a number of options to select from. Do you want to have a total figure of a given number of cells? Do you want to add a percentage to a previously declared figure, for example add Value Added Tax (VAT) to a sales figure and so on?

In the example the use of the word '*SUM*' instructs Excel to carry out a specific task; the SUM function adds values or ranges of cells.

The detail contained within the parentheses are known as 'arguments' and identifies the cells that the calculation is to be based upon.

The calculation '=SUM(B4:D4)', when placed in cell E4, means 'display the sum of cells B4, C4 and D4 in cell E4'. The cell in which the formula is created is the one in which its result will be displayed.

Take note

The colon (:) is used to separate the references of the cells at the ends of a range. Excel is not case sensitive when entering formulas, you may use uppercase, lowercase or mixed.

How to enter the formula

Basic steps

1   Click in the cell E4

2   Type in the equal (=) sign followed by the word 'sum' (you can use upper or lowercase)

❑   Do not leave any spaces when entering the formula details

3   Enter the opening parenthesis (which will enclose the cell references

❑   At this stage the formula should appear '=sum(

4   Click in cell B4 and drag the cursor over to cell D4

As you drag the cursor, a broken outline appears around the cells. The detail in cell E4 also reflects the movement of the cursor and inserts the cell references into this cell.

5   When the three cells B4, C4 and D4 have been selected, release the button

❑   Your worksheet should resemble this

	A	B	C	D	E
1			QUARTERLY SALES FOR WINTER 1999		
2					
3		January	February	March	Quarterly Sales
4	FOOTWEAR	2,976	2,367	2,989	=sum(B4:D4
5	CLOTHING	4,356	2,340	3,452	
6	TOILETRIES	2,350	2,956	2,870	
7	MISC	1,300	1,456	1,299	
8					
9	Total				
10	Monthly Sales				

❑   The formula is not yet complete. When the button was released, you were returned to cell E4

6   Type in the closing parenthesis) to complete the formula and then press [Enter]

❑   The formula =sum(B4:D4) appears in the Formula bar and the result 8,332 in cell E4

7   Re-select cell E4

8   Place the cursor over the lower right corner of the cell and when it changes to a thin black cross, click and drag down to cell E10

9   Release the button

❑   This action carries the formula down to the other cells and adjusts it accordingly.

As the cursor is moved down the column, Excel carries out the calculation and inserts the result in the respective cells.

10 Re-select cells E5 to E7 in turn and check the Formula bar to see the changes

E10		=	=SUM(B10:D10)	
	A	B	C	D	E
1		QUARTERLY SALES FOR WINTER 1999			
2					
3		January	February	March	Quarterly Sales
4	FOOTWEAR	2,976	2,367	2,989	8,332
5	CLOTHING	4,356	2,340	3,452	10,148
6	TOILETRIES	2,350	2,956	2,870	8,176
7	MISC	1,300	1,456	1,299	4,055
8					0
9	Total				0
10	Monthly Sales				0

The above example now shows all the calculations completed. There is a small problem however. Cells E8 and E9 indicate a zero (0) value and, as it is unlikely that any values will be entered in the reference cells, the presence of the zeros are an unnecessary distraction.

11 Select cell E8 and drag the cursor down to include cell E9 in the selection

12 Press [Delete]

❑ The zero values will be removed

Using the Undo command

If you make a mistake and delete the wrong figures, don't panic, use the Undo command.

Basic steps

1 Click on the Undo icon down-arrow on the Standard toolbar

2 Select the appropriate option

In this instance it would be the top word 'Clear' and the deleted zeros (0) would be reinstated. Do not reinstate the deleted items at this stage.

Inserting additional Formula

The overall worksheet is still not complete. The formula for the 'Monthly Sales' has yet to be entered.

Basic steps

1 Select the cell B10 and type the formula =sum(B4:B7)

2 Move the cursor down to the lower right corner of the cell

3 When the cursor changes to a thin black cross, click and drag the cursor to the right to include cells C10 and D10 in the selection

4 Release the button when you reach cell D10

❑ The totals will be calculated and entered in the worksheet

❑ Notice that as you dragged the cursor to the right, the zero value in cell 'E10' was changing to reflect the increase in totals

Your worksheet should resemble the example shown.

E10		=	=SUM(B10:D10)	
	A	B	C	D	E
1		QUARTERLY SALES FOR WINTER 1999			
2					
3		January	February	March	Quarterly Sales
4	FOOTWEAR	2,976	2,367	2,989	8,332
5	CLOTHING	4,356	2,340	3,452	10,148
6	TOILETRIES	2,350	2,956	2,870	8,176
7	MISC	1,300	1,456	1,299	4,055
8					
9	Total				
10	Monthly Sales	10,982	9,119	10,610	30,711

Summary

Let's take a moment to review the calculations and what they represent.

Quarterly sales:

The first calculation '=**sum(B4:D4)**', totalled up the footwear sales for the months of January, February and March and displayed the result in cell E4.

When the cursor was dragged down from E4 to E7, the formula in cell E4 was being transferred to the selected cells and adjusted to show the results of the Clothing, Toiletries and Misc sales.

Excel changed the cell references to correspond to the relevant rows. Select the cells E5, E6 and E7 in turn to see the changes made in the formula, which is displayed in the formula window.

The second calculation '=**sum(B4:B7)**', totalled the sales per month and displayed the result in cell B10.

When the cursor was dragged across from B10 to E10 the formula was transferred and adjusted.

Excel changed the cell references to correspond to the relevant columns. Select the cells C10, D10 and E10 in turn to see the changes made in the formula, which are displayed in the formula window.

The result shown in cell E10 actually reflects two totals – that of cells B10 to D10 and E4 to E7.

Save any changes to the worksheet and then close it by selecting **File > Close** on the menu bar.

Practical exercise

Re-open the workbook 'ECDL1'

Tip

Open the File menu, and if you have not opened many other workbooks since last working on *ECDL1*, you will find it in the lower area of the menu. If it is there, click on it and it will open.

Task

The aim is now to apply all of the additional text and formatting already applied to worksheet *ECDL2* to this worksheet, *ECDL1*, i.e. bold, column width, etc.

Refer to the previous pages and enter the relevant new text, complete with formatting, performing any adjustments as necessary.

Insert all the formulas in the respective areas of *ECDL1*.

When you have completed all the formatting and formula changes to *ECDL1*, save the changes but do not close the workbook. The worksheet should resemble the one shown.

	A	B	C	D	E
	E10		=	=SUM(B10:D10)	
1	QUARTERLY SALES FOR AUTUMN 1999				
2					
3		October	November	December	Quarterly Sales
4	FOOTWEAR	3,980	3,285	4,120	11,385
5	CLOTHING	5,740	5,566	5,990	17,296
6	TOILETRIES	2,541	3,500	2,654	8,695
7	MISC	1,500	1,750	1,458	4,708
8					
9	Total				
10	Monthly Sales	13,761	14,101	14,222	42,084

Inserting new rows and columns

At some stage you will find that you need to insert a new column or row in your worksheet. The procedure to insert additional columns and rows is quite simple.

Basic steps

❑ To insert rows:

1 Ensure that *ECDL1* is open

2 Right-click over the row heading – 7 in this case

3 From the pop-up menu select Insert

	A	B	C	D	E
	A7		=	MISC	
1	QUARTERLY SALES FOR AUTUMN 1999				
2					
3		October	November	December	Quarterly Sales
4	FOOTWEAR	3,980	3,285	4,120	11,385
5	CLOTHING	5,740	5,566	5,990	17,296
6	TOILETRIES	2,541	3,500	2,654	8,695
7	MISC	1,500	1,750	1,458	4,708
	Cut				
	Copy				
	Paste	13,761	14,101	14,222	42,084
	Paste Special...				
	Insert				
	Delete				
	Clear Contents				
	Format Cells...				
	Row Height...				
	Hide				
	Unhide				

❑ The worksheet will roll down one row and a new row 7 will appear. The previous row 7 will be re-numbered as row 8. The worksheet should now resemble the example shown.

	A	B	C	D	E
	E7		=		
1	QUARTERLY SALES FOR AUTUMN 1999				
2					
3		October	November	December	Quarterly Sales
4	FOOTWEAR	3,980	3,285	4,120	11,385
5	CLOTHING	5,740	5,566	5,990	17,296
6	TOILETRIES	2,541	3,500	2,654	8,695
7					
8	MISC	1,500	1,750	1,458	4,708
9					
10	Total				
11	Monthly Sales	13,761	14,101	14,222	42,084

4 Select cell E7 – note that the formula bar is empty. When a new row is inserted, any formulae in the previous row/column are not carried over. This has to be done manually.

4: Spreadsheets

165

5 Select cell E6 and place the cursor over the lower right corner

6 When it changes to a thin black cross, drag it down to carry over the formula to cell E7

7 Release the button – confirmation that the formula has been carried over is the presence of the zero (0) in cell E7 and the formula appearing in the Formula bar

	E7		=	=SUM(B7:D7)	
	A	B	C	D	E
1	QUARTERLY SALES FOR AUTUMN 1999				
2					
3		October	November	December	Quarterly Sales
4	FOOTWEAR	3,980	3,285	4,120	11,385
5	CLOTHING	5,740	5,566	5,990	17,296
6	TOILETRIES	2,541	3,500	2,654	8,695
7					0
8	MISC	1,500	1,750	1,458	4,708
9					
10	Total				
11	Monthly Sales	13,761	14,101	14,222	42,084

8 In row 7, enter the following new details:

Cell A7, HOSIERY
Cell B7, 1256
Cell C7, 1045
Cell D7, 1145

Notice as you move from cell to cell entering the Monthly Hosiery figures, the Quarterly Sales figures in cell E7 and the monthly sales figures are being automatically updated with each move.

9 Save the changes to the worksheet

	E7		=	=SUM(B7:D7)	
	A	B	C	D	E
1	QUARTERLY SALES FOR AUTUMN 1999				
2					
3		October	November	December	Quarterly Sales
4	FOOTWEAR	3,980	3,285	4,120	11,385
5	CLOTHING	5,740	5,566	5,990	17,296
6	TOILETRIES	2,541	3,500	2,654	8,695
7	HOSIERY	1,256	1,045	1,145	3,446
8	MISC	1,500	1,750	1,458	4,708
9					
10	Total				
11	Monthly Sales	15,017	15,146	15,367	45,530

Inserting columns

We will now insert a column in the ECDL1 worksheet. The new column will be used to display an Average Sales figure and is to be located between the column for 'December' and the 'Quarterly Sales' figures.

When a new column is to be inserted the following should be considered and compensated for. Excel will insert a column in the area selected and all columns, including the highlighted column, located to the right of this position will be moved one column to the right.

The new column is to be inserted between the current columns D and E.

Basic steps

1 Right-click over the column E header

2 From the pop-up menu select Insert

❑ Excel will insert a new column E and move the original one to the right, becoming column F

Additional text and formula

Now that we have the new E column, enter '*Average Sales*' into E3. Complete all necessary formatting so that the new column title conforms to the others.

The formula that we are about to create will calculate the average monthly sales for the items in cells B4 to D4. This formula will be placed in cells E4 to E8.

3 Select cell E4 and type: '=AVERAGE(B4:D4)'

❑ Excel recognises the word AVERAGE and will perform the calculation,

(3980 + 3285 + 4120) / 3 = 3795.

4 Drag to copy the formula down to cell E11 – as you copy it to each cell Excel carries out the calculations and displays the results.

5 Highlight the cells E9 and E10

6 Clear the cell contents by pressing [Delete]

Summary

Inserting rows and columns is easy but do remember:

• Formulas are not carried over to the new column or row

• Some re-formatting will most likely be necessary

The completed worksheet should appear as shown.

	A	B	C	D	E	F
1	QUARTERLY SALES FOR AUTUMN 1999					
2						
3		October	November	December	Average Sales	Quarterly Sales
4	FOOTWEAR	3,980	3,285	4,120	3,795	11,385
5	CLOTHING	5,740	5,566	5,990	5,765	17,296
6	TOILETRIES	2,541	3,500	2,654	2,898	8,695
7	HOSIERY	1,256	1,045	1,145	1,149	3,446
8	MISC	1,500	1,750	1,458	1,569	4,708
9						
10	Total					
11	Monthly Sales	15,017	15,146	15,367	15,177	45,530

Reformatting currency cells

It was decided when we started the first worksheets that we would not display any decimal places in any of the currency cells of a value of less than one pound. In other words no pence would be shown. We will now re-format the worksheet to show any pence that may be included in the calculations.

We will also re-format column F, where appropriate, to display the currency pound (£) sign.

Basic steps

1 Ensure that *ECDL1* is open

2 Highlight the cells B4 to E11 by clicking in cell B4 and dragging down and across until all the cells are highlighted

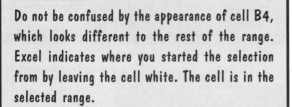

	A	B	C	D	E	F
1	QUARTERLY SALES FOR AUTUMN 1999					
2						
3		October	November	December	Average Sales	Quarterly Sales
4	Footwear	3,980	3,285	4,120	3,795	11,385
5	Clothing	5,740	5,566	5,990	5,765	17,296
6	Toiletries	2,541	3,500	2,654	2,898	8,695
7	Hosiery	1,256	1,045	1,145	1,149	3,446
8	Misc	1,500	1,750	1,458	1,569	4,708
9						
10	Total					
11	Monthly Sales	15,017	15,146	15,367	15,177	45,530

Take note

Do not be confused by the appearance of cell B4, which looks different to the rest of the range. Excel indicates where you started the selection from by leaving the cell white. The cell is in the selected range.

---

3 Release the mouse button

4 Right-click over the highlighted area

5 From the pop-up menu select Format Cells...

6 At the Format Cells dialog box select the Number tab

7 Click on *Currency* in the Category pane

8 The display will change to that shown – make the changes as listed

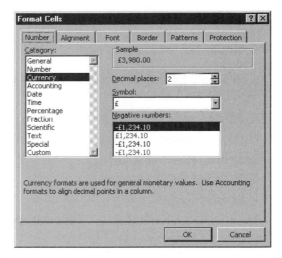

9 In the Decimal places slot select 2

10 Click the arrow in the Symbol slot and select the £ sign

11 Click OK for the changes to be implemented

It is possible that the formatting changes may result in one or more cells not displaying their content correctly as shown in this example.

	A	B	C	D	E	F
1	QUARTERLY SALES FOR AUTUMN 1999					
2						
3		October	November	December	Average Sales	Quarterly Sales
4	FOOTWEAR	£3,980.00	£3,285.00	£4,120.00	£3,795.00	11,385
5	CLOTHING	£5,740.00	£5,566.00	£5,990.00	£5,765.33	17,296
6	TOILETRIES	£2,541.00	£3,500.00	£2,654.00	£2,898.33	8,695
7	HOSIERY	£1,256.00	£1,045.00	£1,145.00	£1,148.67	3,446
8	MISC	£1,500.00	£1,750.00	£1,458.00	£1,569.33	4,708
9						
10	Total					
11	Monthly Sales	£15,017.00	£15,146.00	########	£15,176.67	45,530

The problem here was caused by the cell contents occupying a greater space than was available in the cell display area. The content is not lost, simply not displayed correctly. This can be easily overcome by simply adjusting the cell width.

You should now see that having adjusted the format to display two decimal places, the 'Average Sales' column is now actually displaying decimal values where appropriate.

Further formatting

We will now practice the same procedure but on his occasion we shall select one column.

Basic steps

1 Click in cell F4 and drag down to cell F11 to highlight the block

2 Right-click over the highlighted cells

3 From the pop-up menu select Format Cells…

4 Select Number and Currency

5 Perform the same formatting changes as outlined previously

❑ The final layout and display of the worksheet should be as shown here

	A	B	C	D	E	F
1	QUARTERLY SALES FOR AUTUMN 1999					
2						
3		October	November	December	Average Sales	Quarterly Sales
4	FOOTWEAR	£3,980.00	£3,285.00	£4,120.00	£3,795.00	£11,385.00
5	CLOTHING	£5,740.00	£5,566.00	£5,990.00	£5,765.33	£17,296.00
6	TOILETRIES	£2,541.00	£3,500.00	£2,654.00	£2,898.33	£8,695.00
7	HOSIERY	£1,256.00	£1,045.00	£1,145.00	£1,148.67	£3,446.00
8	MISC	£1,500.00	£1,750.00	£1,458.00	£1,569.33	£4,708.00
9						
10	Total					
11	Monthly Sales	£15,017.00	£15,146.00	£15,367.00	£15,176.67	£45,530.00

6 Save the changes to the worksheet

Sorting data

There will be occasions where you may wish to present the data in a worksheet in a different order, for instance you may wish to display the worksheet *ECDL1 Monthly Sales* in ascending order, by commodity. This is a sort of text and data combined, with the emphasis placed upon the simple requirement of displaying the result in ascending order.

Excel can perform more complex sorts and the method of applying the sort action is different in each case. We will carry out a simple sort first, using the **Sort** icons on the Standard toolbar. Before we start you should be aware of how Excel performs the action.

Default sort orders

Excel uses specific sort orders to arrange data according to the value, not the format, of the data.

When you sort text, Excel sorts left to right, character by character. For example, if a cell contains the text 'A100', the cell will place that after a cell that contains the entry 'A1' and before a cell that contains the entry 'A11'.

In an ascending sort, Excel uses the following order.

♦ Numbers are sorted from the smallest negative number to the largest positive number

♦ Text, and text that includes digits are sorted in the following order:

0 1 2 3 4 5 6 7 8 9 ' - (space) ! " # $ % & ( ) * , . / : ; ? @ [\ ] ^ _ ` { | } ~ + < = > A B C D E F G H I J K L M N O P Q R S T U V W X Y Z

♦ In logical values, FALSE is sorted before TRUE

♦ All error values are equal

♦ Blanks are always sorted last

In a *descending* sort, this sort order is reversed except for blank cells, which are always sorted last.

For further information, use the online Help.

Sorting data using sort icons

Basic steps

To make these changes to the worksheet:

1 Click in cell A4 and drag down to cell D8

2 Release the mouse button

3 Locate these icons on the Standard toolbar

Ascending ➡ [A↓ Z↓ / Z↓ A↓] ← Descending

4 Click the Sort Ascending button – the highlighted area will rearranged to display the data as shown in the example.

	A	B	C	D	E	F
1	QUARTERLY SALES FOR AUTUMN 1999					
2						
3		October	November	December	Average Sales	Quarterly Sales
4	Footwear	£3,980.00	£3,285.00	£4,120.00	£3,795.00	£11,385.00
5	Clothing	£5,740.00	£5,566.00	£5,990.00	£5,765.33	£17,296.00
6	Toiletries	£2,541.00	£3,500.00	£2,654.00	£2,898.33	£8,695.00
7	Hosiery	£1,256.00	£1,045.00	£1,145.00	£1,148.67	£3,446.00
8	Misc	£1,500.00	£1,750.00	£1,458.00	£1,569.33	£4,708.00
9						
10	Total					
11	Monthly Sales	£15,017.00	£15,146.00	£15,367.00	£15,176.67	£45,530.00

All the corresponding cells will automatically recalculate their respective values in relation to the changes brought about by the Sort action.

5 Click in a blank cell to remove the highlight

This was an alphabetical sort based upon the commodity names and not their values.

6 Save the changes to the worksheet

Complex sorts

We are now going to carry out a Sort that will change the order of the values, based on the month columns, to ascending order. This will then display each commodity by value, rather than in alphabetical order. This is a Numeric Sort, whereas the previous one was an Alphabetical Sort.

Basic steps

Still using the ECDL1 workbook:

1 Select the cell range A4 to D8

❑ This cell range is shown here and we will compare it on completion of the Sort action.

3		October	November	Decemeber
4	CLOTHING	£5,740.00	£5,566.00	£5,990.00
5	FOOTWEAR	£3,980.00	£3,285.00	£4,120.00
6	HOSIERY	£1,256.00	£1,045.00	£1,145.00
7	MISC	£1,500.00	£1,750.00	£1,458.00
8	TOILETRIES	£2,541.00	£3,500.00	£2,654.00

2 From the Menu bar select Data > Sort. The Sort dialog box will open. Investigate the drop-down arrows, which will open lists based on the current worksheet. Do not click on OK yet.

3 Copy the settings shown in the example

4 Leave the last Then by option empty

5 Click OK for the Sort action to be carried out

Shown here is the result of the Sort. Compare this result to that shown before the Sort action was applied.

3		October	November	December
4	HOSIERY	£1,256.00	£1,045.00	£1,145.00
5	MISC	£1,500.00	£1,750.00	£1,458.00
6	TOILETRIES	£2,541.00	£3,500.00	£2,654.00
7	FOOTWEAR	£3,980.00	£3,285.00	£4,120.00
8	CLOTHING	£5,740.00	£5,566.00	£5,990.00

The Sort shown here was performed on the numeric values while retaining the commodity identity for each value. If you had selected the range B4 to D8 and then performed a Sort using the toolbar icons, values would have been rearranged but would have not kept the commodity names with the correct numeric values and therefore the result would be wrong.

6 Save the changes to the worksheet

Copy and paste between workbooks

There may come a time when you require a row or column that appears in one worksheet to appear in other workbooks.

It would be tedious to re-type all the detail a second time to insert it into another workbook. There is however a quick way of inserting the information and this is by using the 'Copy and Paste' features found in Excel.

For this exercise we are going to copy a row and a column.

Basic steps

1 Open both *ECDL1* and *ECDL2* workbooks and make *ECDL1* active, i.e. the one that you can see and use – to confirm this, check the Excel title bar at the top of the screen. The active workbook name will appear as shown.

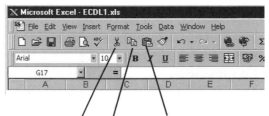

The Cut, Copy and Paste icons are on the Standard toolbar.

Alternatively, open the **Window** menu. In its lower section there are the file names of the currently open workbooks. The file name with the tick (✓) along side it indicates that it is the active workbook – the one currently in use.

We are going to copy the *Hosiery* row and the *Average Sales* column from the workbook *ECDL1.xls* to *ECDL2.xls*.

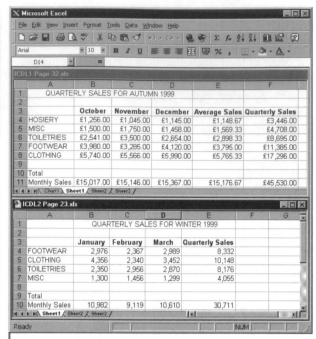

Take note

You may recall that in Chapter 2 we learnt that we could display two windows, or more if required, in the application window. In this case because the two workbooks are quite small, we could easily show them simultaneously and this will make the next action easier.

At present both workbooks, *ECDL1* and *ECDL2* are open. You may have to experiment at this stage because we are unsure how your application and workbook windows are configured.

The aim is to have your workbook window Control buttons displayed as shown here. At this setting, the workbook window will display its borders and it is these that we are about to adjust.

If the workbook Control buttons are displayed as shown here, click the centre button to change the window display to that as described above.

Adjust each of the workbook windows in turn, by placing the cursor over the lower right corner of the workbook border. When it changes to a double-headed arrow, left-click, hold and drag the border up to about half way. Release the mouse button and repeat the action on the other workbook, except this time, work from the top of the workbook and drag it down.

Shown in the example is what we wish to achieve. Ensure that *ECDL1* is the top workbook.

Pasting a row

Before we start copying data from one workbook to another, we will first synchronise the workbooks so that the commodities appear in the same rows. This will reduce the likelihood of any errors.

Basic steps

1   Ensure that *ECDL2* is the active workbook
2   Select the range A4 to D7
3   From the menu bar select Data > Sort
4   When the dialog box opens copy the settings shown in the example
5   Click OK to perform the sort

3		January	February	March	Quarterly Sales
4	MISC	1,300	1,456	1,299	4,055
5	TOILETRIES	2,350	2,956	2,870	8,176
6	FOOTWEAR	2,976	2,367	2,989	8,332
7	CLOTHING	4,356	2,340	3,452	10,148
8					
9	Total				
10	Monthly Sales	10,982	9,119	10,610	30,711

6 Re-select workbook *ECDL1* and select row 4, '*Hosiery*'. Copy it using either the right-click Copy option or by selecting Edit > Copy

7 Change to workbook *ECDL2* and right-click over row 4

8 From the pop-up menu select Insert Copied Cells

❑ Copying the row from one workbook to the other has resulted in our worksheet displaying various figures in the wrong columns and this must be corrected before we proceed

9 Click in cell E4 and press [Delete] to remove the cell contents

10 Click in cell F4, then move the cursor to the lower area of the cell

❑ The new row 4 has carried over the details of row 4 in *ECDL1*. This includes the *Average Sales* figures, which appears in the wrong cell, E4. The *Quarterly Sales* figure for *Hosiery* is now in cell F4. Column F is not currently used in this worksheet.

11 When the cursor changes shape to an arrow, click and drag it across into the empty cell E4

12 Release the button and the data will be transferred into E4

Copying columns

When we created the workbook *ECDL2* we placed the worksheet title, '*Quarterly Sales for Winter 1999*' in cell B1. Whereas when we created the workbook *ECDL1* the worksheet title was placed in cell A1.

The reason for changing the location was to highlight a problem often encountered when copying between workbooks and/or worksheets. If you encounter a problem when attempting to copy columns, re-check the overall layout of the worksheets and you will often find that there is a difference in the general layout of such items as titles etc.

The difference in the location of the header is the problem. We cannot insert a new column because of it, but we can overcome it quite simply.

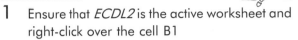

Basic steps

1 Ensure that *ECDL2* is the active worksheet and right-click over the cell B1

2 From the pop-up menu select Cut

3 Move the cursor down to an area below the data and select an empty cell, e.g. A20

4 Right-click over it and from the pop-up menu select Paste – the title will be moved to the new location

We can now start copying a column from one workbook to another

5 Make *ECDL1* active and click on the column E header to select the column

6 Copy column E

7 Switch workbooks so that you are working in *ECDL2* and right-click over the column E header and select Insert Copied Cells…

The original column E will now move to the right and become column F, while the *Average Sales* figures column will now become column E.

We now want to move the title back up to the top of the worksheet, above the data.

8 Right-click over it and select Cut

9 Right-click over cell A1 and select Paste

That completes the copying of rows and columns.

Inconsistency in formatting

There will now be some inconsistency in the overall formatting and appearance of the *ECDL2* worksheet. Reformat as required for an overall consistency and in line with that of the workbook *ECDL1* and save the changes to the worksheet, then close it.

Creating and saving charts

A picture paints a thousand words and it is certainly true that you can often see and understand more from a picture than a description.

Facts and figures are often hard to absorb and understand, but Excel can greatly assist in their presentation through the use of charts and graphs.

You can use charts to make it easier to spot trends, highlight important changes and compare individual figures. Using charts in reports and presentations will display numerical data to your audience in a format that is easy to see and understand.

When you create a chart, each row or column of data on the worksheet makes up a *data series*. Each individual value within a series is called a *data point*.

The chart range can include row and column headings, which are used as category labels and legend text. If the range does not include headings, Excel creates default headings.

In Excel you can either embed a chart in your current worksheet, or create it on a separate chart sheet.

An **embedded chart** is a chart *object* in the worksheet. When you want the chart and the worksheet data viewed or printed together, you should use an embedded chart.

A **chart sheet** is a separate worksheet in the workbook that contains only the chart. If you want to use the chart by itself (for example, in a presentation) you should use a chart sheet.

Both kinds of chart are linked to the worksheet data and updated automatically if the data is changed.

The Chart Wizard

The Chart Wizard assists you in creating a chart by leading you through a series of dialog boxes that allow you to choose different options for the chart. You can quickly learn the essentials of creating a chart using the Chart Wizard. For example, if you have never created a chart to demonstrate monthly sales, the Chart Wizard will guide you through the process, step by step.

As you progress, the terminology used above and what it means, will soon become more apparent. The aim is to introduce you to the charts and how they are constructed, using a Wizard. You can return to each chart in time, to experiment and make changes so that you develop a greater understanding of them.

Pie charts

We are now going to create a pie chart.

Pie charts can only show one data series, either one row or one column. They cannot show multiple rows and multiple columns of data.

Basic steps

❑ We only need one workbook for this exercise.

1 Open *ECDL1* and ensure that the window is maximized

2 Select the range A3 to B8 – this is the data, which will be used to create the chart

		October
4	HOSIERY	£1,256.00
5	MISC	£1,500.00
6	TOILETRIES	£2,541.00
7	FOOTWEAR	£3,980.00
8	CLOTHING	£5,740.00

3 Click the Chart Wizard icon [img] on the Standard toolbar

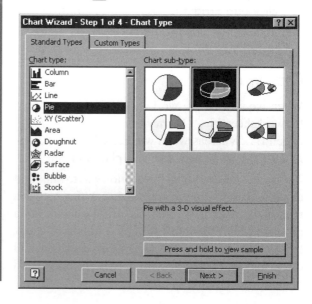

- ❏ The Chart Wizard will now open as shown
- 4 Select *Pie* in the Chart type pane
- 5 In the Chart sub-type select the 3D version

Tip

You can preview what the data will look like by clicking and holding down on the preview button.

---

6 Click Next – at this stage you are offered a number of options

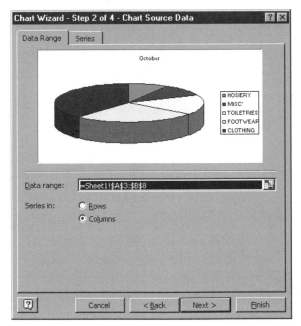

7 Accept the default setting, with a legend box to the right of the chart and click Next

- ❏ The next window to open will let you create Titles, Legends and Data Labels for the chart.

Take note

An explanation of the $ symbol is covered on page 181. Ignore it for now. Experiment with the settings, but return them to those shown in the example.

---

8 Ensure that the Title tab is selected. Highlight whatever text may appear in the chart title slot, and type '*October Sales 1999*'

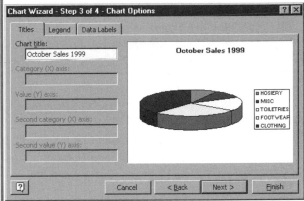

9 Select the Legend tab. This offers you the option of having a legend and a choice of legend positions. Copy the selections shown.

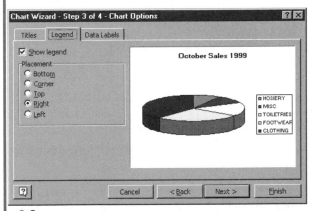

10 Click on the Data Labels tab and select Show Percentage then click Next

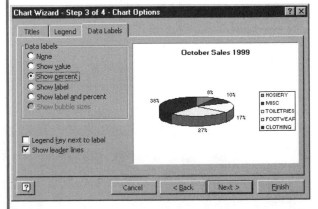

11 You will be offered two options as to where the chart should reside. Select As new sheet and click Finish

The chart will now appear on its own sheet and will have been allocated a default name of '*Chart1*'.

Close the *ECDL1* workbook and save any changes if prompted.

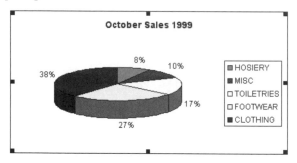

Creating a second chart

We will now create a second chart, this time using the *ECDL2* workbook.

Basic steps

1 Click in cell A3 and drag down and across to cell D8 to highlight this area of data

2 Hold down the Control (Ctrl) key and click on cell F3 and drag it down to cell F8

☐ This will select the data within this range while retaining the previously highlighted data

3 Release the mouse button

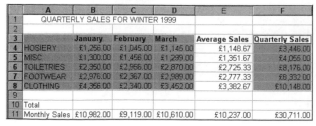

---

4 Click on the Chart Wizard icon

5 At Step 1, on the Standard Types tab, from the Chart Type pane select *Column*

6 From the Chart sub-type pane click on the first image on the second row then click Next

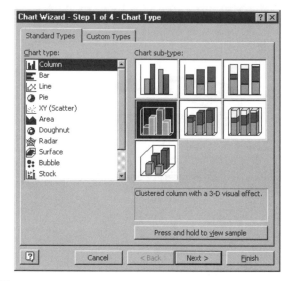

7 At Step 2, ensure that the Data Range tab is selected

8 Click the Columns option and see how the chart is displayed

9 Click the Rows option and note the difference in the way the chart is displayed. Retain this selection and click Next

10 At Step 3, ensure that the Titles tab is selected and type '*Quarterly Sales Winter 1999*' in the Chart title slot

11 Click on the Legend tab, ensuring that the Show Legend box has a tick in it

12 In the Placement area select *Right*

13 On the Data Labels tab, select *None* and click Next to move on

14 At Step 4, Chart Location, select As object in – the adjacent slot should indicate *Sheet 1*

15 Click Finish

❑ The Chart Wizard will close and the chart will appear on the current sheet

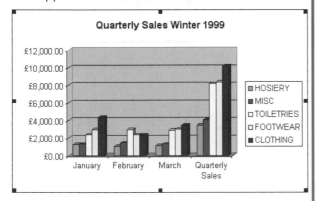

Changing the axis scale

An axis is a line on the side or bottom of the plot area, providing a frame of reference for measurement or comparison in a chart. Normally, data values are plotted along the vertical *y* axis, and categories are plotted along the horizontal *x* axis.

Check out the completed chart, in particular the y axis, which shows the sales values. The value starts at £00.00 and increases in £2000 increments, up to £12,000. You may want the values displayed differently, colour applied to font, etc.

Basic steps

To make a change to any axis:

1 Right-click over it

2 From the pop-up menu select Format Axis

3 At the Format Axis dialog box, ensure that the Scale tab is selected

❑ Note the word Auto. Below it are a number of tick (✓) boxes. If ticked, their values are automatically assigned, subject to the values in the worksheet. The absence of a tick signifies that the value has been set manually.

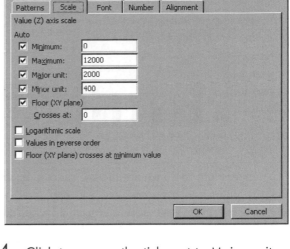

4 Click to remove the tick next to Major unit

5 Type in '1000' then click OK to observe the change to the chart

6 Follow the same procedure and change it back to '2000'

Other options

Check each area of the axis dialog box and experiment changing the scale, such as **Values in reverse order** to observe the effect. Also investigate the other options including font, alignment, etc.

Check the same on the categories axis and other areas of the chart, such as the title, text box and so on.

Once a chart has been created, it is not set in stone as the last exercise has just proven. You can return to the chart time and again and change various aspects of it. Keep this in mind, as it could save you a great deal of time in the future.

Moving a chart

You may find that having inserted the chart, it was not placed where you want it and it may even be hiding or covering some of the data.

When the chart appears on the worksheet it should already be selected. You can confirm this by the presence of a dark outline surrounding the chart with small squares, known as *handles*, at intervals in the rectangle.

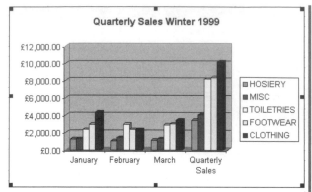

Quarterly Sales Winter 1999

The squares and the lines around the chart indicate that the chart has been selected and can now be moved around the worksheet or resized as required.

Basic steps

To move the chart:

1 Ensure it is selected

2 Move the cursor up to the chart rectangle until it changes its shape to that of a single arrow

3 Click and drag in the direction that you want the chart to go, in this instance move it below the data. The cursor will change to ✛

4 When the chart is in the correct location, release the button and save the changes

To resize a chart

It is possible to either increase or decrease a chart's size.

Basic steps

Save the changes to the worksheet and then:

1 Select the chart by clicking over an area of the chart that has no detail in it

❑ The outline rectangle and handles, will appear

2 Slowly pass the cursor over the handle at the lower right-hand corner of the chart. The cursor will change its shape to ↘

3 Click and slowly drag it to the upper left corner

❑ Save the worksheet and then experiment moving and sizing the chart

Also experiment by selecting the components that comprise the chart. For instance right-click over the **Legend** of the chart and a pop-up menu will appear from which you may format the Legend.

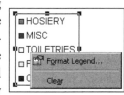

Save the changes and keep the workbook open for the next section, which covers printing worksheets and charts.

Summary

Charts can produce very good displays and visually impart information extremely effectively. However, overloading the chart can defeat the objective of imparting information. You should experiment using all aspects of the chart feature to learn which chart best suits the task and information for the occasion.

Printing worksheets

Headers and Footers

Before printing the worksheet and chart we will first create a Header and Footer for it. Headers print at the top and Footers print at the bottom of every page in a printout and they contain descriptive text such as title and page numbers.

Basic steps

To insert headers and footers:

1 Open *ECDL2.xls*
2 From the menu bar select File > Page Setup
3 At the dialog box, click on the Header/Footer tab

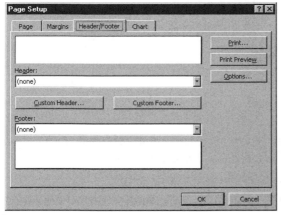

4 Select Custom Header...

❑ The dialog box shown will open

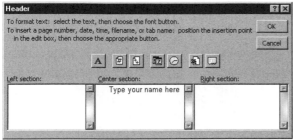

5 Place the cursor in the Center pane and type in your name
6 Click OK to close the Header dialog box

7 Click on the drop-down arrow of the Footer pane
8 Select *Page 1* from the drop-down list
9 Click the Print Preview button to check the layout

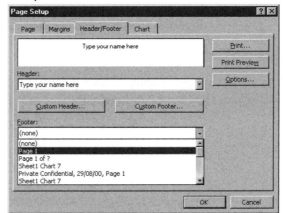

Print preview

You will be presented with an outline of the worksheet, complete with the chart, for you to determine if the layout is satisfactory and that the page contains all the required elements.

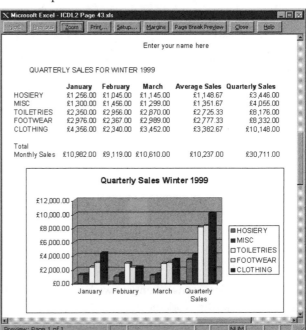

Check that the layout is similar to the example shown. If you are presented with the chart without any data, you most likely have the chart selected in the worksheet. Exit Print Preview and you will be returned to the worksheet. Deselect the chart and click on the Print Preview icon again.

Should the preview document appear small, click the **Zoom** button and the view size will increase. Clicking Zoom once more will reduce the view size.

Close the Print Preview window, as we are now ready to print the worksheet and save the changes.

Changing the page layout

Because workbooks usually contain many columns of data, most are printed in Landscape.

Basic steps

1   From the menu bar select File > Page Setup
2   At the dialog box, ensure that the Page tab is selected
3   In the Orientation section select Landscape

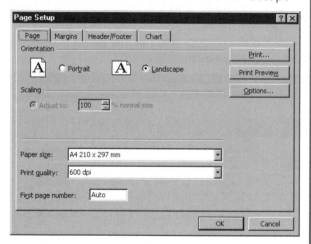

4   If you want to preview the layout, click the Print Preview button
5   Click OK

Printing selected areas

There may be occasions when you wish to print only a selected area of a worksheet.

Basic steps

Method 1

1   Ensure that *ECDL1* is open at *Sheet 1*
❑   You may have given this sheet another name when carrying out an earlier exercise
2   Select the range A3 to D8
3   Select File > Print Area > Set Print Area

Page Setup...		
Print Area	▶	Set Print Area
Print Preview		Clear Print Area
Print... Ctrl+P		

❑   Excel will now place a dashed line around the range A3 to D8 indicating that it is the content which will be printed

3		October	November	December
4	HOSIERY	£1,256.00	£1,045.00	£1,145.00
5	MISC	£1,500.00	£1,750.00	£1,458.00
6	TOILETRIES	£2,541.00	£3,500.00	£2,654.00
7	FOOTWEAR	£3,980.00	£3,285.00	£4,120.00
8	CLOTHING	£5,740.00	£5,566.00	£5,990.00

❑   You may wish to Preview the document to confirm the selection fits the page
4   Select Print from the File menu or click the Printer icon on the Standard toolbar
❑   You will notice that the selected area still has the dashed line around it

To clear the line it is necessary to:
5   Select File > Print Area > Clear Print Area

Method 2

1   Ensure that *ECDL1* is open at *Sheet 1*
2   Select the range A3 to D8
3   Select File > Print
4   At the Print dialog box, in the Print what section click the Selection button

❑   You can, at this stage Preview the print task
5   Click OK to print the selection

- The selected area in the worksheet is still highlighted. To remove the highlight:

6 Click on any blank cell of the spreadsheet

This option is a much quicker method to use.

Adjusting the margins

There will be occasions when it will be necessary to adjust the pre-set margins. This may be necessary to create a uniform margin around the printed document or because a small amount of text/data was missed off the document printout.

Basic steps

1 Select File > Page Setup
2 At the Page Setup dialog box, ensure that the Margins tab is selected

- The values in the example are set to centimetres. Experiment adjusting the margins

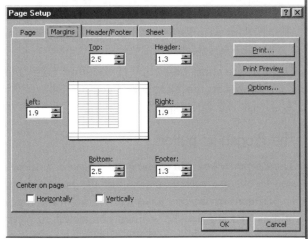

- Before clicking OK to accept the changes, investigate the Center on page options. Note that as each is selected the image changes to reflect the option chosen

The **Center on page** option will often create a more acceptable document layout and presentation without too much effort. Experiment with the available options and print one or two copies of the worksheet using both of the options available.

An alternative method

1 Select File > Print Preview
2 Ensure that you can see the complete document on the screen, If not, use the Zoom control to adjust the view.
3 From the Print Preview menu bar select Margins

- The margins will be displayed on the screen, including the Header and Footer areas, and any text in them

4 Move the cursor over any of the margins and it will change shape.

- Over the top or bottom margins it will be $\updownarrow$
- Over the left or right margins it will be $\leftrightarrow$

5 Click and drag it left or right, or up or down, as appropriate – Excel will not allow you to drag the margins off the page completely

6 When the desired or maximum movement position is reached release the button

Reducing the worksheet to fit one page

If making adjustments to the margins does not have the desired effect, then you have the option of reducing the overall document size.

Quite often you may find that the worksheet, or the selected area, will not quite fit onto one page when printing. Excel provides a means of overcoming this problem. However, because our worksheets are currently small in size, we must first create a situation to test this feature.

Basic steps

1 Ensure that *ECDL2* worksheet is open and *Sheet 1* is displayed

- If necessary resize the chart to occupy 5 columns wide and 16 rows deep

2 Move the chart so that the upper left corner is located in the cell H1
3 Click on a blank area of the worksheet
4 Select Print Preview

179

- ❏ You should now find that only part of the chart is visible
5 Select Setup from the Print Preview menu
- ❏ A dialog box will open

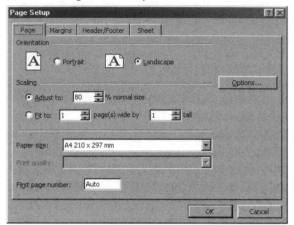

6 Ensure that the Page tab is selected and that the Orientation is set to *Landscape*

7 In the area entitled Scaling, ensure that the Adjust to option is selected

8 Click on the down arrow to the right of Scaling to reduce the size of the print area to 80%

9 Click OK

You are now returned to the Print Preview window and as a result of the adjustment, the whole chart should now appear in the preview.

10 Click the Print button on the Print Preview menu bar

11 At the Print dialog box, click OK to print the worksheet

Experiment with this feature by changing the scale and then print the worksheet after each adjustment and compare the results.

Printing a worksheet

Basic steps

1 Ensure that *ECDL2.xls* is open
2 From the menu bar select File > Print
3 The Print dialog box will open and it is from here that you select your print requirements

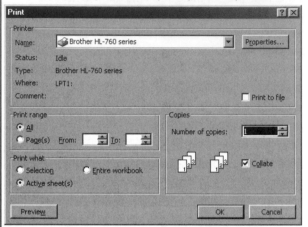

4 In Print what, ensure that the Active sheet(s) option is selected

5 If more than one copy is required enter the number in the Number of copies slot

6 Click OK to print the worksheet

The Properties button

The Properties button in the Print dialog box allows you to change various aspects of the print output. Experiment in due course to learn more of the capabilities relating to the printer connected to your computer.

Save the changes and close the workbook.

Relative and absolute references

Relative references

When you create a formula, references to cells or ranges used in the formula are usually based on their position relative to the cell that contains the formula. For instance, if cell E4 contains the formula '=B4', Excel finds the value three cells to the left of E4 which is cell B4. This is *relative referencing*.

	A	B	C	D	E
1					
2					
3		October	November	December	1/4 Sales
4	CLOTHING	£5,740.00	£5,566.00	£5,990.00	=B4
5	FOOTWEAR	£3,980.00	£3,285.00	£4,120.00	
6	HOSIERY	£2,541.00	£3,500.00	£2,654.00	
7	MICS	£1,500.00	£1,750.00	£1,458.00	
8	TOILETRIES	£1,256.00	£1,045.00	£1,145.00	

When you copy a formula that uses relative references, the references in the pasted formula update and refer to the different cells. In the example, the formula in cell E4 has been copied to cell E5. The formula in cell E5 has changed to '=B5', this refers to the cell that is three cells to the left of E5.

	A	B	C	D	E
1					
2					
3		October	November	December	1/4 Sales
4	CLOTHING	£5,740.00	£5,566.00	£5,990.00	=B4
5	FOOTWEAR	£3,980.00	£3,285.00	£4,120.00	=B5
6	HOSIERY	£2,541.00	£3,500.00	£2,654.00	
7	MICS	£1,500.00	£1,750.00	£1,458.00	
8	TOILETRIES	£1,256.00	£1,045.00	£1,145.00	

If you move the formula, the cell references change relative to where the formula is moved to.

Using this method, where practical, Excel will create the Relative References automatically for you.

Absolute references

Absolute references do not change when used in formulas. The reference cell remains fixed because the particular value in the reference cell does not change when applied to other values. Two examples of the use of an absolute reference are:

*   Fluctuating currency exchange rates, where the current rate changes after a period of time. When

the exchange rate is changed only the one figure, the absolute reference, has to be changed to reflect the overall change in the rate.

*   Commission, usually awarded at a fixed rate for a given period of time. If the basic salary is increased, the commission percentage will usually remain the same, which is the absolute reference.

When entering an absolute reference in a cell the '$' sign is used to instruct Excel that this is an absolute reference and therefore is fixed, i.e. 'A15'.

So far within the course you have used relative references with one exception which was when you created the charts. When we selected the range A3 to D8, Excel converted the range to an absolute reference. Excel will also automatically convert a named range (see page 171) to an absolute reference. It is important to remember this when working with named cells and ranges.

Creating an absolute reference

We are going to create an absolute reference based on our worksheet 'ECDL1'.

The scenario is that it is company policy that each branch manager will receive a 2.5% commission based on the overall monthly sales figures.

Basic steps

1 Open the *ECDL1* and ensure that *Sheet 1* (or if you renamed it, *Autumn 1999*) is selected

2 In cell A13 type 'Managers'

3 In cell A14 type 'Commission'

4 In cell A15 type '2.5'

5 In cell B14 and enter the formula '=B11/100 * A15'

An explanation of this formula follows:

♦ Cell B11 is the monthly sales figures for October on which the commission of 2.5% is to be based

♦ The B11 figure £15,017.00 is divided by 100 to determine what 1% is, in this instance £150.17p

♦ The commission rate is 2.5% stored in cell A15. Therefore multiplying the value £150.17 by that figure, we arrive at the commission of £375.43.

You should now have the figure £375.43 in cell B14. However if you have the sum £375.*425*, don't worry. This is due to the cell formatting which we are about to change.

6 Use the AutoFill method to carry the formula over into cells C14 and D14

7 Perform any formatting necessary, i.e. format cells to display the '£' sign and two decimal places

❑ Excel has rounded the pence upward from .425 to .43 in cell B14.

Take note

An absolute reference is a cell reference that does not change when copied to a new location. A relative reference is a cell reference that is adjusted when the formula is copied to other cells.

In certain circumstances you can use a mixed reference in a formula. This subject is outside the scope of this course and you should investigate mixed references using online Help.

	B14	▼	=	=B11/100*A15	
	A	B	C	D	E	F
1	QUARTERLY SALES FOR AUTUMN 1999					
2						
3		October	November	December	Average Sales	Quarterly Sales
4	HOSIERY	£1,256.00	£1,045.00	£1,145.00	£1,148.67	£3,446.00
5	MISC	£1,500.00	£1,750.00	£1,458.00	£1,569.33	£4,708.00
6	TOILETRIES	£2,541.00	£3,500.00	£2,654.00	£2,898.33	£8,695.00
7	FOOTWEAR	£3,980.00	£3,285.00	£4,120.00	£3,795.00	£11,385.00
8	CLOTHING	£5,740.00	£5,566.00	£5,990.00	£5,765.33	£17,296.00
9						
10	Total					
11	Monthly Sales	£15,017.00	£15,146.00	£15,367.00	£15,176.67	£45,530.00
12						
13	Managers					
14	Commission	£375.43	£378.65	£384.18		
15		2.5				

Named cells and ranges

So far you have used cell addresses, i.e. A15, C15, etc., to refer to cells. There is another and sometimes more convenient method of referencing cell and ranges of cells. This method is known as *Naming*.

Excel allows the use of named cells or ranges in formulas. Named cells and ranges can be moved, copied or entered, just as ordinary references.

Using the absolute referencing that you have just created, you could give it a name, such as *Commission* and use that reference in other worksheets.

When an adjustment in the commission rate is required, the adjustment only has to be made at the one location, in this instance in the workbook *ECDL1*, *Sheet 1*, cell reference A15. The adjustment will automatically update all referenced worksheets.

There is however a minor problem. Previous months' commission, which will have already been paid at the previous rate will be amended by the change and show an incorrect figure. There are methods of dealing with this situation, however this topic is not discussed within this course but is discussed in the online Help.

We have talked about naming cells or ranges of cells, so how do we do it? We will use the absolute reference recently created in the *ECDL1* workbook.

Basic steps

1 Ensure that the workbook *ECDL1* is open and that you are at *Sheet 1* or *Autumn 1999*

2 Select cell A15

3 Click in the Name slot on the Formula toolbar – this will already have the cell reference A15

4 The cell reference will be highlighted ready for you to overtype the existing name, in this instance 'A15'

5 Type in a name, in this instance *Commission* and press [Enter]

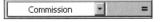

❑ If you have several names in a workbook you may not recall them all. If this is the case:

6 Select Insert > Name > Paste

7 When the dialog box opens click on the name

We will now create a new calculation based on the absolute reference name and the Total Monthly Sales figure in cell F11.

8 Select cell A17 and type 'Manager's'

9 Select cell A18 and type 'Quarterly'

10 Select cell A19 and type 'Commission'

11 Select cell B19 and type the formula '=F11/100*Commission' and press [Enter]

You should have the result £1,138.25. You may have to format the cells as previously to display the result as shown.

Excel recognised what the name *Commission* was and the absolute reference was used in the formula to perform the calculation.

12 Save the changes and close *ECDL1*

Putting it all together

We are now going to create a third workbook, using the data from the existing workbooks, with the aim of practising what we have already learnt and introducing a number of new procedures and functions.

Open a new workbook and save it as *ECDL3*.

Copy and paste between workbooks

Basic steps

1 Open *ECDL1* and rearrange the display so that you can view both *ECDL1* and *ECDL3*

2 From *ECDL1* select the cells A3 to D11 only

3 Copy the cells. The Copy action will be confirmed by the presence of the dashed border around the selected cells

4 Switch to the new workbook *ECDL3*

5 Click in cell A3 then click the Paste icon to insert the data from *ECDL1* into *ECDL3*

6 Perform any formatting adjustments as required, such as the column widths, etc.

❑ Check the cells 'B11' to 'D11' and you will see that the formulas for these cells have been carried over to the new worksheet.

7 Close *ECDL1* and open *ECDL2* and readjust the screen display so that you can see both workbooks

Before we start, we must ensure that both of the workbooks are synchronised and are displaying the data in the same sequence, otherwise we could insert data in the wrong location and sequence.

Each workbook should be displaying the commodities in the following order:

A4	Hosiery
A5	Misc
A6	Toiletries
A7	Footwear
A8	Clothing

If your workbooks are different perform a 'Sort' as described earlier.

8 From *ECDL2* select the cells B3 to D11 only and copy them

9 Switch to *ECDL3*

10 Click in cell E3 and Paste the contents from *ECDL2*

11 Close *ECDL2* and maximize the *ECDL3* window

❑ Do not make any changes to the formatting

Uniform cell sizing

Instead of setting each cell width individually we can set the width for all cells in one action.

Basic steps

1 Select all the cells in the range B3 to G11

2 Select Format > Column > Width

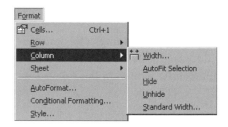

❑ The Column Width dialog box will open. The current value will be highlighted:

3 Type '12'

4 Click OK

❑ All the columns will now expand and have uniform width

Inserting column headings

Basic steps

We are now going to insert three additional column headings:

1. In cell H3 type 'Half Yearly'
2. In cell I3 type 'Average'
3. In cell J3 type 'Percentage'

Format new cells

Basic steps

1. Adjust the cell range H3 to J11 to a column width of 12 as described previously
2. Select the range H3 to J3
3. Embolden the column titles
4. Select the range B3 to J3
5. Centre the text by clicking on the Center icon on the Formatting toolbar
6. In cell C2 type 'Autumn'
7. In cell F2 type 'Winter'

Tip

Notice the justification for these two cells is set to Left Align. Remember that numbers are automatically set to Right Align, the default setting.

Selecting non-adjacent cells

Basic steps

To select the two cells C2 and F2:

1. Left-click in the cell C2
2. Hold down [Control] and click in the cell F2
3. Release [Control] and mouse button

If you find that the cells C2 and F2 have not been selected, this is probably due to the wrong key being selected, possibly [Shift]. If this did occur, click on any blank area of the worksheet to deselect the highlighted range and try again.

4. Click the Center icon and the Bold icon
❑ We will now add a title to the worksheet but before we type it in we will format the cell.
5. Right-click over cell D1, and from the pop-up menu select Format Cells…
6. On the Font tab select Bold, size 12, and change the colour to *Red*
7. Click OK
8. In cell D1, type '*Autumn/Winter Sales 1998/ 99*' and press [Enter]

Take note

The cell immediately picks up the formatting changes as you type in the text. Preformatting can often be quicker than typing in the text, then having to select it all and then make the changes. Whichever method used is a matter of personal preference.

❑ The title appearance is untidy, so we will merge and centre it:
9. Select the cells D1 to F1 and click on the Merge and Centre icon on the Formatting toolbar
10. Save the changes

Entering the formulas

We are now going to enter the required formulas in the new cells and we will be using the AutoFill feature to carry the formulas over to other cells as necessary.

The half yearly total

The first formula is to calculate the monthly sales for each commodity and have the results appear in column H as appropriate.

Basic steps

1　Select cell H4
2　Type '=sum(B4:G4)' and press [Enter]
3　Select cell H4 and place cursor over the lower right corner
4　Click and drag down to, and include, cell H11
5　Release the mouse button and the formula will be carried over to these cells
6　Select the two cells H9 and H10 and delete the contents

Using the average function

We are going to calculate the average for a group of sales figures.

Basic steps

1　Select cell I4
2　Enter the formula required to calculate the Average figures: '=AVERAGE(B4:G4)'
❑　If you select the range, rather than type the reference, be careful not to include the half yearly totals
3　Use the AutoFill method to carry over the formulas down to, and including, I11
4　Select cell I9 and I10 and delete the contents
❑　Carry out any formatting if necessary

Take note

Do not, at this stage, be concerned by the error message that appeared in these two cells. Error messages are dealt with later in the course.

The percentage figure

We are now going to create a formula to display the half yearly sales figures of each commodity as a percentage of the overall half yearly total (cell H11).

Before we enter any formulas, it is necessary to understand how Excel handles percentages and how this will affect the entering of formulas. Excel takes any value that appears in a cell that is preformatted to display the contents as a percentage and then multiplies that value by 100. We will use the workbook *ECDL3* as the example.

Basic steps

1　Select any blank cell, without any formatting applied
2　Enter the formula '=H4/H11*100'

The result should be 9.039755512 and if you then format the cell as a percentage, to display the result with the % symbol, the result would change to 903.98%, which is wrong. Excel has multiplied the value in the cell by 100, (9.039755512 * 100=903.98) which is clearly incorrect.

3　Delete the above example
❑　We will now enter the formulas required to display a percentage return:
4　Select cell J4
5　Type in '=H4/H11' and press Enter

This formula will give a result of 0.09039756. Do not be tempted to make any adjustments to the formatting just yet, we will do this later.

Excel will not permit you to use the AutoFill feature to carry the formula over the other cells. The following error message will appear if you attempt it,' #DIV/0!'.

6　Select cell J5 and enter the previous formula replacing H4 with H5
7　Repeat this action in cell H6, H7 and H8 amending each cell reference as appropriate

Formatting the percentage column

The results displayed in the respective columns are not displayed as percentages, in the true sense, but shown as decimal places. We will now adjust the column to display the value as a percentage figure and to include the '%' symbol. This will immediately assist the user/reader to identify the value in that column as a percentage figure.

Basic steps

1 Select the cells J4 to J8 inclusive

2 Right-click over the cells and from the pop-up menu select Format Cells…

3 At the Format Cells dialog box , ensure that the Number tab is selected

4 From Category pane select *Percentage*

5 Set the Decimal Places slot to 0

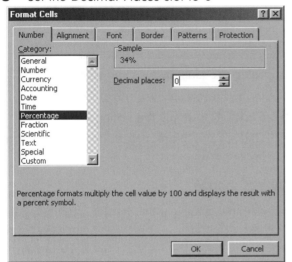

6 Click OK to apply the formatting

❑ The result should now be displayed as shown

Half Yearly	Average	Percentage
£6,892.00	£1,148.67	9%
£8,763.00	£1,460.50	11%
£16,871.00	£2,811.83	22%
£19,717.00	£3,286.17	26%
£27,444.00	£4,574.00	36%

7 Save the changes

Take note

Excel has rounded up the percentage figures and you must always consider this when working with percentages. If you were to total up the figures in the above example, you will have a total of 104, which is clearly wrong.

Once you have saved the changes reformat the column to show 2 decimal places and observe the difference. When you have finished experimenting, close the workbook but do not Save the changes when prompted.

Creating an absolute reference

We are now going to create an absolute reference as we did in the previous exercises.

Basic steps

1 Re-open *ECDL3*

We will again use the example of a manager's commission based upon the overall monthly sales.

2 Select cell A13 and type 'Manager's'

3 In cell A14 type 'Monthly'

4 In cell A15 type 'Commission'

5 In cell A16 type '1.5'

6 Select cell B15 and enter the formula to create an absolute reference based on the content of cell A16 (1.5)

❑ Remember to add the '$' sign to 'A16' to convert it to an absolute reference, i.e. 'A16'

7 Using the AutoFill feature, carry the formula over to the cell range C15 to I15

❑ Apply any other formatting to ensure an overall continuity of style and layout

8 Save the changes to the worksheet

Additional information

Once a month, the company, whose simplified account we have recently created, decreed that the sales information should be circulated to a number of personnel so that they can see how sales are progressing. It has been decided that there should be a distribution list inserted as part of the worksheet and when each person on the list has seen the sales figures, they will annotate the sheet indicating that they have read the data.

Basic steps

1 Type in the data as listed below

In cell A18 type 'Name'
In cell A19 type 'Sales/Harding'
In cell A20 type 'Finance/Golding'
In cell A21 type 'Planning/Ross'
In cell A22 type 'Operations/Winter'
In cell A23 type 'Directors/Holden'
In cell A24 type 'Directors/Collins'
In cell C18 type 'Date seen'
In cell D18 type 'Signature'

2 Select the cell range A18 to D18 inclusively

3 Embolden the text and save the changes

4 Select cells A18 and B18 and Merge and Centre them

5 Repeat for the name cells below this range

❑ The alignment of the names needs adjusting:

6 Select the cell range A19 to A24 and click the Left Align icon on the Standard toolbar

❑ The names will now align to the left and look much better

Applying borders

It is often beneficial to insert borders around areas or sections of data or text. Not only does this highlight a particular section, it also avoids any ambiguity in respect of what section the data represents. In our example we may wish to separate the sales figures from the analysis figures.

Basic steps

1 Select the cell range A2 to D16 inclusively

2 Right-click over the selection

3 From the pop-up menu select Format Cells...

4 Select the Borders tab

It is important that the sequence that follows is adhered to, to ensure first-time success.

5 Click the down-arrow by the Color slot and from the colour palette select *Light Blue*

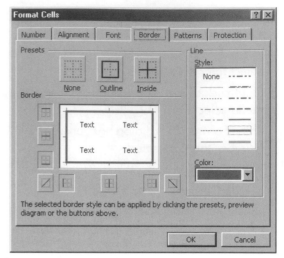

6 Select the Line Style as shown above

7 In the Presets section, select *Outline*

8 Click OK to apply the settings.

9 Click in any blank cell to deselect the high-lighted area

Another border

We will now create another border surrounding the 1999 sales figures.

Basic steps

1 Select the cells E2 to G16 inclusively

2 Right-click over the area

3 Select Format Cells... from the pop-up menu

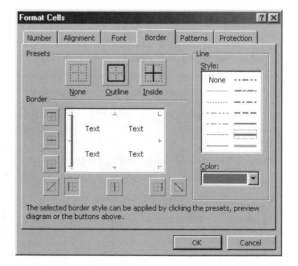

4 At the Format Cells dialog box ensure that the Borders tab is selected

5 Select the colour *Red* for the new border

6 Select the same Line Style as previously

We are now going to individually select each border line. Consult the example which is an enlargement of the Border line options window.

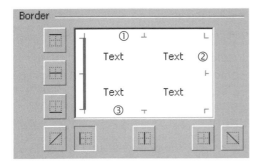

Remember that the thick line represents the right vertical line of the border surrounding the 1999 figure. This now becomes the left-hand vertical line of the new border.

7 Left-click once on the areas indicated by the symbol ① then on ② and finally on ③

After clicking on each area, the appropriate line will be added to the border.

8 Click OK to apply the changes and deselect the highlighted area

You should now have the 1999 sales figures surrounded by a red border with a blue line dividing each sales section.

Exercise

Using the method described above, create a border around the following cell ranges:

> The cell range H2 to J16 inclusively (choose your own colour)
>
> The cell range A18 to D24 inclusively, on this occasion select the double line style (choose your own colour)
>
> When complete, save the changes to the worksheet

You should experiment with the features available within the Borders dialog box to become proficient in their use and produce attractive worksheets.

Find and Replace

If you have completed the Word module, then you will have already been introduced to the Find and Replace feature. This will search the currently open file for occurrences of a word, a series of words or data, which you may then replace. If the search produces a result which is not what you are looking for, then you can simply select the **Find Next** button to continue the search. This will continue until the end of the file is reached. At this stage you may close the dialog box or start a new search, using different criteria.

Setting up the criterion

Basic steps

1 Ensure that the workbook *'ECDL3'* is open

We are going to conduct a combined Find and Replace action. You can use the Find feature on its own to simply locate text or data. You will recall that we recently added a list of names to the worksheet. This list now requires updating due to staff changes.

2 Select Edit from the menu bar

3 Select the Replace option. The Find and Replace dialog box will open.

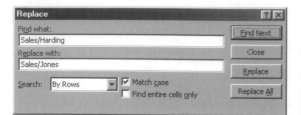

4 Type 'Sales/Harding' in the Find what slot

5 Type 'Sales/Jones' in the Replace with slot

6 Click Find Next

Excel will start the search and on finding the first instance of the text, stop and highlight it.

7 If this is the required text, and in this instance it should be, click Replace

Or

8 If the text found was not the text or data that you required, click Find Next – Excel will look for the next occurrence. If this is what you were looking for, click Replace

The Find and Replace dialog box will remain open and you may continue the Find and Replace action or close it.

9 Click Close to close the box

The Find feature

Select **Edit > Find** to start this feature. It functions in a similar manner to the Find and Replace option, but is only used to find words or data and at this stage you cannot replace them. However, you can quickly switch to the **Replace** option by simply clicking on the **Replace** button.

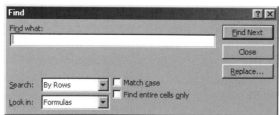

Clicking **Replace** changes the dialog box to the **Find and Replace** dialog box.

To use the feature in the Find mode, you simply type in the word or data value in the **Find what** slot and click on the **Find Next** button.

As with the Find and Replace feature, you can set a search criterion using the options available as shown in the example.

Exercise

We will now use ECDL3, worksheet 1 to locate a name.

Basic steps

1 From the menu bar select 'Edit > Find'

or

use the shortcut key combination of Ctrl+F.

2 At the Find dialog box, in the Find what slot, type 'hosiery', all in lowercase letters

3 Ensure that the Match case box does not have a tick in it

4 Click Find Next

Excel will now search the worksheet and if it locates the word 'hosiery', it will select the cell containing the word and adjust the spreadsheet so that you can see the appropriate cell.

Summary

We have, over the period of this course, created a number of workbooks and in each instance they have all been small and contained limited data. It would therefore be easy to locate any item, in any of the workbooks, without resorting to the Find feature. However, if the workbooks contained numerous rows and columns all filled with data, finding data may then become a chore and the Find and Replace feature would then become an extremely useful tool.

Both of these features are extremely useful and worthy of further investigation.

Take note

Be wary of using the Replace All button, which will replace all occurrences of the word or data. If the search criteria was not set correctly, some mistakes may well occur.

A half yearly sales chart

Our worksheet is beginning to look quite detailed now but remember the observation raised earlier, '*A picture paints a thousand words*'.

Basic steps

We will now create a chart based on a collection of the available data.

1 Ensure that *ECDL3* is open

2 Select the cell range A3 to G8 inclusively

3 Click on the Chart Wizard icon

4 Construct the chart as shown in this example (the chart is to appear on the current worksheet)

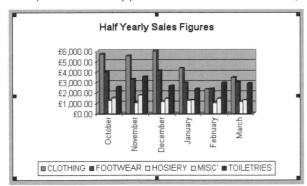

5 Position it with its upper right-hand corner in cell J17

We have a temperamental Managing Director who has some presentational likes and dislikes. The MD want a colour in the background.

6 Move the cursor to the lower left chart area and pause – a Tool Tip will appear to identify the area that you are pointing at. It should be the Chart Area

7 Double-click on this area

❑ The Format Chart Area dialog box will open

8 Select the same options shown in the example

9 Apply the changes by clicking OK button

10 Move the cursor around various areas of the chart, for instance over the Chart Title area

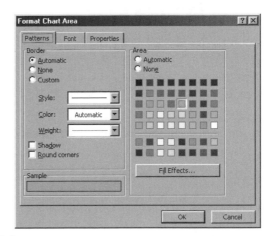

11 Pause over this area and when the Tool Tip appears, double-click and the Format Chart Title dialog box will open

❑ We will not make any changes to this area now, but remember how you accessed it

12 Close the box by clicking Cancel button

What we actually want to do is remove a word from the Chart Title. There should still be a border around the title text. This indicates that the Chart Title area is in fact a text box and you can manipulate the text.

Half Yearly Sales Figures

13 Click into the box at the end of the word 'Sales'

❑ A flashing text cursor will appear

14 Use [Delete] to remove the word 'Figures'

Half Yearly Sales

15 Click on a blank area of the worksheet and the change will be applied

If you are not happy with the colour selection made by Excel for the columns, these too can be changed. Simply double-click on a column, and from the **Format Data Series** dialog box, select a colour.

It is possible to identify what each column represents simply by placing the cursor over the column in question. A pop-up window will appear as shown in the example.

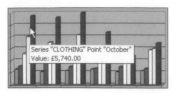

Move the cursor around the chart and identify the following areas:

Chart area   Plot area   Chart Title
Legend   Walls   Value axis
Category axis

All of the above can be selected and modified in various ways, after the chart has been created.

Automatic update

If any changes are made to the worksheet, i.e. a sales value is increased or decreased, the chart will automatically reflect the change.

Change the sales value of £1,256.00 for *Hosiery* for *October* to £5,670.00 and watch the chart update when you press [Enter] to accept the change. Now return the value to £1,256.00 and the chart will again be updated.

Deleting a column

The Managing Director has decided that the column titled *Average* is of no consequence as the data is artificial and should be removed.

Basic steps

1   Right-click over the column header

2   Select Delete from the pop-up menu

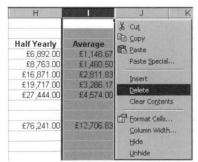

The column will be removed and the Percentage column will move to the left to fill the gap and become the new column I.

Create a second chart

Basic steps

Yet another change of plan. The MD has decided that he would like to see a chart included that will display the half yearly sales figures for 1999.

1   Select the cell range A4 to A8 and H4 to H8, using [Control] to make the selection.

2   Create a 3D Pie chart as shown in the example

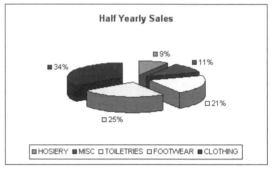

3   Re-size and position the new chart so that it will fit directly below the distribution list

4   Select Print Preview to check the overall layout of the worksheet before printing it

❑   If you find that the page is set to portrait (shortest side horizontal)

5   Select Setup on the Print Preview menu bar

6   At the Page Setup dialog box, select the Page tab and select Landscape then click OK

You will be returned to the Preview window, where you may find that an area of the second chart is not visible in the Print Preview.

Two options exist; either reduce the overall chart size, which may reduce the readability of the worksheet when printed, or remove less important information from the worksheet.

After some discussion it was decided that the distribution list should be removed.

7   Select the range A17 to D24 and press [Delete]

You should now find that all of the content has been removed but the border is still there. Before you do anything else:

8 Click the Undo icon or press Ctrl+Z to restore all of the contents

9 With the cell range A17 to D24 still highlighted, select Edit > Clear > All

10 Click anywhere on a blank area of the worksheet to remove the highlight

Tip

The contents and border are deleted in one action using this method. Keep this method in mind when you wish to delete a selection that includes a border.

11 Move the second chart up to fill the recently vacated space and in line with the top of the original chart

12 Change the second chart background to a colour of your choice

13 Experiment with the options from the Format dialog box to round the corners of each chart

14 Create a stylish fill using the Fill Effects button

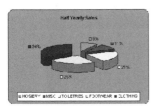

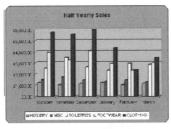

Inserting symbols

There may be an occasion when a particular symbol or sign, such as the Yen symbol '¥', is required but is not available from the keyboard set-up that you are currently using.

There are two ways to insert a symbol and if you are going to use symbols regularly it will be worth while learning the codes for them. Use the code in the same way that you use the shortcut keys, such as **Ctrl+S**.

For instance using the key combination **Alt+0162** (using the numeric keypad) will produce the symbol '¢' or **Alt+0165** will produce the symbol '¥'. These symbols are available from the System font.

The alternative method is to switch the Font type from the Formatting toolbar drop-down list. The problem here is that you must still know which keys on the keyboard will produce the required symbol.

Similarly if you only wish to insert a particular symbol in a cell, try this exercise.

Basic steps

1 Select the cell range J4 to J8 inclusive

2 Click on the Font drop-down list on the Formatting toolbar

3 Change the font to *Wingdings* and the size to 14

4 Click on any blank area of the worksheet to remove the highlight

5 Select each cell, indicated below and type in the letters indicated for each cell:

Cell J4	type:	capital letter L
Cell J5	type:	capital letter K
Cell J6	type:	capital letter K
Cell J7	type:	capital letter J
Cell J8	type:	capital letter J

So we have an accountant with a sense of humour, because you should now have a series of smiley and not-so-smiley faces next to the Percentage figures as shown below:

☹   ☺   ☺   ☺   ☺

The Character Map

The example shown here is the Windows Character Map and it is by selecting this that various Font keystrokes can be identified to achieve the above.

Basic steps

To open the Character Map:

1 Click on the Start button
2 Select Programs > Accessories > System Tools > Character Map

In the example shown the font selected is *Wingdings* and the smiley face is the choice.

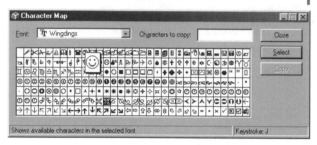

The lower right corner of the window will display the keystroke for each character when selected. 'J' will produce the smiley face.

Some characters can not be reached by simple keystokes. For these you must use the [Alt] key and a code number, typed in from the numeric keypad, for example **Alt+0165** will produce the Japanese currency symbol, the Yen '¥'. Remember to use only the numeric keypad for the code figures.

Experiment with this feature and maybe make a list of certain symbols that you are likely to use.

Changing an existing chart type

Occasionally, some time after you have created a chart of one style, for instance a 3D column chart, it may be considered necessary to change it to another type, e.g. a bar chart. Care should be taken when changing the chart as sometimes the detail used in it, such as the labels, may not lend themselves to the changed chart display.

Always remember that, if things do not turn out the way you expected, **STOP** and then click the 'Undo' icon or use the keyboard shortcut keys 'Ctrl+Z' to restore the original element.

Alternatively you could save the workbook with a different name and work on that version as a safe-guard without fear of losing the original chart if things do not work as planned.

Basic steps

1 Select the pie chart that displays the half yearly sales figures
2 Ensure that you select the chart and not an element of it (look for the border and the presence of the resizing handles)
3 Select Chart > Chart Type
4 At the Chart Type dialog box, ensure that the Standard Types tab is selected
5 Select *Bar* from the Chart Types
6 From the top row select the top left chart and click OK
❑ Perform any re-formatting and you should have a chart resembling the example shown

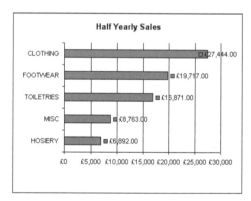

An alternative method

If you find the above method does not achieve the aim, select the chart and click the Chart Wizard icon.

The Chart Wizard will now open and you have the option of changing various areas of the chart other than just the chart type.

You do not necessarily have to use the Wizard to make certain changes. You can individually select items on the chart and move, change the size and colour independent of other areas of the chart.

Save the changes and keep the workbook open.

Deleting a chart

After all the time and effort put in to creating the half yearly sales 1999 chart the MD has decided that it is no longer relevant and wants it removed.

Select the chart and press [Delete], it's as easy as that.

Inserting clip art or other images

There will be occasions when you may wish to insert a piece of clip art, or an image, in the worksheet to draw attention to a section or to emphasise a point.

We are now going to insert a piece of Clip Art that is included with the Microsoft Office Suite.

Take note

Because of the manner in which the Office suite of applications is installed, not all of the clip art may be available to you. Use your discretion and select an appropriate item from what is available.

Basic steps

1 Select Insert > Picture > Clipart – the Microsoft Clip Gallery window will open

2 In the Search for clips slot, type '*People at work*' and press Enter

There are many images listed in the category 'People at work' and not all can be displayed at once. To view more images, scroll down to the bottom where you will see the Keep Looking icon. Click on it and more images will appear.

3 Select the image

4 Click Insert ClipArt

5 Close the dialog box and the image will appear in the worksheet.

In our case, the image represents the senior salesperson showing the successful six months' sales.

Summary

That completes the '*Putting it together*' section, which combined all of the previous elements of Excel, some of which were used in a slightly different manner. You also learnt new features and facilities available within Excel.

You should now practise any areas that you are unsure of or did not fully understand, remembering to use the online Help system. Experiment with the different features to gain more experience and confidence ready for your examination.

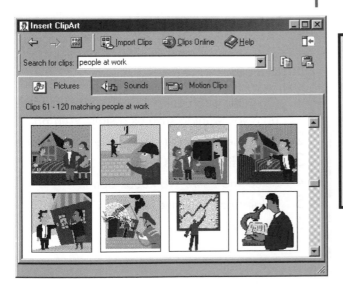

Tip

Remember that the image can be moved or resized as required. The techniques are the same here as in Word — refer back to page 126 for more on inserting graphics.

Saving in other file formats

With Excel 2000, you can save workbooks in formats other than the default .xls. We are going to discuss two of the many options – Web Page and Text (txt).

Web Page

With the increasing importance of the Internet and e-commerce, the ability to save a workbook in a format suitable for publishing on the Internet, or company intranets, will assume increasing importance with time. Excel offers you two options for Web publication – *static Web page* and *interactive Web page*.

You can turn data, charts, PivotTables and entire workbooks into Web pages so that people how do not have Excel can read the data, provided that they have Internet Explorer 4.01 or higher and Office Web Components (part of Office 2000) installed.

We will only cover the static Web page. For information on Interactive Web pages, use the online help.

Static Web page

A static Web page can include an entire workbook, including all of its worksheets, complete with sheet tabs and worksheet formatting such as fonts, colours, etc., and any embedded charts. Individual charts, or selected ranges, can also be published as Web pages.

How is it done?

First we are going to re-save the workbook, 'ECDL3', using a different name. The reason for this is so we can make a number of changes to it and then save it in a format that can be used on the Internet or viewed with a web browser such as Internet Explorer.

Take note

By converting the worksheet to other formats some of the formatting may be lost in the conversion. Always review the converted file to ensure it still displays the data in a suitable manner.

We are first going to save a copy of the worksheet with a different name so that we still have a full working copy of the worksheet as a backup.

Basic steps

1　Ensure that *ECDL3* is open

3　From the menu bar select File > Save As

3　At the Save As dialog box, type 'ECDL4'

4　Click Save

Take note

By saving the worksheet in HTML you are increasing the scope of distribution, by making the document available to others who may not have Excel, but do have an Internet browser.

Creating a static Web page

If you have any experience of creating a Web page, using Office 97, you will find this procedure quite different. Please don't be tempted to jump the gun.

Basic steps

1　Open the workbook 'ECDL4', which holds the data you want to save as a static Web page.

2　From the File menu select Save as Web Page

3　A modified Save As dialog box will open.

4　Select the *Entire Workbook* option

5　Retain the suggested name 'ECDL4.htm'

6　Click Save

Saving as a text file

We are now going to save a workbook as a text file so that a word-processor or text editor can read it. However, only one worksheet can be saved in a text file, so ensure that the correct one is displayed before you start. If you wish to save multiple worksheets, each must be saved as an individual text file.

If still open, close 'ECDL4' and open the workbook 'ECDL3' and delete any images or charts that may exist. We only require the data area.

Viewing the HTML file

Basic steps

1 Open Internet Explorer or other Web browser

2 As soon as the browser opens, click the Stop icon to stop your default home page loading

3 Select File > Open

4 At the Open dialog box, click the Browse button and locate and open the file

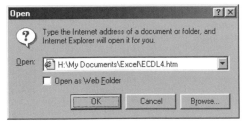

5 Click OK

❑ Your browser will open and display the file

It is possible that the workbook and chart did not fit on the page completely. If this is the case, use the scroll bars to move the page up and down or left and right as necessary.

When you have finished reviewing the worksheet, close the browser.

Basic steps

1 From the menu bar select File > Save As

2 At the Save As dialog box, drop-down the Save As type list and select *Text (Tab delimited)(*.txt)*

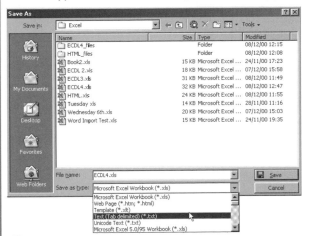

3 Do not change the name, simply click Save

❑ A message box will advise you that you can only save single sheets in this format. As the workbook only has one sheet, this is not a problem in this instance.

4 Click OK.

❑ The file will now be saved in the '.txt' format

If you attempt to close Excel with a text file still open, you will be warned that it is not in Excel 2000 format and asked if you want to save your changes. You do not, so click the **No** button.

Various other formats exist and should be investigated as required. Do however be careful when saving a worksheet in a different format or version.

Opening the text file in Word

You may want to open the text file just created to check and see what it looks like, and whether changing its format has resulted in any loss of data or changed its layout.

Basic steps

1 Open Microsoft Word
2 Select File > Open or click the Open icon

3 Navigate to where you stored the text file

❏ The Open dialog box will by default show only those files with the Word extension of '.doc'. To locate your text file, remember it will have a '.txt' extension, so you must first change the file type option.

4 Click the Type of file drop-down arrow to open its list

5 Select *Text Files* – your file will appear in the file pane

6 Double-click on it and it will open

❏ You will probably find that the data is mixed up and its layout has been lost. If this is the case:

7 Select Page Setup and change the orientation to *Landscape*

When you have finished checking the contents, close Word and proceed.

Further formatting

There remain a number of formatting features that you should be aware of.

Basic steps

- ❑ To complete this section, open the workbook *ECDL2* and ensure that you are at *Sheet 1*
- 1 Select the cell range A1 to G12 inclusively
- 2 Copy the range
- 3 Switch to *Sheet 2*
- 4 Select cell B2 and paste in the copied range
- ❑ Do not perform any formatting changes at this stage

Adjusting cell width and height

Basic steps

- ❑ We are going to uniformly adjust the height of the cell range B3 to G12:
- 1 Highlight the range B3 to G12
- 2 Select Format > Row > Height
- 3 At the Row Height dialog box, change the Height to 14 and click OK

Row Height

Row height:	14
	OK
	Cancel

- ❑ The cell range will remain highlighted

Adjusting the row width

Basic steps

We will now uniformly adjust the cell width:

- 1 Select Format > Column > Width
- 2 Type in 15 then click OK
- 3 Save the changes and keep the worksheet open

Changing the currency symbols

Throughout this book we have used the English '£' sign. You may be using a different symbol, appropriate to your location or work. Irrespective of which symbol you use by default, you may sometimes create worksheets which use other currency symbols.

We are going to change the worksheet to display the currency data as US dollars ($). The same procedure can be used to change the symbol to any other currency symbol.

Basic steps

- 1 Select the cell range C5 to G12
- 2 Right-click over the range and select Format Cells... from the pop-up menu
- 3 At the Format Cells dialog box ensure that the Number tab is selected
- 4 Select *Currency* in the Category pane
- 5 Click on the down arrow by the Symbol slot
- 6 Select *$ English (United States)* then click OK

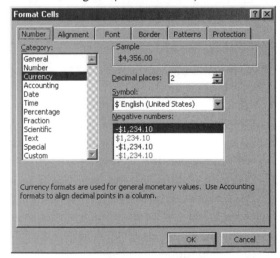

- 7 Deselect the cell range and you will see that the '$' symbol is now displayed
- 8 Save the changes

199

Date formats

Excel can display dates in a number of different format styles. To demonstrate this we will add three areas to the worksheet. Each will be formatted differently, simply as illustrations. You would not normally use different styles on the same worksheet.

Basic steps

- ❑ Ensure that ECDL2 sheet 2 is selected
- 1 In cell B14 type 'Updated'
- 2 Right-click on C14 and select Format Cells...
- 3 Ensure that the Number tab is selected
- 4 In the Category pane select *Date*
- 5 In the Type pane select the option shown here

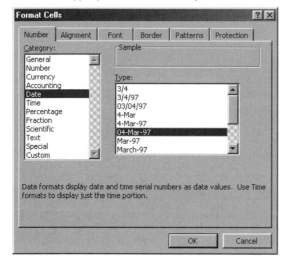

- 6 Click OK to apply the format
- 7 Ensure that cell C14 is still selected
- 8 Type '04/07/00', then press [Enter] and Excel will display the date in the chosen format
- ❑ Do not be concerned that the date is wrong. This is only an example of the format, the correct date will be inserted.
- 9 Follow the same procedure to apply to D14 the Date format indicated here

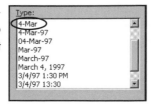

- 10 In cell D14 type '05/07'
- ❑ The date will appear as '5-Jul'
- 11 Apply this format to cell E14
- 12 Enter today's date into E14.
- ❑ Note the difference in the date format compared to the previous example

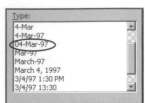

Copy data within a worksheet

We have used the Cut, Copy and Paste commands a number of times during this course to achieve various tasks. One was not mentioned. You can copy any section of data, text, chart or image within a worksheet and paste it in a different location within the same worksheet.

Why would you want to do this? An occasion may arise when you want to experiment with a particular set of data, without fear of losing the original source data.

We will copy a data section and paste it in another location to illustrate how simple it is. Ensure that you have *ECDL2*, *Sheet 1* open.

Basic steps

- 1 Select the range A4 to F8 inclusively
- 2 Copy the selected range
- 3 Move down the worksheet, leaving at least 10 blank rows
- 4 Paste the selected range in this new location
- 5 Experiment changing the formatting options, such as the currency symbol, cell and row width and heights
- 6 When satisfied with the results, ave the changes

Summary

Clearly there exists a wide variety of preformatted options and you should investigate all of them.

The Spell Checker

We have very little to spell check in the current worksheet, however, there will be occasions when there will be considerably more detail. The Spell Checker will function just as effectively on a large worksheet as it does on a smaller one.

The Spell Checker in Excel functions in a similar manner to the one in Word.

Exercise

To test the Spell Checker we will deliberately misspell two words and see if it will pick-up the errors and advise the correct spelling.

Basic steps

1 Open 'ECDL2' and select Sheet 1 is selected

2 Change the words 'CLOTHING' to 'LOTHING' and 'MONTHLY' to 'NONTHLY'

3 Select cell A1 (otherwise Excel will start the check from whichever cell is currently selected)

4 From the Tools menu select Spelling. The Spell Checker dialog box will open.

❑ Excel may pick up our word 'MISC'. If it has, it will offer a number of options, which you may ignore if you are satisfied with the original word, 'MISC'. We will choose to ignore it

5 The Spell Checker will identify 'LOTHING' as not being in its dictionary. It has offered the word 'LOATHING' as an alternative. This is not what we want, and we have two options.

❑ Notice that the word in the Change to slot is highlighted. This can be changed.

6 Type in the correct word 'CLOTHING'

7 Click Change.

❑ Excel will continue the Spell Check and should pick up 'NONTHLY'. In this case has offered 'NINTHLY'. This is again not what we want, so perform the same procedure as before.

8 In the Change to slot, type the word 'MONTHLY' and click Change.

❑ Eventually the Spell Checker will reach the end of the worksheet and advise you that it has completed the task.

9 Click OK to close the dialog box

Adding words to the Spell Checker

There will be occasions when the Spell Checker will identify a word which is correctly spelt, but is not in the Spell Check dictionary. When this happens, first check that the spelling is correct and then click the **Add** button. Excel will include it in its dictionary.

Take note

If the word that was added to the dictionary was spelt all in lowercase letters, for example 'mine', when it is later spelt as 'Mine' the Spell Checker may not recognise the word with a capital letter 'M'. You will have to enter each variation of the word and its spelling.

A Word of caution

The Spell Checker is good but if you misspell a word in the context of your meaning, but that word is actually spelt correctly in another context, the Spell Checker may not pick it up as incorrect. The Spell Checker within Excel, unlike Microsoft Word, does not have a Grammar Checker, which may have recognised a grammatical error.

Error messages

Excel, along with other applications, will produce error messages when you attempt to perform an action/task that it fails to understand or cannot do. There will be occasions when no error message will appear and the task may well be completed and the result is incorrect. You must then determine what has happened, or not happened, as the case may be.

Error messages will attempt to guide and give advice when possible and you should always read the message carefully and follow the suggestions offered.

Common Error Messages

The error message may not always be helpful. To assist you we have listed a number of common error messages and their meaning.

Take note

Further explanations of error messages are available in the online Help system.

Error	Meaning	Fix it
####	The column is not wide enough to display the value	Widen the column
#VALUE	Wrong type of argument or operand (for example calculating a cell with the value #N/A)	Check operands and arguments so that the formula doesn't divide by zero
#NAME	Formula is referencing an invalid or non-existent name	Make sure the name exists or correct the misspelling
#N/A	Usually means no value is available or inappropriate arguments used	In a lookup formula, ensure that the lookup table is sorted correctly
#REF	Excel cannot locate the referenced cells. For example the referenced cells have been deleted	Click Undo immediately to restore references, then change formula references to convert formulas to values
Circular	A formula refers to itself, either directly or indirectly	Click OK , then look at the status bar to see which cell contains the circular reference
#DIV/0!	Formula is attempting to divide by zero	Check the values or cell reference so that the formula doesn't divide by zero

Excel and other applications

Information stored within an Excel spreadsheet can very easily be copied or linked to any of the other applications to be found within the Microsoft Office Suite 2000.

A chart or data can be inserted in a Word document, an Access database or a PowerPoint presentation.

It is also possible to import data from an Access database into Excel. Excel has excellent data handling and analysis tools, which can be used to manipulate raw data.

Exchanging data between Excel and Access

To analyse the data from a Access table in Excel, you can use features in Access to export the data automatically to a new Excel workbook. You can also import worksheet data into Access from Excel. If you want only a few records from an Access table, you can open the table and copy and paste selected records into Excel.

If you're working in Excel and have installed and loaded the AccessLinks add-in, you can convert a list to an Access database file. For more information about add-ins use the on-line Help system.

If you have completed the module on Microsoft Word, you will recall that we covered importing information in Chapter 3.

Exchanging data between Word and Excel
Copy worksheet cells into a Word or PowerPoint document

Basic steps

1   On your worksheet, select the range you want to copy
2   Click Copy
3   Switch to your Word or PowerPoint document
4   Click where you want to insert the cells
5   On the Edit menu in Word or PowerPoint click Paste Special
❑   To paste the cells so that you can size and position them like a picture:
6   Select Microsoft Excel Worksheet Object
❑   To paste the cells in Word as a table you can resize and format:
7   Click Formatted Text (RTF)
❑   To paste the cells as text separated by tabs:
8   Click Unformatted Text
❑   To keep only the current result of the formula:
9   Click Paste
❑   To keep the copied information up-to-date if the original data changes in Excel:
10 Click Paste link

Take note

In PowerPoint, the Paste link option is available only if you select the Microsoft Excel Worksheet Object format.

If you select the Microsoft Excel Worksheet Object and Paste options, only the visible data in the cells appears in the embedded picture. If data is cut off, double-click the object, and resize the columns to show all the data. If you paste a worksheet object, the linked picture reflects the column width and other formatting of the original cells as they appear in the source workbook.

If you select the Paste link option, the result is pasted as a linked object. If you select the Microsoft Excel Worksheet Object and Paste options, the result is pasted as an embedded object. For more information about linked and embedded objects use the on-line Help and type in the word 'export'.

If you linked the cells and might later want to include additional rows or columns, first name the range in Excel. Then copy the range and paste the cells as a linked object into Word or PowerPoint. If you add more data to the range in Excel, you can redefine the range name to include the additional cells. The new data is added to the linked object the next time you update the link.

5 Databases

Introduction to Access

What is a database?

The term *database* refers to a collection of information organised in such a manner as to make the information easily accessible. The structure of the database should be simple in order to make the storage and retrieval equally easy. Some examples of databases in everyday use, which people may not think of in terms of a database are:

- A telephone directory
- A dictionary
- A catalogue

In the business world when one refers to a database, it is usually the following that are being referred to:

- Stock control records
- Customer accounts
- Personnel records

An example of a database table is shown here. The database comprises of a series of columns with headings, known as *field names*, which relate to the content of each column.

In this example there are six different column headings and makes what is known as a *record*.

The six columns here contain cells, known as *fields*, where the information relating to each column is stored.

In conclusion, the example database is made of columns, which contains the fields. Fields usually contain only one item of information, for instance a postal code. Fields are grouped together in rows and each row may contain a varied number of fields within the same database. Each row is known as a record and each record relates to one entry in the database, such as a client's contact details, as here.

Viewing and editing data

There are three ways in which you will work with data.

- **Input** where you store data in a record, in the database
- **Editing** where you require a means of editing or updating the data within the tables
- **Searching** where you require a means of searching and viewing the records found.

These tasks are performed using the following components of the database.

Tables are the backbone of the database and contain the information stored within it. Data is stored in tables from where it can later be edited or used.

Tables enable you to view several records, arranged in rows on the screen. Tables are not the normal method of viewing data.

Forms are the usual method of entering or editing data contained within tables. You can create forms that combine data from one or more tables and a table may have more than one form associated with it.

Forms, subject to their design, are used to view one record at a time and are dependent upon tables.

A table row   Field name   A table cell

Name	Surname	Tel	Fax	Town	Post Code
Michelle	O'Leary	01934 418261	01934 418261	Glasgow	G2 6YH
Keith	Champion	0171 548 7285	020 8521 5621	Hackney	NW12 7RQ
James	Bates	01705 293176	01705 293176	Portsmouth	PO3 2PL
Joe	Smith	01705 275193	01705 275213	Portsmouth	PO5 2DG
Peter	Bloggs	0181 329 1122	0181 329 1123	Richmond	TW9 1QP

Queries are used to edit or enter data. The purpose of a query is to select data using a set of criteria. Once the data has been selected, it can then be edited using a datasheet view of a table or form view, find data or used to create other Tables and Forms.

Reports produce paper copies of the information for distribution. A report may have multiple tables associated with it. They can be produced with the information displayed in a table format or as single columns, or you can design the report layout completely.

They can be set up to perform calculations and print out the results.

Access is a powerful *relational database* which allows multiple Tables and Forms to be created and linked together according to a given set of criteria.

For the purpose of this module we will not be building relational databases, only simple databases. These can be expanded into relational databases at a later stage, if so required.

Take note

There are two ways (views) that you can look at a table, form, report or query.

Design view is the term used when you are creating the table, form, record or query. You cannot input or edit data in this view.

Datasheet view and Form view are used when you change from the Design view and are used to input or edit data.

Access Wizards

Some wizards offer you pre-designed databases. With some input from you, they will assemble the database, complete with Tables, Forms and Reports.

Other wizards will create single items, such as Forms or Reports. You will encounter these Wizards in due course as you progress through the course work.

Wizards reduce effort and time and may in the early stages of learning assist you in designing certain

types of databases. You should investigate the options available from the wizards in Access.

Access database terminology

As you progress with this module, you will probably encounter new terminology, which is used to describe specific items or actions within the Access database. Every attempt will be made to explain its meaning and function when it is introduced, however should you encounter anything that you are unfamiliar with, use the online Help and search for the item and see what Microsoft has to say on the subject.

Database design

Before you start creating tables, forms, reports and queries, it is worth spending some time thinking about the information that you are going to work with and how you will want it handled and displayed.

The most important lesson to learn, as you create a database, is good design. Without good design, you will find that you are constantly modifying the tables and forms and you may find it difficult to extract information from your database. As a database developer, the first problem is to gather the information requirements. What information do you want to store and what will you want to extract from this?

Drafting the database design

You should spend some time drafting the database, starting with the report, assuming that you will want to publish the information in paper format. Mentally picture the information that you will have and how you will want it displayed in the report. Think logically, and then draw it on paper.

Follow on by drawing the table, with the field names, then with designing the layout of the forms, all on paper, before finally committing to build the database within Access.

Do not rush this process. Constantly cross-reference the report to the form and the form to the table.

This method will identify your requirements and remove the likelihood of errors which would occur if you did not spend time beforehand thinking of the design and layout.

Access Online Help

Before we go any further, a quick word on the online Help in Access.

There are two methods of viewing the online Help. By default the Office Assistant is activated and available for use.

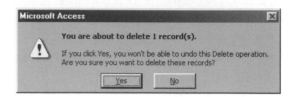

The second method of accessing online Help is to turn off the Office Assistant and use the Help menu of toolbar icon to open this dialog box.

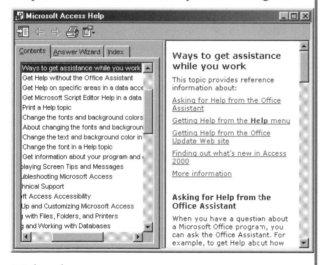

Dialog boxes

Dependent up on which method you are using, you will also find that different style dialog boxes will sometimes appear.

If you have the Office Assistant active and decide to delete a record in a table, the following dialog box will open.

If you have the Office Assistant switched off and carry out the action described above, this dialog box will appear.

Using online Help in this course

It is assumed that you are currently using the default option and have the Office Assistant active. This is the choice of Help generally used in this module.

However, the aim is to practice you in using both methods of online Help, so you will often be referred to the online Help for further information on a discussed topic and occasionally we will turn off the Office assistant to access that Help. Instructions will be given on how to achieve this at the appropriate time.

More information

See Chapter 3, Word processing, for more information on the Office Assistant and customising toolbars.

Starting Access

Access can be started in a number of different ways.

The simplest is from the **Start** > **Programs** menu

You can also start Access from the Office shortcut toolbar, if it was included in the installation of Office.

If the Microsoft Office toolbar is not available you can also create a shortcut on your Desktop, see Chapter 2.

The application window

Below is the Access application window. It shows the default start-up display.

The application window looks very much like any other application window in respect of the general layout, title bar, etc.

The Access dialog box

The Microsoft Access dialog box is displayed when Access first opens and offers you several options.

Create a new database using:

This will open a database which has no tables or forms in it. You will need to create these objects.

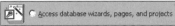

We shall build a database with the assistance of a Wizard. There are 47 Wizards to choose from.

Shown below this option is a list of the most recently opened databases. If the database you require is listed here, simply double-click on it and it will open.

If the file that you require is not shown in the list, double-click on the **More Files** option and locate the file through the **Open** dialog box

Title bar   Menu bar   Database toolbar

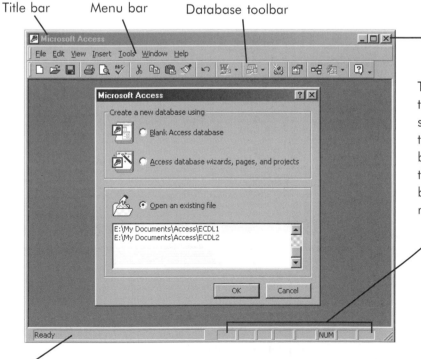

Application control buttons

This area will change, subject to your actions. At present it is showing NUM, indicating that the number lock on the keyboard is active. This means that the numeric keypad can be used to insert numbers rather than for navigation.

Status bar

Creating a database

Before Access will open a new blank database you must first allocate it a name.

Basic steps

1 Select File > New
❑ The New dialog box will open
2 Double-click on the Database icon (or select it and click OK)
❑ The File New Database dialog box will open. Access automatically creates a name for you in the File Name slot. It is suggested that you use your own descriptive names rather than simply accept the one offered by Access. The name is already highlighted, which means that it will be overwritten when you type in your choice of name.
❑ In this instance, we will save the new database to the floppy drive, simply to illustrate how to do it. Databases can become quite large over a period of time and it would be more prudent to save future databases to the hard drive.

3 In the Save in area click on the down arrow and select *3½ Floppy (A:)*
4 Click in the File name slot and type 'ECDL1'
5 Click Create
❑ The Database window will now open

6 In the Objects bar select Tables
7 Right-click over *Create table in Design View* and select Design View from the shortcut menu

Constructing the table

The **Design View** window will open. It is from here that you will create the relevant fields for the database.

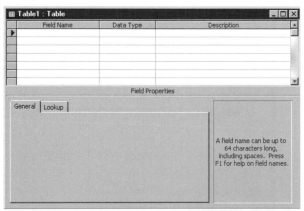

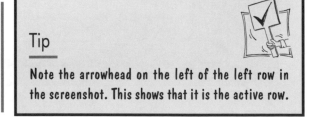

Tip

Note the arrowhead on the left of the left row in the screenshot. This shows that it is the active row.

210

Before entering any text, an explanation of the three columns shown in the window.

Field name

This is the column header, which will appear in the table.

Data type

When the cursor is moved into this field a drop-down arrow will appear. Click on it to open up a list of options, which are used to designate and format the column content.

The Field Name and Data Type each have default and optional setting. For instance the default setting for the Field Name, if the Data Type is Text, is 50 characters. This can be increased to 255 characters or decreased as appropriate.

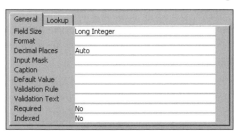

Take note

You will learn more of these Properties as we progress. Remember that the online Help is available for further information.

Description

The use of this field is optional. It is provided for you, the database developer, to enter notes or explanations of the fields and properties for future reference.

Entering the field names

Basic steps

1 Type in the Field Names, with the Data Type options as indicated

Field Name	Data Type
ID	AutoNumber
First Name	Text
Last Name	Text
Date of Birth	Date/Time
Salary	Currency
No of Children	Number

2 Use the [Tab] key to move forward from field to field

3 To select the data type, click on the down-arrow which appears as you move from the Field Name to the Data Type cell

Tip

To move back to the previous field, press the [Shift] and [Tab] keys simultaneously.

We will not be using the Description area at this stage.

Field properties window

You may have noticed that, as you were entering the field data in their respective columns, something was happening in the lower left-hand area of the Table window. This area is known as the Field Properties.

At this stage we will make two changes to the default settings that Access has inserted:

4 Click in the Field Name *No of Children*

5 In the Field Properties select Default Value

6 Delete the value of 0 (zero) and leave this field blank

7 Do the same for the *Salary* field

The example shown is what your completed table should now look like in Design View when all of the field names and properties have been entered.

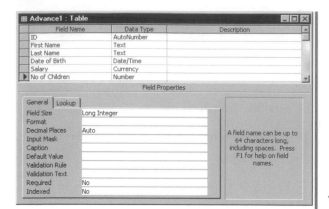

Take note

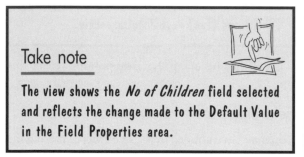

The view shows the *No of Children* field selected and reflects the change made to the Default Value in the Field Properties area.

Once you have entered all the fields:

8   Click the Close button in the upper right corner of the table window

9   You will be prompted to save the table. Click Yes – if Office Assistant is on, you will see a different style prompt

Microsoft Access

Do you want to save changes to the design of table 'Table1'?

[Yes]   [No]   [Cancel]

10   At the Save As dialog box, enter the name *ECDL Table1* and click OK

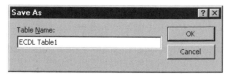

Save As   ? ✕

Table Name:
ECDL Table1   OK   Cancel

❑   A further dialog box will open and warn you '*There is no primary key defined*'

Microsoft Access
There is no primary key defined.

Although a primary key isn't required, it's highly recommended. A table must have a primary key for you to define a relationship between this table and other tables in the database.
Do you want to create a primary key now?

[Yes]   [No]   [Cancel]

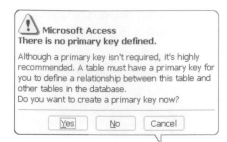

11   We do not require a primary key at this stage, so click No

This box will now close and you will be returned to the database window.

Primary and secondary keys

When you later progress to creating more complex databases, you will be designing in ways that link various tables together, hence the term *relational database*. The linking of tables involves designing each table to be linked, with a field common to both tables.

Take note

Although this means deliberately duplicating some data in the database, it is better to duplicate a limited amount of data than have a long set of fields within the database.

The linked fields are usually described as *Primary* or *Secondary keys*.

Primary keys

The power of a relational database system such as Access comes from its ability to quickly find and bring together information stored in separate tables using queries, forms, and reports.

In order to do this, each table should include a field or set of fields, called the *Primary key*, that uniquely identify each record stored in the table. Once you designate a Primary key for a table, to ensure uniqueness, Access will prevent any duplicate or Null values (ones which do not contain any data) from being entered in the Primary key fields.

In a personnel database, for example, each person has a unique National Insurance Number. This number would be the entry for a field, which would be assigned as the Primary key.

In time, this field would be used to link data to other records, in other tables within the database.

Secondary keys

If you want to link data from one table to another table you will need to include a field in the second table that corresponds to the Primary key in the first table. This field is then known as the Secondary key.

This example was taken from an database, called *Northwind* which is supplied with Access.

In the example, the table called *Suppliers* has a field called *Supplier ID* and it is the Primary key for the table. In the *Products* table there is

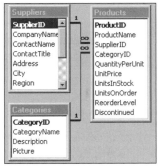

also a field called *Supplier ID* which is a Secondary key and creates the link between the two tables.

It is worth investigating this database further. It can be found in the folder *Program Files\Microsoft Office\Office\Samples* and contains many good examples of database ideas and design.

For more information on the subject of Primary and Secondary keys, investigate the online Help system.

The database window

Think of the database window as a box containing a card filing system, with seven object headings. The items stored in each section can be determined by clicking on each object heading in turn, i.e. Tables, Queries, etc.

All items that make up the database are stored within this window. Here's how to locate a table.

Basic steps

1   Click on the Table tab
2   Select *ECDL Table1* in the database window

3   Click Open.

❑   The table will open in the Datasheet view. You can now start to enter data into the table

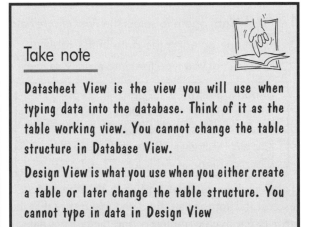

Take note

Datasheet View is the view you will use when typing data into the database. Think of it as the table working view. You cannot change the table structure in Database View.

Design View is what you use when you either create a table or later change the table structure. You cannot type in data in Design View

Our new, but still empty, table should look like this.

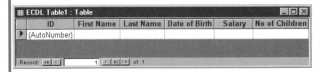

Entering data in a table

In the ID column you will see that Access is displaying word 'AutoNumber'. You will recall that this was the Data Type selected for this field at the design stage. As soon as any detail is entered into the First Name column, Access will automatically allocate the ID number.

Basic steps

1 Enter the data shown into the table. Type in the name 'Simon' and notice that as soon as you enter its first letter, a new record appears below the one you are entering data in.

2 To move to the next field, press [Tab]. The cursor will move to the *Last Name* field. Continue entering the data relating to Simon Smith until you reach the last field *No of Children*. Remember, if you overshoot, press [Shift] and [Tab] to move back to the previous field.

3 After entering the number 3, at the end of the first line, press [Tab]. The cursor will move to the *ID* field and start a new record

4 Press [Tab] again to select the *First Name* field

5 Continue entering the data in the table.

6 Ensure that you type the date exactly as shown

Simon	Smith	12 Jan 71	£950	3
James	Bond	31 Oct 67	£1250	0
David	Jones	16 Aug 77	£1130	2
Angela	Mathews	18 May 70	£1180	0
Cherry	King	11 July 72	£1270	1

If you make a mistake typing in the above detail, reselect the appropriate field and make sure that the error is removed completely and the correct data is entered. When we later come on to the subject of queries, any mistake here may result in the query not returning the correct data.

When you have finished typing in all the data, check the manner in which Access actually displays the date, which for Simon is displayed as 12/01/71. You actually typed in 12 Jan 71, which is the way we want the date to be displayed in the table, not as Access has displayed it.

Changing the data type format

We will now ensure that Access displays the date the way we want it. To make any changes to the table we must revert to the Design View of the table.

Basic steps

1 Click the Design View icon ▼ on the Formatting toolbar

❑ The table will now change to the Design View

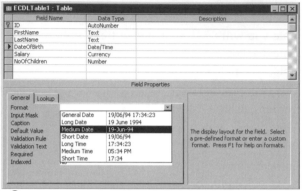

2 Click in the *Date of Birth* field

3 Move down to the Field Properties area

4 Ensure that the General tab is selected

5 Click in the Format slot

❑ Once the cursor is in the slot, a drop-down arrow will appear in the right area of the field

6 Click once on the arrow and a list will appear

7 Select the date style and format as shown

8 Click the Datasheet View icon 🔲 ▼ on the toolbar

9 You will be prompted to save the table – click Yes

❑ The table will change to Datasheet View

Check that the format of the date is displayed, it should now follow the format 12-Jan-71.

Navigating from record to record

You will recall that, when inputting data into a table, you use **[Tab]** to move from one field to the next, until such time as you reach the end of the record. When you next press **[Tab]**, the cursor will move to the beginning of the next record. This method, if used to navigate between records, is long, laborious and inefficient. There is a more efficient way to move between records and that is to use the navigation buttons located along the bottom of the table as shown in the example.

First
Back one
Current record number
Forward one
Last
Create new record
Number of records

Adding records to an existing table

We will now add a further three records.

Basic steps

1 Click in the *First Name* field of the empty row
2 Type in the data shown here

George	Brown	13 Jan 55	£940	0
Joe	Hopeless	01 Apr 81	£890	2
Peter	Brown	31 Jul 79	£930	3

Printing a table

We will now print the table, however it is advisable to preview the document before actually printing it.

Basic steps

1 Select File > Print Preview
❑ The preview window will open, an example of which is shown on the next page

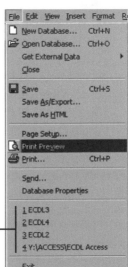

Access remembers the last four databases that were used and stores their names in the File menu. Click on a name to open the database.

Print preview

Confirm that the layout is similar to this example. If the document appears too small, click on the magnifying glass icon on the Print Preview toolbar. The cursor will change to a symbol of a magnifying glass and the image will increase in size. Click the same icon again to decrease the image size.

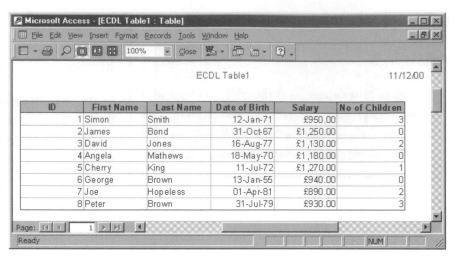

You could also place the cursor over the preview window and if the symbol had a '+' sign within the circle, clicking over the image would enlarge it. If the symbol had a '-' sign within the circle, clicking over the image would reduce it.

2 Select Close on the Print Preview Toolbar

3 When the window closes, select File > Print

❑ The Print dialog box will now open

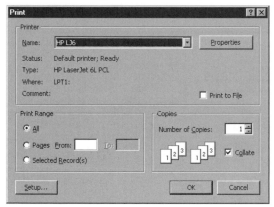

4 Ensure the correct printer is selected (which will be different from that shown in the example)

5 Click OK

Print properties

Various changes can be implemented from within the Print dialog box. We will not investigate these options at this stage, however you should at a later stage read the handbook relating to your printer and practise making changes to the way the document can be printed.

Saving a copy of a table

It is possible to export the table to another database or to save a copy of it, under a different name, within the same database. Why would you want to do this?

You may wish to create a new table, using a structure similar to the existing table. Copying the table will save considerable time and effort and you may only have to carry out minor modifications to the new table structure.

Another reason is that you may wish to modify the current table but are unsure of the result. By copying the table you will not lose data should the changes fail or if they do not have the desired effect.

Basic steps

To save the table within the same database:

1 Close the table

2 Ensure that the appropriate table is selected, in this case, 'ECDL Table1'

3 Select File > Save As

❑ The Save As dialog box will open

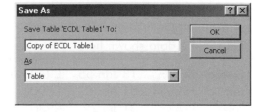

☐ Access will offer you a name beginning with 'Copy of' followed by the name already assigned to that table. In this instance the suggested new name is '*Copy of ECDL Table1*'.

4 It is recommended that you accept the suggested name, because it is then easier to identify the origin of the table. Should you wish to change it, simply type in the new name.

5 Click OK to accept the suggested name

You will be returned to the database window, which will now display in the Tables tab both copies of the table.

Renaming Access objects

You may wish to rename a table, or a form, query or report, at some stage of your work.

Basic steps

1 Close the item

2 Select it in the database window – in this case, *Copy of ECDL Table1*

3 Right-click over the name

4 Select Rename from the pop-up menu. The menu will close and the name will now have a flashing cursor within it

As the name is already highlighted, simply type in the new name and the old one will be over-written.

5 Enter the new name '*ECDL Table2*'

6 Press [Enter] for the change to take place

Open
Design View
Print...
Print Preview

Cut
Copy

Save As...
Export...
Send To ▶
Add to Group ▶
Create Shortcut...
✕ Delete
Rename

Properties

An alternative method

You may also rename an item by choosing **Rename** from the **Edit** menu. Select the item to be renamed then select **Edit > Rename**, and proceed as as described previously.

Indexing

In Access, an *index* is a pointer or indicator. You can create indexes based on a single field or on multiple fields. Multiple-field indexes enable you to distinguish between records in which the first field may have the same value.

If you have a database that is comprised of addresses and you regularly run searches on the postal code, then you would place an index on the postal code field.

By indexing fields, searches are performed much quicker. The computer only has to read the pointer information rather than read each record in the database until it finds the required field.

Basic steps

1 Right-click over *ECDL Table1*

2 From the pop-up menu select Design View

3 When the table opens in Design view, select the *Last Name* field

4 Click in the Indexed slot of the Field Properties pane

5 A drop-down arrow will appear – click it

6 From the list select Yes (Duplicates OK) – there may be people with the same surnames and had the other option been selected, you would not have been permitted to enter the same name twice.

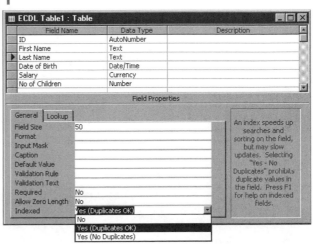

The 'Duplicates OK' option allows any number of 'Browns', 'Smiths', etc. which are spelt the same, to be entered in the database.

7 Click on the Datasheet View icon

8 When prompted to save the changes, click Yes

❑ You will now be returned to Datasheet View

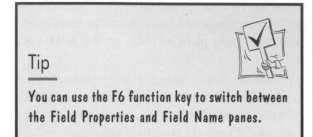
Deleting records

There are times when you may have to delete a record from a database. Although deleting records is sometimes necessary, it is a major action to undertake and should be approached with caution.

Basic steps

❑ The *ECDL Table1* should still be open

1 Select George Brown's record, by clicking on the grey square to the left of the name

2 Select Edit > Delete Record or right-click over the record and select Delete Record

❑ You will be prompted with a warning you that you are about to delete a record

Microsoft Access
You are about to delete 1 record(s).
If you click Yes, you won't be able to undo this Delete operation.
Are you sure you want to delete these records?
Yes   No

3 We do want to delete the record, so click Yes

❑ Clicking No would restore the record

When the record was removed, the lower record was rolled up to close the gap.

ID	First Name	Last Name
1	Simon	Smith
2	James	Bond
3	David	Jones
4	Angela	Mathews
5	Cherry	King
7	Joe	Hopeless
8	Peter	Brown
(AutoNumber)		

Record: 1 of 7

There are now 7 records

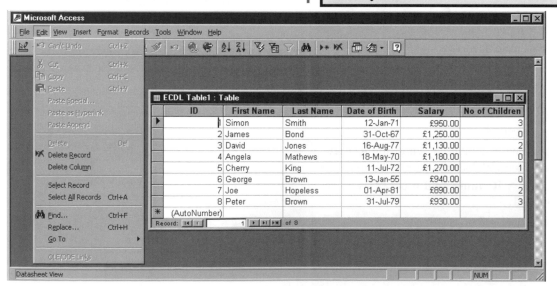

Microsoft Access

File Edit View Insert Format Records Tools Window Help

	Can't Undo	Ctrl+Z
Cut	Ctrl+X
Copy	Ctrl+C
Paste	Ctrl+V
Paste Special...
Paste as Hyperlink
Paste Append
Delete	Del
Delete Record
Delete Column
Select Record
Select All Records	Ctrl+A
Find...	Ctrl+F
Replace...	Ctrl+H
Go To
OLE/DDE Links

ID	First Name	Last Name	Date of Birth	Salary	No of Children
1	Simon	Smith	12-Jan-71	£950.00	3
2	James	Bond	31-Oct-67	£1,250.00	0
3	David	Jones	16-Aug-77	£1,130.00	2
4	Angela	Mathews	18-May-70	£1,180.00	0
5	Cherry	King	11-Jul-72	£1,270.00	1
6	George	Brown	13-Jan-55	£940.00	0
7	Joe	Hopeless	01-Apr-81	£890.00	2
8	Peter	Brown	31-Jul-79	£930.00	3
(AutoNumber)					

Record: 1 of 8

Datasheet View   NUM

Sorting records

An excellent feature of databases is that you can present the same information in a variety of ways. You may wish to display the information in the *ECDL Table1* with all the *Last Name* fields in alphabetical, ascending order.

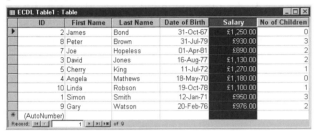

Basic steps

1 Select the field that you wish to sort on, by clicking on the column name

❑ To sort into alphabetical order of names:

ECDL Table1 : Table					
ID	First Name	Last Name	Date of Birth	Salary	No of Children
1	Simon	Smith	12-Jan-71	£950.00	3
2	James	Bond	31-Oct-67	£1,250.00	0
3	David	Jones	16-Aug-77	£1,130.00	2
4	Angela	Mathews	18-May-70	£1,180.00	0
5	Cherry	King	11-Jul-72	£1,270.00	1
7	Joe	Hopeless	01-Apr-81	£890.00	2
8	Peter	Brown	31-Jul-79	£930.00	3
* (AutoNumber)					

Record: 1 of 7

2 Click the Ascending Order icon ⬇ on the Standard toolbar

❑ The records will be sorted in ascending alphabetical order of the data in the *Last Name* field

ECDL Table1 : Table					
ID	First Name	Last Name	Date of Birth	Salary	No of Children
2	James	Bond	31-Oct-67	£1,250.00	0
8	Peter	Brown	31-Jul-79	£930.00	3
7	Joe	Hopeless	01-Apr-81	£890.00	2
3	David	Jones	16-Aug-77	£1,130.00	2
5	Cherry	King	11-Jul-72	£1,270.00	1
4	Angela	Mathews	18-May-70	£1,180.00	0
1	Simon	Smith	12-Jan-71	£950.00	3
* (AutoNumber)					

Record: 1 of 7

Insert additional records

We will now add a further two records to the database to increase it in size. Enter the data, as shown, in the next blank records in the table.

Gary	Watson	20 Feb 76	£976	2
Linda	Robson	19 Oct 78	£1100	1

Re-sort the table in ascending order on the *Last Name* field.

Moving fields

After constructing the table you may prefer to have two particular columns next to each other. Here, we want the *Salary* to be next to the *Last Name* column.

Basic steps

1 Select the *Salary* header to highlight the column

ECDL Table1 : Table					
ID	First Name	Last Name	Date of Birth	Salary	No of Children
2	James	Bond	31-Oct-67	£1,250.00	0
8	Peter	Brown	31-Jul-79	£930.00	3
7	Joe	Hopeless	01-Apr-81	£890.00	2
3	David	Jones	16-Aug-77	£1,130.00	2
5	Cherry	King	11-Jul-72	£1,270.00	1
4	Angela	Mathews	18-May-70	£1,180.00	0
10	Linda	Robson	19-Oct-78	£1,100.00	1
1	Simon	Smith	12-Jan-71	£950.00	3
9	Gary	Watson	20-Feb-76	£976.00	2
* (AutoNumber)					

Record: 1 of 9

2 Click and hold down on the *Salary* column header

❑ A white line will appear to the left of the column and a small rectangle below the cursor.

3 Drag the cursor towards the *Last Name* field.

❑ As you move the cursor a black line will appear between the *Last Name* and the *Date of Birth* fields.

4 Release the mouse button

❑ The column will move adjacent to the *Last Name* field

Take note

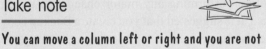

You can move a column left or right and you are not restricted to moving it just one column's width.

ECDL Table1 : Table					
ID	First Name	Last Name	Salary	Date of Birth	No of Children
2	James	Bond	£1,250.00	31-Oct-67	0
8	Peter	Brown	£930.00	31-Jul-79	3
7	Joe	Hopeless	£890.00	01-Apr-81	2
3	David	Jones	£1,130.00	16-Aug-77	2
5	Cherry	King	£1,270.00	11-Jul-72	1
4	Angela	Mathews	£1,180.00	18-May-70	0
10	Linda	Robson	£1,100.00	19-Oct-78	1
1	Simon	Smith	£950.00	12-Jan-71	3
9	Gary	Watson	£976.00	20-Feb-76	2
* (AutoNumber)					

Record: 1 of 9

Viewing the data

At present, if we wish to view details relating to any of the personnel listed in our database we have to view this information in a table. The above table only has six fields and is reasonably easy to view and use. Imagine if the table included the addresses of the personnel and the names of their wives or husbands, where appropriate and any other relevant detail. Not all of it would fit into the display window and you would be constantly using the scroll bars. Not particularly user-friendly, however we will correct this in due course.

Modify the database structure

It is possible to modify the database structure after it has been constructed and even when it has been in use for some time. However, with careful thought and consideration, at the design stage, modification of the structure of the database should be kept to a minimum and modifications should be carefully thought out before being undertaken. This is particularly important when working with relational databases where knock-on effects may not have been considered or realised.

Changes to the structure might include adding new fields, deleting fields, and changing field properties.

Recommendation

Before performing any major changes to the database, it is suggested that you create a Backup copy of the database.

Deleting fields

We are not going to change the structure of the database but should you need to do so in the future, follow these procedures.

If the modification requirement is to remove a Field which is no longer required, select the required database Table and then select **Design View**. Select the unwanted field by clicking to the left of it and from the menu bar click on **Edit > Delete Row**.

Take note

This may initially be a little confusing. We started out to delete a field but the command used was **Delete Row**. However, remember to modify a table you must be in Design View. Table Design View has a row for each field in the table, which contains the Field Name, the Data Type and Description.

Access will warn you that deleting the field will result in a loss of data. It allows you either to carry on and delete the field or to cancel the operation.

If you decide to carry on with the deletion, the selected row will then be deleted. Close the Design View and when prompted save the changes.

If a form was based on the table, it may now be necessary to modify the form and delete the corresponding field there. Forms are introduced next.

Inserting fields

We will not, at this stage, alter the database, but it is possible to insert additional field(s). It is done from the Table Design View, in a similar manner as when constructing the original Table. Inserting additional fields will have repercussions on such items as Forms, Queries and Reports. If you require the new field to be included on a Form or Report, you will have to either re-create the item from scratch, or more likely manually insert it, which is discussed later in the course.

Summary

Always create a copy of the database before making any changes to its structure, particularly if you are considering deleting fields with the resultant loss of data. There may be numerous factors to consider and one such factor could be that the field to be deleted is a Primary or a Secondary key linking various tables.

There is no reason not to change the structure of a database if so required and after due consideration and investigation of the consequent effects.

Creating a form

Forms are the main method of entering and editing data. Forms are based upon one or more tables and usually display one record at a time, unlike tables, which display multiple records simultaneously. To create a form, a table has to be constructed first.

Forms can be constructed using a Wizard or from the Design View mode.

Creating a form using a Wizard

Basic steps

1 Close *ECDL Table 1* – save changes if prompted
❑ This will return us to the Database Window
2 Click Forms in the Objects bar
3 Double-click *Create form by using a wizard*.

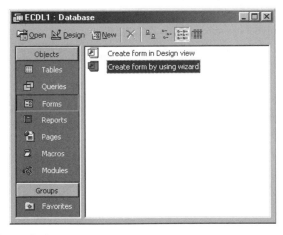

A reminder

A Wizard is a semi-automated method of creating items or functions within Access and is an ideal way of creating the Form that we require for our database.

The Wizard will at various stages prompt you for information to assist with the design and construction of the Form. You can back track on the selection for each option, if you change your mind, by clicking **Back** . This will return you to the previous stage.

Forms can also be produced without the use of the Wizard, by selecting **Design View** from the **New**

Form dialog box and you may well adopt this method in due course, but remember, all of the thought and planning must be done beforehand.

Selecting the form fields

The first dialog box lists the fields available from *ECDL Table1*. You can select all the fields, or certain ones. In this instance all the fields are required.

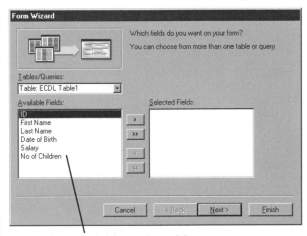

Fields available in the table

Fields are selected and moved from the **Available Fields** list to the **Selected fields** list. The fields can be selected and moved individually or moved together. Any fields that appear in the **Selected Fields** list are the ones which will appear on the form.

The **Tables/Queries** slot lists the table that the form will be based upon. You can change the selection at this stage if required. However, please read the details below before performing any actions.

These lower two buttons move fields back from the **Selected** to the **Available Fields** list.

Basic steps

1 To move a single field, select it and click ▸
❑ We want all the fields. Simply click ▸▸. All the fields will be moved to the Selected Fields pane

221

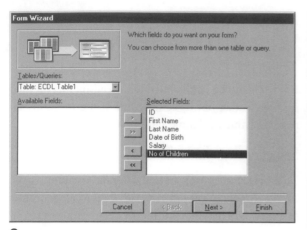

2 Click Next

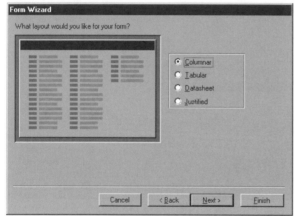

3 Select each layout option in turn – it will be displayed in a preview

4 Select Columnar and click Next

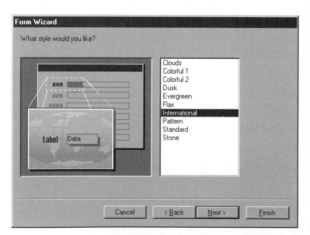

❏ The next box will offer you different selections of background styles for the Form. As you select each style, it will be previewed in the style pane.

6 Select Standard and click Next

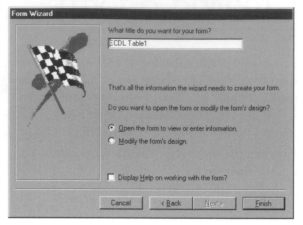

❏ The next box will prompt you for a name :

7 Call this form 'ECDL Form1'

❏ Do not change the options offered

8 Click Finish

The Wizard will now produce the completed Form.

Navigating the records in Form View

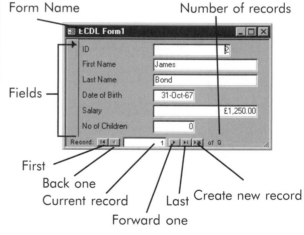

Form Name — Number of records

Fields —

First
Back one
Current record
Forward one
Last
Create new record

Practise moving through the database viewing the records. Remember what the control buttons do, and they can save considerable time with a large database.

❏ Close the Form

At this stage only the Database window should be open. This will remain open, irrespective of whether you are using a Table, Form or Query. You can minimise the window if it becomes a distraction.

❏ Do not close the database at this stage, as you require it for the next chapter

Creating and performing queries

Queries arc used to extract specific information from a database. They can also be used to create new tables based upon the information extracted (and perform a number of other tasks not covered in this course).

Queries are a powerful tool and we are only going to discuss some of their functionality. You should use the online Help for further information on their use.

We are now going to create a query, which will extract information from the database within the criteria that we specify.

Basic steps

1 Ensure all tables and forms are closed and that the Database window is displayed

2 In the Objects bar select Queries

3 Right-click over *Create query in Design view* and from the pop-up menu select Design view

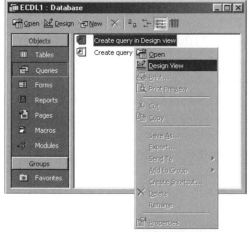

❑ The Query Design window will now open, with the smaller Show Table dialog box in front.

4 From the Show Table dialog box select *ECDL Table1*

5 Click Add then Close

❑ The details of the table will be transferred to a smaller box in the upper left corner of the Query Design window.

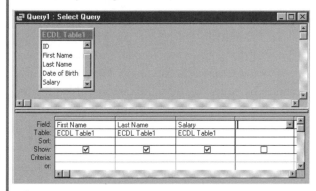

6 In the field list, select *First Name*

7 Click and drag the field over to the first column

8 Drop it in the first row

9 Repeat with the *Last Name* and *Salary* fields, placing them in the columns as shown above

We are going to set up the query to extract all the personnel who have a salary over £1000, using *operators* to assist us. Before we proceed any further there follows a quick explanation of some of the operators that can be used in Access.

Query operators

Operators are essential to queries. They are found under a number of different headings, subject to the functions they perform or in what context they are used.

Operators indicate that an operation, or task, has to be performed on one or more items. The following are some of the more common examples.

The = (equal) operator will return a match, or in database talk 'True', if two expressions being compared are the same. For example, if used in the query that we are just creating, we would enter the following in the *Salary* Criteria slot '=1000'. The query would look for any figures, in all the Salary fields, that are equal to 1000.

If none of the salaries were equal to 1000, then the query would return a 'False' result. If any salaries are found to be equal to 1000, the query will list them.

Access uses a variety of operators. These are the most common.

Mathematical operators

There are seven mathematical or arithmetic operators:

*   multiplication
+   addition
-    subtraction
/   division
\   integer (whole number) division

mod modulus (remainder from whole number division)

^   exponentiation

Relational operators

There are six relational or comparison operators, which compare two values or expressions:

=	Equal
<>	Not equal
<	Less than
<=	Less than or equal
>	Greater than
>=	Greater than or equal

Returning to our example: if we entered the criteria in the Salary row as 'greater than or equal to' (>=),

the query would give a return on any person whose salary was 1000 or greater.

The ECDL course syllabus does not require you to learn query operators in depth, we only use them in very simple queries. It is suggested that for more information on using operators, you should consult the online Help. When the Help dialog box first opens, a number of operators are listed at the very beginning of the Help topic list. You should also look up 'Order of Precedence'. Learn the order of precedence for using operators, as some common errors encountered by users are often due to incorrect use of operator precedence.

Basic steps

To create the query criteria:

1   Click in the Criteria field under the *Salary* column

2   Type in the greater than (>) symbol

❑   Do not leave any spaces, after the '>' sign

3   Type in '1000'

4   From the Query Design toolbar click the Run Query icon ▮

Field:	Salary
Table:	ECDL Table1
Sort:	
Show:	☑
Criteria:	>1000
or:	

Access will now search the database for all personnel with salaries over £1000 and present the information in a table format.

Query1 : Select Query

First Name	Last Name	Salary
James	Bond	£1,250.00
David	Jones	£1,130.00
Angela	Mathews	£1,180.00
Cherry	King	£1,270.00
Linda	Robson	£1,100.00

Record: 1 of 5

This figure indicates that 5 records were found that meets the criterion set up in our query

Saving query

Because we may want to run the query in the future, we will save it.

Basic steps

1 Click the Close button on the top right of the window

2 You will be asked if you wish to save the query. We do, so click Yes

3   At the Save As dialog box, call the query 'Salary>1000'

4 Click OK to save it

You will now be returned to the Database window and will see the query name in the Queries tab. Any queries that you create will appear in the Queries tab.

Exercise 1

Create a Query which will extract all the personnel listed in *ECDL Table1* who have 2 children (Note: Use the equals (=) sign not the greater than sign (>))

Include the *First Name*, *Last Name* and *No of Children* fields in the query as well

Save the query and call it '*Children*'

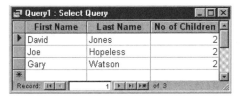

Exercise 2

Modify the query *Children* to extract the information on all personnel who were born after May 76 and who have 2 children.

When prompted save the query.

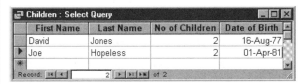

Summary

That completes this section which introduced you to simple queries. You will encounter more queries as the module progresses.

Further information can be found in the online Help and you should investigate the more advanced features available to you using queries.

Reports

At some stage during the use of the database you may require some, or all, of the content to be printed for distribution. You could simply print a copy of the table but it may be quite large and due to its layout will not lend itself to easy reading.

The way to print data is to produce a report. The report can be created using a Wizard or you may decide to create it yourself using the Design view. In this instance we are going to create a report based on *ECDL Table1* using a Wizard.

Creating a report

Basic steps

1   Ensure that all tables, forms or queries are closed and that the Database window is open
2   In the Objects bar, select Reports
3   Right-click on *Create report by using a wizard*
4   From the pop-up menu select Design View

The Report Wizard will open and it is from here that you will construct and assemble the Report's content.

5   Click the drop-down arrow and a list of tables and queries will appear

6   Select *ECDL Table1*
7   Click OK

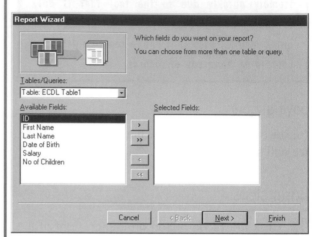

❑   We will now select the fields that are required in the report:
8   Select *First Name* and click ▸ to move the field to the Selected Fields list
9   Repeat for *Last Name* and *Salary*
10 Click Next
❑   The next window will now ask you if you want to add any grouping levels

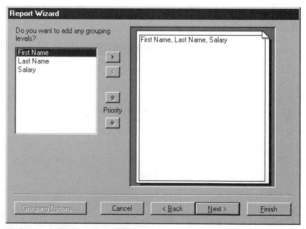

11 You can experiment with this later but for now ignore it – click Next

The wizard will now present you with a dialog box from which you may sort the records. We will only concern ourselves with the 'Salary' field for now.

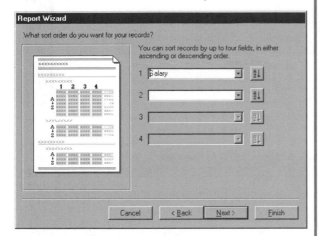

12 Click the drop-down arrow and select *Salary*

❑ Access will now sort the report based on the *Salary* field in ascending order

13 Click Next to move to the next dialog box. This will offer you a choice of layout. For example, do you want the fields laid out in Columnar or Tabular form, with Orientation as Portrait or Landscape?

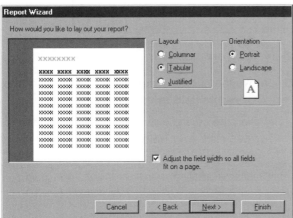

14 Leave the settings as Tabular and Portrait. Also, leave the tick in the Adjust field box. This will not affect us at this stage, but you should be aware of this facility.

15 Click Next to move to the dialog box. This will offer you a number of options relating to the layout style.

16 Make the same selection as shown in the example – *Soft Gray*

17 Click Next

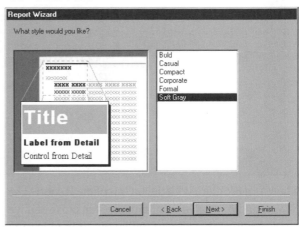

The last window of the Wizard series, offers you a number of options.

18 Type *Salary* for the report title (note that Access has already allocated it a name based upon the table name and that it is highlighted)

❑ You are also offered the opportunity to Preview the Report', which is the default setting, or Modify the report's design

19 Ensure that Preview the Report is selected

❑ Have the online Help displayed whilst working with the report

❑ We do want to see what the Report will look like before proceeding any further, so:

20 Click Finish – The Preview window will open

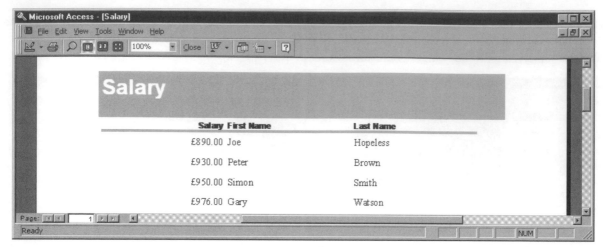

There is a problem with the layout of the Report. The *Salary* and *First Name* columns are too close and we need to adjust this area of the layout. It is in Design View that we can make changes to the layout of the Report.

Modifying the report layout

Basic steps

1   Click the Design View icon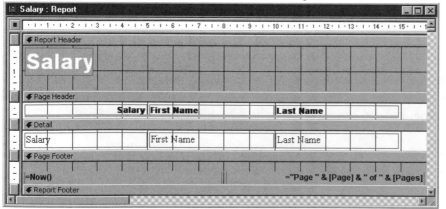

❑   Shown below is the image of our report in Design View. It is from here that we will make two changes and insert extra space between the *Salary* and the *First Name* fields.

2   Press and hold down [Shift]. This will allow you to make multiple selections

3   Click on the *First Name* field in the Page Header section

4   Keeping [Shift] down, click on the *First Name* field in the Detail area

5   Releasing the button and [Shift]. Both fields will remain selected. Note that each has a frame around it with a number of small rectangles, the re-sizing handles, within the frame.

Below are enlarged examples of the two fields discussed with the re-sizing handles visible.

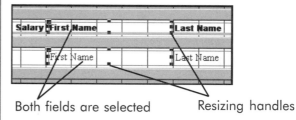

Both fields are selected   Resizing handles

6   Move the cursor over the centre handle of the *First Name* field in the Detail area

7   When the cursor changes to a double-headed arrow, click and hold the button down

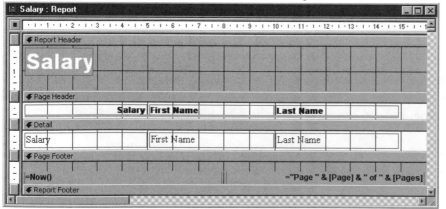

Report in Design View

8 Using the background squares as guides, drag the cursor approximately one square to the right and release the mouse button,

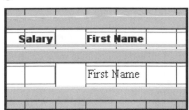

9 Click on the down-arrow adjacent to the View icon

10 From the drop-down list select the 'Print Preview' icon

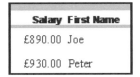

The image will revert to Print Preview and you will see that there is now a reasonable amount of space between the two fields.

Before and after changes

Examine the two examples and you will clearly see the difference in respect of the spacing.

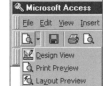

Salary	First Name
£890.00	Joe
£930.00	Peter

Before   After

11 Close the Print Preview window and close the *Salary* report

12 If prompted save the changes

Printing the report

Basic steps

1 Select the Reports tab on the Database window

2 Select the *Salary Report*

❑ You can print the report without opening it

3 From the menu bar select File > Print

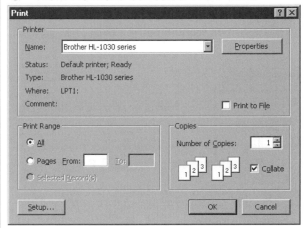

4 Ensure that the correct printer is selected – your display will be different to that shown here.

You can print just one page or all the pages within the report. As our report only contains one page you need not make any changes in the **Print Range** area.

If you require more than one copy, you should adjust the figure in the **Copies** area.

5 Click OK

After a short pause your printer should begin printing the report.

Exporting to another database

You may recall that earlier in the course we saved a copy of the *ECDL Table1* and renamed it *ECDL Table2*. During the course of saving the table we were offered the opportunity to export it to another database. This is what we shall now do. We are going to use the existing database *ECDL1* and create a new database, which we will call *ECDL2*.

Basic steps

1   Close all tables, forms or reports including the Database window

2   Select File > New, double-click on the Database icon and save it as *ECDL2* on the floppy disk

❑   The dialog box will now close and the Database window for the *ECDL2* database will open. We do not require this window open at the moment, so close it.

❑   Ensure that the floppy is in the disk drive

3   Select File > Open, and at the Open dialog box select *3½ Floppy (A:)*

4   Open the database *ECDL1.mdb*

5   At the Database window, select the Tables tab and click on the file *ECDL Table2*

6   Select File > Export

7   At the Export Table dialog box, select 'ECDL2.mdb' and click Save

❑   A further dialog box will offer you two options of how to export the table:

Export the table with *Definition and Data*

Export the structure, or *Definition only*

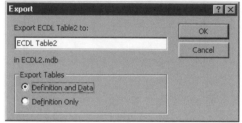

8   Select Definition and Data and click OK

❑   Access will now export a copy of the table from *ECDL1.mdb* to *ECDL2.mdb*

9   Close the *ECDL1* Database window

10 Select File>Open

11 Double-click on *ECDL2.mdb*

12 At the Database window, select the Tables tab – you should now find a copy of *ECDL Table2* present. Open it by double-clicking on its name

Take note

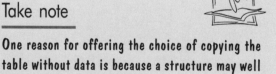

One reason for offering the choice of copying the table without data is because a structure may well be suitable for a series of tables, often with just minor amendments. This can be much quicker then creating a new table from scratch.

Adding records to ECDL table2

Add the following records to the table:

Raymond	Jennings	21 Mar 65	1350	3
Marie	Rosenbloom	30 May 56	1175	2
Frank	Robinson	25 Sep 57	1225	5
Richard	Carson	15 Dec 60	1452	4
Clare	Steine	21 Dec 61	1245	2
Rosemary	Kline	15 Jul 59	1236	0

Your table should now look like the example below.

Changing the table structure

As previously mentioned, it is possible to add new fields to a database should the need arise. In this case we want to be able to differentiate between the male and female staff and list personnel by gender when required. A simple way to do this would be to add to another field which we will call *Gender*.

Basic steps

1 With *ECDL Table2* open, click on the Design View icon on the toolbar

2 Place the cursor in the blank line under the field *No of Children*

3 Type 'Gender'

4 In the Data Type column accept the default setting of *Text*

5 Switch to the Field Properties pane

6 Press [F6] or click in the Field Size slot

❑ We are only going to enter a single letter in this field in the database, therefore we will change the default field length from 50 to 1.

7 Delete the default of 50 and type in 1

8 Click the Datasheet View icon

9 Save the changes when prompted

You will now see the *Gender* field located to the right of the *No of Children* field.

Take note

You may have noticed that although we set the field size to 1 there is more space in the field displayed. This is to accommodate the length of the field name.

Testing the field size property

Place the cursor in the *Gender* field for Simon Smith and type in the word 'Male'. You should find that you will only be permitted to enter the first letter. Access will not tell you why you cannot type further text.

Table layout

It would make more sense to have the *Gender* field located after the *Last Name* field. Move the *Gender* field there (to refresh your memory, see page 206).

(to refresh your memory, see page 206)

ID	First Name	Last Name	Gender	Date of Birth	Salary	No of Children
1	Simon	Smith	M	12-Jan-71	£950.00	3
2	James	Bond	M	31-Oct-67	£1,250.00	0
3	David	Jones	M	16-Aug-77	£1,130.00	2
4	Angela	Mathews	F	18-May-70	£1,180.00	0
5	Cherry	King	F	11-Jul-72	£1,270.00	1
6	George	Brown	M	13-Jan-55	£940.00	0
7	Joe	Hopeless	M	01-Apr-81	£890.00	2
8	Peter	Brown	M	31-Jul-79	£930.00	3
9	Raymond	Jennings	M	21-Mar-65	£1,350.00	3
10	Marie	Rosenbloom	F	30-May-56	£1,175.00	2
11	Frank	Robinson	M	25-Sep-57	£1,225.00	5
12	Richard	Carson	M	15-Dec-60	£1,452.00	4
13	Clare	Steine	F	21-Dec-61	£1,245.00	2
14	Rosemary	Kline	F	15-Jul-59	£1,236.00	0
(AutoNumber)						

ECDL Table2 : Table

Record: 14 of 14

The sample table with its additional data and the new field (after it has been moved)

5: Databases

231

Complete the *Gender* column appropriate to the names in the *First Name* field.

- Save the changes and then close the table.
- Ensure that the Database window is open.

Exercise 3

Create a query to list all females

Create a query based on the *ECDL Table2* that will produce a list of the females listed in the table.

Include the following fields in the query:

- First Name
- Last Name
- Gender

The criterion should be on the *Gender* Field.

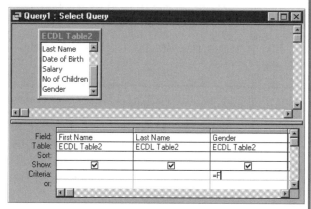

Run the query and you should find that it will return a table (as shown) with five females listed.

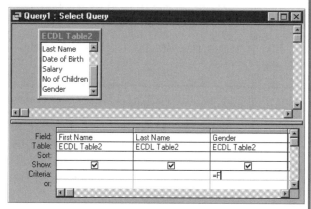

Exercise 4

Modify the query

Return to Design View and modify the same query.

Include the *No of Children* field without any criteria and run the query. The result is shown here.

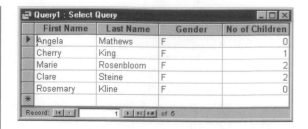

- Save the query as *Females* and close the query window.

Exercise 5

Extract males with children

There will be occasions when we create a query and use a particular field to extract the data, but do not require that field to appear in the query result. You can exclude the field quite easily.

We are going to demonstrate this using the *Gender* field.

Examine the example shown and you will see the tick in the box on the **Show** line. Notice the *Gender* field has been removed.

Click on the box, to clear the tick. It is a 'toggle' – click on the box again and the tick will reappear.

The query

Create a new query using *ECDL Table 2* which will list all the males with children.

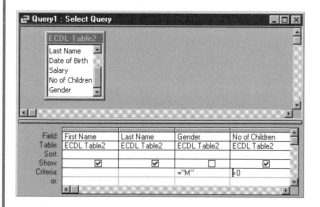

Base the query on the following fields:

- First Name
- Last Name
- Gender
- No of Children

Set the criteria as shown

The result

Note that the *Gender* field is not shown, but its inclusion was essential to the query to differentiate between the sexes. The listing is obviously an all-male group and therefore the inclusion of the *Gender* field would have been superfluous.

• Save the query as '*Males*'.

First Name	Last Name	No of Children
Simon	Smith	3
David	Jones	2
Joe	Hopeless	2
Peter	Brown	3
Raymond	Jennings	3
Frank	Robinson	5
Richard	Carson	4

Record: 1 of 7

Exercise 6

Create a report based on a query

Basic steps

1 Close all the windows that may be open, except for the Database window.

2 Select the Reports tab and right-click over *Create report by using a wizard*

3 Select Design View

4 Ensure that the name '*Query: Males*' appears in the Table/Query slot

5 Work through the Wizard, adding all the fields to the Selected Fields, sorting on *Last Name* and choosing the *Soft Gray* style, but leaving other settings at their defaults. At the last stage, accept the suggested name of *Males* and click Finish

6 Preview the report, make any adjustments necessary and then print out a copy of it.

Exercise 7

Deleted records and queries

The aim of this exercise is to demonstrate how an existing query will always return an up-to-date listing and not one from the time it was created.

Before we run the query, we will first delete something from *ECDL Table2*. Open the database *ECDL2*, then open the table *ECDL Table2* and delete the records for the following personnel:

David Jones

Frank Robinson

Re-run the query

Close the table and from the Database window select the **Reports** tab.

Click on the *Males* report and click on **Preview**.

Compare the copy printed when the report was first run, before any records were deleted, to the preview copy now on screen. The screen copy reflects the changes, and the two records have gone.

What this indicates is that the Report always re-runs the query upon which it is based, before displaying any data, so that the information contained in the Report is always current and reflects the database at that time.

Close the Preview window and close the *ECDL2* database.

Putting it all together

We are now going to create a third database, using an existing table as its foundation, and then perform a number of more advanced operations involving the use of Forms, Filters and Images.

Before we perform the export, we are going to create a new database. Follow the procedure detailed on page 208 to create a new database, called *Advanced*, and to export into it ECDL Table2, calling the new table *Advance1*.

Adding additional fields

We are now going to add fields to the existing structure. The additional detail will be addresses for the existing personnel and the date they started working for the company.

Basic steps

1   Open the exported table *Advance1*

❑   Before we start, we shall tidy the database so that it lists the personnel in numerical order

2   Click on the *ID* column in Datasheet View

3   Perform an Ascending Sort

4   Switch to Design View

⊞ Advance1 : Table	
Field Name	Data Type
ID	AutoNumber
First Name	Text
Last Name	Text
Date of Birth	Date/Time
Salary	Currency
No of Children	Number
Gender	Text

5   Place the cursor in the empty field below the *Gender* field and type:

Address1	Text	Field Size default
Address2	Text	Field Size default
Town	Text	Field Size default
Post Code	Text	Field Size 10
Employment	Date/Time	Medium Date

The amended database

Your table in Design View should now look like with the additional fields.

⊞ Advance1 : Table			_ □ ✕
Field Name	Data Type	Description	
ID	AutoNumber		
First Name	Text		
Last Name	Text		
Date of Birth	Date/Time		
Salary	Currency		
No of Children	Number		
Gender	Text		
Address1	Text		
Address2	Text		
Town	Text		
Post Code	Text		
Employment	Date/Time		

Take note

You may find that Access has moved the 'Gender' field back to its original position, if it has do not worry and leave it there.

6   Save the changes and switch back to Datasheet View

If you cannot see all the table fields at the same time, maximise the table window.

The address list

Switch to Datasheet View and copy the details on the opposite page carefully and check them when you have finished, as we will be using them later to create queries. The *ID* numbers are included to assist you to identify the correct records and should not be entered.

Adjusting the column widths

We will adjust the table column widths to display all of the field contents.

There are a number of methods available and one is similar to that used in Excel.

ID	Address1	Address2	Town	Post Code	Employment
1	123 Upper Forest Rd	Burden	Doncaster	HN5 5RT	14 Feb 91
2	23 Chase Rd	Lofturn	Doncaster	HN6 8TR	16 Jun 85
4	97 Crumlin Ave	Lee	Manchester	MN2 9SD	27 Jul 92
5	2/34 Cheshire House	Swinbury	Sheffield	SF4 8GF	23 Oct 91
6	2 Buxton View	Swinbury	Sheffield	SF3 5FD	12 Dec 78
7	8 Glen Close	Upper Maple	Buxton	SD6 8JK	22 Feb 98
8	12 Winston Churchill Ave	Lee	Manchester	MN3 9FF	30 Jun 96
9	23 Calne Close	Lofturn	Doncaster	HN3 7JK	14 Jul 87
10	12 Rose Lane	Upper Maple	Buxton	SD3 5FD	11 May 79
12	45 Downton Road	Cross Keys	Buxton	SD3 4BG	14 Oct 86
13	55 Elm Drive	Upper Maple	Buxton	SD3 2AW	04 Aug 84
14	234 Skye House	Lee	Manchester	MN4 8YH	05 Sep 76

Basic steps

Method 1

1 Right-click on the column header for *Address1*
2 From the pop-up menu select Column Width
3 From the dialog box, select Best Fit

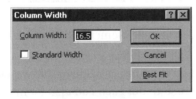

The column will now automatically adjust its overall width to display the widest column contents.

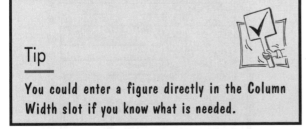

Tip

You could enter a figure directly in the Column Width slot if you know what is needed.

Method 2

1 Place the cursor over the junction of the column to be adjusted
2 When the cursor changes its shape, drag it left or right until the required width is obtained

These are similar methods to those used in Excel to change the cell widths. If necessary, adjust any column widths.

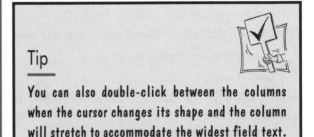

Tip

You can also double-click between the columns when the cursor changes its shape and the column will stretch to accommodate the widest field text.

Table layout

Clearly using the table to view data is not the most effective method. For example, if the field widths are all adjusted to view each field fully, you have to make excessive use of the scroll bar.

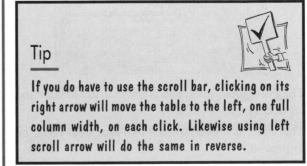

Tip

If you do have to use the scroll bar, clicking on its right arrow will move the table to the left, one full column width, on each click. Likewise using left scroll arrow will do the same in reverse.

Forms usually display data one complete record at a time and are therefore the ideal tool for viewing and inputting data.

Using a Wizard to create a form

We have already created a Form using a Wizard and will do the same on this occasion, modifying it to suit our requirements. As we have previously created a Form, the full procedure will not be listed here, although new procedures will be explained.

Basic steps

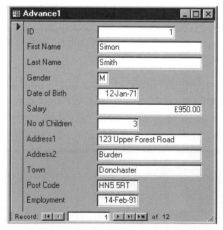

1   Close all windows, saving changes if prompted, do so, until only the Database window is open
2   Select the Form tab
3   Click the New button
❑   From the next series of dialog boxes select:
4   Form Wizard and *Advance1*
5   We require all the fields on the form
6   Choose *Columnar* layout and *Standard* style
7   Accept the suggested name
8   Click Finish

Access will now generate the form, which should resemble the one shown here.

The Form looks good and is easier to use to view and input data than a table.

There are, however, one or two areas that could be improved.

Certain fields are too big for the content.

This can happen when too little thought is given to the table or form design.

In our case it was intentional.

Points like this can be rectified without too much effort and we will make the changes shortly.

Form design view

Forms, like Tables and Reports, can be viewed in Design View and that is where changes can be made to layout and properties.

With the Form still open, click on the 'Design' icon located on the toolbar.

Take note

You may find that in addition to the form when you are in Design View, the Form Properties dialog box opens. Do not concern yourself, at this stage, if it did open.

Shown here is the Design View of the form and at the moment it is the field elements that we are interested in and will shortly move or resize.

Each field on the form is made up of two elements, which are linked, but each can also be manipulated independently.

The elements are:

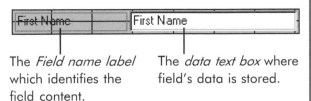

The *Field name label* which identifies the field content.

The *data text box* where field's data is stored.

Moving and resizing fields

There are a number of ways that you can resize or move fields. We will look at the manual method.

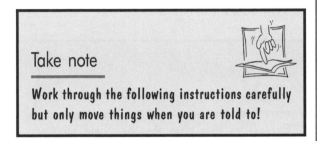

Take note

Work through the following instructions carefully but only move things when you are told to!

Identifying the elements

Click the *ID* field data text box and when selected, you will see resizing handles appear around it. Resizing handles are used to increase or decrease the length or width of the selected field or label.

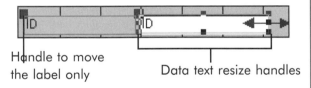

Handle to move the label only

Data text resize handles

You can move the field name label or the data text box independently of each other.

Look to the top left corner of the field name label – there is a small square.

Place the cursor over the square and it will change its shape to that of a small hand with a pointing index finger. If you Click and drag, only the field name label will move, the data text box will remain in its original location.

Clicking on the *ID* field name label will also result in resizing handles appearing around it and it can also be resized if necessary.

We will be doing this shortly.

To move both the field name label and data box, left-click over the appropriate field and when the cursor changes its shape to a small open hand, drag the field to the required location.

Tip

Remember that in any Design View, it is up to you to save the changes. It is suggested that until such time that you become confident, after each change you make, assuming that it has resulted in the desired effect, you save the change.

We will now adjust the *ID* field data box and reduce its length.

Adjusting a field length

Basic steps

1 Select the *ID* field data text box

2 Point to the right middle resize handle

3 When the cursor changes to a horizontal double-headed arrow, click and hold

❑ Using the grid in the background as a guide:

4 Carefully drag the cursor to the left to reduce the field length to one square length

5 At the appropriate point, release the button

6 Save the changes by clicking the Save icon on the toolbar

Adjusting multiple fields simultaneously

There are a number of fields that we are going to change and when finished, they will all have the same length. These changes are made in the Field Properties dialog box and can only be accessed when the form is in Design View. We should now be in Design View and the box may already be open, however we will describe two methods of opening it for future reference.

237

Opening the Field Properties box

Basic steps

1 Close the Properties box
2 Right-click over a field and from the pop-up menu select Properties
❑ Or double-click on any field and it will open

The Field Properties box

We will change two fields so that they are the same length as the *Salary* field and rather than change each field individually, we will change all of them in one go. This is known as a multiple selection.

Before we can make the change, we must first determine what the Salary field size is.

Basic steps

1 Return to the form and double-click on the *Salary* data text box
2 At the Properties box ensure that the Format tab is selected
3 Find the Width slot and make a note of the size

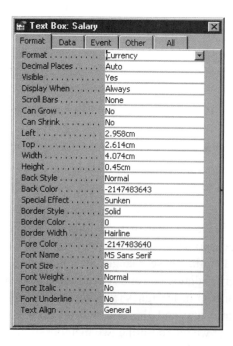

In this instance the size is given as 4.074cm. If the size or measurement unit on your computer is different, do not worry, make a note of what is shown.

❑ Now that we know the size, return to the form and we shall now select the other fields
4 Depress and hold down [Shift]
5 Select the *Date of birth* and *No of Children* field text boxes – as you click on each text box, it is included in the group selection
6 When all are selected, release [Shift]

Now check the **Width** slot in the **Properties** box and you will find it empty.

Take note

Because we have more than one field selected, what you see in the Properties box represents the properties shared by all of the selected fields.

7 Click in the Width slot and enter '2.037cm'
8 Watch the form and then press [Enter]
❑ The three text boxes will now all be set to the same length in one go
9 Switch from Design View to Form View to see the result of the change
❑ Keep the Properties box open

Changing the form name

When the Form was created the suggested name *Advance1* was accepted and it now appears on the title bar. However the name has little meaning in relation to the content, which are personnel records.

We will now change the form caption as it appears on the title bar and to do this we must now access the form's Properties box.

Selecting the form's Properties dialog box

As the name implies, the Field Properties box that we have used so far relates only to the fields that appear on the form. However, another properties box exists which relates to the form itself.

This is the **Form's Properties** box and it is here that we can make the change to the form caption. There is a particular method of opening this box.

Basic steps

1 Switch to Design View

2 Click in the square circled here – a solid block will appear in the square

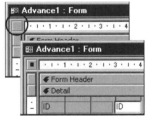

❑ Return to the Properties box and confirm that the correct box has opened. Check the name at the top – it should read *Form*.

3 Ensure that the Format tab is selected

❑ The item that we require is listed as Caption. It is currently displaying the suggested name *Advance1*.

4 Double-click over the word *Advance1*

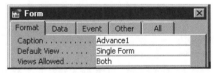

5 Type the new name '*Personnel Records*'

6 Switch back to Form View

❑ The form will now display the new caption *Personnel Records*

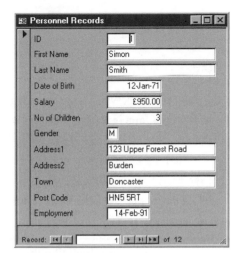

7 Save the changes

Changing the form background

We will now change the Form background colour.

Basic steps

1 Switch to Form Design View

2 Ensure that the Properties box is open

3 Click once on a blank area of the Form as indicated in the example

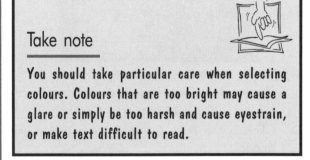

Blank area – without labels or text boxes

Take note

In the example on the previous page, showing a cut-down view of the form in Design View, you will see that the title bar still shows *Advance1* – the form name. What we changed was **not** the Form name, but the Form Caption. Do not confuse these two items. If you want to change the Name to match the Caption, you can, as described previously.

The Properties box should now look like this.

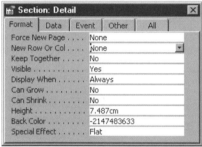

4   Locate the Back Color line.
    The number -2147483633, is Microsoft code for the colour light grey

5   Click in the Back Color slot – a button will appear

6   Click on the button and the Color palette will open

❑   Note that the light grey colour button is shown as depressed which indicates that it is the currently selected colour

7   Select the colour located on the same row, one to the left of the light grey button

8   Click OK

9   Switch to Form View

❑   The colour change will be applied. The colour is quite dark but label text can still be read without eyestrain. (Experiment with this later).

10 Save the changes

Resizing the form

We are going to reorganise the general layout and location of the form fields to create more space so that later we can add an image to the form.

We will first resize the form.

Basic steps

1   Switch to Form Design View

2   Place the cursor over the lower right-hand corner – your background colour may at this stage, not quite reach the corners as shown in the example. Do not concern yourself about it now.

3   When the cursor changes to a double-headed arrow, Click and drag it to the right

Check the ruler located immediately below the Form title bar. If you are using metric measurement, release the mouse button at the 16cm (approximately 6½ inches) mark on the right.

Take note

Each item on the form, such as a text box or label has its own properties and when selected, in the Design View, will be accompanied by its own Properties box.

240

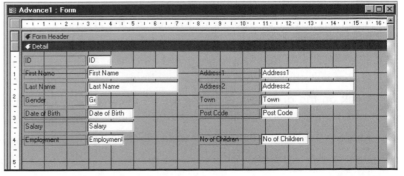

4   Place the cursor over the top edge of the Form Footer

5   When it changes its shape to ↕ click and drag it down to the 9.5cm mark on the left ruler

6   Place the cursor over the right edge of the green background area of the form

7   Drag it out to the right until your form resembles the example shown

Relocating fields on the form

We are going to move the address fields first and to do this we will make a multiple selection and move the fields simultaneously. It is suggested that you read this next section first before attempting to move the fields.

Basic steps

1   Make sure you are in Design View

2   Click on the *Address 1* text box

3   Depress and hold down [Shift] and select each of the remaining address fields

4   Move the cursor over the selected fields – it should change its shape to resemble a flat black hand.

At this point:

5   Click and drag the selected fields up and to the right, as shown in the example

6   Align the fields using the background grid and other fields

7   Release the mouse button

8   Click on a blank area of the Form to deselect the address fields

9   Rearrange the remaining fields until your form resembles the example shown

10 Save the changes

11 Switch to Form View

❑   Do not worry about the overall layout at this stage. We will be performing further changes to it shortly

241

Changing the tab field selection order

Using the Tab key is probably the most efficient method of selection, or movement, between fields when entering data. You already have your hands on the keyboard entering data in to the database and it is time-consuming to move your hand from the keyboard to the mouse to select the next field.

Therefore, there should be a logical order to the Form layout with a progressive movement from one field to the next.

The cursor should already be in the *ID* field. If not, click in it so that the cursor starts at the top of the form. Use [Tab] and select in turn each of the fields. Pay particular attention to the selection sequence.

You should find that the cursor starts at the *ID* field and moves through a logical selection sequence until it reaches the *Last Name* field, from where it jumps across to the *Date of Birth* field.

Think back to the Form layout before we moved any of the fields. The Tab sequence of selection is following the previous layout and order of the fields.

We know that the movement functions logically until we reach the *Last Name* field and it is from this point that it is out of sequence. This can be overcome easily.

Basic steps

1 Select Design View

2 From the View menu select Tab Order...

❑ The Tab Order dialog box will open. It is from this box that we can re-arrange the Tab selection order.

3 Ensure that the Detail option is selected

4 Click on the grey square to the left of the *Gender* field

❑ The field will now be highlighted and the cursor will change to a single arrow-head

5 Click on the grey square by the *Gender* field and drag the field to below the *Last Name* field

6 Release the mouse button to drop the *Gender* field into its new location

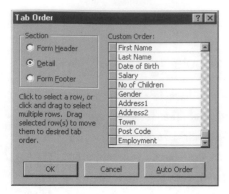

7 Click OK

Testing the tab order

Switch back to Form View and using [Tab], confirm that the change has been implemented and tab through all of the fields. Things are still not quite correct.

8 Return to Design View

9 Move the *Employment* field so that it is under the *Salary* Field

10 Move the *No of Children* field to the last position, underneath the *Post Code* field

Switch back to Form View and test the Tab order of selection. When you have confirmed the logical order of selection using [Tab]:

11 Save the changes

Import an image or graphic file

A database of personnel records could be greatly enhanced by the inclusion of a photograph of each person listed. We are now going to further modify the Form layout to accommodate a photograph.

Remember that Forms are based on Tables and before we actually import an image, some modification to the table is required first.

Basic steps

1 Close the form and save any changes if prompted

2 Open the table *Advance1* in Design View

3 Place the cursor in the empty field below the *Employment* field

4 Type '*Picture*'

5 In the Data Type box select *OLE Object*

6 Switch to Datasheet View and save the changes when prompted

❑ Scroll to the last field in the Table and you will find the new field *Picture*

Because this is a fictional database, we do not actually have any personnel and therefore no photographs. We are going to import a number of clip art images – the procedure is basically the same.

7 Right-click over the *Picture* field for Record 1 and from the pop-up menu select Insert Object

8 At the Insert Object dialog box, ensure that the Create New button is selected

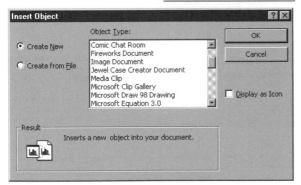

9 From the Object Type pane double-click on *Microsoft Clip Gallery*

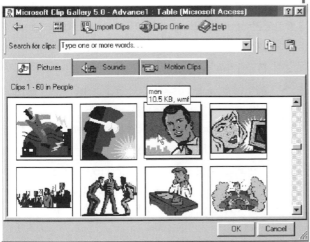

❑ The Microsoft Clip Gallery box will open

10 Scroll down and click on the *People* icon

11 Right-click over the image shown in the example and select Insert. This image will be inserted into the *Picture* field

12 Perform the same actions for Records 2 and 3, selecting a different character for each field

13 Close the table

14 Re-open the Form in Design View.

Picture fields in forms

Forms handle Picture fields just like any other data field and had the Picture field existed when we initially created the Form, it too would have been included along with all the other fields created by the Wizard. We have already modified the Form layout once and we are about to do the same again to accommodate the Picture field.

Basic steps

1 With the form open in the Design View, ensure that you have plenty of spare space in the lower area of the form – if necessary open out the form by dragging the borders out.

When we previously wanted to select a number of adjacent fields, we selected each field individually. On this occasion we are going to select all of the fields and we can do this quickly by using the shortcut key method.

2 Press [Control] and [A] simultaneously (Ctrl+A)

❑ All of the fields will now be selected. This is confirmed by the presence of the resize handles appearing around all the fields.

3 Place the cursor over the selected fields. When it changes shape to that of a flat hand:

4 Click and drag all of the fields down to occupy the lower half of the Form area

5 Click on a blank area of the Form background to de-select the fields

6 Save the changes

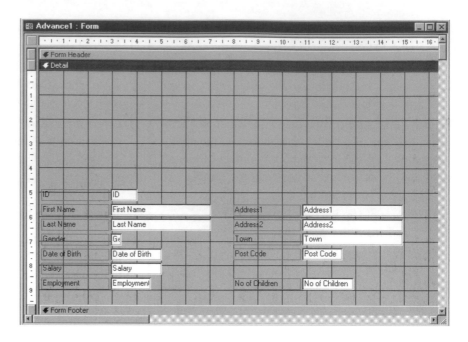

Inserting a Picture field

When we created the form the Form Wizard did the work for us. You may decide to create a Form without the assistance of a Wizard and decide the layout of the fields and any controls.

To insert the *Picture* field in the form, you require access to a list of all the fields available in the table upon which the form is going to be based. Access provides you with a Field List which is accessible from the Standard toolbar.

Basic steps

1 Go into Design View and click on the Field List icon ▣ on the toolbar

❑ The Field List box will open. Note that the name in the title area is *Advance1*. This is the name of the table which the form is based on.

The list contains all the fields in the table, all of which, excluding the Picture field, are already included in our form.

To include the *Picture* field in our form:

2 Click on the *Picture* field name and drag it across to the form

4 Release the mouse button when the field is over the centre of the blank area

❑ The field, and its label, will appear on the Form

5 Close the Field List by clicking on the Close button on its title bar

❑ The Picture field may be larger than we require, so we will set the field size

Basic steps

If the Properties dialog box is not already open:

1 Right-click over the *Picture* field

2 From the pop-up menu select Properties

3 At the Properties box opens select the Format tab

4 Change the Width and Height settings to 3cm

5 Close the Properties box

❑ The changes will be applied to the *Picture* field

There is no requirement for a label identifying the Field as 'Picture' so we will delete the Label.

244

Basic steps

1 Click on the Label
2 Press [Delete]
3 Reposition the *Picture* field so that it occupies the upper left area of the form
4 Save the changes
5 Switch back to Form View

Changing the Picture Properties

When in Form View you will find only that a limited amount of the image can be seen in the *Picture* field. We will rectify this by adjusting the field's properties.

Basic steps

1 Return to Design View
2 Open the *Picture* Properties box
3 Ensure that the Format tab is selected
4 Click in Size Mode slot – which should be showing *Clip*

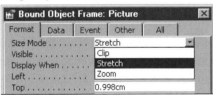

Bound Object Frame: Picture					✕
Format	Data	Event	Other	All	

Size Mode . . . . Stretch
Visible . . . . Clip
Display When . . . . . . Stretch
Left . . . . Zoom
Top 0.998cm

5 Click the drop-down arrow that appears to the right of the slot to open the list
6 Select *Stretch*

Tip

If you want to know more about the Stretch option, click into it and press [F1]. This will bring up the online Help and display help about this option. You can use the same technique to find out more about the options in any dialog box.

7 Switch back to Form View
❑ Check the *Picture* field and you should find that the image fills the field and can be fully seen
8 Save the changes

Understanding the image options

The **Stretch** option is not ideal for our use. This is because it sizes the object to fill the object window and may distort the image.

This is not important while we use clip art items. However, if we were using better quality images, i.e. photographs, then we would not want to see any signs of distortion.

The Zoom option better meets our requirements. Zoom displays the entire object, resizing it as necessary without distorting the proportions of the object.

Repeat the last set of steps to change the choice to Zoom.

If necessary, adjust the form border so that your form now resembles the one shown here.

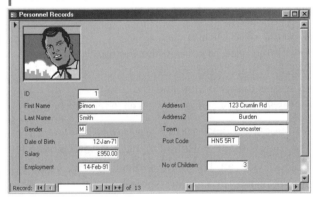

Using the record selection navigation controls, located in the lower area of the form, move through the records that you have assigned images to.

As you select a different record the image changes to represent each person list in the record. The images would in reality be the photograph of each individual.

Tabulation selection of the image

There is no logical reason for wanting to select the *Picture* field. We only require the field to change its display when the record changes. We can opt to switch off the Tab selection option within the Properties box.

Basic steps

1   Return to the Form Design View
2   If the Field Properties box is not open double-click on the *Picture* field
3   Select the Other tab
4   Locate the Tab Stop option and change this to No

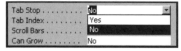

Tab Stop	No
Tab Index	Yes
Scroll Bars	No
Can Grow	No

5   Save the changes

Understanding object frames

A bound object frame

The frame used to contain the Picture was a Bound Object Frame, which means that the frame contains an image that is bound and fixed to the record and correspondingly changes when each record changes.

An unbound object frame

The opposite of a Bound Object is an Unbound Object. Use an Unbound Object Frame when a picture on a form or report is required and which you expect to update frequently. For example, if an image is used as the background to a form, it remains constant and does not change when different record are selected.

Using the form to enter data

As previously mentioned, it is the form that you will use most to input or edit data and we will now practise using a form.

Please review the section on form navigation controls (see page 210) if you are unsure of how the navigation controls function as they are important to this section.

Basic steps

1   Ensure that you are now back at Form View
2   click on the New Record button (circled)
    A new blank record will open

3   Enter the following details in the relevant fields
    Collin   Forbes   M   25 Nov 67   £1450
    12 Aug 88   36 Farm Fields Avenue
    Cross Keys   Buxton   SD5 8BG   4

You will notice that the cursor started in the *ID* field and we had to tab down to the *First Name* field before we could type in the data. Because we have little control of what goes into the *ID* field, there seems little point in it being included in the Tab order.

4   Switch to Form Design View
5   Click on the *ID* field and set its Tab Stop to *No*, as you did for the *Picture* field
6   Save the changes

Form text formatting

You will have noticed that various fields have different alignment applied, subject to the field data type.

♦   Text is normally left-aligned, but numbers are right-aligned, as are the currency and date fields.

The data type assigned to the fields are carried over to the form, but the formatting can be changed if required. We will experiment and change the alignment for a number of fields.

Basic steps

1   Ensure that you are in Design View and that the Properties box is open
2   Select the fields *Address1*, *Address2*, *Town* and *Post Code* (remember to use [Shift] to make multiple selections)
3   Ensure that the Format tab is open in the Properties box

4   Click in the Text Align slot – this   should be showing *General*

5   From the drop-down list select *Center*

6   Save the changes

7   Switch back to Form View to view them

Changing the label backgrounds

Any item that appears on the Form can have its Properties changed.

Basic steps

1   In Design View select all labels of the fields below the *Picture* field (i.e. all those on the left of the form)

2   Open the Properties box and select the Format tab

3   Click in the Back Color slot and open the Color Palette

4   Select *Light Grey*

5   Click OK to apply the change

6   Close the Color Palette

7   Switch back to Form View

☐   Compare the display and readability between the two sets of Labels that are now displayed

8   Save the changes

Changing the text box backgrounds

Basic steps

1   Switch back to Design View

2   Ensure that the Properties box is open

3   Select all of the address data text boxes

4   Change the Back Color property to red

5   Change the Fore Color property to blue

6   Switch back to Form View to see the changes

You can if you wish revert to the original default colours. This exercise was performed to illustrate the flexibility and choice available for customisation and possible pitfalls of colour clash.

Summary

You should investigate the Properties box in greater depth. The customisation and options available are numerous. When you progress to more advanced form design with the inclusion of control buttons, it is the Properties box where the control and manipulation of these and other items are setup.

Using the Replace feature

If you have completed either the Word or Excel modules, you will already be familiar with the Replace feature which functions in Access in the same way.

Basic steps

1   Open the *'Personnel Records'* Form

2   In Form View select Edit > Replace

3   At the Replace dialog box, type in the text and apply the settings as shown in the example

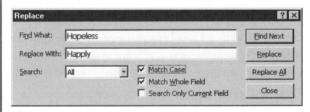

4   Click Find Next

5   When the only entry of the name Hopeless is found, click Replace

6   Close the dialog box and save the changes

Form filters

You will recall that we created a number of queries earlier in the course to extract certain information that met a given criterion. Forms have a Filter option which can be used in a similar manner as queries. Form filters are described later but first Microsoft's explanation of Filters vs. queries.

The Microsoft explanation

The basic similarity between selecting queries and filters is that they both retrieve a subset of records from an underlying table or query. How you want to use the records that are returned determines whether you use a filter or a query.

Use a filter to temporarily view or edit a subset of records while you are in a Form or Datasheet View.

Use a query if you want to do any of the following:

◆ View the subset of records without first opening a specific Table or Form

◆ Choose the Tables containing the records you want to work with and add more Tables at a later date

◆ Control which fields from the subset of records are displayed in the results (remember the tick box)

◆ Perform calculations on values in fields

Form filter options

There are three simple ways to filter records.

If you can easily select in the form, sub-form, or datasheet, an instance of the value you want the filtered records to contain, use *Filter by Selection*.

If you want to choose the values you are searching for from a list without scrolling through all the records in a datasheet or form, or if you want to specify multiple criteria at once, use *Filter by Form*.

If the focus is in a field in a form or datasheet and you just want to type in place the exact value you are searching for or the expression whose result you want to use as your criteria, use *Filter for Input*.

For complex filters, use *Advanced Filter/Sort*. See the online Help system for further information.

Where are the filters?

You can only apply form filters when in Form View. Before we can apply any type of filter action, we must first identify the locations and items that apply and then later remove the filter(s).

As with most Windows-based applications, you can access the controls in a number of different ways, for instance the toolbar has a number of filter icons. For quick access however, all of the filter options are listed in the **Records** menu, when the form is open.

Sort icons

You will already be familiar with the two icons, ![sort icons]. These are the Sort buttons which were introduced in Excel and used earlier in this course. The icons will sort selected data in either ascending or descending order.

Toolbar filter icons

There are three icons on the Form View toolbar ![filter icons].

◆ The first icon activates Filter by Selection

◆ The second icon activates Filter by Form.

◆ The third is a toggle. In the example it is in the Apply Filter mode and when clicked on, its appearance changes to that of a depressed button and is then in the Remove Filter mode.

The Records menu

All the available Filter options are also accessible from the Records menu and are shown in the example here. You should practise using either of the selection methods.

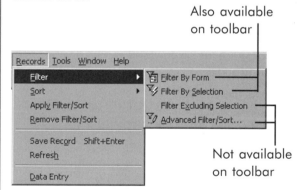

Also available on toolbar

Not available on toolbar

Exercise 8

Filter by selection

We are going to apply a Filter that will return all the records for a particular town, in this instance 'Buxton', and the procedure to be used is Filter by Selection. This means that we are going to first find the name of the town by scrolling through the records, using the navigation buttons, until we find the first occurrence of the town name 'Buxton'.

Basic steps

1 Ensure that the *Advance1/Personnel Records Form* is open in Form View

2 Click in the *Town* field

3 Scroll through the records to find '*Buxton*'

4 Click on the Filter by Selection icon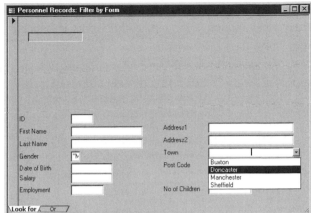

❑ Access will quickly filter all unwanted records and when complete, you can scroll through the selection. Check the Status bar and you will see that Access shows how many records met the criterion 'Buxton', in this instance 5.

❑ The filter will remain in force, indicated by the Remove Filter icon appearing depressed, until such time that you remove the filter.

5 Click the Remove Filter icon

❑ This will restore the full database. The icon will revert to its Apply Filter mode.

Filter by form

To perform a Filter by Form, you must first click on the Filter by Form icon. This is a different procedure to that used when we applied a Filter by Selection. Here, we first select the Filter type, then apply the criterion.

Basic steps

1 Check the toolbar and if the icon is in Remove Filter mode, click it to clear the Filter.

2 Click the Filter by Form icon

3 Return to the form

The form will be blank, except you may find that Access has retained some of the previous filter criterion, e.g. 'Buxton'. If this is so, select the field and press [Delete] to remove the criterion.

We are going to create a Filter criterion based on the *Gender* and *Town* fields. The aim of the exercise is to find all of the males, who live in Doncaster.

4 Click in the *Gender* field, then click the drop-down arrow which appears, to open the list

5 Select the letter 'M'

❑ Do not concern yourself if only an element of the field content is visible at this stage

6 Click in the *Town* field, open its drop-down list and select 'Doncaster'

7 Click on the Apply Filter icon on the toolbar

❑ Access will filter the records and indicate the number that met the criteria, in this instance 3.

8 You can now scroll through the records

9 When you no longer require the filter result click to restore the full database

At present we no longer require the Form so close it down and if prompted, save any changes.

Logical operators in queries

When we created the queries earlier in this course, we used arithmetic and comparison operators to sort and extract the required information.

There is another group of operators, known as logical operators.

Order of precedence

When more than one operator is used in a query, each part is evaluated and resolved in a predetermined order called *operator precedence*.

When a query contains operators from more than one category, arithmetic operators are evaluated first, comparison operators next and logical operators last.

249

Comparison operators all have equal precedence; they are evaluated in the left-to-right order in which they appear.

You can enter additional criteria for the same field or different fields. When you type expressions in more than one Criteria cell, Access combines them using either the **And** or the **Or** operator.

- If the expressions are in different cells in the same row, Access uses the **And** operator, which means only the records that meet the criteria in *all* the cells will be returned.

- If the expressions are in different rows of the design grid, Access uses the **Or** operator, which means records that meet the criteria in *any* of the cells will be returned.

Creating a query using logical operators

The aim here is to retrieve the names of any personnel that live in 'Buxton', in the post code area 'SD3'. As you have already created a number of queries, the procedure will not be fully itemised.

Basic steps

1 Open the database *Advanced*
2 In the Objects bar select Queries
3 Right-click over *Create query in Design view* and from the pop-up menu select Design view
4 In the Show Table dialog box select the Tables tab and double-click on the *Advance1* table
5 Click the Close button
6 Enter 'Buxton' as the criteria in the *Town* fields – the (") signs are added automatically

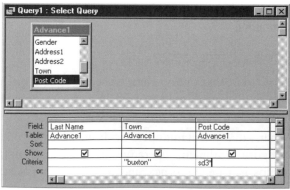

7 For the *Post Code* criteria type 'sd3*' – the asterisk (*) is as a wild card and Access interprets this to mean: *Search for data that starts 'sd3' and is followed by any other characters.*

If we had not included the asterisk sign as an element of the criteria, the query would not have located any data matching it, because there are no *Post Code* fields just with 'sd3'.

8 Run the query and it will return this result:

Query1 : Select Query		
Last Name	**Town**	**Post Code**
Rosenbloom	Buxton	SD3 5FD
Carson	Buxton	SD3 4BG
Steine	Buxton	SD3 2AW

Record: ◄ ◄ 1 ► ►► of 3

9 Return to Design View and check the contents in the Criteria field for the *Post Code* – you will find that Access has changed it to *Like "sd3*"*

The Like operator is a *pattern-matching* operator and the query looked for all of the data that matched 'sd3'. However, there are no Post Codes that comprise only of 'sd3' but because of the presence of the asterisk sign Access interpreted it as to mean 'include any remaining data not specifically specified in the query criteria'.

10 Save the query as 'Wildcard'

Testing the query

To confirm and demonstrate the need for the wildcard asterisk, we will now change the query.

Basic steps

1 Delete all of the *Post Code* criteria
2 Type a new criteria 'sd3'
3 Re-run the Query
❑ It will return an empty table
4 Close the query. Do not save the changes

Multiply criteria

In the exercise that follows, we will create a query, which will return a list of all those personnel who live in 'Buxton' and 'Manchester'.

Basic steps

1 Create the query

2 Save it as 'Two towns'

❑ Set up your query to match that shown. Note that the Sort (in the *Town* column) is set to *Ascending*. This means the list will be sorted in ascending order of *Town*

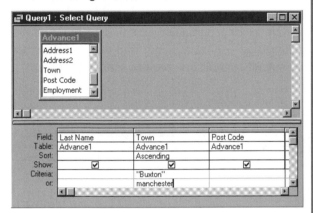

To select Ascending:

3 Click in the field and a drop-down arrow will appear in the right corner

4 Click on the arrow and from the drop-down list select *Ascending*

5 Run the query and it will return a list as shown here:

	Last Name	Town	Post Code
▶	Forbes	Buxton	SD5 8BG
	Steine	Buxton	SD3 2AW
	Carson	Buxton	SD3 4BG
	Rosenbloom	Buxton	SD3 5FD
	Happly	Buxton	SD6 8JK
	Kline	Manchester	MH4 8YH
	Brown	Manchester	MN3 9FF
	Mathews	Manchester	MN2 9SD
*			

Record: ◀ ◀   1   ▶ ▶◀ ▶* of 8

Online Help

Do remember to use the online Help in Access, which will often assist you with a practical example.

Take note

You are not constrained to using two town names. If your database is extensive and you wish to retrieve details based on more than one location, type the additional name in the cell below the one that currently has 'Manchester' listed.

A point of interest

If you are interested in developing your database development skill, you may be interested to see how Access converts your use of logical operators. This section is not part of the course and is shown only as an interest point.

Basic steps

1 Ensure that you are in Query Design View

2 Click the View down-arrow

3 From the drop-down list, select SQL View

❑ This window will open

```
SELECT Advance1.[Last Name], Advance1.Town, Advance1.[Post Code]
FROM Advance1
WHERE (((Advance1.Town)="Buxton" Or (Advance1.Town)="manchester"))
ORDER BY Advance1.Town
```

What you are looking at in the example is Microsoft Access Visual Basic, the programming language of the application.

As previously stated, this is shown as an interest point only. If you plan to develop your Access skills you will often encounter Visual Basic and the example illustrates how Access converts your input to Visual Basic.

That concludes the section on applying Filters and Query operators. Only the basics have been covered. Filters and Queries are powerful tools and if used correctly can produce and create extremely useful results, for a variety of different purposes.

Create a report

We will now create a report, with the aid of a Wizard, then change the layout of one or two fields within it. The report will be based on the *Advanced* database.

The report will list all personnel but will not include all the fields in the database. We will create a two-level report which will group the personnel by their *Town* and then in ascending order of *Salary*.

Basic steps

1. Close any open forms or tables
2. In the Objects bar select Reports
3. Right-click over *Create report by using wizard* and from the pop-up menu select Design view
4. In the Table/Query slot, select *Advanced*
5. Select the fields in the order *Last Name, First Name, Date of Birth, Employment, Salary, Address1, Address2, Town* and *Post Code*
6. Click Next
☐ In the next box we will set the grouping levels:
7. Select *Town* in the left pane, then click ▸ to move it to the right pane

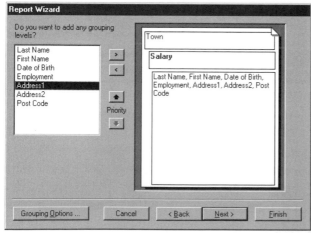

8. Select *Salary* then click ▸ to move it to the right pane
9. Click Next
10. We will not make any changes at the next box. We will let the grouping sort the detail for us.

Click Next
11. At the box dealing with the layout, select *Block*, change the Orientation to *Landscape* and click Next
12. For the Style, select *Formal* and click Next
13. Change the name to '*Personnel Records*'
14. Accept the selection of Preview the Report and click Finish

Access will now create and then open the Report in Preview mode. Look very carefully at the overall layout, paying particular attention to the Address fields. You will quite likely find that some are not completely visible and require some adjustment.

The report title   Field label boxes

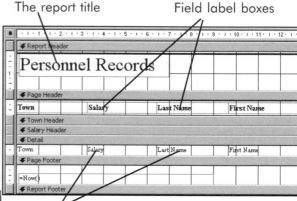

The data field boxes, in which the details will appear. These are aligned with the titles above.

Revision

Shown here is a cut-away view of a Report in Design View and an explanation of the different areas.

If you wish to move a data field text box, the corresponding field title text box must be moved at the same time or the fields will not align on the printout.

Always move or re-size text boxes slowly and carefully until you become more proficient at this task.

Resizing report fields

We are going to move or adjust a number of fields. The *Salary* field is large and we require more space to accommodate other fields.

Basic steps

1 Switch to 'Design View'
2 Click on the *Salary* text box in the Detail area
3 Hold down [Shift] and click on the *Salary* label box in the Page Header area
4 Release both [Shift] and the mouse button

Tip

Whilst moving or re-sizing fields, use the grid squares shown in the background, as guides.

---

5 Click on the right middle re-sizing arrow of the data text box and drag to the left until the *Salary* fields occupy two grid squares

Both of the boxes relating to the *Salary* field were resized

6 Release the button and deselect the two fields
7 Select all of the label and text boxes relating to the fields *Last Name, First Name, Date of Birth* and *Employment*
8 Place the cursor over any of the selected fields
9 When it changes shape to a flat hand, click and drag all the fields to the left until they are close to the right edge of the *Salary* field
10 Release the button and deselect the fields
11 Select the label and text boxes relating to the *Address1* field
12 Resize both fields by expanding them to the left
❑ This is a r*esize* not a *move* operation. Use the left side middle resizing handle of the text box.
13 Drag the text box up to the right side of the *Employment* text box and release the button
14 De-select the fields

15 Switch back to 'Preview' mode
❑ Check the overall layout of the Report. You will find that there is more work to be done. However, before we proceed we will perform two other changes.

We do not require two Address title fields and the *Address1* title is grammatically incorrect. We are going to change the title to 'Address'.

Basic steps

1 Switch to Design View
2 Double-click over the *Address1* field under Page Header
3 At the Properties box, ensure that the Format tab is selected
4 Click into the Caption slot and delete the figure '1' of 'Address1'
6 When completed, close the Properties box

Deleting a report field

We do not require the *Address2* label, so select it and delete it. There is still one adjustment required and this is because part of the Post Code field is not fully displayed.

Basic steps

1 Select the *Address2* data text box
2 Click on the right-hand side middle resizing handle and drag to the left, decreasing the field size approximately one square
3 When you are satisfied, release the button
4 Select both of the *Post Code* boxes and resize them, using the handles on their left side
5 Click and drag the handles to the left, up to the *Address2* data text box
6 Release the mouse button
7 Switch to Print Preview

Check that the overall layout is to your satisfaction, if not, perform out any final adjustments until such time that you are totally satisfied with the results.

❑ The actions just performed highlight a small failing in Access when the Wizard constructs the report for you in as much that it did not insert sufficient space between the fields. It is still quicker, in some instances, to use a Wizard than creating the Report from scratch.

8 Save the changes

Inserting an additional report field

You may wish to create a report including some detail that is not included in the database on which the report is based.

We are going to create a completely new box to go in the report.

Basic steps

1 Ensure that the report is open in Design View
2 If the Toolbox is not already open, click on the Toolbox icon  from the Report Design toolbar

The Toolbox will open and it is from here that more advanced controls can be selected and included in reports or on forms.

We are going to add a label box to the Report to type your name into.

Included in the Toolbox is a Wizard icon which resembles a magic wand. This icon is a toggle and switches the Wizard option on or off. We will not use the Wizard, so if it appears to be depressed, which indicates it is 'on', click on it once to turn it off.

3 Left-click on the Label icon _Aa_ – we will draw a box using this
4 Place the mouse cursor in the upper right corner of the Report Header – this is the same

---

Take note

As you move the mouse, the cursor repeatedly changes its shape.

---

area, but opposite to where the Report Title, *Personnel Records* is located.

5 Cick and drag to the right for 5 squares, aligning it with the top of the Report Header, exactly the same as the *Personnel Records* box
6 Keep the left button pressed and drag it down one square
7 Release the mouse button when the label box is drawn (do not over-run the background)
❑ You now have an *Unbound Label box* on the report.

Take note

'Unbound' means that the detail displayed in the boxes is not taken from the database. You control the box contents, in this instance your name.

---

8 Type in your name
9 Switch back to Preview mode

Check the layout. Adjust the position of the text box to conform to the overall Report layout.

Tip

To change the font type or size, right-click over the box and from its **Properties** dialog box, select the **Format Tab**. Change the font as required.

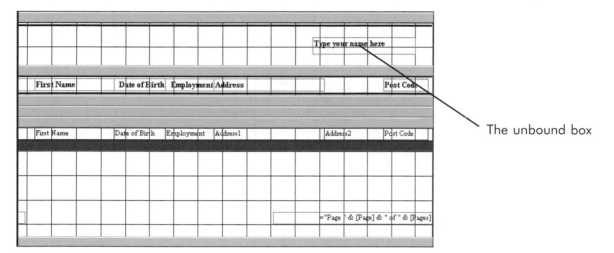

The unbound box

The final product

Check that your Report looks similar to the one shown on page 244.

The various boxes are spaced so that the detail in them can be read easier.

You will find the way Access creates the report and aligns text and figures can cause some occasional presentational problems. This is another reason why you should develop your skills and create your own Report layouts.

You may have noticed that your report has the date and page numbering. Access, by default, inserts this automatically without you having to do anything.

Report properties

A report, like tables and forms, has a properties dialog box and you can change several of the default settings from here. We will not be covering this subject, but you should experiment with the report layout to gain experience and knowledge on the subject.

The reason for including the additional unbound text field was to show that there are a number of other controls and options available, which you can use to add to or modify forms and reports. This is an area that you should investigate in greater detail using the online Help.

Summary

That completes the work on this report. If any of the lines look rather thick or are appearing in the printed document or in the preview as double lines, you will have to re-adjust each text box affected until the overall appearance is to your satisfaction.

❏ Save and close the report

Personnel records

Type your name here

Town	Salary	Last Name	First Name	Date of Birth	Employment	Address		Post Code
Buxton	£890	Happly	Joe	01-Apr-81	22-Feb-98	78 Glen Close	Upper Maple	SD6 8JK
	£1,175	Rosenbloom	Marie	30-May-56	11-May-79	12 Rose Lane	Upper Maple	SD3 5FD
	£1,245	Steine	Clare	21-Dec-61	04-Aug-84	55 Elm Drive	Upper Maple	SD3 2AW
	£1,450	Forbes	Collin	25-Nov-67	12-Aug-88	36 Farm Fields Ave	Cross Keys	SD5 8BG
	£1,452	Carson	Richard	15-Dec-60	14-Oct-86	45 Downton Rd	Cross Keys	SD3 4BG
Doncaster	£950	Smith	Simon	12-Jan-71	14-Feb-91	123 Upper Forest Rd	Burden	HN5 5RT
	£1,250	Bond	James	31-Oct-67	16-Jun-85	23 Case Rd	Lofturn	HN6 8TR
	£1,350	Jennings	Raymond	21-Mar-65	14-Jul-87	23 Calne Close	Lofturn	HN3 7JK
Manchester	£930	Brown	Peter	31-Jul-79	30-Jun-96	12 Winston Churchill Ave	Lee	MN3 9FF
	£1,180	Mathews	Angela	18-May-70	27-Jul-92	97 Crumlin Ave	Lee	MN2 9SD
	£1,236	Kline	Rosemary	15-Jul-59	05-Sep-76	234 Skye House	Lee	MH4 8YH
Sheffield	£940	Brown	George	13-Jan-55	12-Dec-78	2 Buxton View	Swinbury	SF3 5FD
	£1,270	King	Cherry	11-Jul-72	23-Oct-91	2/34 Cheshire House	Swinbury	SF4 8GF

Miscellaneous customisation

Access, like the other applications included within the Office Suite, can be customised to your personal preferences and way of working. Exercise caution when first investigating and implementing changes, always explore and use the online Help before undertaking any changes to ensure that the effect is clearly understood.

Toolbars

You will have noticed that when an application changes from one view to another, or changes from Table to Form or Report, that the toolbars change to one that is applicable to the particular item open at that time.

Some toolbars are 'docked', fixed in one position, while others appear over tables, when open in the Design View. These are often referred to as 'Floating Toolbars' or 'Palettes'. You can control the appearance of a toolbar, both when it appears and which icons are displayed on it.

Currently it is suggested the only change you should attempt is to display one or more toolbars, other activities should be left until you become more proficient in the use of the application.

Basic steps

With Access running and a Table open:

1 Right-click over a toolbar on display

❑ A menu will appear. The tick next to Table Datasheet indicates that the toolbar is currently on display. There are two other toolbars that could be displayed and you can, if so required, display them in addition to the Table Datasheet toolbar.

Formatting (Datasheet)
✓ Table Datasheet
Web

Customize...

To display an additional toolbar:

2 Left-click adjacent to the required toolbar

❑ A tick will appear. The menu will close and the toolbar will appear. The last option listed in the menu is 'Customize'. Choosing this option will open up the 'Customize' dialog window.

You should read the online Help section on this subject before attempting this particular customisation.

Customisation

Tables

When designing Tables it is often tempting to leave the default value of text fields set to 50 characters long. Plan and think out the design and future requirements and set the field lengths to a suitable figure. If all text fields are left at the default setting of 50, the effect will be seen when working with Forms based on the Table. Field lengths on the Form will often be too long and will then require adjustment, resulting in unnecessary time and effort on your part.

Forms

Remember that the Form has many properties of its own. The fields and other objects on the Form also have their own properties. You can customise all of these. Closely investigate the Properties box for each item to determine what you can, or cannot, change.

257

Reports

Reports produced by the Wizard are often adequate and at some stage you will prefer to organise the overall layout yourself. Choose Design View from the New Report dialog window, instead of the Wizard option. This option is available when designing tables and forms and you can develop your skills in this area later.

Advanced databases

For the future, learn how to create relational databases and understand the functionality of such databases. Investigate the sample database, *Northwind*, supplied with Access and see how linking of data is undertaken thus creating a relational database.

Designing a database

There will always be a requirement to modify a database to some degree. However, the time taken drafting the requirements and drawing the tables, forms and reports before opening Access will not have been wasted.

Summary

Access is a powerful Relational Database Management System (RDBMS) and offers the user a considerable number of options in the way data is presented. This course is an introduction to it and by now you will have realised the potential of it. If you have identified a suitable use for Access, within your work or home environment, you are urged to learn more advanced techniques and skills for deploying Access databases.

6 Presentations

Introduction to PowerPoint

PowerPoint is a presentations application and is included within Office 2000. It is used to create computerised presentations, known as *slide shows*.

What can PowerPoint do for you?

- The application can be used to produce a slide show on screen that will run unattended and in a continous loop.

- Its preformatted templates will you in the construction and design of a presentation.

- It also has a range of coloured backgrounds and text formattings that will suit most situations and presentations, but which can be easily and quickly changed to suit a particular audience.

- You can also prepare a presentation to be given as 35mm colour slides instead of the computer.

- You can produce banners and overhead projector transparencies, in colour and black and white.

- You can produce presentation handouts, which will include miniature copies of your slides and notes for the presenter.

The course objective

The course objective is to create a number of slides, which will introduce a new member of staff to a department within a company.

We will use these slides to produce an on-screen presentation. You will also be introduced to the drawing tools to be found within PowerPoint.

Starting PowerPoint

PowerPoint can be started in a number of different ways. The simplest is from the **Start > Programs** menu

You can also start PowerPoint from the Office shortcut toolbar, if it was included in the installation of Office.

If the Office toolbar is not available you can also create a shortcut on your Desktop, see Chapter 2.

When PowerPoint first starts, you will be presented with this dialog box.

It offers a number of options:

- **AutoContent wizard** brings up a number of templates from which you may select a topic suitable to your requirements.

- **Design Templates** offers you a series of coloured background Presentation Designs.

- **Blank presentation** will open up another dialog box from which you may select a number of preformatted slides without any backgrounds or text and headings applied. It is this selection which we will make shortly.

- **Open an existing presentation** will open a previously-saved presentation.

Click **OK** to action your selection, or **Cancel** to close the dialog box without carrying out any action.

❑   Leave the dialog box open and proceed

- Always remember that Windows applications, including PowerPoint, can be customised by you in many ways, therefore not all of the examples included with this course will be identical to your display. This should not distract from using the courseware. The images used in this courseware were taken from a version of PowerPoint using default settings. Simply follow the instructions given and you will achieve the required result.

Opening an existing presentation

Before we proceed and create a new presentation from the beginning, we will first open an existing presentation and make a number of changes to it and then save it for future use. This will also give you the opportunity to see what a presentation may look like, its format and layout.

We have included a short presentation on the CD supplied with this book, but as it is on CD it is currently set to 'read-only'. This means that you can open and read the file, but cannot save any changes that you may make to it.

To enable you to save the changes perform the following.

Removing the read-only attribute

Basic steps

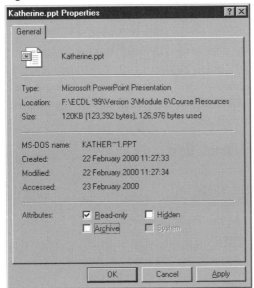

1 Using Windows Explorer create a new folder within *My Documents* on your hard disk drive
2 Call it '*ECDL Course*'
3 Locate the *Course Resources* folder on the CD
4 Copy the file *Katherine.ppt* to your *ECDL Course* folder
5 Right-click over the file in your folder

---

6 Select Properties and click on the General tab.
7 At the Properties box click on the Read-only slot and the tick will be removed
8 Click OK to apply the change and close the box

You will now be able to save the changes that we are about to make to the presentation called 'Katherine'.

Opening the presentation

Basic steps

1 You should have Power-Point running and the start-up dialog box open
2 Select Open an existing presentation then click OK

3 At the Open dialog box, navigate your way to the *ECDL Course* folder and open it
4 Double-click on *Katherine.ppt* and it will open

The file, *Katherine.ppt*, outlines some background detail on a person called Katherine Richards. You will have more dealings with this person later, however, for the time being we will use this opportunity to learn how to move from slide to slide, add detail to a slide and then save the changes, and expand on the existing detail on Slide 2.

Moving between slides

The slide shown in the example here is Slide 1, the first slide of the presentation. If your view of the

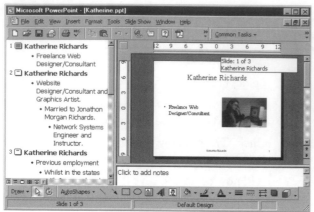

presentation is different to that shown above, left-click on **View** on the menu bar and select **Normal**.

We are going to add some information to the presentation. It is to go at the end of that which already exists on Slide 2. There are a number of ways in which you can move between slides. We are going to use the scroll bar indicated above.

Basic steps

1 Click on the scroll bar slider and drag it down

❑ Notice the pop-up message that appears. This identifies the current slide and how many there are in the presentation. It also tells you the slide title, in this case, Katherine Richards.

2 Drag the scroll bar down until the pop-up message tells you that you are at Slide 2

3 Release the mouse button

❑ You should now have this slide on your screen

Katherine Richards

- Website Designer/Consultant and Graphics Artist
    - Married to Jonathon Morgan Richards
        - Network Systems Engineer and Instructor

Katherine Richards   2

The slide is a preformatted slide, which uses bullet points to emphasise main headings and sub-sections.

4 Place your cursor at the end of the last line (ending '*Instructor*') after the full stop

5 Press [Enter] to insert a new line

When you clicked on the slide, a hatched frame appeared. This indicates the size of the text box that you have just selected (we will return to this subject later in the course).

You will have noted that the existing text is indented to the right and with each different indentation, the text is of a different size.

When you pressed [Enter] the new line started immediately below the previous line and retained the same level of indentation.

Bullet indentation

We are going to add more detail, relating to a different subject and therefore we have to change the indentation to a higher level than currently selected.

There are a number of ways that you can increase or decrease the level of indentation and we will use the [Tab] and [Shift] keys.

Basic steps

1 To increase the indentation to the right, or *Demote*, press [Tab]

2 To decrease, or *Promote*, the indentation level, press [Shift] and [Tab] simultaneously

Practise these options later, but for now just press the [Shift] and [Tab] keys simultaneously, once and the indentation level will move to the left and the cursor will now align under the level starting with the word 'Married'.

Additional detail

Basic steps

1 At the new indentation level type 'Two children'

2 Press [Enter] to insert a new line

We now have to change the indentation level once again, as the next text to be entered is a sub-heading of text you have just typed in.

3 Press [Tab] once to demote the indentation to the right

4 Type 'Richard, 8 years of age'

5 Press [Enter] once to insert a new line

❑ Do not change the indentation level

6 Type 'Samantha, 6 years of age'

7 Press [Enter] once more, to insert a new line

8 Press [Tab] key once to further indent the line

9 Type 'Both children in boarding school in the UK'

Your slide should now match the example shown

Katherine Richards

- Website designer/consultant and graphics artist.
  - Married to Jonathon Morgan Richards.
    - Network Systems Engineer and Instructor.
  - Two children:
    - Richard, 8 years of age.
    - Samantha, 6 years of age.
      - Both children in boarding school in the UK.

Katherine Richards   2

---

10 Save the changes and close the presentation

❑ Remember this presentation as you will use it later in the course

❑ We are now going to close PowerPoint and then restart the application

❑ From the menu bar click on File > Exit and PowerPoint will close

The reason for closing the application is to ensure you know how to do it, but when we restart PowerPoint we will be back at a good starting point for the next stage of the course.

That completes this section and you will now realise that you can change an existing presentation, even one that you did not create, without too much difficulty.

Creating a presentation

New slide show scenario

We are now ready to create a new presentation. To do this, you require some background information, which you will use to create the presentation.

The following is the information you require and includes an explanation as to why the presentation is being assembled.

Background information

You will recall that the course objective is to create a number of slides to introduce a new member of staff to a department within the company. This new member of staff is in fact a new departmental head, hence the presentation to a particular department.

Our fictitious company, called *Tec-com*, specialises in computer training and recently underwent quite a major expansion and investment. Until recently *Tec-com* only ran courses for companies and the public in general on the most common computer applications. However, due to the recent investment and expansion they have introduced computer network courses.

The original members of staff who taught general applications were not qualified in computer networking and a whole new department was formed within the company to teach these courses. The introduction of this department has resulted in an increase in staff, who naturally specialise in networking, along with back-up and support staff.

The company has also invested a considerable sum of money in a number of different network systems which will support the instruction of students and allow them to install and run various types of networks during the courses.

We now have the outline details of the company. Read the following to find out more about the new departmental head.

- Jonathan Morgan Richards is the new employee. Jonathan prefers to be known as Jon - note the spelling. Jon is 38 years of age and is a married man with two children.

Family details are:

- Jon's wife is Katherine, known as Kathy (who works as a consultant Web designer). This is the Katherine referred to in the earlier presentation.

- Kathy and Jon have been married for ten years.

- Kathy and Jon have two children, Richard, 8, and Samantha, 6. (Both are at boarding school.)

Jon's education qualifications:

- Comprehensive education.

- University: B.Sc. Computer Science.

Jon's background and previous employment:

- Jon later went on to qualify as:

- A Certified Novell Engineer.

- A Microsoft Systems Certified Engineer and is also qualified as a Microsoft Certified Professional in a number of MS Office applications.

- Jon completed a number of years working in the field, designing and supervising the installation of various types of network systems, during which time he found himself instructing support staff on how the network was assembled and functioned.

- Jon realised that he had a skill in teaching network subjects and then spent some time attending college to learn more of the methods of instruction.

- Jon was initially employed in the UK with a large multinational company: Samson's United Systems, as a network systems engineer.

- During this time he accepted an assignment to the company's US office, where he was headhunted by an American organisation, Anglo-American International, who specialised in developing remote controlled computerised systems.

- After some two years, Jon found, interesting though the work was, he much preferred the hands–on experience of networking and people contact and returned to the UK where he joined the staff of one of the new converted banks, Collins PLC, as the deputy systems engineer.

◆ It was during this time that Jon's interest in teaching was re-awoken and he gained the Microsoft Certified Trainer qualification.

◆ Jon was later to be approached by a recruitment agency and asked if he would be interested in a career divergence, retaining the network aspect but with an emphasis on training. Jon agreed to the offer and that brings us up to date.

We are going to create a new presentation, starting from scratch, but using a number of the pre-format-ted slides available within PowerPoint.

❑ Re-start PowerPoint by selecting Start > Pro-grams > Microsoft PowerPoint

Selecting a slide

Basic steps

1 At the start-up dialog box, select Blank presen-tation and click OK

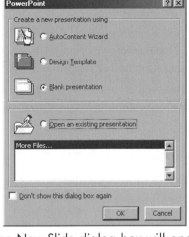

❑ The New Slide dialog box will open

2 Select the slide indicated and click OK

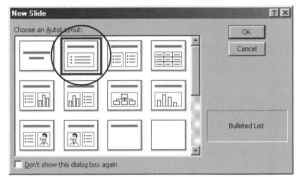

❑ PowerPoint will now open the slide. This is known as *Normal View*.

We can now edit the slide to our requirements.

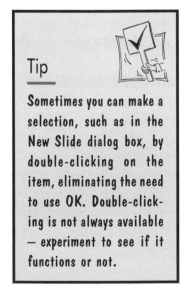

Tip

Sometimes you can make a selection, such as in the New Slide dialog box, by double-clicking on the item, eliminating the need to use OK. Double-click-ing is not always available – experiment to see if it functions or not.

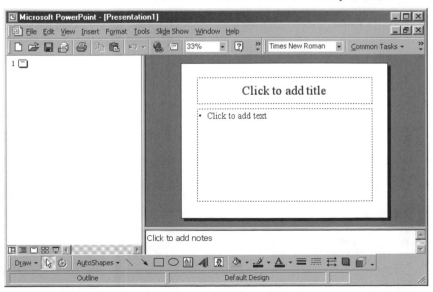

Saving the presentation

You will require a new formatted floppy disk for this next section. Place the disk in your A: drive. We will Save the presentation before we proceed any further.

The Save routine is the same as in Word, see page 94. Save the new presentation on the A: drive, naming it 'Jon's intro'.

Editing the Slide Master

There are a number of sub-headings that we want to appear on all the slides and the way to do this is to edit the Slide Master.

Think of the Slide Master as being similar to using Headers and Footers in Microsoft Word.

Any object that is placed in the Slide Master will appear on every slide.

You can also change the default formats and styles using the Slide Master and create a unique, personal slide.

The Slide Master view

We require the following items to appear on each slide.

* The company name, Tec-com
* The date the presentation was made

Basic steps

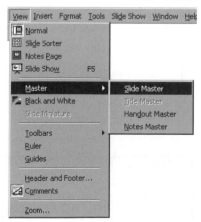

1 Select the slide
2 Select View > Master > Slide Master

3 Double-click over <date/time> to highlight it

4 Select Insert > Date and Time
5 At the Date and Time dialog box select the format as shown in the example and click OK

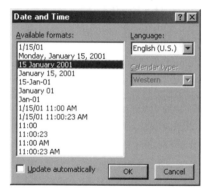

❑ We will now add the company name and number the slides

6 Double-click over the <footer> area and type in 'Tec-com plc'

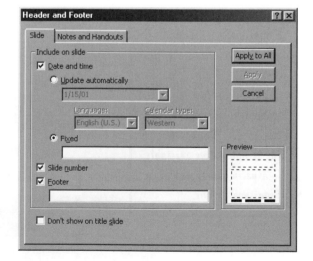

7 Double-click over the <#> area

8 Select View > Header and Footer

9 At the Header and Footer dialog box select the Slide tab

10 Tick Slide Number and Footer

11 Click Apply to All

12 Save the changes and select View > Normal

Take note

You will not be able to see the changes for the page numbering format until you return to the Slide View. PowerPoint will automatically insert a slide number, much as Word does for page numbering.

Editing the slide title

We are now ready to enter the title for the first slide. The example shown is the upper area of our current slide, and is known as the Title text box.

Basic steps

1 Click once in the Title area and the display should change to show a flashing cursor

> Click to add title

> |

2 Type in 'Staff Briefing'

3 Click anywhere on the slide other than in the title area and the display should change to this

> Staff Briefing

4 Notice that title box no longer has the hatched frame around it

Take note

The Title font is Times New Roman, size 44 pt, centred within the title text box. You can change these settings, but we will retain them for now.

❑ We will now move on to the lower area of the slide. It is here that we are going to type in the aims and objectives of the briefing. This section is pre-formatted as a bullet point list.

> • Click to add text

The bullet point text is pre-formatted as Times New Roman at 32 pt. You can change the style of the bullet point to an arrow, hand or other symbols. How to do this is discussed later.

5 Click over the words *Click to add text*

6 Type 'Aims and Objectives' and press [Enter]

❑ A new bulleted line will automatically be inserted. PowerPoint always inserts a new line based on the previous selection.

7 Press [Tab] – the cursor will be indented and moved to the right. PowerPoint will reduce the text size, in this instance to 28 pt.

8 Type 'Introduction of departmental head' and press [Enter]

9 Press [Tab] to further indent the text

❑ Note the different bullet points at each indent level

10 Type in 'Jon M Richards' and press [Enter]

❑ PowerPoint has inserted a new line based on the previous line, but here we want to return to the style used on the line starting 'Introduction'. Previously we used [Shift] and [Tab] to promote but this time we will use an icon.

On the Formatting toolbar are these two icons . They are used to decrease (Demote) or increase (Promote) the amount of indent.

267

11 Click the left arrow – the indent will be pro-moted and move one tab setting to the left

12 Enter 'Introduce Departmental Organisation'

13 Retain the same settings and type 'Instruc-tional Programme'

14 Save the changes

This is how your slide should now look.

> # Staff Briefing
>
> • Aims and Objectives.
>   – Introduction to departmental head.
>   • Jon M Richards.
>   – Introduce Departmental Organisation.
>   – Instructional Programme.
>
> 23 March 2000   Tec-com plc   1

Insert an additional slide

We will now insert a second slide.

Basic steps

1 From the menu bar select Insert > New Slide

2 At the New Slide dialog box select the *Text & Clip Art* slide as shown.

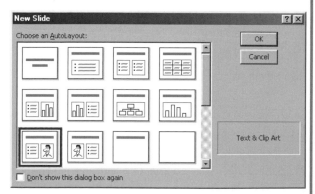

❑ This slide is pre-formatted with a title area, a bullet area and a graphic placement box.

3 When the new slide opens, click in the title area and type 'Staff Briefing'

4 Click in the bullet area and type 'Jonathan Morgan Richards'. This text may not all fit on one line, and PowerPoint may automatically move the word 'Richards' to another line.

❑ We want the name all on one line, so we need to adjust the box.

5 With the bullet list area selected, move the cursor over the sizing handle as shown

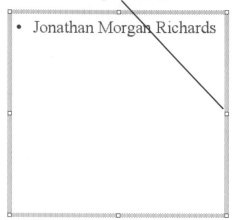

6 When it changes its shape to a horizontal double-headed arrow, click and drag, slowly, to the right until all the words fit on the one line

7 Release the mouse button.

The bullet list frame may have overlapped the Clip Art frame. If so, adjust the Clip Art frame, dragging its left border to the right until it is clear.

Carry on typing in the bullet list text, as shown below. Ensure that you indent the relevant sections, as shown and then Save the presentation

> # Staff Briefing
>
> • Jonathan Morgan Richards
>   – Prefers to be called Jon
>   – 38, married with 2 children
> • Qualifications:
>   – Computer Science degree
>   – Microsoft MCSE and MCP
>   – Microsoft Certified Trainer
>   – Novell CNE
>
> 25 July 1999   Tec-com plc   2

Inserting a clip art image

We should include a photograph of Jon so that everyone will know who he is.

However, because we may not all have the same imagery available on our computers we will need to improvise.

Insert a suitable image of people at work from the Microsoft Clip Gallery and adjust the size to fit the frame, using the same techniques as for inserting clip art in Word (see page 127)

Using the tool on the Drawing toolbar, add a circle around one of the characters and an arrow pointing from the name 'Richards' to the circled person.

The circle should be formatted with the *No Fill* option. (See page 129 if you need a reminder about the Drawing tools.)

Your slide should resemble the example shown.

> ### Staff Briefing
>
> - Jonathan Morgan Richards
>   - Prefers to be called Jon
>   - 38, married with 2 children
> - Qualifications:
>   - Computer Science degree
>   - Microsoft MCSE and MCP
>   - Microsoft Certified Trainer
>   - Novell CNE
>
> 25 July 1999   Tec-com plc   2

We still have to include Jon's employment history and to do this we require another new slide.

Insert a new slide based on the Bulleted List blank slide, and type in the details shown in the example. Save the changes

> ### Staff Briefing
>
> - Jonathon Morgan Richards
>   - Employment History
>   - 1987 - On leaving university, recruited by multi-national company: Samson's United Systems
>   - 1993 - Joined Anglo-American International, worked stateside for two years
>   - 1995 - Returned to UK and joined the newly converted bank: Collins plc
>   - 1999 - Tec-com
>
> 23 March 2000   Tec-com plc   3

Summary

We used several different pre-formatted slides to create our slides, which highlights their flexibility. A pre-formatted slide does not restrict you in changing the overall layout of the slide.

In the next section we will use a slide designed to create an organisational chart.

Tip

Beware of creating clutter on the slide. Keep the slide tidy and do not overload it with text.

Creating an organisation chart

We have now reached the stage of the presentation when the organisational structure of the new section is to be discussed. PowerPoint has a slide designed to create organisational charts with the minimum of effort and fuss.

Basic steps

1 Select Insert > New Slide
2 At the New Slide dialog box double-click on the Organization Chart slide
❏ You should be presented this slide

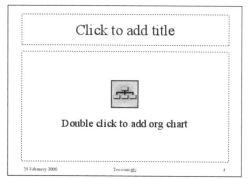

3 In the title text box type in 'Staff Briefing'
4 Save the changes

5 Double-click over the icon
6 The Microsoft Organization Chart window will open. Adjust it to a suitable size, so that you can see all of the detail contained within it

Typing text in chart boxes

To enter text into the boxes left-click once inside the appropriate box and start typing. The box will open out as shown in the screenshot. We will only use the first two lines, so ignore the remaining lines. They will disappear when the box closes.

To move from one line to another, i.e. to move from the Name line to the Title line, click **[Tab]**.

Start by clicking on the uppermost box and type in the detail shown in the example below. Continue until all the details as shown have been completed.

Chart Toolbar: Use these icons to add additional boxes to the existing chart.

We are not going to make any changes to the existing chart at this stage.

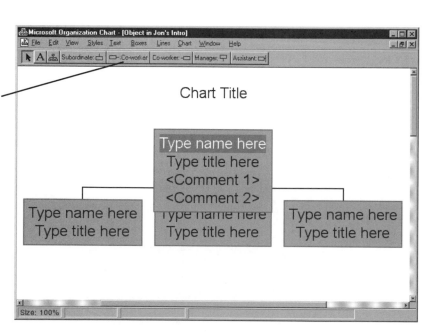

270

It would be advantageous to inform the staff of all the changes and additions to the company, so we shall now add another two boxes.

Inserting additional chart boxes

Basic steps

1 Select the Subordinate icon on the Chart toolbar

❑ The cursor will change to

2 Click inside the box that you want to attach it to, in this instance, the Jan Meinard box …

❑ The box will attach itself as shown

3 Click on the new box to open it

❑ We will only use the first two lines

❑ Complete the chart as shown

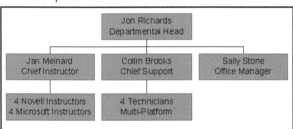

Deleting chart boxes

An unwanted box can be deleted easily. Just select it and press [Delete].

Saving the chart

It is possible to save an organisational chart as a separate file which can be used in other applications, for example Word or Excel.

Basic steps

1 Select File > Save Copy As

2 At the Save Chart dialog box, save the chart on the 3½ Floppy (A:) drive as 'Tec-com Chart'

3 Open the File menu and select Update Jon's Intro then close the chart window

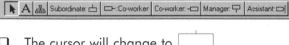

You are now returned to the normal PowerPoint window, complete with the chart on display.

♦ Note the sizing handles around the chart image and the changes that occur to the cursor depending upon where it is in relation to the chart or sizing handles.

♦ Move the mouse cursor over the chart image and the cursor will change to a four-headed arrow. This indicates that the chart can be moved around to a different position on the slide.

♦ Move the mouse cursor over any of the sizing arrows and it will change to a double-headed arrow, which indicates that the chart can be re-sized to your requirements.

♦ If you wish to change any of the detail, simply double-click over the chart and you are returned to the Chart window, where any editing can be performed.

♦ Save the changes to the presentation.

Take note

DO NOT save any changes to the presentation from this point onwards unless specially instructed to do so by this courseware.

Experiment with re-sizing, moving and re-opening the Chart window. DO NOT save any changes that you may make during any experimentation.

When you are satisfied and have finished experimenting, close the presentation and click **No** when prompted to save changes.

Slide Sorter view

We are now going to reopen the presentation. You may recall from the other courses that the application remembers which files were used most recently. The same applies to PowerPoint.

Basic steps

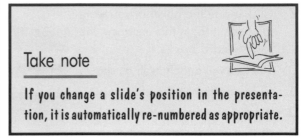

1 From the menu bar select File
2 Click on the presentation name in the lower area of the list
❑ The presentation will open at Slide 1. We want to move to Slide 4 and this is the ideal opportunity to introduce the Slide Sorter View. In the lower left-hand area of the presentation window you will find a number of icons.

Normal View   Slide Show View

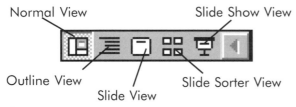

Outline View   Slide Sorter View
        Slide View

3 Click on Slide Sorter View

❑ The screen will change to that shown in this example. The Slide Sorter View displays all the slides in the presentation in a miniature format. It is from this view that you can change the position of slides or insert a new slide in the appropriate position within the presentation.

Slide numbering

Examine the Slide Sorter View and you will see that each slide is numbered and closer inspection will reveal that the number is also present on the slide itself. Remember the changes that we made to the Slide Master earlier? The numbering is created as and when you insert a new slide into the presentation.

Take note

If you change a slide's position in the presentation, it is automatically re-numbered as appropriate.

Practice

Basic steps

Save the presentation and then:

1 Select Slide 4 – the one that contains the chart
❑ The image will have a thick border around it.

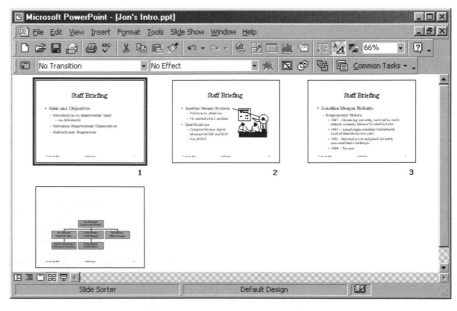

2 Click and hold over the image – the cursor will change to an arrow with a small rectangle

3 Drag the cursor to the left until it is between the first and second slides then release the button

You may have noticed that as the cursor was dragged to the left, when it arrived between the various slides, a vertical line appeared between the slides. This indicates that you may, if so desired, release the button and the slide will be moved to that location.

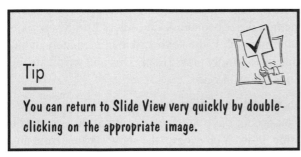

Tip

You can return to Slide View very quickly by double-clicking on the appropriate image.

Practise the above actions, but do not Save any changes at this stage.

An alternative method

Basic steps

1 Right-click over the slide that you wish to move

2 Select Cut from the pop-up menu

3 Move to where you want the slide to appear, right-click and select Paste

When you feel confident with these procedures, close the presentation but do not save the changes when prompted. The reason for not saving the changes at this stage is that we wish to retain a common presentation throughout the course, because there is still more to be done.

Basic steps

1 Re-open the presentation

We are going to modify the chart so:

2 Double-click on Slide 4 to change to Slide View

3 Double-click on the chart to open the Microsoft Organization Chart window

4 Highlight the words *'Chart Title'*

5 Type 'Network Instructional Group'

❑ The text appears quite small

6 Highlight the text and from the Chart menu bar select Text > Font

7 At the Font dialog box change the font size from 14 to 36 and style to Bold

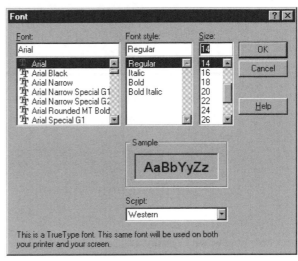

8 Click OK

9 Select File > Update Jon's Intro

10 Select File > Close and Return to Jon's Intro for the changes to be implemented

11 Save the changes

Practice slide show

At this stage it would be well worth checking the overall appearance of the presentation when run as a Slide Show.

What is a Slide Show? It is the combination of all the slides assembled in the presentation, shown at full screen size, without any of the menu bars, toolbars, etc. being visible to the viewer.

Slides can be either manually changed or set to run automatically. We will only use the manual method during this presentation.

Starting the Slide Show

Ensure that you have Slide 1 on display, otherwise the Slide Show will start from whichever slide is selected and not all of the slides will seen.

Click on the Slide Show icon located in the lower area on the screen.

Once the Slide Show icon has been selected, the first slide will fill the screen and should resemble the example shown.

Staff Briefing

- Aims and Objectives:
    - Introduction of departmental head
        - Jon M Richards
    - Introduce Departmental Organisation
    - Instructional Programme

25 July 1999   Tec-com plc   1

At the moment we are at Slide 1 and it is now up to you to decide when to move onto the next slide.

To move on to the next slide, either:

- Click on the mouse anywhere on screen

or

- Click on the button in the lower left area of the screen. A pop-up menu will appear and it is from this menu that you may control the Slide Show. Use these options to move back and forward through the slides, or to go to a particular slide number.

Next
Previous
Go ▶

Meeting Minder...
Speaker Notes

Pointer Options ▶
Screen ▶

Help
End Show

Another option of particular interest is the **Pen** which allows you to do free-hand drawings on a slide, whilst running the presentation.

For more information on the use of the Pen and other options, use the on-line Help.

Terminating the slide show

During the course of running a Slide Show, you may decide to terminate the show before reaching the end, the last slide. You may decide to use the pop-up menu method described above and select **End Show**. Another method, if the keyboard is immediately available, is to simply press **[Esc]**. This will terminate the Slide Show at once.

An alternative slide show method

You do not have to have selected Slide 1 to start a Slide Show. You can run the show starting from any slide in the presentation. For instance, you may have just edited a slide and want to confirm that the change has had the desired effect.

Basic steps

1   In Slide Sorter or Slide view, select Slide 2
2   Select Slide Show > View Show
❑   The Slide Show will start from Slide 2

You can then either run through the remaining slides or terminate the show.

Summary

Now that we have previewed the presentation, it is apparent that we have not included any details of Jon's family.

In addition the slide background was rather plain, in fact plain white. We can improve this situation quite easily because PowerPoint has a number of pre-formatted background designs.

We will investigate these designs but before we proceed, select **Save** to ensure the file is current. Another reason for saving the presentation at this stage is that we are going to experiment applying a background design, but will not retain it within 'Jon's Intro' presentation.

Applying a design

A PowerPoint Design consists of a background colour or image and formats for the different levels of text. Applying a design is a quick way to give a slide a more professional look.

Ensure that you are viewing Slide 1.

Tip

A quick way to return to the first slide is to use the Shortcut Ctrl + Home. Ctrl + End will take you to the last slide in the presentation.

Basic steps

To apply a design:

1   Select Format > Apply Design Template

❑   The Apply Design dialog box will open

It is from this dialog box that the design selection is made.

The apply design window

We are only going to discuss the basics of selecting a design, you should experiment later to learn the other features and options available.

2   Select *Dad's Tie.pot* and click Apply

This design will give you a good idea of the colour aspects. Do not save any changes at this stage.

Closely examine your slide now that the design has been applied and you will find that some changes to the style and layout have occurred, for instance:

- The title *Staff Briefing* was originally centred in the title text box, but is now left aligned

- Some text boxes extend beyond the slide

PowerPoint stores all the default designs in a folder called *Presentation Designs*

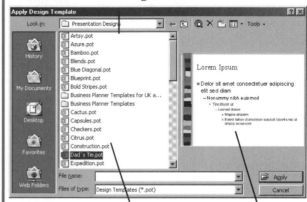

Design names – the selected design is *Dads Tie.pot*. The *.pot* extension identifies the file as a presentation design.

Preview of what the design will look like.

Formatting individual slides

It is possible to format individual slides with different colour displays and though we are not going to cover this option here, you should be aware of it.

To format an individual slide, select it and then from the menu bar, select **Format > Slide Color Scheme**. Experiment with this option at a later time.

Tip

Check every slide after a design has been applied, as it may have areas of formatting that will clash with your original slide layout. If your Slide Show is to be run from an OHP, practice the Slide Show on the projector. They usually have a background colour, often blue, which may cause colour clashes with your display. Practice may not always make perfect, but it will help eliminate embarrassing moments for the presenter.

6: Presentations

275

Saving with a different name

Basic steps

1 From the menu bar select File > Save As
2 At the Save As dialog box, type in the name 'Jon's Intro2' and click Save
❑ Note the new name in the title bar
3 Close this presentation and re-open the original, *Jon's Intro*, which has the plain white background and no design applied

We will insert the slide relating to Jon's family, make some changes to the font, and apply some colour.

Inserting a new slide

Basic steps

1 Change to the Slide Sorter View
❑ The new slide is to be inserted between Slides 3 and 4
2 Click in the area between them
3 Select Insert > New Slide
4 At the New Slide dialog box double-click on the Bulleted List slide to return to Slide View where we will start entering the family details

Take note

The slides have automatically been re-numbered, where appropriate. The new slide is now Slide 4 and the previous Slide 4 is now Slide 5.

5 Click in the slide title area
6 Type 'Staff Briefing' (or copy and paste it from a previous slide)

The bullet list area is what we eventually require, but we want an additional, separate text box as well. The problem is, where will it fit without overlapping the already existing two areas? At the moment it cannot fit without overlapping, so we are going to resize the bullet list area first.

7 Click anywhere over the bullet list to select it
8 Place the cursor over the top, middle resize handle
9 When the cursor changes to a double-headed arrow (not the four-headed arrow, which is used to move the box) click and drag it down to just below the words 'Click to add text'

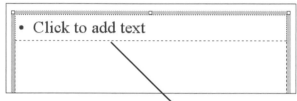

• Click to add text

Resize the box to this level

We will now insert a new text box between the two existing areas. Ensure that the Drawing toolbar is displayed, if not select **View** > **Toolbars** and select **Drawing** from the pop-out menu.

Basic steps

1 Click the Text box icon 🔲 on the Drawing toolbar – the cursor will change to a thin inverted cross ⊥
2 Click between the two existing text boxes and drag the cursor down and to the right to create the additional text box

Staff Briefing

• Click to add text

3 Release the mouse button – be careful at this stage not to click outside of the text box area because if you do, the text box will simply disappear. This is due to the fact that there is no text inside it and PowerPoint thinks that it is no longer required and deletes it.
4 Type 'Jon's Family'
5 Save the changes

Changing fonts and creating borders

The subject of font type and size is discussed in Chapter 3, Word processing. If you have not yet completed this module, it is suggested that you look at that chapter to learn more on this subject.

When you insert a new text box, PowerPoint will automatically format it as left justified. The font type is the same as that used throughout the presentation, i.e. Times New Roman, at 24 pt.

If you investigate the three text boxes on this slide, you will find that they have the same font type, i.e. Times New Roman, but each is a different font size. The convention is that the title is the largest and it is set to 44 pt. The new text box is set to 24 pt whilst the bullet list is set to 32 pt.

However, the text box font size, 24 pt, is too small, as we want this font to be the same size as the bullet list.

Basic steps

1 Highlight the text '*Jon's Family*'
2 Right-click over the selected text and from the pop-up menu select Font
3 At the Font dialog box, change the Font Size to 32 and click OK
❑ The font type can be changed in this box
4 With the text still highlighted, click on the Centre icon on the Formatting toolbar
❑ The text will become centred in the text box

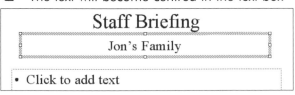

Applying colour to text

Basic steps

With the text still highlighted:

1 Select Format > Font
2 At the Font dialog box click on the down-arrow by the Color slot and select More Colors
3 From the colour wheel select a red tone and click OK

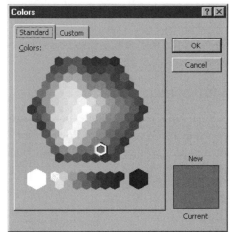

4 Close the Font dialog box by clicking OK

The colour will be applied to the text. You can use this method to apply colour to text anywhere in your presentation.

Take note

You can also make the changes by highlighting the text and then right-clicking over the selection. When the pop-up menu opens, select 'Font' and the same dialog box will open.

Changing text case

At times you may find that you have a line of text in uppercase (all capitals) and decide to change it all to lowercase or a mix of both. There is a quick method of doing this.

Basic steps

1 Highlight text that you wish to change

2 Press [Shift]+[F3] – the text will change from upper to lower case

3 Press [Shift]+[F3] again – it will change to a mix of upper and lower case

4 Press [Shift]+[F3] again – it will return to all uppercase

❑ Remember this, it's a good time saver and it works in Word as well

Applying borders

You can, if you wish, include borders around the various types of boxes used in PowerPoint. We will include a border around the text box that we recently created.

Basic steps

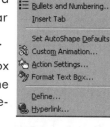

1 Select the text box by clicking in the text area

2 Right-click over it and a pop-up menu will appear

3 Select Format Text Box...

4 At the Format Text Box dialog box, ensure that the Colors and Lines tab is selected

5 Select red as the line colour

6 Adjust the remaining settings in your dialog box to conform to that shown in the example

7 Click OK and save the changes

❑ You will be returned to Slide View

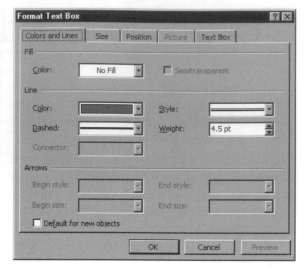

The text box should still be selected – click anywhere on the slide to deselect it. You can now clearly see the border surrounding the box.

The border around the text box may be too long for the amount of text it contains, so we will now re-size the box.

Basic steps

1 Click on the box border to select it

2 Place the cursor over the middle resize handle on the left border of the box

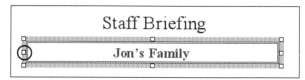

3 Click and when the cursor changes to a double-headed horizontal arrow, drag to the right

4 Adjust the size until you are satisfied with the way the text appears within the box, but leave a little space at each end of the text.

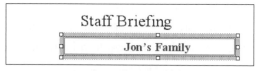

❑ Compare this image to the previous example. The box now appears to have moved to the right side of the slide. It has not actually moved but was simply re-sized.

5 Point to the border – not a handle

6 When the cursor changes to a four-headed arrow, click and drag the cursor to the left until the box appears central below the slide title

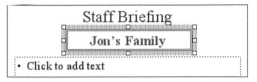

7 Save the changes

❑ Keep this slide in view because we still have some work to do

Copying between presentations

We are now going to copy some of the information from the presentation called *Katherine*, to this presentation. There are several reasons for doing this.

◆ To illustrate how easy it is to copy between different presentations

◆ To maintain an overall consistency in presentational styles

◆ To ensure the accuracy of the information

◆ To create a new presentation, by combining information from other presentations

Basic steps

1 Open the presentation *Katherine.ppt*

2 Move to Slide 2

We are going to copy the slide's information:

3 Select all the bullet list text, from 'Website' down to the end of the slide

4 Copy the text, using the shortcut Ctrl+C

Switching between presentations

5 Open the Window menu – in its lower area you will see the names of the open presentations, in this instance *Jon's Intro* and *Katherine*. The tick next *Katherine*, indicates that this is the active presentation.

Window	Help
New Window	
Arrange All	
Fit to Page	
Cascade	
Next Pane	F6
1 Jon's Intro.ppt	
✓ 2 Katherine.ppt	

6 Click by the appropriate name (*Jon's Intro*)

Inserting the copied information

With 'Jon's Intro' presentation active and on screen:

7 Ensure that the new Slide 4 is visible

8 Place the cursor in the bullet list

9 Using the shortcut Ctrl+V, paste in the detail copied from the *Katherine* presentation

You may find that that the copied information overflows or extends below the current slide area. Do not concern yourself about it at this stage, we are about to make a number of changes to the text and this will rectify the situation.

Deleting text

Basic steps

1 Place the cursor at the left of the first line

2 Press [Enter] to insert a new line

3 Press [Tab] key to demote that line

4 Move the cursor back up to the blank line

5 Type '*Katherine, prefers to be called Kathy*'

6 Highlight the line starting at '*Married*' and the one beneath, starting 'Network'

7 The text is no longer required, so delete it

8 Press [Backspace] to remove the blank lines

❑ If necessary, adjust the text box size so that all of the first bulleted text appears on one line

❑ Your slide should match the one shown

Staff Briefing

Jon's Family

• Katherine, prefers to be called Kathy.
  – Website Designer/Consultant and Graphics Artist.
  – Two children.
    • Richard, 8 years of age.
    • Samantha, 6 years of age.
      – Both children in boarding school in the UK.

23 March 2000   Tec-com plc   4

---

9 Save the changes to *Jon's Intro* and keep it open as it is required for the next section

10 Close the *Katherine* presentation

Practice slide show

We are now at the stage ready to run the presentation as a Slide Show to check the layout and appearance of the slides. Ensure that you have the first slide on display, so that the show will run from the beginning. Start the show with **Slide Show > View Show** then navigate through the slides (see page 264).

Tidying up

On completion of the Slide Show you may find that the chart on Slide 5 appears small on the screen. If so, you can increase the size easily.

Basic steps

1 Ensure that the chart slide is displayed

2 Select the chart by clicking over it

3 Click over the top left-hand sizing handle and drag up to the left

4 Release the button when the border of the box is approximately 3cm from the left of the slide

❑ If the chart is still not quite large enough, perform the same actions, only this time:

5 Select the lower right-hand sizing handle and drag it out to the lower right of the slide

Re-run the Slide Show to ensure that you are happy with the final size and positioning on the slide.

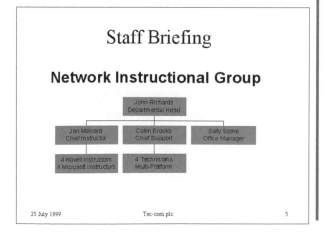

Staff Briefing

Network Instructional Group

John Richards
Departmental Head

Jan Meinard
Chief Instructor

Collin Brooks
Chief Support

Sally Stone
Office Manager

4 Novell Instructors
4 Microsoft Instructors

4 Technicians
Multi-Platform

25 July 1999   Tec-com plc   5

Slide 4, Jon's family details, has an oddity on it. The problem area is the first line of the bullet list, '*Katherine, prefers to be called Kathy*'.

'*Katherine*' is the correct size, but the remainder of the text, should be of a smaller font size.

6 Highlight the text '*prefers to be called Kathy*' and change the font size to 24 pt

❑ The use of red for both the text and text box 'Jon's Family' was not a good choice, so:

7 Select the text box

8 Change the border to blue

9 Save the changes to the presentation

That completes the creation of the presentation *Jon's Intro* for the moment, but do not close it yet. We require it for the next section.

To highlight and practise one or two other procedures, we are going to re-open the *Katherine* presentation and introduce a number of features and formatting options not yet covered.

Cutting and pasting text and images

Ensure that the presentation *Jon's Intro* is open and is the active one. Re-save it with a new name, calling it '*Modified*', so that the original presentation is unaffected by the changes that we are about to make.

We require the *Katherine* presentation open as well, as we will be moving text and images between the presentations.

Basic steps

1 Open the *Katherine* presentation

2 Switch to the *Modified* presentation

3 Switch to the Slider Sorter view

4 Click to the right of Slide 5

5 On the menu bar select Insert > New Slide and double-click this slide

6 When it appears in the Slide Sorter view, double-click on it

7 In the Title box type '*Practice Slide Only*'

8 De-select the text box

9 Select the Text Box tool on the Drawing toolbar

10 Draw a rectangle in the left area of the slide by dragging down and to the right but stopping just short of the centre of the slide

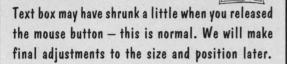
❏ Your slide should resemble the example shown – if the new text box image is not in the same position, do not worry. You can adjust it later.

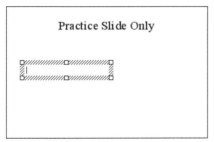

11 Switch to the *Katherine* presentation

12 Go to Slide 2

13 Select and copy the first line of the text in the bullet list starting 'Website Designer'

14 Switch to the 'Modified' presentation

❏ The new text box should still be selected.

15 From the menu bar select Edit > Paste

❏ The text will appear in the text box. Adjust the box size so that your text layout matches this.

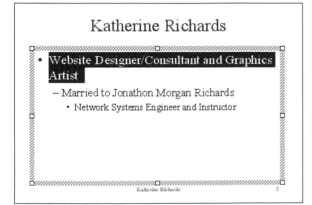

Moving an image

We are now going to move an image.

Basic steps

1 Switch to the *Katherine* presentation

2 Select Slide 1

3 Right-click over the image and from the pop-up menu select Cut

4 Switch to the *Modified* presentation

5 Go to Slide 6 and right-click over the empty right area of the slide

6 From the pop-up menu select Paste

The image should now appear in approximately the same location as it occupied in the other presentation, and should retain its size. If the image size requires adjustment, right-click over it, select **Format Picture** and change the picture size as appropriate.

Convert a text box to a bullet box

We need to label the image of Katherine Richards so that anyone viewing the slide can know who she is.

We will convert the text box to a bullet list and include her name.

Basic steps

1 Select the text box

2 Place the cursor at the start of the first line, to the left of the word 'Website'.

3 On the Formatting toolbar, click on the Bullet list button

❑ The text box will be converted to a bullet list box. You will most likely find that the text is too close to the bullet point. We can adjust this.

4 Ensure that the Ruler is displayed

❑ This should match this example. Note the positions of the indent indicators (circled).

5 Click on the lower triangle and drag it to the right

6 When its position matches the example here, release the mouse button

7 Leave the cursor where it is (between the bullet point and the word 'Website')

8 Press [Enter] to insert a new line

❑ The existing text will move down one line and leave an empty space. At this stage you will not see a bullet point in the empty space.

9 Click in the space above the word 'Website'

❑ You should now see the bullet point. The text box is ready to have further text inserted.

10 Switch to the *Katherine* presentation and go to Slide 1

11 Highlight and copy the text in the slide title, 'Katherine Richards'

12 Return to the *Modified* presentation

13 Ensure that the cursor is still on the empty bullet point line

14 From the menu bar select Edit > Paste

❑ The name will appear in the text box and your slide should now match the example.

Practice Slide Only

- Katherine Richards
- Website Designer/Consultant and Graphics Artist

---

15 If necessary, change the font size

15 Save the changes to the *Modified* presentation only

Copying a image between presentations

We have recently moved an image from one presentation to use in another. We could have easily just copied the image and pasted it wherever we required and that is what we shall do now.

Select and copy the image on Slide 6 of the Modified presentation and paste it into Slide 1 of the Katherine presentation. You will find that the original image is still present because in this instance the Copy command and not the Cut command was used.

Copying an image within a presentation

You have seen how easy it is to copy, or move, an image and text between presentations. You should be aware that it is just as easy to do the same, within the same presentation.

Katherine's image is still in the Clipboard. Go to Slide 4 of the *Modified* presentation (*Jon's Family*) and paste the image into the empty area to the right of the text box.

The image will be placed in approximately the same location it occupied on the source slide. However, it has overlapped the existing text extensively.

If you attempt to resize the text box, the text will overrun the slide area.

If the image and the existing text clash, the simplest thing to do is to delete the image.

Select the image and press **[Delete]**.

Import an image from a different file

You may have a file, such as a Word document, sent to you that contains an image or text that you wish to use in a presentation you are creating. The procedure is little more than a Copy and Paste action.

To assist in this procedure, we have included a Word file in the *Course Resources* folder on the ECDL CD and it contains two images that we will use.

We will use cut and paste procedures to import the images from the Word document and place them on the Slide Master so that the images appear on every slide in the presentation.

Basic steps

1 Ensure that the presentation *Jon's Intro* is open and that you have Slide 1 displayed

2 Select View > Master > Slide Master

3 Start Word and open *Import Image.doc* in the *Course Resources* folder on the CD

❑ When it opens, you will find that the document contains two images, the European Union and UK Union flags.

4 Right-click over the middle of the UK flag and select Copy from the pop-up menu

5 Switch to PowerPoint and Paste the image into the title text box, setting it to the left of the text and on a line with it.

6 Return to the Word document

7 Select and copy the European Union flag

8 Switch back to PowerPoint

9 Paste it the image appears into the right-hand side of the title text box.

❑ If necessary, adjust the image sizes to those shown in the example

---

 Staff Briefing

---

10 From the menu bar select View > Slide

11 Check each slide in the presentation to ensure that the two images do not obscure any detail on any of the slides. If there is a problem, note what is required and return to the Slide Master view and adjust the offending image(s).

12 Save and Close the presentation

Copying a slide between presentations

To date we have copied, moved and deleted text or images between different presentations. You can also copy or move complete slides.

Basic steps

1 Open the *Modified* presentation and display Slide 2

2 Select all of the items on the slide (either select Edit > Select All or use the shortcut Ctrl+A)

3 Copy the selections, using the shortcut Ctrl+C

4 Switch to the *Katherine* presentation

5 Select Slide Sorter view

6 Insert a new blank slide between Slides 2 and 3, so that the new slide becomes Slide 3

7 Double-click then right-click over the new slide

8 From the pop-up menu select Paste

You will now have a copy of all the objects of the slide from the other presentation in the current one.

Take note

There are other – and sometimes better – ways of copying a slide from one presentation to another. Look up 'Copying slides' in the online Help.

Duplicating a slide

You will sometimes find that you have created a slide layout, which is unique and specific to a certain presentation, only to find later that you want to use the slide again with all of its objects and formatting.

To reproduce the slide from the beginning is time consuming and unnecessary.

PowerPoint has a feature called **Duplicate**, which can be found in the **Edit** menu.

Basic steps

1 In the *Modified* presentation select Slide Sorter view

2 Select the slide that contains the image representing Jon

3 Select *Edit > Duplicate*

❑ A duplicate slide will be inserted next to the original. You can move it to another position, if necessary, and edit it as required.

Deleting a slide

We do not require the duplicate slide and only performed the procedure to show how easy it was. Select the slide and use **Edit > Delete Slide**.

• If the wrong slide was deleted, stop immediately and use **Edit > Undo** or **Ctrl+Z** to restore it

Outline view

Outline view shows the structure and main text of the presentation, and is probably the best view in which to organise and develop its content.

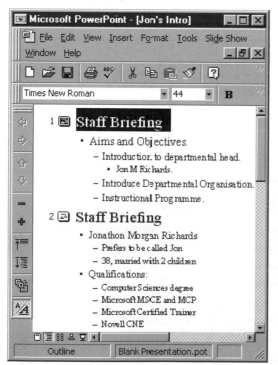

You can type an outline directly, start with one from the AutoContent Wizard, or import an outline from Word.

For each slide you have its number and title, with up to five indented levels of body text. You can use normal editing and cut-and-paste techniques to add or rearrange points within a slide, or to move slides, and the Outline toolbar has its own special tools to help you organise your presentation. Use these to change indent levels, move points or slides, show or hide formatting, or to expand or collapse the text on display.

The Common Tasks toolbar

This toolbar has now been combined with the Formatting toolbar and no longer appears as a floating toolbar. It is now a permanent feature of the Formatting toolbar.

New Slide... Slide Layout... Apply Design...

The commands available will save you quite a lot of time when you are creating a presentation and are worth investigating further.

284

Creating charts in PowerPoint

PowerPoint presentations can include charts, similar to those used in Excel workbooks, which are either produced from within PowerPoint directly or imported from another application.

In this section we are going to create a simple chart from scratch, using PowerPoint facilities and save it in its own presentation which you may wish to reuse later for practice. Save any open presentations and then close them.

Basic steps

1 Select File > New from the menu bar
2 Double-click on 'Blank Presentation'
3 At the New Slide dialog box double-click on the *Chart* slide shown in the example

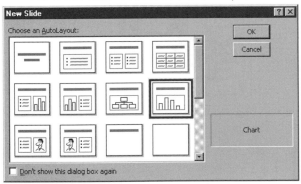

4 Save the presentation as 'Chart'

The chart slide is divided into two areas:

- The slide title area
- The chart area, which is a separate smaller application within PowerPoint. To start it you have to double-click on the image of a chart

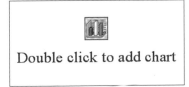

Double click to add chart

5 Give the slide the title '*Creating a Chart*'
6 Double-click on the image of a chart

❑ The chart application will run and your display will change to this. Note the two distinct areas.

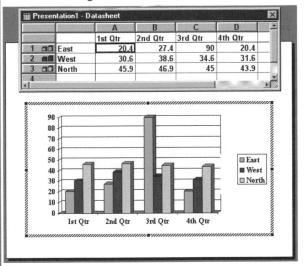

The datasheet

In the upper area of the example is the datasheet. This contains the data on which the chart will be based.

- Each row has a colour assigned to it – the colour is used to indicate the item in the chart
- The datasheet has sample data in it. This can be overwritten or deleted as required.

Check the toolbars and you will find that the Standard toolbar now displays chart specific icons. Investigate and identify the functions of the icon by pausing over each and reading the tool-tips.

The chart

Below the datasheet is an example chart based on the data currently displayed.

Our chart

We are now going to create a new chart, which will record and display the results of five fund raising events for a local charity.

Editing the datasheet

Before we can proceed, we must first clear the example data in the datasheet.

Basic steps

1 Click the rectangle where the row and column headers meet – this will select all the cells

2 Right-click anywhere over the sheet and select Clear Contents from the pop-up menu

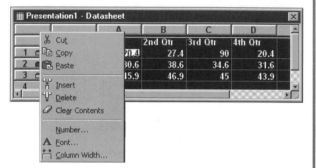

3 Click in the first empty cell of row 1

4 Type in the headings shown in the example – note how they are added to the chart legend. If the text overruns into the next cell, the column widths can be adjusted using the same techniques as in Excel (see page 156)

5 Continue to enter the event details. Note that as you type, the chart is being created.

		A
1	Fancy Dress	150
2	Summer Fair	347
3	Autumn Ball	245
4	Fireworks night	95
5	Christmas draw	368

❑ At the moment, the chart values could represent anything, when they are currency. We will format the cells to display the £ symbol.

6 Click on the column A header to select the column

7 Right-click over the column and select Number from the menu

8 At the Format dialog box, select Currency and make your settings match the example

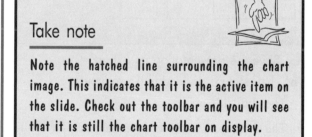

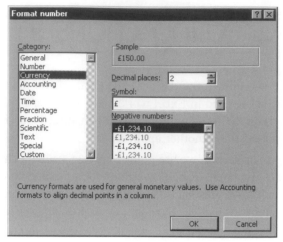

9 Click OK and save the changes

10 Click on the title bar of the datasheet and move it so that you can see the chart. If it matches the example, close the datasheet.

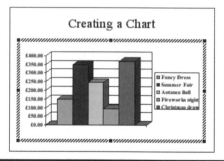

Creating a pie chart

We have created a 3D bar chart but we actually require a pie chart. At the moment our data is displayed by rows and this is indicated by the presence of the symbols next to the row numbers.

You may recall from chapter 4 that pie charts can only show one data series, either one row or one column.

To change the chart to a pie chart, we must first change the data axis to column.

Basic steps

1 Click this icon 📊 on the toolbar

2 Check the datasheet and you will see that the symbols have been removed from the rows and that column A now has a symbol next to it.

3 Click the down arrow by the Chart Type icon

4 From the menu select the 3-D Pie Chart

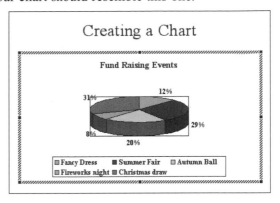

Displaying values

The chart will now be changed to that of a 3D chart. However, by default PowerPoint does not display any slice values and as our chart is not currently very informative we shall display the percentage values.

Ensure that the chart is still active. If not, double-click on it make it active.

Basic steps

1 Select Chart > Chart Options

2 At the Chart Options dialog box, ensure that the Titles tab is selected

3 Type in '*Fund Raising Events*'

4 On the Legend tab, tick (✓) the Show Legend slot and select the Bottom option

5 Go to the Data Labels tab and click Show percent

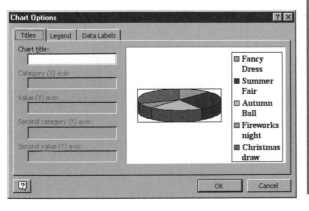

6 Click OK to apply the changes and save the presentation

Your chart should resemble this one.

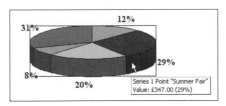

Look closely at the Pie chart and you will see that it has a border around it that can be distracting. It can easily be removed. However, before we do that let's look at the Pie chart a little more closely.

At the moment the percentage values are displayed and you could, if required, display the monetary values of each slice. Be careful, however, of over-loading the chart with too much detail.

Place your cursor over the dark blue slice shown as 29% and pause. Another small window will open displaying the actual monetary value. Check each of the slices in the same manner.

We will now remove the border around the pie chart.

Place your cursor over the main chart area and pause. If the cursor is in the correct area, a message will appear advising you that you are pointing at the Plot Area. If you find that another message appears, move the cursor off the area all together and try again.

7 Right-click and from the pop-up menu select For-mat Plot Area

❑ The Format Plot Area dialog box will open

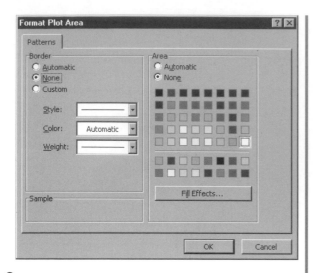

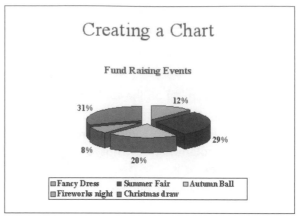

8   In the Border pane, select the None option

❑   Note that you can make numerous changes to the plot area from this box if required

9   Click OK and save the presentation

Open out the pie chart

You can add more visual impact by separating each of the slices that make up the chart.

Basic steps

1   Place your cursor over the 29% slice

2   Click and drag down and to the right

❑   The chart will open out revealing each slice as an individual item. When you are satisfied with the appearance of the chart, release the mouse button.

Your slide should resemble that shown

3   Save the changes and close the presentation

Summary

That completes the introduction to charts. It is suggested that you use this presentation to practise making changes to the chart. Remember, the various elements that make up the chart, such as the title, legend, chart area and the chart itself, are all selectable. Changes can be made to each, including font type, size and colour and orientation. The various backgrounds can have a colour and pattern applied.

Use the online Help to learn more on this subject and experiment.

The next section also covers the use of charts and imports data from a Microsoft Excel workbook that is used to create a bar chart.

Software integration

Information used within a PowerPoint presentation can easily be copied or linked to any of the other applications in the Office Suite. A chart or data can be inserted in a Word document, an Excel worksheet or an Access database. It is also possible to import data from these applications into PowerPoint.

Import a spreadsheet and create a chart

We will now import an Excel worksheet, which, when double-clicked on, will open Excel, without you leaving PowerPoint. This allows you the flexibility to change, or update the data without having to open Excel. You must have Excel on the computer that will run the presentation and have access to the file, either on the same computer or over a network.

We will also create a chart in PowerPoint using the imported Excel data. To assist with this section of the course we have included an Excel file in the *Courses Resources* folder, called *ECDL1.xls*.

Inserting an Excel worksheet

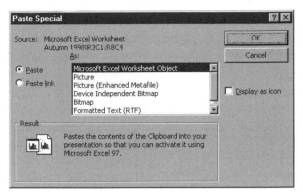

Basic steps

❏ Ensure that the *Modified* is open and you have Slide 6 displayed
1 Insert a new Title-only slide as shown
2 In the title text box type 'Autumn Sales 1999'
3 Open Microsoft Excel
4 Locate the folder *Course Resources* on the course CD and open the file *ECDL1.xls*
5 Select and copy the cells A3 to D8 inclusive
6 Return to PowerPoint, at the new slide
7 Select Edit > Paste Special
8 The Paste Special dialog box will open. Check that the detail relates to your file and click OK

The Excel worksheet will, after a short pause, appear on the slide. It will almost certainly be too small so use the resizing handles to resize the image to occupy the left area of the slide.

9 Save the changes

Take note

If you want to change any of the data in the sheet, double-click over it in PowerPoint and Excel will be launched. You will not see the full Excel application display, but only the immediate cell area that you copied across to PowerPoint. Carry out any changes to the data and when finished left-click on any blank area of the slide to return to normal Slide View in PowerPoint.

Inserting a chart

We will now insert a chart based on the data contained in the Worksheet.

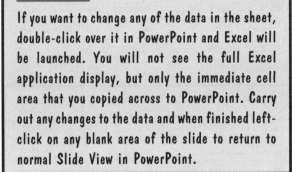

Basic steps

❏ Ensure that the *Modified* is open and you have Slide 7 displayed
1 Double-click over the worksheet data – Excel will be launched as described

6: Presentations

289

2 If not already highlighted, highlight the cells A3 to D8 inclusive

3 Using the short-cut keys Ctrl+C, copy the cells

Take note

The broken line surrounding the selected cells indicates the cells have been copied.

---

4 Click on any blank area of the slide to exit Excel – if you forget to do this, the chart will not appear on the PowerPoint slide but will be displayed in the Excel worksheet.

5 Select Insert > Chart

❑ PowerPoint will display an example chart and, more importantly, the Datasheet window. For the time being concentrate on the Datasheet.

	A	B	C	D	E
	1st Qtr	2nd Qtr	3rd Qtr	4th Qtr	
1 East	20.4	27.4	90	20.4	
2 West	30.6	38.6	34.6	31.6	
3 North	45.9	46.9	45	43.9	
4					

6 Clear the contents (as shown on page 286)

7 Right-click over the sheet

8 Select Paste

Take note

You may find that a message box will appear and warn you that the data in the clipboard is not the same size and shape. You can ignore this, so click OK. The data you copied from the Excel worksheet will now appear in the Datasheet.

❑ When the data appears in the Datasheet, close it by clicking the Close button. The example chart will now change to represent the data that you have just copied in.

290

9 If the chart is too large and overlaps the sheet, resize it and move it to the right of the slide.

10 Save the changes

Your slide should now resemble this example.

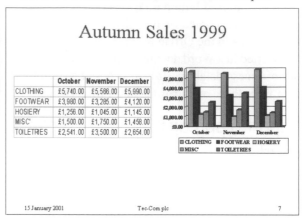

Including the datasheet

You can, if required, include the datasheet on the chart slide.

Ensure that the chart toolbar is on display; if not double-click over the chart. Click on this icon ⊞ and the datasheet will appear, usually below the chart.

Try it now. It is not wanted at this time, so click on the same icon again and it will be removed.

Changing the chart type

You can change the chart from a column chart, to any other type supported by PowerPoint.

Basic steps

1 Right-click over the chart and from the pop-up menu select Chart Object > Open

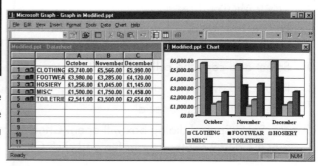

2 At the Microsoft Graph dialog box, click on the down arrow on the right of the Chart Type icon on the Standard toolbar

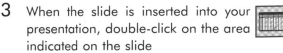

3 From the drop-down menu select the chart of your choice (but remember the constraints of using a pie chart)

❑ Close the Microsoft Graph dialog box and the change will be applied to your chart

Importing Word tables

We will not use this feature, it is mentioned only for information. PowerPoint features a slide layout that includes a placeholder for a table that you would use if you wanted to include a Word table in the presentation.

Basic steps

1 Click on the New Slide button on the Common Tasks toolbar

2 At the New Slide dialog box opens, double-click on the *Table* slide

3 When the slide is inserted into your presentation, double-click on the area indicated on the slide

❑ The Insert Word Table dialog box will open and it is from here that you set the number of columns and rows that you require in the table

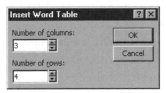

4 Click OK once you have completed your selection

❑ The dialog box will close and you will then see a cut-down view of a Microsoft Table

❑ Experiment with this feature later. If you use tables regularly, it will be invaluable to you

Summary

That completes the chapter on software integration. Practise the areas that are of interest to you and remember that further information is available from the online Help.

Additional text and slide formatting

There are still a number of text and slide formatting options that we have not yet covered and we will now address this area, using the Modified presentation. However, before we start, a word of explanation. This section is primarily an exercise in formatting options within PowerPoint and has little relationship to the slides created earlier.

Basic steps

❑ Ensure that the *Modified* presentation is open and that you have the last slide on display

1 Insert a new Title only slide

2 In the title text box type 'Text Formatting'

3 Insert a new text box the same width as the title box and type into it the text as shown here

---

Text Formatting

An example of plain formatting, 24 pt.

Another example with Bold and Underling applied

Another example with shadow applied.

Another example with superscript and subscript applied.

Another example right aligned.

Another example centre aligned.

Another example left aligned.

23 March 2000   Tec-com plc   8

---

4 Select each line of text in turn and apply to it the formatting to match the text, using these methods

❑ For Bold and Underlining use the shortcuts Ctrl+B and Ctrl+U

❑ For the Shadow, Superscript and Subscript effects, right-click and select Font. Tick the appropriate checkbox.

❑ To set the alignment, use the shortcuts Ctrl+R (right-aligned), Ctrl+E (centred) or Ctrl+L (left-aligned); or the alignment icons on the toolbar

---

Using the Shadow option

Initially you may find it difficult to discern any difference between plain text and text with the shadow option applied. Shadow is more effective with different font types, sizes and the use of colour.

We can examine the effects more closely if we zoom in, and enlarge the area of interest. Zoom in to 200% and experiment with the font and colour settings for the shadow text.

Changing line spacing

A further option that you should be aware of is the line spacing. We will first look at the default spacing, using our Text Formatting slide.

Basic steps

❑ Go to Slide 8, set the Zoom level to *Fit* and locate the slide centrally on the screen

1 Highlight the first three lines of text

2 Select Format > Line Spacing

3 At the Line Spacing dialog box, click the up-arrow next to the Line Spacing slot until you reach the figure 2

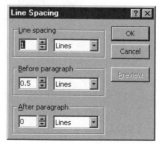

4   Change the Before paragraph value by click-
    ing the up-arrow until you reach the figure 1

5   Click the Preview button and observe the
    changes

❏   We will not apply the changes to our slide – this
    section was solely to illustrate how easy it is to
    change the line spacing.

6   Click the Cancel button

❏   Investigate the other line options at a later date

Finer control

The increments at which the figures change in the
line-spacing box permit you good control over various aspects of line spacing. You also have the option
of changing the line spacing option from lines to font
size points. Select the unit of measurement from the
drop-down list to the right of the values in the **Line
Spacing** dialog box.

Tip

**Experiment with the line spacing option, because
it is a means of cheating. You will have the odd
occasion when you find that text will not fit on the
slide correctly and overruns at the bottom. You
may not want to insert another slide just for one
line of text as it would spoil the continuity and
style of the presentation. So, by adjusting the line
space a little, you will find that you can cheat and
get that last line on the slide.**

Changing bullet points

We will now change the format of the bullet points in
Slide 1 of the *Modified* presentation.

Basic steps

❏   Ensure that the *Modified* presentation is open
    and Slide 1 is displayed

1   Place the cursor to the left of the first word
    'Aims' of the first line

2   From the menu bar select Format > Bullets and
    Numbering

❏   Go to the Bullet tab and click Character

3   Select *Webdings* in the Bullets from slot

4   Select the image shown in the example

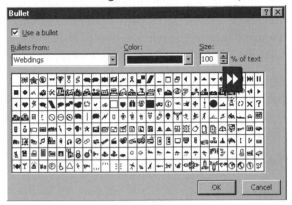

5   Click OK

❏   Change each bullet point, as shown in the
    example, using the same procedure.

Staff Briefing

⯈Aims and Objectives.
   ▸ Introduction to departmental head.
     ● Jon M Richards.
   ▸ Introduce Departmental Organisation.
   ▸ Instructional Programme.

23 March 2000   Tec-com plc   1

Take note

**All of the bullet point symbols used in the example
are from the Webdings font. You can however mix
bullet points from different font lists.**

Save the changes and keep the presentation open as
we are now going to perform a number of drawing
exercises.

Drawing simple shapes

PowerPoint has are a number of simple freehand drawing tools. You have already used some to create lines and circles in the recently created presentation. We are going to use one or two of these tools to highlight what can be created with relative ease.

Software integration

The tools that are about to be described are the same tools used to produce drawings in Microsoft Word, Excel and PowerPoint.

Drawing using the AutoShapes feature

Earlier in the course we used the drawing toolbar to draw a circle and a straight line and we discussed how to display the Drawing toolbar (see page 117). If the toolbar is not visible, open it now.

Drawing basic shapes

We will start by drawing a number of simple basic shapes using AutoShapes. AutoShapes are available from the Drawing toolbar. When selected, a number of options are available.

Basic steps

1   Insert a new title slide.
2   Click AutoShapes on the Drawing toolbar
3   Point to Basic Shapes and select the shape indicated
❑   The cursor will change shape to that of a small cross
4   Place the cursor over a blank area of the slide
5   Hold down [Shift] while you click and drag the cursor to create the AutoShape – [Shift] will keep the shape in proportion

❑   Don't draw too large a shape as we will be drawing a number of different shapes shortly
6   Release the mouse button
7   Select the same AutoShape and draw another shape, but this time do not use [Shift] – as you drag the shape out you will find that you can personalise the shape.
8   Draw a shape similar to the image shown

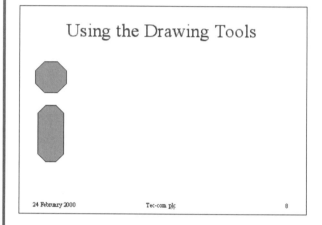

What is a colour fill?

You can fill objects with solid or gradient colours, a pattern, a texture, or a picture. If you change an object's fill, you can easily change it back to its default. All shapes have a fill, usually white. This means the fill colour is not always apparent.

When you drew the shapes you may have found that a colour fill had already been applied. This depends upon how your system is configured.

Basic steps

To change the many properties of a shape:
1   Right-click over the lower shape
2   From the pop-up menu select Format AutoShape
❑   The Format AutoShape dialog box will open
3   Select the Colors and Lines tab

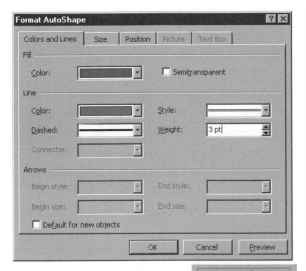

Add, change, or remove an object shadow

The images that we drew are flat and we can improve the appearance by adding shadow.

You can add a shadow to any object, including text boxes and you can set its size, direction, and colour.

When you change the colour of a shadow, it does not affect the object.

You can also add shadows to the borders of pictures, or give an object an embossed or engraved effect.

Basic steps

To apply a shadow:

1 Select the first of the drawn objects

2 Click the Shadow icon ▣ on the Drawing toolbar

❏ The Shadow menu will open and offer a number of options for how and where you want the Shadow to appear

3 Click the Shadow Settings... button

❏ This will open the Shadow Setting dialog box, where you can adjust the depth and colour

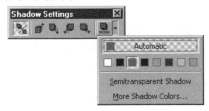

4 Select the Shadow Setting option as indicated

5 With the object still selected, click the Shadow button again and return to the Shadows Settings – this time select More Shadows Colors...

6 At the Colors dialog box select an orange tone and observe the effects on the object.

❏ The reason for selecting an orange colour for the shadow was to emphasise the effect because the contrast is greatly heightened, though the true effect of the shadow is lost.

To change the colour fill:

4 Click the Color down-arrow in the Fill section and select a colour

5 From the same menu click on Fill Effects...

6 At the Fill Effects dialog box, open the Pattern tab, select a pattern and click OK

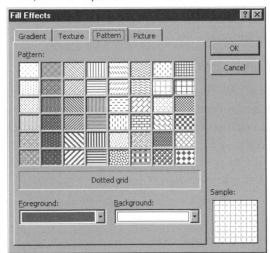

To change the line style and colour:

7 In the Line section select a colour

8 Change the line weight and style to that shown in the example above

9 Click OK to apply the changes

❏ The AutoShape should look like this

Rotating or flipping a drawn object

Objects can be rotated or *flipped* (reflected).

Basic steps

1 Select the second of our drawn objects

2 Click the Draw button on the Drawing toolbar

3 Select the Rotate or Flip option

❑ This menu will open. Its options, include the ability to control the rotation

4 Select Rotate Right

❑ Observe the effects on the selected object

Take note

If you find that you cannot select an option, ensure that you have selected the object. Experiment with the options, in particular the Free Rotate feature, which gives you greater control over the rotation of to the object.

Drawing lines

Another feature of the Drawing toolbar is the Line drawing tool, which enables you to draw straight or diagonal lines, with the ability to later change the weight and style of the lines, including changing a plain line to either a single or double-ended arrow.

In addition to straight lines, also available are Freeform, Curve and Scribble drawing tools. You should experiment with each of these tools in due course, however for now we will use the Freeform tool to illustrate its flexibility and potential.

Basic steps

1 From the AutoShapes > Basic Shapes menu select the isosceles triangle

2 Draw a shape approximately 4cm by 4cm

3 Change the fill to any colour other than the default fill colour

❑ We are going to draw another triangle, over the top of the existing triangle:

4 From the Drawing toolbar select AutoShape > Line

5 Select the Freeform tool

6 Click on the lower right corner of the triangle, then drag the cursor to the top corner of the triangle and click, drawing a line

7 Drag the cursor down to the lower left corner and click

8 Drag the cursor back to the lower-right corner, and left-click for the final time

❑ This action will produce a closed object, in this case a triangle

You will see the effect immediately because the default colour fill is applied to the newly drawn object and the original triangle will disappear. It is still there but obscured by the new object.

9 Place the cursor over your triangle

10 When the cursor changes to a four-headed arrow click and drag the object off the other triangle

Object stacking

If you draw an object over a previously drawn object, the newly drawn object will obscure the original one. Placing one object over another is known as *stacking* and the order of precedence in respect of object visibility is determined by the order in which each object is drawn.

You can change the order of appearance in the stack of any or all of the objects.

Basic steps

1 Place one triangle partially over the other

2 Select the triangle that is partially obscured

3 From the Drawing toolbar select Draw > Order

4 Select the Bring to Front option

This exercise was used to illustrate how simple it is to create your own drawn objects and to introduce the Freeform tool, which can be used to draw complex shapes.

Experiment with these features as they are extremely useful. You will become more aware of their potential as you develop your drawing skills.

Using the Scribble tool

Basic steps

1 Separate the drawn objects so that there is space between all of them

2 Open the AutoShape > Lines menu and click on the Scribble tool

❑ The cursor now resembles a pencil

3 Holding the mouse button down, draw a line that passes over each of the objects, re-turning to the start point but stopping just short of it. Do not join the lines

4 Release the mouse button

5 Click the Line Style icon and from the menu select the 6 pt line weight

6 Click the Dash Style icon and select the dot-dash style as in the example

7 Click the Line Color down-arrow, then click the More Line Colors button and from the color wheel select a colour that we have not yet used in any of our drawing objects

Take note

If you simply click the **Line Color** icon, the colour is shown on the icon will be applied to the line.

❑ The line can be moved and re-sized in the same way as any other object

The final product

The example shows how your drawing slide should look, after all the objects have been drawn, moved, re-shaped and have had various colours applied.

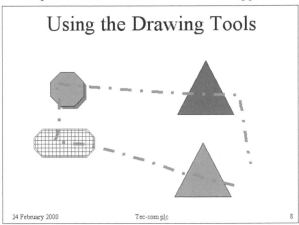

Creating a group

This very useful feature allows you to create a group by combining a number of independent objects. This is important if you create a shape, consisting of a number of individual shapes, which you later may wish to move or re-size. Without the ability to group them, you would have to move each object individually, which is time-consuming and will disrupt the positioning of the objects in relation to each other.

We will use the drawing slide and create a group of all of the drawn objects on that slide.

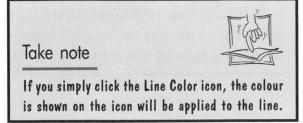

Basic steps

1 Click on one of the objects

2 Hold down [Shift] and click on the remaining three objects and the line

3 Right-click over the group

4 From the pop-up menu select Grouping > Group

297

❑ Each of the object's re-sizing handles will disappear and a new group will appear, encompassing all of the objects, which now resembles a single entity.

Take note

Care must be exercised when selecting smaller objects such as lines, particularly when there are several objects to be included, otherwise an item may be omitted from the group selection.

To confirm that all of the objects have been included in the group and that the object behaves as one, place the cursor over any object and when it changes to the 'move cursor' symbol, left-click and drag the object around the slide.

All of the objects should now behave as a single object. Should this not be the case, you may have missed one or more objects, so re-create the group as described above.

Ungroup objects

Basic steps

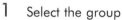

1 Select the group
2 Right-click and select Grouping > Ungroup

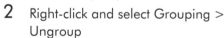

❑ All the objects will be returned to their original state

Experimentation
The Drawing tools require experimentation. Try out the various tools later – remember to try the 3D shapes and adjust the lighting effects.

Slide show review

Run the Slide Show and review the presentation as many of changes have been applied to it. Check each slide in turn.

It will soon become apparent that some of the slides have no relevance to the theme of the presentation.

We could easily delete the offending slides but this is a good opportunity to introduce you to another feature of PowerPoint.

Hide slides

You can create or modify a presentation to suit different audiences without deleting slides. This is done by hiding individual slides.

Basic steps

1 Switch to Slide Sorter View
2 Right-click over the slide that contains the spreadsheet imported from Excel
3 From the pop-up menu select Hide Slide

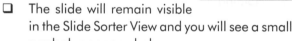

❑ The slide will remain visible in the Slide Sorter View and you will see a small symbol appear, below the lower-right corner of the slide. The symbol indicates that the slide is set as hidden and it will not appear in the Slide Show.

4 Re-run the Slide Show, remembering to start at Slide 1, and you will see that the slide does not appear in the presentation.

Hide all of the slides that are not relevant to the

Take note

To reveal the hidden slide again, right-click on it in Slide Sorter View and click the Hide Slide button. This is a toggle – either 'on' or 'off'. When the button is depressed it is switched 'on'.

Applying animation to slides

Select Slide 2 and run the Slide Show to review that individual slide. There is a lot of information on the slide, as well as the image, and the information covers two specific subjects, i.e. introduction of Jon and then his qualifications.

Ideally you should reveal each subject individually to the audience. This will allow you to retain your audience's attention on the subject being discussed, without the distraction of Jon's qualifications being visible, as well as taking questions from the floor.

When you have covered the first topic on the slide, you then reveal the next topic and so on.

PowerPoint has an animation feature that allows you to customise how the topics or images will appear throughout the presentation.

Basic steps

1 Ensure that Slide 2 is displayed in Normal View
2 Right-click over the bulleted text box
3 From the pop-up menu select Custom Animation…
❑ The Custom Animation dialog box will open

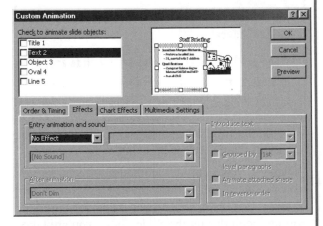

Initially the **Animation order** pane will be empty, as none of the objects have had any animation applied.

To the right of the dialog box is a miniature copy of our slide, with a hatched outline surrounding the text box. This indicates that the animation will be applied to that object.

It is in the lower area that you create the animation effects and determine how they will be displayed.

4 Select the Effects tab and click on the Entry animation and sound down-arrow

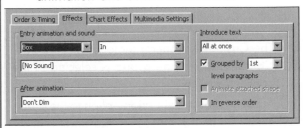

5 Click in the slot by 'Text 2' in the Check to animate slide objects
❑ Make your dialog box settings match those in the example at the bottom left of this page
6 Click the Preview button – the miniature slide will display the effects of the animation
7 Click OK to apply the animation
❑ Run the Slide Show to see the effects of the animation
8 When the slide is displayed, click and the first piece of text will appear, then click again and the second piece will appear below the first

There is a problem with the slide as it stands at the moment and that is with the image. It is there, on display, as soon as the Slide Show started, out of sequence. We will overcome this problem and apply an animation effect to it as well.

The image is one item, but there is the matter of the circle and the line which are two separate items, making a total of three items requiring animation.

❑ We do not want each item appearing individually, so create a group of all three items now
9 Right-click over the image group and select Custom Animation

299

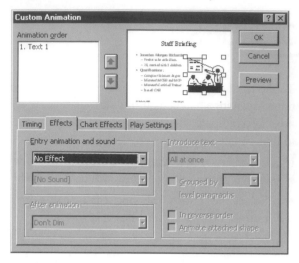

❏ The Custom Animation dialog box will open. Note that the image group is selected in the preview window

10 Apply the Box In animation option to the group

11 Select the image and apply the same settings

12 Click OK to apply the animation and close the dialog box

❏ You can improve on the way the text appears and make your audience concentrate even more on each topic in the text box by dimming out text when you have finished discussing it.

13 Ensure that Slide 2 is displayed in Normal View

14 Right-click over the text box and select Custom Animation

❏ At the dialog box opens, ensure that the Effects tab is selected. In the lower area you will see the After animation option, which, at the moment, displays the message *Don't Dim*.

15 Click on the down-arrow and select a light grey colour

16 Click OK button to apply the change

Re-run the Slide Show on Slide 2 only and observe the changes. The effect of dimming out text, once it has been discussed, is a good aid to presentations, and instruction, as it removes some of the distraction for the audience.

We used a light grey colour because our background colour is white. If you apply a design to your presentation, you will have to experiment to determine which colour will work best with the design colours.

Changing an animation effect

To change an applied animation is simple. You just select the object, re-open the Custom Animation dialog box and select a different animation. We will change the animation on the group on Slide 2 to *Peek From Right* and the effect for the bulleted text box to *Fly From Bottom-Left*. Re-run the Slide Show on Slide 2 only and observe the changes.

Take note

You must always practise the Slide Show fully and plan which animations to use, in relation to your subject, size of display screen, etc.

Some animation effects can be a distraction because they do not move smoothly and appear to jerk or judder.

When you have an effect applied to a slide and, as in Slide 2, the text appears in two or more distinct actions, this is known as a 'Build'.

How did the animation work, was it smooth, was the text a little blurred as it came in?

When you have applied animation effects, as you have to Slide 2, particularly the text box, you should be aware that if you were to select **Previous** from the pop-up menu during the Slide Show, you are taken back through each animation build. Run the Slide Show and go as far as Slide 3 then select the **Previous** command. Keep doing this until you reach Slide 1 and observe what happens at Slide 2

Slide transition

A transition is a special effect, which is used to introduce a slide during a presentation. You can set how the slide will appear and vary the speed of the effect.

Basic steps

1   Switch to Slide Sorter view
2   Right-click over a slide
3   From the pop-up menu select Slide Transition
❑   The Slide Transition dialog box will open

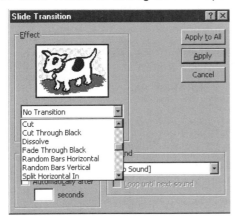

4   Click on the down-arrow in the Effect area
❑   A drop-down list will appear. This list contains all of the transition effects

5   Select any transition effect
6   Click Apply
❑   Do not change any of the other options. The effect will only be applied to the selected slide
7   Select a different slide and carry out the same procedure, but applying a different effect
❑   Do this to a number of the slides and decide which effect you prefer

Run the Slide Show and when you want to change slides, left-click and the next slide will appear until such time that you either terminate the Slide Show or reach the last slide.

Summary

That completes the section on animation and transitions. We have not covered all the features available and you should experiment, particularly with the Timing aspects, to gain maximum use and benefit of the feature.

There is quite a lot of information in the on-line Help on the subject of animations. Start up Help and open the Index tab. Type in the word 'animation' and you will be presented with a number of options. It is suggested that you select the option 'creating animated slides' first, then work your way through the remainder and practice the effects as you gain in experience.

Previewing and printing

PowerPoint offers you several ways to print presentations. For maximum benefit, use a colour printer, but remember the cost factor if you are printing a presentation with many slides. The options are:

* Print each individual, full size slide, either on paper or on Overhead Transparency film

* Print handouts for your audience, which contain miniature versions of your slides to take away at the end of the presentation (each handout may have two or more, and up to a maximum of six, slides per page)

* Print speaker notes - you can create, and print, speaker notes, as you create the presentation, for use by the presenter

Printing the presentation

Ensure that you have Slide 1 on display.

Basic steps

1   Select File > Print from the menu bar

❑   The Print dialog box will open

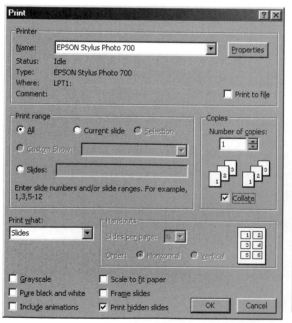

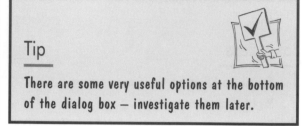

Tip

There are some very useful options at the bottom of the dialog box — investigate them later.

2   Click the down-arrow by the Print what slot

❑   This list contains the main print options

3   Select the *Notes Pages* option from the list

4   For the Print Range select *Current slide*

5   Click OK

❑   Your print out should resemble this example

The area at the bottom is for presenter's notes — these are not seen in the slide show

Printing OHP transparencies

Should you decide to create a number of slides for use with an overhead projector (OHP), you will usually make the necessary selections from within the printer's Properties box.

In the next example is a page from an Epson Stylus Photo 700's Properties box. You will see that it has a print option to use OHP film, shown as *Ink Jet Transparencies*. (You must of course have the correct OHP transparency film in your printer before you can actually print a transparency.)

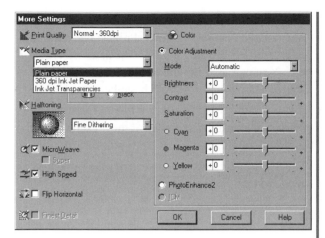

Changing the output format

When we created our first presentation, we accepted the default styles and formats, without changing anything. By default, we created a presentation for use on a computer display. We could, if we wanted create a presentation using the 35mm film format.

You can also change the orientation of slides or printouts from here. The default setting for slides on screen is *Landscape*; the default for printed notes, handouts and outlines is *Portrait*.

Basic steps

1   Select File > Page Setup

2   At the Page Setup dialog box, click the drop-down arrow next to the Slides sized for slot

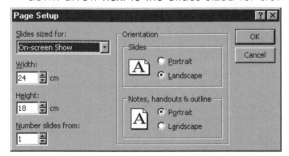

3   Make your selection from the list – *On-screen show* is the default

4   In the Orientation area set the orientation for Slides and for other printouts

5   Click OK

Previewing the presentation

You can preview the presentation in a number of different ways.

From the menu bar select **View**. Listed in the upper area of the menu are a number of different view options.

In the example shown opposite the **Normal** view option appears depressed, indicating that it is the currently selected view.

Click on the **Slide Sorter** option and see how PowerPoint displays this particular view of the presentation.

You can create a presentation or edit existing slides using this view.

You have already used the **Slide Sorter** option, so jump to the **Notes Page** and see how it is displayed.

The last option, **Slide Show**, has been used already. You will in time develop your own preferred way of working, like using the Slide View to create slides, but do remember all the options available.

Creating speaker's notes

Basic steps

1   Open the *Jon's Intro* presentation and go to Slide 1

2   Select View > Notes Page

3   Change the Zoom level to 100%

4   Scroll the page down to the notes section

5   Click in the text box marked '*Click to add text*'

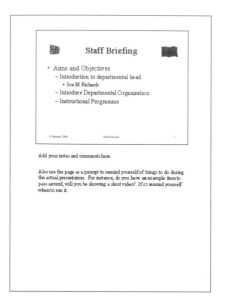

Spell checking the presentation

As we have been using PowerPoint it has automatically been performing a Spell Check as we typed in text. You can also run the Spell Checker yourself to double-check that no errors have been overlooked.

If you run the Spell Checker while in Outline View, you can see a high percentage of the presentation text simultaneously.

The Spell Checker is used in exactly the same way as in Word (see page 98).

6   Type in your notes

7   Save the changes to the presentation

Tip

Use the notes pages as prompts to remind yourself of things to do during the presentation. Do you have a sample to pass around? Will you be showing a short video? If so remind yourself when to do it.

PowerPoint and the Internet

Save a presentation as a Web Page

PowerPoint not only enables you to save your work directly in HTML format, but also allows you to open your HTML slides directly into PowerPoint. You can then edit and save them again in HTML. As you will see, this is not only easy but saves time, as it eliminates the need to convert the presentation each time.

We will open the presentation Katherine.ppt, re-save it using a different name and then convert it for publishing on the Web. When a presentation is converted for use on the Web, a number of files and images are created. In order to keep all of them together, we will first create a new folder in which to store them all.

Basic steps

1 Open Windows Explorer
2 Click on the folder *My Documents*
3 Select File > New > Folder from the menu bar
4 Call the new folder '*web presentation*'
5 Close Explorer

Take note

If you are familiar with PowerPoint 97 and its Internet Assistant, don't skip this section, because Microsoft have completely revamped and changed the Internet aspect of PowerPoint 2000.

Saving as a Web Page

Basic steps

1 Open *Katherine.ppt*
2 Select File > Save as Web Page

3 When the Save As dialog box opens navigate to the Web Presentation folder.
4 In the File name slot type 'Web Presentation'
5 Click Save

Its as easy as that. You now have a Web-based PowerPoint presentation.

Previewing the presentation

Select File >Web Page Preview. PowerPoint will launch your Internet Browser and the presentation will appear as shown here. Investigate each of the buttons located along the bottom of the window.

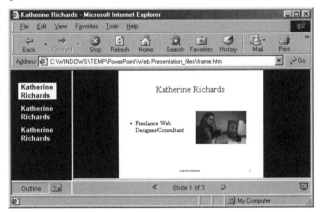

Running the Slide Show

Basic steps

1 Click the Full Screen Slide Show button
   The presentation will open in Full screen view, as if in PowerPoint'
2 Click on the slide to move to the next slide.
   When you reach the end of the Slide Show, a blank black screen is displayed. Click once more to exit.

Customising a Web Presentation

This procedure appeared to offer little or no option in the way of customisation and completed the process without any input. You can however apply some customisation to the presentation.

Basic steps

1 Select File > Save as Web Page
2 Click Publish – the Publish as Web Page dialog box will open and it is from here that you apply customisation.

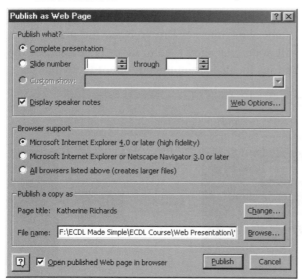

3 Click Web Options... for additional options

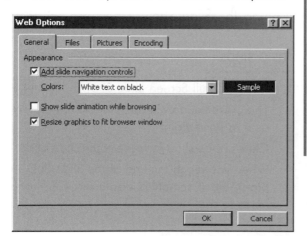

Take note

Pay particular attention to the Picture options relating the browsers and the picture format. Use the online Help for further information.

Point of Interest

When presentation was saved, it was given the name *Web Presentation*. Open Windows Explorer and navigate to the web presentation folder. You should find, in addition to the presentation with its .htm extension, a folder called *Web Presentation_Files*. PowerPoint created this folder during the process of saving the presentation. Open the folder and you should find that it contains 18 objects, all of which combine to make up the overall presentation.

Remember, you can create a link to the presentation, rather than keep using Windows Explorer to locate the file, and store that link in the Internet Explorer Favorites. See page 321 in the Internet module to find out how to add a link to your favorites.

Saving in different formats

You should be aware that you can save a presentation using formats, other than the PowerPoint 2000 default.

Basic steps

1   Open the *Jon's Intro2* presentation – we will not over-write the current presentation
2   From the menu bar select File > Save As
3   Change the name to '*Old Format*'
4   Click Save
❑   The new name will appear on the application title bar
5   Re-select File > Save As, however on this occasion keep the same name but click on the drop-down arrow of the Save as type slot

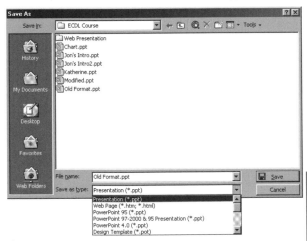

6   Scroll down to *PowerPoint 95* and click on it
7   Click Save
❑   You will be warned that the file already exists. This is true, we created the file only a short while ago with the intention of replacing it using a different file format
8   Click on 'Yes' to effect the change
❑   You will see another message box informing you that PowerPoint is saving the file, using the PowerPoint 95 format

Take note

If you save a presentation, created in a PowerPoint 2000 format, using an older format such as PowerPoint 95 or as a Rich Text File (rtf), you may find that elements of the presentation will have changed or even been lost and some controls may not function.

With each release of an application upgrade, new functionality is often introduced that is not available in the previous version. Think twice about using an older or different file format.

If you want to give a colleague, who does not have PowerPoint, a copy of your presentation consider saving it as an HTML file.

There is another alternative, which is outside the scope of the course, and it is the 'Pack and Go' feature. To learn more on this subject, use the online Help and in the Index slot type in the word 'pack', and then select 'Pack and Go Wizard' option.

7 The Internet

The Internet

The following module introduces the concepts of the Internet and the World Wide Web. The module has been split into two sections: *The Internet* will show you how to navigate the World Wide Web to find information and Websites of interest, and *Electronic Mail* will demonstrate how to send e-mail.

The Internet module has been designed using the Microsoft Internet Explorer browser version 5.5. If you are using a different browser version or type, you may find some differences between the images (screen shots) in the exercises and what you see on your computer, however the concept of the exercise and results should be the same.

Similarly, the Electronic Mail module has been designed using Microsoft's Outlook Express version 5. If you are using a different version of Outlook Express or different e-mail software you may find some differences.

Internet Explorer 5.5 (IE5.5)

You may install a free copy of Internet Explorer 5.5 from the CD that accompanied this book. Simply, insert the CD into your computer and follow the on-screen instructions. If you do not have a CD or experience any difficulties please contact BCD.

If you are unsure what browser software version you are using, please seek advice.

Exercises

Within this module you will be presented with a series of exercises demonstrating many features of the Internet.

These exercises typically involve going to a Website on the Internet and performing various tasks.

If you do not currently have an account with an ISP, you can perform an automated process to sign-up by inserting the CD that accompanied this book and following the on-screen instructions.

If you are unsure whether to proceed, either browse through the course first, omitting the exercises, or contact BCD on (023) 9275 0234 for guidance.

The majority of the Websites used throughout this course support the ECDL course and many feature the ECDL logo on their site.

Whenever you find the ECDL logo on one of these sites, click on the logo and you will be presented with further information and some additional exercises.

Getting started

Internet access these days is much simpler than it used to be, as long as you have these four things

A computer – though we are now also seeing the introduction of televisions which are Internet compliant allowing you to get online though your telephone line and surf the Internet via this medium.

A modem (MOdulator/DEModulator) – is an electronic device that converts binary data from the computer to analogue tones and voltages that are suitable for transmission over standard telephone lines. This will enable your computer to talk over the Internet via your telephone line. Modems are available at different speeds and at different prices. Therefore when deciding which you wish to purchase, you need to balance the cost of the modem against the possible cost of telephone calls, that may need to be longer when using a slower modem.

A telephone line – note that most telephone lines will not allow you to make, or take, telephone calls while you are logged on to the Internet, so you may wish to consider having a separate telephone line for use with the Internet. An alternative is to install an ISDN (Integrated Systems Digital Network) line, which transmits data in a digital format and is therefore capable of communicating at a far quicker rate.

An account with an ISP (Internet Service Provider) – this allows you to connect to the Internet via the service provider's communication equipment ensuring that the speed of access is kept to a maximum. Most service providers now offer a variety of packages at various prices, where the options include a monthly subscription fee, matched against a number of hours of free call time.

Surfing the Internet

A Browser is the software you use to *surf* the World Wide Web. You will be using Microsoft's Internet Explorer 5.5 or higher during this course, however other browser software is available, such as Netscape Communicator.

The most popular part of the Internet is the World Wide Web (WWW). This allows people to publish pages, or Websites, from anywhere in the world. A Website can be viewed at anytime, by anybody, anywhere. The phrase 'surfing the Internet' generally describes undirected browsing in which the user jumps from page to page randomly, instead of searching for specific information.

The best-known Websites are large-scale professional services packed full of information, entertainment and with the capability to purchase items online – anything from buying flowers to booking a holiday. However, anyone can be a publisher on the Internet, and many Websites are the work of small groups or individuals talking about their hobbies or interests.

So how do you get to these and other sites on the World Wide Web?

Once you have all the things listed on the previous page, including an ISP, you are ready to proceed.

Logging on to the Internet

You connect, or log on, to the Internet via your ISP. To log on you need to open your browser window by clicking 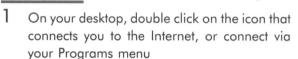, the Internet Explorer icon.

Alternatively, if you do not have any icons that relate to your browser you can, like any application, open the program via your Start menu.

Basic steps

1   Click Start > Programs > Internet Explorer

❏   A menu should open presenting you with a number of Internet options

2   Select Internet Explorer

If you are using a browser other than Internet Explorer, it will have a different name, e.g. Netscape Communicator.

If your browser is configured to automatically connect to the Internet upon opening, you may be asked for a *Username* and *Password*. These will have been supplied by your ISP when you registered with them.

You can configure your computer to save your username and password, so that every time you logon you do not have to type them in. There are security implications though, as then anyone who has access to your computer can use your Internet account without your permission.

During the logon process you will see a dialog box displaying the progress while your username and password are being verified. Once your computer has successfully completed this process, you will be 'on-line' and can now access the Internet and the World Wide Web.

The browser

Once the browser window has opened and assuming you are *on-line* (that is connected to the Internet via your ISP through your telephone line) you will be presented with your *Home* or first page.

Practice session 1

Basic steps

1   On your desktop, double click on the icon that connects you to the Internet, or connect via your Programs menu

2   Enter the Web address http://www.bbc.co.uk/ in the Address line of your browser as shown in the example below

You will be presented with a page from the comprehensive BBC Website similar to the one shown. Note how the site provides both information and an index of the contents including News, Weather, Sport, The Arts and the BBC themselves.

CONGRATULATIONS! You are now 'surfing' the Web.

Practice session 2

3 If you have disconnected from the Internet reconnect as above.

Otherwise:

4 Enter the Website address 'www.cnn.com'

You may find that you are offered the choice of cnn.com or Europe.cnn.com. Select cnn.com for this exercise.

This is the Website of the international news organisation, CNN. Note how their content and style differs from the BBC.

Exercise

5 Enter the Web address 'www.booksrus.co.uk' and note the information available on this Website.

Closing your browser window

When you have finished using the browser window, it is closed in exactly the same manner as other application software. Click on the 'X' at the top-right of the window and the browser will shut down.

Dependent on how your browser is configured you may automatically become disconnected from your ISP, or alternatively you may need to disconnect as a separate action.

Take note

Websites are constantly being updated. If you are directed to one that appears different from the examples here, don't worry. Some sites change their appearance every couple of months.

Navigating the Internet

The Toolbar

You need to get to know the buttons along the top of the browser window to become more proficient in your Web surfing. An explanation of some of the functions and operations of the buttons follows (unfamiliar items are explained later). Working from left to right across the Toolbar:

♦ **Back:** This will take you to the Web page you were looking at last. You will be surprised how often you will want to retrace your footsteps.

♦ **Forward:** If you do go back, then want to return to where you just came from, click this.

♦ **Stop:** Click to stop downloading a page that you picked by accident, or are having trouble loading.

♦ **Refresh:** This will download the page you are currently looking at, all over again. This is useful if some images have failed to load properly, or if the page is likely to be updated frequently.

♦ **Home:** This button takes you to your default Home, or starting, page.

♦ **Search:** This button opens the default search engine within your browser (see page 309).

♦ **Favorites:** This presents you with a listing of your favourite Websites (see page 307).

♦ **History:** This holds links to all the sites you have visited over a set period of time, allowing you to click on the URL and be taken directly there.

♦ **Channels:** This opens up a selection of links to pages or services which use 'push' technology, where data is sent to your browser automatically rather than by request.

♦ **Full screen:** This will display a Web page using all the available screen area.

♦ **Mail:** This will open your mail browser allowing you to access and send e-mails.

♦ **Print:** This will print the current web page on the currently selected printer. There are a number of options to improve the clarity of the print-out, including print all text as black and options to switch off various HTML and graphics features.

In addition, you can return to a site you visited the last time you were on the Web by clicking on the arrow at the end of the box containing the current site address. This will 'drop-down' a list of the sites you have looked at most recently. You can click on the one you want, to go directly there. Most browsers have many other tricks you can use to help you navigate the Internet – experiment with the controls to find out extra features.

Hyperlinks

Hyperlinks are connections between Web pages, or different parts of the same page, and provide a shortcut method of navigating around the Internet.

Links are designed to stand out from the rest of the page. A text link will be highlighted in some way – often in blue underlined text when the rest of the text is black. Links might also take the form of graphics, or pictures. You will soon learn how to spot a link.

Click the mouse button, and the browser will whisk you off to another site or page.

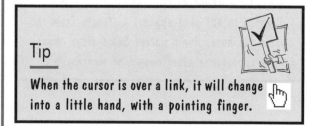

Tip

When the cursor is over a link, it will change into a little hand, with a pointing finger.

Exercise 1

- Go to the Website www.edu.co.uk

- On the page there are two Hyperlinks for the ECDL course, one in the form of text and one as a graphic

- Find one, and click on it to move to the ECDL Web page

- Having done this, use the **Back** button to return to the previous page

- Find the other ECDL Hyperlink and navigate the same ECDL page by clicking on the link again

Exercise 2

- Go to the Website www.e-sporte.com, a Global sports site

- Count how many hyperlinks appear on the Home, or First page

- Check your answer by clicking on the ECDL Hyperlink at the foot of the page

Tip

If you encounter any difficulties whilst using your browser window, Internet Explorer provides you with on-line Help functions.

Browser settings

It is worth mentioning before we view further Websites, that you can modify your browser settings allowing you to both change the appearance of your browser and the Web pages you are viewing. This is done using the **View** option on your browser toolbar.

Web pages

When Web authors and designers create Websites they specify the colour, size, font-type and background colours for each page. However, any of these settings can be overwritten using the View menu option. This is particularly useful if you have limited or impaired vision and find it generally difficult to clearly view a Website.

Basic steps

To change how page colours are displayed:

1 Select Tools>Internet Options
2 Ensure that the General tab is selected and click on Colors
3 Remove the default option Use Windows colors by clicking over the tick box to remove it
4 Specify the colours of the Web page text, background and links

To display text in a different font:

5 On the General tab click Fonts
6 At the Fonts dialog box, select the fonts you wish to use for displaying Web pages

Tip

A quicker method for modifying the text size, is to select View > Text Size and then specify the size you require.

To view Web pages quicker, configure your browser so that images are not displayed. Images are typically what take the longest time to download, so this option can enhance your efficiency when gathering information from the Internet, although the Web pages become less attractive to view.

Basic steps

1 Select Tools > Internet Options then click the Advanced tab
2 In the Multimedia area turn off the option Show pictures

If the pictures on the page you are viewing are still visible after you remove the Show pictures option you can hide them by clicking **View > Refresh**.

316

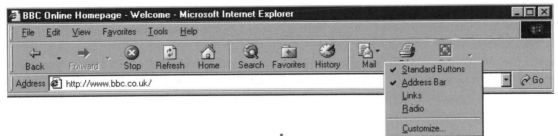

Toolbars

The toolbars that appear across the top of your browser window can be added, modified and removed as required. This enables you to configure the browser so that the items and functions you most regularly use are conveniently located.

Some of the options available to you are listed below:

* To move or resize the Address bar or Links bar you can drag them up, down, left, or right

* To make more room on your screen, you can hide toolbars by right-clicking the toolbar you wish to hide, and then clearing the tickbox next to the toolbar name

* In the same manner you can hide the Address bar or Links section of the toolbar by right-clicking the toolbar and then clearing the tickbox for each item you wish to hide, as above

* Toolbar button labels may be changed by right-clicking the toolbar, selecting **Customize** from the pop-up menu and altering **Text options** in the drop-down menu box

Take note

Within the Multimedia area you also have the options to **Play animations**, **Play videos** and **Play sounds**.

Once you have cleared the **Show pictures** or **Play videos** option, you can display an individual picture or animation on a Web page by right-clicking its icon and then clicking **Show Picture**.

Some sites are constructed solely of images and therefore the option detailed would result in a totally blank page.

URLs

URLs (usually referred to as Website addresses or domain names) are everywhere these days – in newspapers, on television and even on your breakfast cereal packets. Whilst they may appear daunting at first, they provide a sensible and structured way to present Internet addresses in a way that can be understood and remembered.

URL – stands for Universal Resource Locator and is the address of a Website.

Addresses will nearly always begin with **http:// www**, followed by more letters, dots and slashes. You don't always need to remember the whole address. Most browsers do not need you to type in the **http://** part; you can just start with the **www**.

Following the **www** you will then usually find the organisation or company name of the publisher of the site. For example you would expect IBM computers to start **http://www.ibm.** or the Wembley site to start **http://www.wembley**.

Finally, the extension at the end of the URL will indicate the type of organisation who has published the Website. For example:

- International businesses end with the extension **.com** (Commercial)
- Non-commercial organisations end **.org**
- Network and Internet specialists use **.net**

These are referred to as *global domains*.

Where sites are country specific the extension is followed by a country code. For the United Kingdom this is **.uk**. Other examples include **.de** for Germany, **.us** for USA, **.fr** for France and so on.

Within the United Kingdom:

- Commercial sites end **.co.uk**
- Government sites end **.gov.uk**
- Academic sites **.ac.uk**
- Non-profit sites use **.org.uk**

On occasions a URL may have an extension that works in the same way as a subfolder within Windows Explorer.

For example the Website **www.footballclubs.com** contains information relating to a number of different football clubs around the world. As well as going directly to the site and finding the pages relating to Manchester United football club, you can enter the URL **www.footballclubs.com/manutd** directly into your address box.

For businesses (and individuals) considering having an Internet site, the domain name they use is of great importance.

Whilst a business might be called *Smith Brothers International Export Agency*, the domain name **www.smithbrothersinternationalexportagency.com** is not only hard to fit on a business card but also easily prone to mistyping! Similarly shortening the name to **www.sbrosintlexpagnc.com** is not only meaningless but also difficult to remember.

A very good name would be **www.smith.com**, however, as more and more organisations are getting Websites, the availability of domain names is becoming less and less, as they are issued on a first come, first served basis.

Many domain names that are considered prestigious due to being simple, memorable or relating to large industries, are being bought and sold for many millions of pounds. However many good names are still available for considerably less.

Take note

The above relates only to domain names which have already been registered and are being resold by a third-party. If a domain name is still available the cost of registration is only a few pounds.

Basic steps

1　Connect to the Internet
2　Enter the Web address: www.a1domain.com
3　Select Registration > Check Domain
4　Enter in the box 'worldbanker.com'
❑　You will see that this domain name has already been registered and is unavailable

Exercise

Using the rules regarding domain name structures, discussed in this chapter:

◆　Find the Website of *Marketstall*, an international business

◆　Find the Website of *Axcess*, a UK based charity

◆　Find the Website of *MP-3*, a UK based business

◆　At the Website *www.a1domain.com*, within the *Check Domain* page, search to see if your company name or personal name have been registered with either a '.com' or '.co.uk' extension. If they have consider, and search for alternative domain names you could use which would still be both memorable and meaningful.

◆　On the same site go to the *Prestige Domain* page and from the list of names, find those most appropriate to your industry or interests.

Take note

Domain names can only consist of letters, numbers and the '-' (hyphen) symbol. It makes no difference whether the letters are in upper or lower case.

Home page

Every time you go on to the Internet your browser opens with your default 'Home' page. This is the Website that you can select as your starting point. Your browser will have come with a default Home page already set, however you can change this to a page of your choice.

If ever you get lost on the Internet, clicking the 'Home' button at the top of your browser window will return you to your default home page.

Note that depending upon which browser version you are using you may notice differences from the examples below.

Practice session

Basic steps

1 Go to www.bcdtraining.com

2 Select Tools > Internet Options

3 At the Internet Options dialog box select the General tab

4 In the Home Page area, click the Use Current button. The URL for the bcdtraining.com site is now the address specified

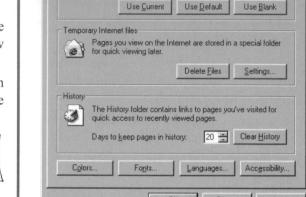

5 Click Apply and then OK

The bcdtraining.com site is now your default home page and will appear every time you logon to the Internet via your browser, or click the 'Home' button at the top of the browser window.

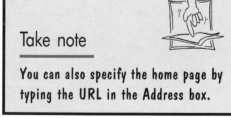

Take note

You can also specify the home page by typing the URL in the Address box.

Exercise

♦ Visit www.thebrochure.com and set this site as your default Home page

♦ Visit any other site (e.g. www.bcdtraining.com) and then return to The Brochure site (your default Home Page) by using the Home button on your toolbar

Favourite sites

As you start to use the Internet on a regular basis, you will want to find a quick way of getting to your favourite sites without having to remember lists of Website addresses. One of the most useful functions on the toolbar at the top of your browser is **Favorites** in Internet Explorer (or **Bookmarks** in Netscape Navigator). This provides a way of storing the addresses of Websites you like.

When you arrive at a site you want to bookmark, simply click the **Favorites** button, then click the **Add to Favorites** selection. If your bookmarks list starts to get out of hand, you will be able to rearrange it into folders and files, so you can have one for news, one for weather, one for your hobby, and so on.

Practice session

The illustrations that appear throughout this practice section are all taken from Microsoft Internet Explorer (IE) 5. If you are using IE 4, you can still carry out this exercise although you will find that the dialog boxes that open at each stage are slightly different, but still allow you to carry out the instructions and complete the exercise.

Basic steps

1 Find the Website of madesimple.co.uk
2 Select Favorites on your browser toolbar
3 Click Add to Favorites

4 At the Add Favourite dialog box, type *Made Simple books* in the Name slot, then click OK

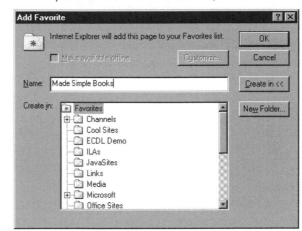

5 Click on Favorites again, but this time select Organize Favorites

❑ You will be presented with the Organize Favorites dialog box which lists all your folders and favourite sites

6 Select *Made Simple books* and click the Move to Folder button

7 At the Browse for Folder dialog box, click on the *Cool Sites* folder, then OK

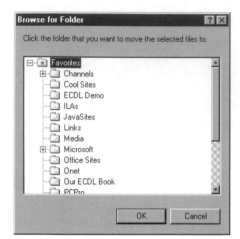

❑ The dialog box will close and you will be returned to the Organize Favourites box

8 Locate the *Cool Sites* folder and left-click on it

When the folder opens, you will see *Made Simple Books* is now in the folder.

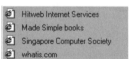

To view the Website:

9 Click on Favorites, select the *Cool Sites* folder, and then double-click on *Made Simple books*

Exercise

♦ Go to the Website hyperlink:
   http://www.e-sporte.com and add it to your list of favourites named *e-Sporte*

♦ Organise your list of favourites so that *e-Sporte* is kept in the *Sport* folder

♦ Go to the Website hyperlink:
   http://www.e-lounge.co.uk and add it to your list of favourites named *e-Lounge*

♦ Organise your list of favourites so that *e-Lounge* is kept in the *Search Engines* folder

Take note

Depending upon which ISP's browser you are using, these sites may already be in your favourites. If this is the case attempt the exercise with an alternative Website of your choice, e.g. http://www.manutdfc.com

Search engines

Many newcomers to the Internet worry about how they are going to find the addresses of Websites that might be of interest to them. There is no equivalent of a phone book for the Internet, but you will find it remarkably easy to find what you are looking for.

The nearest you will get to a telephone book is one of the major search engines. A search engine is a directory of millions of Web pages that have been indexed to allow you to track down topics by typing in keywords.

Basic steps

1 Go to Ask Jeeves at www.askjeeves.com
2 Type into the search slot '*What is the Capital of Peru*' and click the Ask button
❑ Ask Jeeves will return a list of Websites that may contain the information you require based on the question you entered, from both within its directory plus matches from other search engines.
3 Check the answers by clicking on the Ask button next to the Website lists

Exercise
◆ Find out what is meant by the computer term 'ADSL'
◆ Find a list of restaurants in Blackpool
◆ Find out what the population of New Zealand is

Advanced searches

Ask Jeeves allows you to ask questions in plain English, for example 'where can I find a nice restaurant in Sheffield'. The results returned, however, are based upon answers already stored in the Ask Jeeves directory.

An alternative is to use one of the more traditional search engines such as Yahoo. Here the answers are extracted from many millions of Websites all over the world, meaning greater selection although potentially less relevance to your requirement.

Yahoo, like the majority of search engines requires you to enter your query as a series of keywords rather than in plain English. Therefore to ask the same question as you did with Ask Jeeves you would simply enter the words 'Restaurant' and 'Sheffield'. The international Yahoo site can be found at **www.yahoo.com**, whilst the UK specific version is at **www.yahoo.co.uk**.

You will find that on many occasions the results of your search will either be too large to be of any use to you, or will return pages that are not relevant to the information you require. For example a search on the word 'Computer' is liable to return many thousands of pages, while a search on the word 'Rugby' when trying to find information about the businesses in the town of Rugby in England, is likely to return many pages on the sport of Rugby Football.

Therefore the key to useful searching is to be specific as possible in your search criteria. In the examples above, a search on the phrase 'Macintosh Computer Peripherals' will return far fewer, yet far more useful sites. Additionally a search on 'Businesses in Rugby, Warwickshire, England' should return more accurate results.

Another method of returning useful information is to use *logical operators* when performing a search. This information is typically referred to as Advanced Search on most search engines.

The Yahoo *Advanced Search* option is located next to the standard **Search** button. By default, when you enter search criteria, Yahoo uses its Intelligent default search, based on its own method. You will see that on the Advanced Search page you have the ability to change the search method.

◆ Selecting **An exact phrase match**, (see the example overleaf), will only return results containing phrases you specified.
◆ Selecting **Matches on all Words (AND)** only returns results containing all words you specified, but in any order.

323

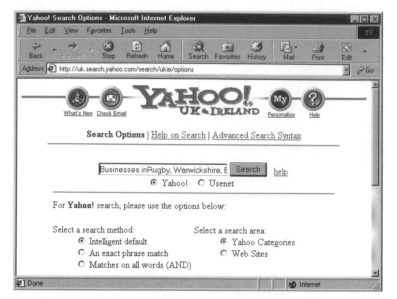

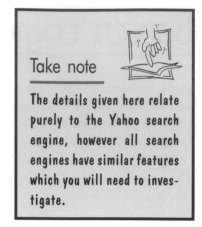

- Selecting Matches on any Word (OR) returns results where any of the words provide a match.

In addition when using the Yahoo search query box you can use what is called Advanced Search syntax. This enables you to tailor search results without having to visit the Advanced Search page, and includes a number of additional features.

There are many types of query syntax available including Required and Prohibited Search Words and Phrase matching.

Attaching a plus symbol (+) or a minus symbol (-) within your search will either require or prohibit words from appearing in the search results, accordingly. For example, attaching the plus symbol to a word requires that the word be found in all of the search results, e.g. Rugby +Sport rather than Rugby would only return information on Rugby Football.

Alternatively attaching a minus symbol in front of the word, requires that the word not be found in any of the search results, for example, using 'python -monty' rather than 'python' would only return results relating to the snake, rather than the television programme.

Using the above criteria, 'python', Yahoo Search Result found 6 categories, 164 sites, and 1 news story for pythons.

To perform a phrase match in a query box is similar to selecting an exact phrase match in the Advanced Search page, and is achieved by putting "double quotes" around the words. This will only find results that match the words in that exact sequence, e.g. "Great Barrier Reef".

Print the search report

You could visit each of the 164 sites found as a result of the search on pythons, or you may want to return to the subject at a later date, but not wish to go through the search routine again. The way to do this is to print the search list.

Click the **Print** button, or right-click over the page and select **Print** from the pop-up menu to open the Print dialog box. Click **OK** and the first page will be printed. If your search returned a large list, you could spend some considerable time printing it.

Exercise

- Go to the Alta Vista search engine featured on the Website hyperlink **www.e-lounge.co.uk**
- Type *Cricket +Sport* and click the Search button.
- Select one of the topics from the list returned and that page will open. This is a good example of how a hyperlink functions.
- If you wish to continue investigating the subject, left-click on the Back button located on the toolbar, or right-click over the page and select Back, and you will be returned to the page which contains the search results.

Information from the Internet

On occasions, you may find information on a Website that you wish to save to your computer's hard disk for future reference. This can be done in several ways.

Download

There are thousands of sites on the Internet offering all sorts of files you can download. Popular examples are the MP3 music files along with movie trailers, to the latest computer game demos. You can download files from any site, simply by finding the file and following the instructions contained on the Web page. As you start the download procedure, you will usually encounter the dialog box shown below.

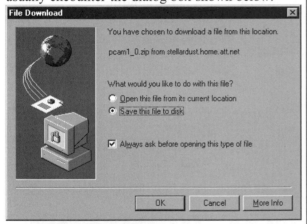

When you have completed your selection, click the **OK** button and the second dialog box will appear.

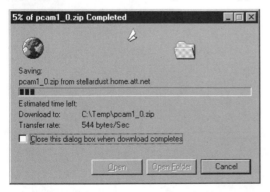

The second dialog box provides a visual progress display of the download, identifies the file being downloaded and where it is being stored.

You can stop a download at any time, simply by left-clicking on the **Cancel** button.

Downloading files can take some time and transfer rates can vary widely. Try to download during off-peak hours, that is early in the morning or late at night.

Create a folder and call it *Download* and always save your downloads in it.

Beware – Files that are downloaded from the Internet may contain computer viruses. See Chapter 1 for more information on viruses.

Practice session

Basic steps

1   Go to the music site www.mp-3.co.uk
2   Click the button to Sign Up with MP3.com
3   Having completed the sign-up procedure, find an area of music you like and select a tune to download
4   Download the Free track and save it to a folder on your computer

You should now be able to play the music using the free software player provided by MP3.com.

♦   MP3.com are currently involved in a US court case, so there is a possibility that this site may not be available by the time you read this.

Save an image

To save an image that is on a Web page you need to click with the right mouse button while your cursor is over the image you require. At this point you will be presented with a menu, shown opposite, which will contain the **Save Picture As** option.

You will need to specify which folder on your hard disk you wish to save the image to.

325

It's easy to copy just about anything from the Internet, but sometimes it may not be legal. Before you copy any text or images, which you intend to use on your own Web page, or, indeed, anywhere public, make sure that you have permission from the original author. If you fail to do this, you could find yourself with a costly legal problem.

Save a Web page

Basic steps

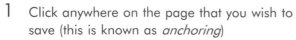

1   Click anywhere on the page that you wish to save (this is known as *anchoring*)

2   Select File > Save As

The page will be saved in HTML format and can be viewed at a later stage using your browser, however it should be noted that this would not save any graphics on the page.

Print a Web page

There may be many occasions where you wish to print from the Internet typically when the page contains a lot of information that you require. Printing a page is a very simple task, although you have a number of options available to you.

Take note

Many pages are constructed using *frames*, so what appears to be a single Web page is actually built from multiple components. Having selected Print you may be asked whether you want to print all the frames, or just the frame that you anchored to.

When printing a page, your first step will be to anchor the page or frame you require by left-clicking in the appropriate place.

Page set-up

If you are unsure whether your printer set-up has been configured correctly for your requirements, you can check by selecting **File > Page Setup** on the

browser menu. The page set-up dialog box will open. This gives you the option of selecting which printer to use, in the event that you have more than one printer connected to your computer. Other options include the page size, orientation, page header and footer and margins.

Having anchored on the frame or page you require, to print the page, either:

❑   Right-click over it (not over an image) and from the pop-up menu select Print

❑   or select File > Print from the browser menu

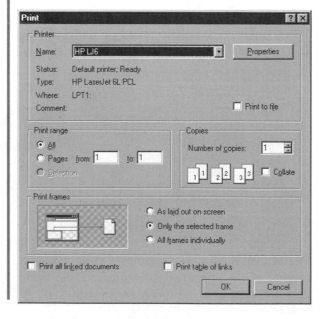

The Print dialog box will open and it is from here that you specify:

- ❑ the Printer to be used
- ❑ which pages you wish to print
- ❑ which frames you wish to print
- ❑ how many copies you require

Additionally, you can also select, by ticking the Print table of Links slot, all the hyperlinks that appear on the page, or even print the pages that the hyperlinks link to.

Exercise

- • Go to the Website **www.thestorefront.co.uk**, anchor on the Home page, and then print the page

- • Go to the Website **www.gamingzone.co.uk**, anchor on the Home page, and then save it in the Internet Exercise folder you created at the start of this module within c:\My Documents or on your A:\ drive.

- • Using Windows Explorer find the page and then double-click on the file to now view the page

E-commerce

E-commerce is the name given to any business whose trading is conducted over the Internet. Typically it refers to Websites selling products or services to the public, however it can also encompass business-to-business dealings.

The advantages of purchasing products via the www include:

- access to a wider range of products than could typically be found in the high street
- reduced cost of products and services due to suppliers reduced overheads
- ability to purchase products from the comfort of your home

Websites selling products typically feature a method of searching for the products you require, either by an index or site search facility; a selection of options and prices for delivery of the product; and a section where you complete your details, including credit card information.

These sites use an encryption method called Secure Socket Layer (SSL), which encrypts your credit card details to ensure the information cannot be intercepted or misused.

Tip

You will know when you have entered a secure area of a Website as a tiny padlock image will appear at the foot of your browser window.

Practice session

Basic steps

1 Go to the Website www.booksrus.co.uk
2 Select the Book shop Amazon
3 Enter in the search box '*ECDL*' and click Go

You will be returned a list of publications that match this criteria:

4 Select 'ECDL Made Simple' by BCD, by clicking on the title
❑ You will be presented with details about the publication
5 Click the Add to Shopping Basket button

If you wished to purchase the book, you would then proceed to check out where you would give your credit card information. However do not proceed any further within this practice session unless you actually wish to purchase the publication

Exercise

- Visit the commerce site **www.thebrochure.com** identify where to buy CDs and search for products of interest to you
- Visit the site **www.thestorefront.co.uk** and compare the cost of PCs on this site with high street prices
- Visit the site **www.manutdfc.com** and compare the selection of merchandise which is available compared to sports shops

E-zines

A good way to keep abreast of topics of interest on the Internet is to subscribe to an Electronic Magazine or *e-zine*. These magazines are delivered by email to your computer and are typically free of charge.

If you would like to subscribe to the e-zine, *What's on the Net* go to the site **www.whatsonthenet.com** and complete the form. You will then start receiving a regular newsletter detailing interesting hints and tips on using the Internet, plus the latest information on trends and services available on the www.

Five sites of interest

Going online is an adventure to start with. Surfing the Web is great fun and can be very informative, but you will soon discover it is the practical uses of the Internet that will make it increasingly central to all aspects of your life.

- Communicating with family, friends and business associates by e-mail is quicker, cheaper and easier than writing letters.

- Online shopping is taking off as companies prepare to do more of their business over the Internet. If you want you can do all your Christmas shopping from the comfort of your living room.

- Sometimes, when buying items such as CDs, books or even a new computer, you will be offered extra discounts for buying online.

- Your children will use computers at school and can use the Internet to help with homework and make e-mail pen-friends in other countries.

Pictured opposite are our top five sites to visit, showing you what the Internet can do for you. Take the opportunity to visit the sites, and also search for a few of specific interest to yourself.

www.bbc.co.uk – British Broadcasting Corporation TV and Radio Website

www.bcdtraining.com – providing comprehensive information relating to the European Computer Driving Licence

329

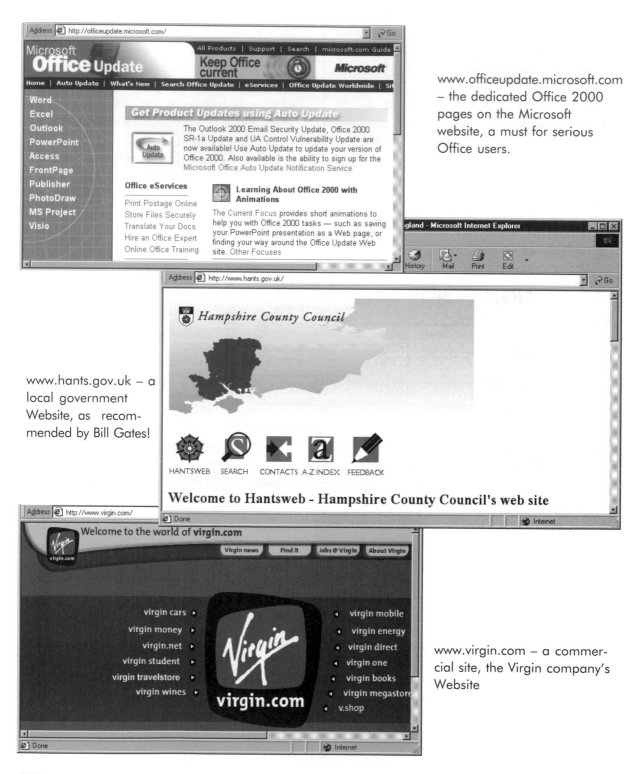

www.officeupdate.microsoft.com – the dedicated Office 2000 pages on the Microsoft website, a must for serious Office users.

www.hants.gov.uk – a local government Website, as recommended by Bill Gates!

www.virgin.com – a commercial site, the Virgin company's Website

Office 2000 Websites

This courseware has been specifically written for Microsoft Office 2000 Professional and you should be aware that Microsoft has two websites dedicated to this version of Office. The first website is based in America. It is updated frequently and usually has the latest news and downloads.

Practice session

1 Open Internet Explorer and go to the address www.officeupdate.microsoft.com

2 Click on Word and investigate the latest news and offers

The second website is located in the United Kingdom. It will duplicate some of the articles that appear on the American site but will also include articles written by the UK OfficeGym team at Reading. The site is customised specifically for UK clients.

Office newsletters

You can sign up at the UK site to be included on the e-mail notification lists. What this means is that if any important changes are made to any product, you will receive any e-mail from Microsoft advising you of the change, how it may affect you and how to install the patch if one is available.

Practice session

1 Go to: www.microsoft.com/uk/office

2 Click on the option to download free Office Add Ons and see what is available

3 You might also want to look at the registration procedure for receiving the e-mail newsletter

Both websites are a good source of information for Office 2000 and well worth investigating.

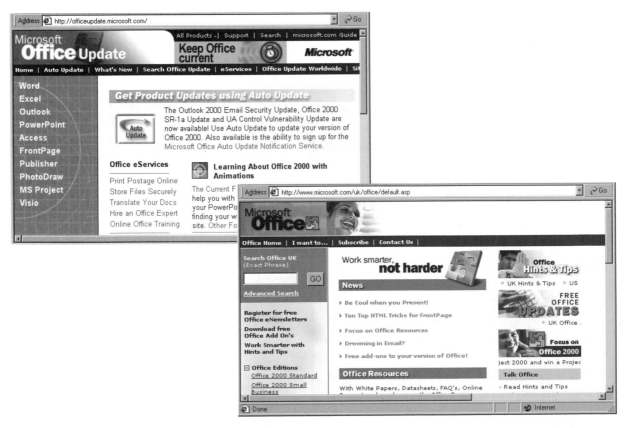

Web site development

Once you have spent a few hours looking at other people's Websites, you might decide you want one too. The following section will show you how to build a very basic Web page, however do not worry, as you will not be required to know this as part of your ECDL test.

Large, professional Websites that have good design and complex functionality are usually designed by professional Web development companies. It is recommended that, if you require a Website for a business or professional organisation, you approach one of the many Web development companies that specialise in all aspects of design.

HTML

Most Web pages that you see on the Internet have been created using a computer language called HTML (HyperText Mark-up Language).

To make best use of any free Web space you have been allocated by your ISP, you will need to learn the basics of HTML. It is simple to learn and with practice you can create Websites quite easily.

HTML works by inserting tags into text. So an HTML file can be written entirely in a normal word processor or text-editing program, like Word or Notepad. Pointed brackets (< >) surround each tag.

Browsers work by reading through the text of an HTML file, and obeying the commands given in the tags. Put simply, the tags tell the browser how to display everything.

Practical exercise

We are going to create a Web site using Notepad.

* Click the **Start** button and select **Programs> Accessories>Notepad**.
* When Notepad opens, you will be presented with a new blank page ready to begin typing in your HTML.
* Before we start, we will save the file. In Notepad, select the **File>Save As** option.

* When the Save As dialog box opens, navigate to the folder where you want to save the file.
* Save the file using the name 'My web Page.htm'.

Take note

It is important to include the period and extension .htm as this specifies the file is an html file and tells your computer that it should be viewed in a browser window.

Using Notepad, enter the following text:

```
<HTML>
<HEAD>
<P><TITLE>My first web page</TITLE></P>
</HEAD>
<BODY>
<P><H1>Welcome to my home page</H1>
</P>
<HR>
<P>There's not much here at the moment, but I
am busy learning more HTML so that I can
create the web site <I>of my dreams.</I></
P>
<P>You can e-mail me by <A
HREF="mailto:me@myaddress.com">  clicking
here</A></P>
</BODY>
</HTML>
```

You can now view the Web page you have just created in two ways.

Using Windows Explorer, locate the file 'My web Page.htm' in the folder you have just saved it to, and double-click on it.

Alternatively, open your Internet Explorer window, and in the address bar type the full path of where your file is, e.g. *C:\My Documents\Internet Exercise\My web Page.htm*, and hit Enter. You should now be viewing the Web page you built.

The final product

HTML reads and translates the coding and displays the web page as shown below.

HTML tags

You will see that most tags have to be opened and closed. The close tag has a forward-slash inserted before the word, so it looks like this: **</HTML>**.

A Web browser will format everything between two matching tags in a particular way. Here's what the tags used in the practice session do:

<HTML> shows this is an HTML document.

<HEAD> identifies the document header – it will not appear in the final display, but holds the title and other information about the document.

<TITLE> gives the page a name. The title will appear at the top of the browser window, and will be used to identify a page in your bookmark list.

<BODY> is the main part of the document – the part that will appear in the browser window.

<H1> is a text heading on the page, size 1 – the biggest text the browser will display. Everything between the <H1> and </H1> will be displayed as a large title on the page.

<HR> draws a horizontal line across the page. It does not need a closing tag.

<P> is to show the start of each paragraph.

<I> makes text *italic* between <I> and </I>.

<A creates a hyperlink to another page or e-mail address. After the 'A' is more code that tells the browser to make a link to a specified e-mail address.

Exercise

- Build a new Web page with a file name of 'ECDL.HTM', saved to the temp folder
- a document header called 'My exercise page',
- a document title of 'ECDL exercise site',
- and the text 'This is my completed ECDL exercise web page. To congratulate me, mail me at', followed by a hyperlink to your mail address of 'yourname@acme.co.uk'.

There are many guides on the Internet to help you learn HTML and assist with Web site design. Remember to keep things simple and add to your knowledge slowly over time.

Web design software

There are many Web authoring tools which allow you to build Websites in a simpler manner than coding in HTML. Users of Windows 95/98 have an application called FrontPage Express, which is ideal for building simple Web pages. This can be found at **Start > Programs > Internet Explorer > FrontPage Express**.

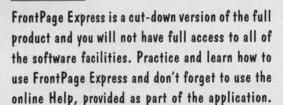

Take note

FrontPage Express is a cut-down version of the full product and you will not have full access to all of the software facilities. Practice and learn how to use FrontPage Express and don't forget to use the online Help, provided as part of the application.

Uploading to the World Wide Web

Having successfully built your Web page(s) you may wish to consider putting your site on to the World Wide Web so that your friends, colleagues and the other 100 million Internet users world wide can see your work! Find out about Web space at your ISP.

333

Electronic mail

Electronic mail or e-mail is a method of sending and receiving messages, from or to a computer or specialist telephone, via the Internet. Sending and receiving e-mail, over the Internet, is extremely cost effective and delivery is usually very quick.

One of the most commonly used programs for sending and receiving e-mail is Microsoft's Outlook Express which is distributed with the Windows operating system.

Take note

Depending on which version of Microsoft Outlook Express you are using and how it is configured, you may view a different page when opening the software than that shown below.

Before we start sending and receiving e-mails, we are going to discuss how you can customise and configure Outlook Express, so that we can perform certain tasks, explore its features and have a common appearance throughout the course.

Starting Outlook Express

You can start Outlook Express a number of ways depending on your computer's configuration. From a shortcut on your desktop, a shortcut on the Windows 98 quick launch section of the taskbar, or from the taskbar by selecting **Start > Programs > Outlook Express**, or **Start > Programs > Internet Explorer > Outlook Express**.

Start Outlook Express using your preferred method and the default-opening page will appear. If your page is different, don't worry, read on and all should become clear.

Changing the view

You can change the way Outlook Express opens and you may find this view more to your liking than that shown below.

Basic steps

1 Select Tools > Options

2 Select the General tab

3 In the General section of the dialog box, tick the 'When starting, go directly to my Inbox folder' slot

4 Click OK

5 From the menu bar select File > Exit and Outlook Express will close

❑ Re-open Outlook Express and you will find that it immediately opens with the Inbox folder displayed

Customising the inbox view

You can further customise how the inbox is displayed as follows.

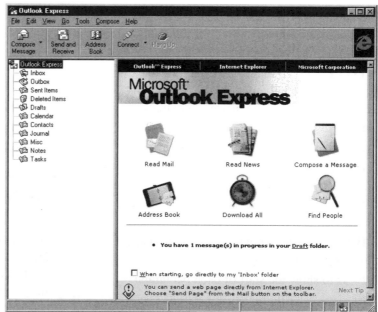

Basic steps

1 From the menu bar select View > Layout and the Window Layout Properties box will open

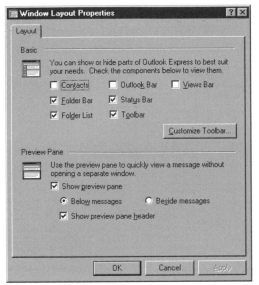

2 Ensure that there is a tick in the Show preview pane slot, if not tick it

3 Click OK and the dialog box will close and the Inbox display will change to that shown below

❑ The Preview pane is located below the e-mail list pane – as you select each message you can preview the text without having to open it

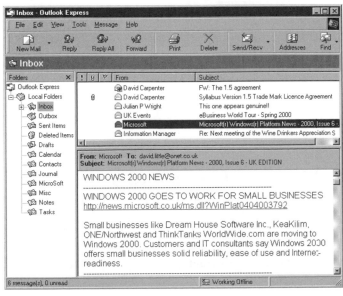

Customising the toolbar display

We have just changed the Inbox view to include the Preview pane. The method used involved us going to the View menu and selecting Layout, then making the changes at the dialog box. There is a quicker way of doing the same job.

We will now place another button on the toolbar, which will carry out all of the actions just described, with a simple click. A further click, on the same button, will change the view back again.

Basic steps

1 From the menu bar select View > Layout

2 At the Window Layout Properties box, click the Customize Toolbar button

❑ The Customise Toolbar dialog box will open

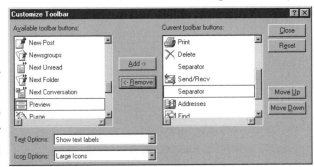

3 In the Current toolbar buttons scroll down and select *Separator*

4 In the Available toolbar buttons locate the Preview button and select it

5 Click the Add -> button.

❑ The Preview button will now appear in the Current toolbar buttons pane

6 Click Close

7 Click OK on the Window Layout Properties box to close the window

Click on the **Preview** button and observe the changes to the Inbox display. Repeat the action and deselect the option and it will revert to its previous display. Ensure that you have the Preview pane on display for the remainder of the course.

Composing a message

Basic steps

1 Click on the New Mail or New Message button on the toolbar

2 The New Message window will open.

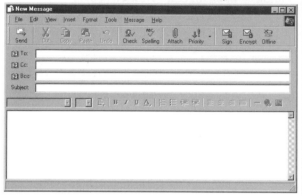

2 Enter the address 'info@bcdtraining.com' in the To box (this will be the recipient)

3 Enter the subject title in the Subject slot

4 Type your message

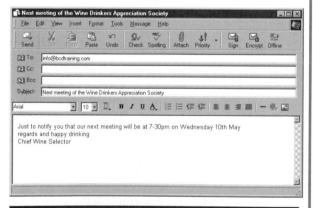

Take note

Type in lowercase, using uppercase only for emphasis. Too much uppercase is considered the equivalent of shouting and is best avoided.

Attaching a file to an e-mail

Files such as a Word document or an Excel spreadsheet can be attached to the e-mail.

Basic steps

1 Click on the paperclip icon on the toolbar

❑ The Insert Attachment dialog box will open

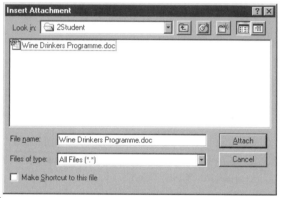

2 Select the file(s) that you wish to attach

3 Click Attach

❑ A new slot will appear below the 'Subject ' slot. The attached file name will appear in it

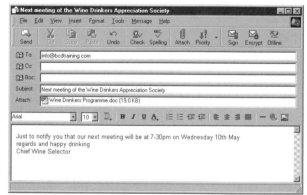

Deleting an attachment

If you find that you have attached the wrong file, or change your mind about sending the file, highlight its name in the **Attach** slot and press **[Delete]**. It will be removed and the 'Attach' slot will disappear.

Auto signature

Depending on the occasion, content and/or style of the e-mail you have written, you may wish to choose the type of signature to use to sign off, i.e. formal or personalised.

Outlook Express has a facility that allows you to create a number of different signatures, which can be reused time and time again, and will automatically insert one with just a click of your mouse button.

Creating a signature

Basic steps

1 From the menu bar select Tools > Options

2 When the Options dialog box opens click on the Signatures tab

3 In the Signatures section click New

❏ The Edit Signatures pane will now become active and it is in this section that you type in your signature

❏ The first signature that you create is designated as the Default. It is suggested that this should be the signature that you use most often

4 Type in your own choice of signature and any other relevant text

5 Click Apply

❏ To create a further signature, simply click New and repeat the procedure

❏ The additional signature will be listed in the Signatures pane as '*Signature #2*'

Take note

If you have more than one e-mail account, you can designate a signature to be used with a particular account. We will not do this. However, should you later decided to designate a signature to an account, open the Options dialog box as described above and click on the Advanced button. Read the instructions and assign a signature as appropriate.

E-mail priority

You can send an e-mail using one of three priorities.

By default Outlook Express assigns *Normal* priority to a message. You can change it so that the recipient knows to either look at it immediately, *High*, or to leave it till later, *Low* priority.

Basic steps

1 In the New Message window, click on the down-arrow of the Priority button on the toolbar

2 Select High Priority

The header section of the message will expand and the **Priority** tag will appear above the **To** slot.

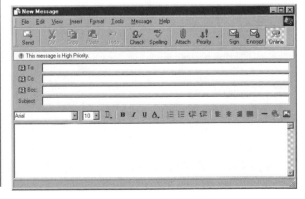

Take note

You can only change the priority setting on a current message.

Using the Spell Checker

Outlook Express uses the Spell Checker and it can be customised by you. You can manually select it each time before you send an e-mail, or you can configure it to carry out a check automatically, before an e-mail is sent.

There are other options that you can change to suit your preferences. For now we will now set-up Outlook Express to automatically carry out a spell check before it sends the e-mail.

Basic steps

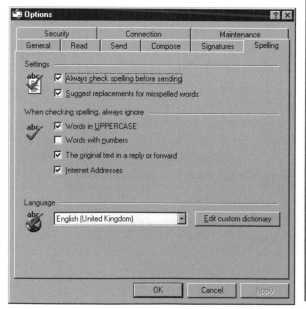

1 From the menu bar select Tools > Options
2 When the dialog box opens, click on the Spelling tab
3 If not already selected, click in the Always check spelling before sending slot and a tick will appear in it

❑ Do not change any of the other options at this time
4 Click OK and the dialog box will close

Sending the e-mail

To send the e-mail click the **Send/Recv** button.

The Outlook Express spell checker functions in the same manner as those used by the other Microsoft Office applications. The spell checker will close once it has finished checking the e-mail.

Your system may be configured to send emails immediately without any further intervention, alternatively a dialog box may open which requests you click the **Connect** button. If the latter is the case, click the **Connect** button to send the e-mail.

Take note

Depending on how Outlook Express is configured, you may find that when you send an e-mail it is actually sent to your Outbox folder, instead of being transmitted over the Internet. You may find this configuration more convenient, as you may create a number of e-mails over a period, and then send them as a batch all at once.

If you have not already explored the Options dialog box, you should do so later where you will find a considerable number of customisable options available, including the configuration above.

To receive e-mail

To receive e-mail simply click the Send/ Recv button on the toolbar. If you are not already connected to your ISP, you will be prompted to connect and when connected, your e-mail will be sent to you.

Whenever you connect, your computer automatically checks your mail box, at your ISP, to see if there is any mail waiting to be collected. If there is, it is sent automatically without you having to do anything.

When you receive emails they are stored in your Inbox. The number of unread messages will be displayed adjacent to it.

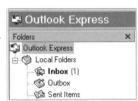

Reading your e-mail

Basic steps

1 To read your e-mail, click on the Inbox folder and any e-mails in it will be listed in the pane opposite

2 Click on the e-mail that you wish to read and the Preview pane will display it

❑ You have not actually opened the e-mail at this stage, you are previewing the text

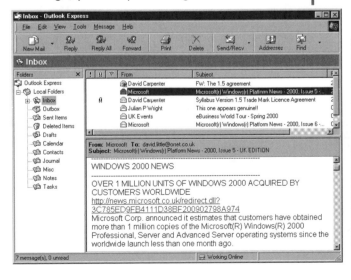

3 To open the e-mail, double-click over it and it will open in its own window

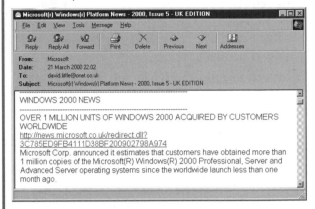

It is from this window that you have full control over the e-mail; you can *Reply*, *Reply to All* or *Forward* the e-mail to another recipient, print the e-mail and much more. The example above shows the same message that we were previewing earlier, now opened in its own window.

When you have finished reading the e-mail, close the window.

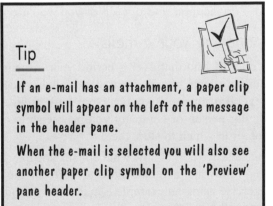

Tip

If an e-mail has an attachment, a paper clip symbol will appear on the left of the message in the header pane.

When the e-mail is selected you will also see another paper clip symbol on the 'Preview' pane header.

Opening and saving attachments

When you receive an attachment you can either read and leave it as part of the e-mail, or you can save it as a separate file for later use.

Basic steps

1 Right-click over the paper clip on the Preview pane header

❑ It will expand to identify the attachment file name and size. To save the attachment:

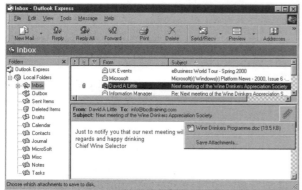

2 Click Save Attachments and the Save Attachments dialog box will open

3 Use the Browse button to navigate to the folder in which you wish to save the attachment

4 Click OK – the Browse for Folder dialog box will close

5 Click Save and the attachment is saved for future use

❑ To open the attachment use the appropriate application and open it as you would any file

Managing your e-mails

You will find that over a period your e-mails will build up, even though you may already have deleted several of them. If you receive e-mails from a particular person or company you may wish to create folder in which to store them.

Because we don't know what e-mails you may have, the following explains how to perform the next exercise using an example e-mail. You should substitute the e-mail, with one of your own.

Filing e-mail

Basic steps

To file mail that you have received:

1 Select the Inbox

2 Highlight the message to be filed

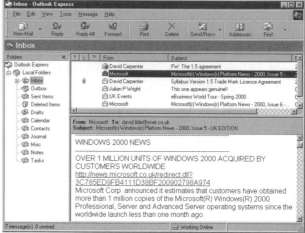

3 Select Edit > Move to Folder

4 At the Move dialog box, select the folder that you wish to move the e-mail to

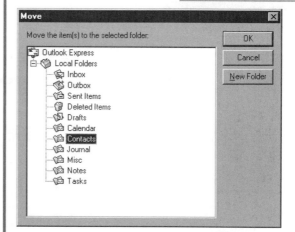

To create a new folder:

5   Click the New Folder button

❑   The New Folder dialog box will open

6   Type in the name '*Microsoft*', or a name of your choice, and click OK

❑   When the New Folder dialog box closes, you will be returned to the Move window

7   Click OK

❑   The dialog box will close and the message will be moved to its new folder which appears in the Folders pane

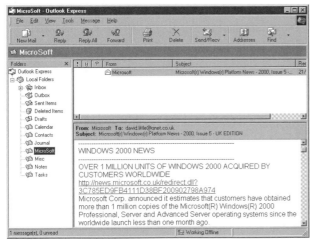

To view the e-mail:

8   Click on the *Microsoft* folder, select the e-mail and the text will appear in the preview pane

Forwarding an e-mail

It is possible to send an e-mail that you have received or composed, to another person who was not on the original address list. This feature can be very useful and a time-saver.

Basic steps

To forward a message:

1   Select the folder and then the message

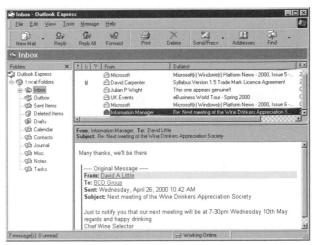

2   Left-click on the Forward button on the toolbar

❑   A further window will open

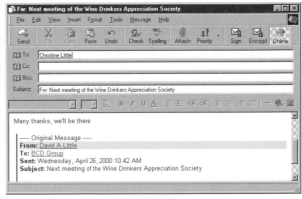

3   Enter the mail address of the recipient in the To slot

4   Enter any other recipient(s) in the Cc: and/or the Bcc: slots

5   Enter your message above the original

❑   You can also amend the Subject content and the message if required

The abbreviation 'Cc' stands for Carbon Copy and sends information to third parties, all of whom see every address. The abbreviation 'Bcc' stands for Blind Carbon Copy and when included in a message, only the sender is aware that the person shown in the Bcc slot has received a copy of the message.

7: The Internet

341

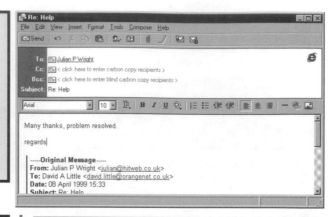

Replying to e-mail

The Reply feature of e-mail is extremely useful. Imagine the scenario: you receive an e-mail and wish to respond to it and include the original message. Do you re-type the entire message again? No, you use the Reply feature.

Basic steps

1 Select the message that you wish to respond to
2 Click the Reply button
❑ Another window will open
❑ Note that Outlook has already completed the address and subject section of the message for you
3 Type in your response
4 When finished click once on the Send button

This feature is extremely useful for a number of reasons, one being that there is little room for error or misunderstanding on the part of any of the recipients if the original text is included in the response. The recipient(s) can easily refer back through the message(s) at any time and re-read the message(s).

Replying without the original message

You may wish to Reply to an e-mail but not include the original message in it, which Outlook Express does by default.

Basic steps

1 From the menu bar select Tools > Options
2 At the dialog box select the Send tab

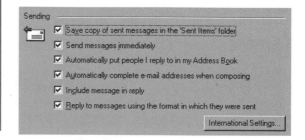

3   Click in the Include messages in reply slot to remove the tick

4   Click on the OK button to apply the change

❏   Open any e-mail and then click on the Reply button and you will now find the message pane is empty

Take note

This option will remain in force until such time that you change it back again and should you use the Reply option from now on, the original message **WILL NOT** be included in your reply.

The Reply All feature

Another Reply feature is the Reply All. If you receive an e-mail, which was sent to a number of people and you wish to respond to it and want all of the recipients to see your responses, you can use the Reply All feature.

Basic steps

1   Select the message and click the Reply All button

❏   The Reply All dialog box will open and you will find that Outlook Express has already inserted addresses from the original message for you

2   In the message pane type in your response above the original message

3   Click on the Send button

❏   Outlook Express will send the message to all the addressees in one go. A real-time saver

Take note

The same set-up rules will apply to Reply All as applied to Reply in respect of including the original message, subject to how you have customised Outlook Express. You can turn this feature on or off to suit your requirements.

Sent Items

Investigate the Folders pane and you will find a folder called Sent Items. By default Outlook Express saves all of your sent e-mails in this folder. You can change the setting from the **Tools > Options>Send** dialog box and removing the tick in the Save copy of sent messages in the **Sent Items** folder box.

To identify the meaning and function of all the different icons used by Outlook Express, locate the 'Tips and Tricks – Message list items for Outlook Express' online Help page and read it later, with Outlook Express open at the Inbox window.

Copy, cut and paste with e-mails

There may come a time when you will want to copy text in an e-mail for use elsewhere. The procedure is quite easy.

Basic steps

To copy a text from an e-mail to another e-mail or application:

1 Open the message

2 From the menu bar select Edit > Select All (or right-click over the text and click the Select All option)

❑ The text will then be highlighted

3 Right-click over the highlighted text

4 Select Copy from the pop-up menu

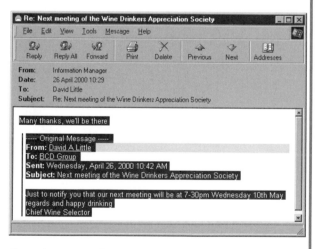

❑ The text will now be stored in the Clipboard ready for further use

❑ The text can now be copied into a different message or a second application, such as Microsoft Word

5 Open a different e-mail and place the cursor in an appropriate location in the text pane and using the shortcut key method of Ctrl+V, Paste the copied text in to this message

You could actually build a completely new message using this method by copying sections from different messages as appropriate. Move on to the next exercise immediately, as we want to use the copied information that is still in the Clipboard to illustrate the next section

Copying between applications

Open Microsoft Word and with a new blank document open, right-click over it and from the pop-up menu select Paste. The text will appear in the document, it's as easy as that. Open another new Word document and type in the following text **exactly** as shown below.

the China Hall Blackburn. John and Mary invite you to celebrate their recent Marriage in Barbados Saturday 10 June 2000 at 7.30pm,

Highlight the text, using the shortcut key method of Ctrl+A, and when highlighted right-click over it and select Copy from the pop-up menu.

Return to Outlook Express and create a new message. When the New Message window opens right-click over the text pane and select Paste from the pop-up menu and the text will now appear in it.

Cutting and pasting within a message

The text that you just copied from Word is somewhat mixed-up and there is no logical order in its layout. This was done deliberately to show just how easy it is to move text around within a message, using the Cut and Paste tools, as follows.

Basic steps

1 Highlight the section of text *the China Hall Blackburn.* including the full stop

2 Right-click and select Cut from the menu

3 Place the cursor at the end of the remaining text, to the right of the comma and insert a space

4 Right-click and select Paste

❏ The text will now appear at the end of the message. Please keep this message open

Copying and pasting within a message

It is just as easy to Copy text from one section of a message and duplicate it elsewhere in the same message, so that the same text appears a number of times.

Basic steps

Using the same message just created to demonstrate the Cut and Paste actions:

1 Copy the text '*Saturday 10 June 2000 at 7.30pm*'

2 Move to the beginning of the text and press [Enter] twice to insert two blank lines

3 Place the cursor at the top of the message on a blank line

4 Right-click and select Paste

❏ The text will now appear at the very beginning of the message

5 Place the cursor at the very end of the message and insert two blank lines

6 Right-click and select Paste

❏ You should now have the date and time of the event at the top, in the middle and at the end of the message

Deleting text

Maybe we have gone a little overboard with the duplicated text. Highlight the last occurrence of the text 'Saturday 10 June 2000 at 7.30pm' and press the 'Delete' key and it is gone. Deleting is as easy as that.

Using the Address Book

You will in time find that you will have accumulated a considerable number of e-mail addresses and it is impossible to recall each and every one of them. Outlook Express has an address book in which you can store all of your e-mail addresses.

To access the address book select **Tools > Address Book** or use the Shortcut of **Ctrl+Shift+B**.

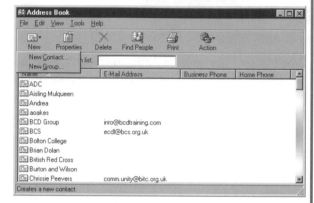

Outlook Express has a feature called Contacts, which is in fact the address book, so all of your contacts, with or without e-mail addresses, will appear when the address book is opened.

Creating a new contact

Basic steps

To record the details of a new contact:

1 Click on the down-arrow of the New button on the toolbar

2 Select New Contact

❑ The Properties dialog box will open. It is in this dialog box that you enter all of your contact's details

3 Ensure that Name tab is selected and click in the First slot

4 Type in 'BCD Group'

5 In the E-Mail Addresses slot type 'info@bcdtraining.com'

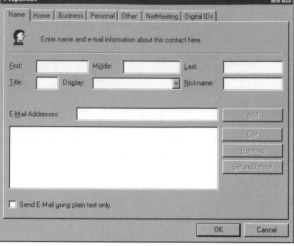

6 Click on each of the tabs and investigate what you can or cannot include

7 Click on the Business tab

8 Type in additional details as shown here

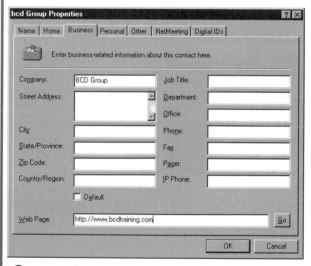

9 Click OK to save the contacts details

❑ The window will now close

Deleting an address

As you accumulate addresses you will find that you are no longer using some, or that some have ceased to exist. You can delete addresses extremely easily.

Basic steps

1 Open the Address Book (remember the shortcut Ctrl+Shift+B)
2 Select the entry *BCD Group* that we just created
3 When highlighted, press [Delete] or click the Delete button on the toolbar

Before the item is deleted you will be prompted to confirm the action:

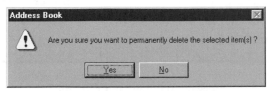

4 Do not delete the address just yet because we want to use it in the next exercise, so click on the No button

Automatic entries

You can customise Outlook Express so that it will automatically insert the details of any contact into your address book when you use the Reply Feature.

Basic steps

1 From the menu bar select Tools > Options
2 Click on the Send tab.
3 Click in the Automatically put people I reply to in my Address Book slot and a tick will appear
4 Click OK to apply the change

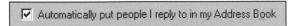

Creating groups/distribution lists

At the beginning of this section we created an e-mail which gave details of a Wine Appreciation Society meeting. What was not clear at that time was how many people there were in the society and how many e-mails would have to be sent to inform the members of the meeting.

Remember, one purpose of a computer is to speed up actions and avoid duplication. Outlook Express has a feature called *Groups*, which lends itself well this. We will create a Group and include the details of all the society members, so in the future when we send out details affecting the society, we will only need to create one e-mail which will go to all the members.

Basic steps

1 Open the Address Book
2 Click New and select New Group

3 Create a meaningful name for the Group (e.g. Wine Appreciation Society)
4 Click Select Members
❑ The next dialog box lists all of your contacts

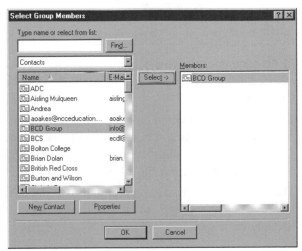

5   In the Name pane click on the BCD Group

6   When highlighted click on Select –>

❑   The BCD Group name will now appear in the Members pane

7   Select any further names from your Contacts list you wish to include then click OK

The Group name will now appear in your address book. To send an e-mail, using the group name, select it, as you would if you were send an e-mail to a single contact. When you send the e-mail, Outlook will deal with the multiple addresses without you having to do anything else.

Replying using the group/distribution list

You can use the Group name to reply to an e-mail. If necessary refer to page 326 for guidance and follow the procedure for replying until such time that the Reply message window has opened.

We will not actually send this e-mail but will list the procedures how to use the Group address in the Reply feature.

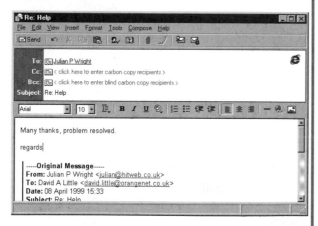

In the example, the Reply address has already been inserted. The Group name can be included in the **To:**, **Cc**: or **Bcc**: slot.

To send it as information only, click the **Cc:** button to open the address book. Locate the group name, click **Cc:** and when the name appears in the appropriate pane, click **OK** to close the address book.

The Group name will now appear in the Cc slot of the message headers. Complete the message and the email is ready to be sent.

Close the message window and remember this was only an exercise, we will not send it. Click on the NO button when prompted to save and the window will close.

Searching for a contact

When you open a New Message window you can, if you remember the address, simply type it in without the use of the address book. However, you can use the address book.

Basic steps

1   Click the To: button

❑   The Select Recipients dialog box will open

To find the person require:

2   Type the name in the Find slot

❑   As you type, Outlook will scroll the list, in the Name pane, to correspond with your typing.

3   When you locate the name, click on it

4   Click on To ->

❑   The name will now appear in the Message recipients pane

If required, repeat the same process to include more names or if you want to include someone in the Cc:

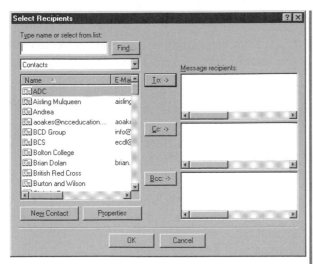

or Bcc: sections, select the name and click on the appropriate button.

5 When you have finished selecting the names, click OK

❑ The window will close and the recipient will appear in the To: slot. It's as easy and as quick as that

The name search feature will save you considerable time as your list of contacts builds up, alternatively you can use the scroll bar to search for names

Searching for an e-mail

Outlook Express does not have a search facility for finding particular emails, unlike the full version of Outlook. However, by managing your e-mails and creating folders for particular groups or subjects you should be able to locate them quite easily. Outlook Express does include a number of features that can assist you in a search.

In the next example, the files have been arranged in date/time order of receipt, starting with the oldest. This was achieved by clicking on the **Received** column header.

Clicking on the Received header again would reorder the e-mails starting with the most recently received.

If you know who the e-mail was from, left-click on the From bar and the list will be reordered, either in ascending or descending, alphabetical order.

A small chevron will appear on the bar, either point up indicating ascending order, or down indicating descending order.

You can also left-click on the Subject bar and reorder the e-mails in ascending or descending alphabetical subject order.

Creating folders in the Inbox

Earlier in the course we created a new folder, in the **Folders** pane of Outlook Express. In this instance we are going to create a new folder in the Inbox.

Basic steps

1 Right-click over the Inbox in the Folders list

2 From the pop-up menu select New Folder

❑ The Create Folder dialog box will open

3 Ensure the Inbox is highlighted

4 In the Folder name slot, type in '*Family*'

5 Click OK and the dialog box will close

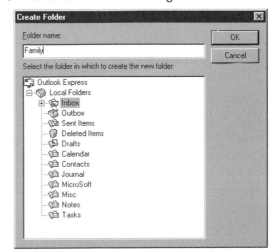

349

The Inbox in the Folders pane may have expanded to reveal the sub-folder that we have just created. If it did not expand, left-click on the plus (+) sign located to its left and it will expand.

At the moment the folder is empty. In the next section we will learn how to move e-mails from one folder to another.

Moving e-mail using drag and drop

Basic steps

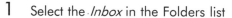

1 Select the *Inbox* in the Folders list
2 Select an e-mail
3 Click and hold the mouse button down
4 Drag the e-mail across to the *Family* folder
5 When over the *Family* folder release the button
❏ Outlook Express will now move the selected e-mail to this folder. This method of move items is known as 'drag and drop'.
6 Click on the *Family* folder to open it and you will now find the e-mail inside
❏ Repeat the above, except this time return the same e-mail back to its original location using the drag and drop method

You can also move e-mails from folder to folder using the same procedure. First open the folder where the e-mail is currently located, select and drag it to the required folder.

Deleting e-mails

If you are accumulating e-mails and you decide that you want to delete several of them:

Basic steps

1 Open the appropriate folder where the e-mails are located
2 Right-click over the e-mail to be deleted
3 From the pop-up menu select Delete
❏ The e-mail will be moved to the *Deleted Items* folder

To permanently delete an item

Basic steps

1 Go to the *Deleted Items* folder
2 Select Delete
3 Select Yes when asked 'Are you sure you want to permanently delete these message(s)'

Deleting an address

We have already touched upon the subject of deleting an e-mail address earlier. We no longer require the BCD Group address: return to page 331, and follow the sequence for deleting items and delete it.

Outlook Express Online Help

As with all of Microsoft's applications, Outlook Express has its own online Help.

Basic steps

❑ To access online help
1 Click on 'Help' on the menu bar
2 Select 'Contents and Index'

Or

3 Press [F1]

The Outlook Express online Help dialog box will open.

The dialog box usually opens with the Contents tab selected, ensure that it is.

4 Click on Tips and Tricks and it will expand to reveal a list of contents
5 Click on the 'Message' list icons for Outlook Express

In the right pane you will now see a list explaining what all of the various symbols and icons mean. This is quite a helpful list, keep it in mind for future reference.

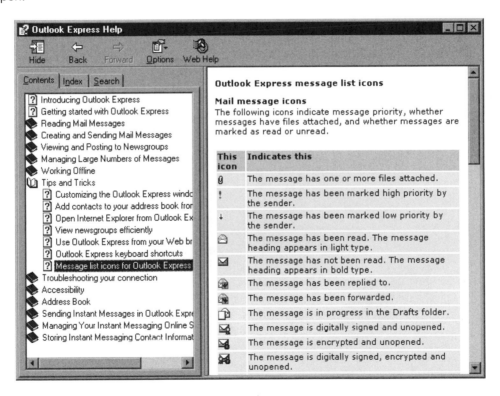

7: The Internet

351

Index